CULTURE, MEDIA, THEORY, PRACTICE

CULTURE, MEDIA, THEORY, PRACTICE
Perspectives

Edited by Ben Dorfman

Series editor Jens F. Jensen

CULTURE, MEDIA, THEORY, PRACTICE
Perspectives
Media & Cultural Studies 3

Edited by Ben Dorfman

Series editor Jens F. Jensen

© The Authors and Aalborg University Press, 2004

Cover: Eva Sofie Rafn
Publisher's editor: Henrik Dalgaard
Layout and print by: Special-Trykkeriet Viborg a-s
Publisher: Aalborg University Press
ISBN 87-7307-729-1
ISSN 1399-1752

Distribution:
Aalborg University Press
Niels Jernes Vej 6B
9220 Aalborg Ø
Denmark
Phone: (+45) 96 35 71 40, Fax: (+45) 96 35 00 76
E-mail: aauf@forlag.aau.dk
Homepage: http://www.forlag.aau.dk

Media & Cultural Studies:
Professor Jens F. Jensen, Series editor
VR Media Lab & Department of Communication
Aalborg University, Denmark

Media & Cultural Studies 1:
Interactive Television. TV of the Future or the Future of TV?, 1999
(Edited by Jens F. Jensen & Cathy Toscan)

Media & Cultural Studies 2
The Aesthetics of Television, 2001
(Edited by Gunhild Agger & Jens F. Jensen)

Contents

6   Contents

"WHAT DOES IT MEAN TO THEORIZE MEDIA?"

"WHAT DOES IT MEAN TO PRACTICE MEDIA ANALYSIS?"

CULTURE, MEDIA, THEORY, PRACTICE – PERSPECTIVES
Introduction

Ben Dorfman
Department af Languages and Intercultural Studies
Aalborg University

The questions of cultural and media theory and analysis are always self-reflective. That is to say that if we accept the relatively common sense assertion theory and analysis are the central tasks of culture and media studies, one is never exempted from the questions of what one is attempting to do and why. To offer an example from my own intellectual background, the opening of Martin Heidegger's *Being and Time* (1927/1962) expresses the situation well: the question of being, asserts Heidegger, "has been forgotten" (21). In other words, the most obvious questions elude us. Nonetheless, we are never able to completely escape their presence. In speaking theoretically and analytically, then, the conditions under which one speaks and the goals driving those articulations in the first place are always present: what are cultural and media theory and analysis, and what are they intended to do? Indeed, we might articulate these questions along a four-fold division: what does it mean to theorize culture, what does it mean to theorize media, what does it mean to practice cultural analysis and what does it mean to practice media analysis?

Now, as a point of qualification, the keen reader will notice that these questions are organized around two essential axioms: (1) that there is a distinction between cultural theory and analysis and media theory and analysis and (2) that there is a distinction between theory and analysis in a general sense – i.e., that, regardless of the topic, the questions of theory and analysis should be posed separately. These axioms are in fact heuristic. As Gilles Deleuze (1972/1977) pointed out, theory and practice are both "relays" to one another, with each exposing the other's limits (206). Similarly, a row of scholars, from Marshall McLuhan (1964/2002) to Manuel Castells (1996-98), have identified culture and media as intrinsically bound to one another. Indeed, these specific scholars tell us that, especially in the age of globalization, both are essential for the various boundary crossings necessary to create visions of the self that extend beyond the traditional identity categories of nation, class, race or gender. What we are saying, then, is that there is no natural distinction between media and culture, nor one between theory and analysis. Rather the very paring of those concepts – culture and media on one hand and theory and analysis on the other – reflects those concepts' involvement in a circuit or continuum that rejoins them as bound problematics. Simply put, to discuss culture in the absence of media is impossible, as is to discuss theory in the absence of analysis, and vice versa.

These qualifications and complications, however, do not prevent the fact that cultural and media theory and analysis represent locales of general concern in the contemporary humanistic environment, and locales that are and perhaps *must be* accessed by the student of culture and media on heuristically separate bases. The reasons for this are multiple: the increasing presence of media in our everyday lives – especially on a mass scales and in electronic forms – the increasing subtlety of media's presence on such an "everyday" level and the need for flexible analytical categories such as the "cultural" to explain experiences in contemporary "global contexts" all provide us with reasons to break down the totalities of the culture-media and theory-practice continuums into smaller and potentially more comprehensible units. Indeed, in the environment of the early twenty-first century, the demand for this move is perhaps stronger than ever. Our view of the pressing and important changing dynamics of geo-political power, for example, comes via the channels of media, new and old – from the print media to television ("old media") to the internet ("new media") and, perhaps quintessentially, the print media *on* the internet (e.g., *The New York Times on the Web* – a blending of new and old media) and then again reviewed by television (e.g., Aaron Brown's "look at the headlines" on CNN's "Newsnight" – a conglomeration of many media styles). Nonetheless, we increasingly hear that changing geo-political dynamics have less to do with nations or even "societies" than "culture" – entities that surely coincide to no small extent with nations and societies, but also have the potential to break nations apart (e.g., the 1991-95 Yugoslav War) and bring together societies that exist on opposite sides of national borderlines (e.g., conceptions of "the West," or an "international" community of Islam).[1] Therein, our four heuristic questions of "what does it mean to theorize media," "what does it mean to theorize culture," "what does it mean to practice media analysis" and "what does it mean to practice cultural analysis" are designed to provide lines of access into the cul-

---

1   Perhaps the most famous (and troubling) of these proclamations was Samuel Huntington's (1996) assertion of a "clash of civilizations."

ture-media and theory-practice continuums in ways that are comprehensible. And, indeed, these are the four questions around which this volume was organized. Researchers associated with the Culture and Media Studies program (CMS) at Aalborg University were posed these questions, and asked to answer them as directly as possible out of their own fields of expertise. Thus, the driving concern behind this volume is, within the context of a functioning research environment organized around problematics in culture and media, what are the differing views of cultural and media theory and analysis that environment presents, what are the views of the *objects* with which cultural and media theory and analysis concern themselves – namely, culture and media – and what thus becomes the nature of that research environment, or its orientation within a more globalized view of culture and media studies?

The responses in this volume are as diverse as the intellectual lineages informing them. That is to say that, using a slightly "older" vocabulary, the "schools of thought" at work in CMS at Aalborg are varied: Bourdieuian sociology, Derridian deconstruction, Jakobsonian linguistics, Labovian sociolinguistics, Faircloughian discourse analysis, Zygmunt Baumann's critical sociology, hermeneutic existentialism and even problematics in historiography and cognitive science. Here, I would simply make an editorial remark and state that such a diversity of influences is the bread and butter of research; the assertion of multiple, received historical perspectives on culture and media that might be assessed, brought into conversation with one another and developed in "conversation" leaves those perspectives as locales providing reasoned choices for the student of culture and media. This gives this volume one of its primary characteristics: the assertion that the best pedagogy in culture and media provides more questions than answers, and that an engagement with basic theoretical and analytical propositions is perhaps the strongest tool in opening such questions.

Nonetheless, such openness becomes problematic to the extent that we are left to wonder what, in the face of such open-endedness, becomes the *program* of Culture and Media Studies in the research environment of Aalborg University? In other words, in the face of open questioning – and, despite the postmodern questioning of intellectual rigidity – what becomes the "training" one receives in a culture and media studies "discipline?" As editor of this volume, I would assert that the answers to these questions come on two levels. First, the "discipline" one receives in CMS at Aalborg is an exposure to essential theoretical and analytical questioning itself. By bringing together multiple intellectual lineages and engaging them in conversation with one another, the faculty associated with the CMS program de facto assert that such critical and open-ended dialogues are essential to engaging culture and media both as academic discourses as well as social and historical "realities." And, in fact, this becomes a major epistemological claim: an understanding of culture and media means an understanding of its discourses, or the range of theoretical and analytical possibilities associated with the ideas of culture and media. In such an understanding, goes this claim, one gains insight into the cognitive options available for the student of culture, or the modes by which one might begin to *think* culture and media as problems.

Such an understanding, however, means that the "discipline" of CMS at Aalborg is self-generating. This stands as the second level of response to the problem of the "training" one receives in the program. That is to say that, in bringing the multiple options involved in thinking culture and media into relief and then bringing them into conversation with one another, the precise dynamics of CMS at Aalborg emerge under their own momentum. Again, from my position as editor, I would define that momentum to this point in two ways:

1. A questioning of the "postmodern paradigm"
By a "questioning of the postmodern paradigm," I mean not postmodernism as something that questions "reality," prevents the making of "statements" or that radically relativizes "truth," but rather as an ontological position. In other words, the effect of many texts classified as "postmodern" is to posit reality as always in its own erasure, or providing conditions that destabilize themselves.[2] Such a position suggests an ultimate transitoriness to analysis. Within the selection of texts presented in this book, culture and media objects are generally portrayed as having greater durability. The tools of analysis are not imagined as somehow undermining the objects of analysis, or leading to their dissolution or negation.

2. The assertion of theoretical and analytical possibilities
By the "assertion of theoretical and analytical possibilities," we are making an assertion that is related to the questioning of the postmodern paradigm. In general terms, the assertion is that not only do we analyze objects with some permanence, and that analysis is not an essentially invasive task, but that methodological deployments should be subject to critique because

---

2   Major texts in this regard would be, for example, Derrida (1967/1995), Foucault (1969/1977) and Lyotard (1983/1988).

methodology should produce results. In other words, analysis has objects, and while maintaining validity as a question in itself, it maintains that validity in order to produce utilizable knowledge.

Now, it should be said that these are not necessarily unusual positions. Many research institutions, if not fields in the humanities in general, are by hook or by crook casting themselves beyond the postmodern paradigm. The titles of the modes of thought "beyond postmodernism" are various: critical realism, cognitive science, ethnomethodology, various stripes of discourse analysis, reflexive sociology and concepts of "new cultural history."[3] However, what gives CMS a great power amidst the larger shifts within the humanities is a deep and abiding respect for the postmodern challenge. Fashioned in the tradition of the best features of Aalborg University as an at-large institution, the essays in *Culture, Media, Theory, Practice: Perspectives* pulsate with a desire to make culture and media theory and analysis matter and do justice, both on intellectual and social scales. This demands a serious encounter with the ontological – which postmodernism provides – and a continued proximity to its questioning.

Clearly, the precise modes and style of the "encounters with the ontological" presented here are multiple. We have, for example, several essays that betray their origins in the Aalborg commitment to knowledge that "matters": direct, informational and no-nonsense in terms of their attempt to generate knowledge that produces positive results. These essays, of which we might especially point to Peter Allingham's, Anders Horsbøl's and Lene Yding Pedersen's, all give us a distinct view of the culture and media researcher making the theoretical deployment. Horsbøl does this by outlining the distinct theoretical options available in his own research area of critical discourse analysis. Foucauldian or Fairclaughian, asserts Horsbøl, discourse analysis is charged to maintain a critique of social power at the same time that it is bound to *learn* from that critique, or put it to use in concrete, utilizable social analysis. Allingham and Pedersen make distinct applications of approaches in their own fields – Pedersen critical and cultural studies and Allingham semiotics and cognitive studies. These applications are made to distinct cultural and media objects – Pedersen's to Yann Martell's popular novel *Life of Pi* and Allingham to advertisements such as those for Elizabeth

---

3   See, for example, López and Potter (2001), Ross (2004), Button (2001), Jørgensen and Phillips (2001), Bourdieu (1992) and Hunt and Biersack (1989).

Arden make-ups. Pedersen's concern is with the connection between the money and cultural economies in a Bourdieuian fashion – is the field of literary production in contemporary culture, she asks, pushing us closer to the aesthetic of a "dream society?" Allingham's concern is that while contemporary advertising exudes a semiotic order, we recognize that order only functions in relation to pre-linguistic cognitive processes. This gives us a matrix that helps us to understand the instantaneity and deception of contemporary aesthetics.

Within this volume, however, Ove Christensen, Christian Jantzen, Steen Christiansen and Ben Dorfman take different tacts in relation to the problematics of culture and media, choosing to make more distinctly methodological statements – i.e., they make theory "as such" their point of entry into the theory-analysis continuum. Ove Christensen advocates a pragmatic encounter with semiotics, cognitive science and, perhaps primarily, Jakobsonian paradigms of communicative "senders" and "receivers." The importance of this is the diversity of demands in specific media and textual-analytical situations – what analytical tools do we need, and what produces explanations of the textual and communicative situations in which we find ourselves? Jantzen (perhaps along with Allingham) is the clearest advocate for cognitive science in this volume. In a stylistically adventurous piece, he makes us aware that in the context of the humanities, it is the great traditions of social theory that cognitive science competes against. Moreover, he asserts that the event of culture is related to biologically-based cognitive evolution and not the development of "Spirit", "context" or "consciousness" in a philosophical or speculative sense. Steen Christiansen reveals the complexities of the theory/analysis connection, taking the classic stance that the two must always be thought at the same time. Finally, Dorfman advocates the development of a "historical approach" to cultural theory and the development of what he calls a "historical phenomenology" of the idea of culture – the assertion that the historical past of a concept provides the dimensions of the possibility of their thought in the present.

Indeed, it is worth pointing out that the "historical approach" to cultural studies reveals a unique set of influences in the CMS program: questions of historiography and the relationship of philosophy of history to cultural studies. To this extent, we are honored to include Benjamin C. Sax's article on the essential approaches to the subject of "cultural history" – a topic which, by way of the historians Jakob Burkhardt and Johann Huizinga, represents one of the oldest traditions with the pale of cultural research. Indeed, the historicity of cultural studies is important for Sax as, in his view, it itself reflects not only its own evolution but also that of related concepts such as "world", "truth," "text" and even "history" itself. Sax's historical approach is accompanied by related thematizations in articles by Tadeusz Rachwal, Jørgen Riber Christensen and Mikael Vetner. Rachwal – who, like Sax, is another friend of CMS whose work we are pleased to be able to include– suggests that repeated and differing engagements with the idea of culture give us its historical "echo," or a way in which we never stop hearing older configurations of the idea. This historicity, however, has a classically post-structural form: "rootless," significatory and producing its own being through the play of language. Not dissimilarly, J.R. Christensen tells us that "grand narratives", or great stories, maintain an essential relationship with historical consciousness and form a second level of view in our intake of electronic visual media – a "pastiche" of texts and signification giving us senses of historically derived meaning. Finally, Vetner makes an invocation of the Foucauldian concept of "episteme," or historical arrangements of knowledge, in an attempt to arrange historically formed fields of meaning in relation to technical objects on a semiotic basis. This becomes another contribution to the idea that culture and media are not simply present events, but have pasts and discourses whose present is informed by that past, as well as subtle – potentially even subliminal – senses of the past at work.

At this point, however, we might identify a departure in the CMS "style." This is on two scales. First, Bent Sørensen provides us with the only true *essay* of the book in the classic sense of the term. Written in elegant, autobiographical style, Sørensen relates the psychic travails of the cultural worker in the literary style – *observateur* in the style of Montaigne, yet haunted by uncanniness, á la Kerouac or Salinger. Interestingly, Torben Vestergaard's style is also not without its wry smile. Coming out of socio-linguistics, Vestergaard's analysis of journalistic media as concerned with two noticeable recent news events betrays the power of language games – languages games whose functioning is central to media communication, and which we must comprehend by way of a reconception of critique in a manner that brings it closer to description. Indeed, Sørensen and Vestergaard's contributions are highly differentiated essays in terms of both their form and content. However, both encourage a gentle humor in relation to cultural and linguistic observation, and significant, if perhaps opposing, views on the role and position of the culture and media observer.

Indeed, we might further the theme that departures in style among the contributions to this volume are accompanied by departures in content. That is to say that it is important to note that, even among thematically linked articles, approaches to given topics can be diverse. Rachwal and Jørgen Riber Christensen present historical knowledge as a matter of reading "underneath" the surfaces we give it. Sax, however, presents historical knowledge as a more of a question of typologies of approaches taken to the cultural past within the humanities, and a hermeneutical self-reflexivity that might offer grounds to accord history pride of place among humanistic approaches to cultural investigation. Presenting another example of "linked" yet "differentiated" thematics, Jantzen posits knowledge as generated in specific situations played out in the present; the cognitive mind, he argues, goes to work in semiotic contexts in the now out of its specifically biologically developed capacities. Dorfman, however, posits that the knowledges of the past have something of a continuing life of their own – this by way of the present's reliance on ideas of the past, or "intellectual history" in a more or less traditional ("canonical") sense. And, cutting across different groupings of articles, we see that Pedersen, Vetner, Vestergaard and Allingham present noticeably different perspectives on how one relates to cultural and media objects –sociologically (Pedersen), semiotically (Vetner), through a semiotics enmeshed with the cognitive (Allingham) and by way of syntax and semantics (Vestergaard). Horsbøl, Ove Christiansen and Steen Christiansen provide us with similar questions concerning methodology – is methodology a question of disciplinary practices, as posed by Horsbøl, the institutional situatedness of theory, as posed by Steen Christiansen or the pragmatic demands of analytical situations, as posed by Ove Christensen? Finally, we have to recognize Sørensen's posing of the question of style: in the end, are not cultural studies always a personal affair, demanding their expression as such?

In the final analysis, then, it may be that CMS, or at least *Culture, Media, Theory, Practice: Perspectives*, is "rhizomatic" – a term connected to the intellectual milieu (postmodernism) many CMS associates are attempting to move beyond, but with respect. The rhizome is "diverse forms" from "ramified surface extension in all directions" (Deleuze and Guattari 1980/1987, 5). As I think is the case with the chapters of this book, we have presentations of unity and diversity that, in accordance with the diverse nature of these ideas, give Culture and Media Studies at Aalborg the dimension of what it is, and give *us* a sense of its uniqueness and its value. By their very nature, cultural and media theory and analysis provide a milieu of folding and unfolding relevances: the "human" and its environment, expression and "thought", form and "content," text and "context." These are relevances that, in fact, make cultural and media theory and analysis more than discourses – they rather make cultural and media theory and analysis discourses that must be engaged in terms of their content such that we might think those things that come under the headings of "the cultural" or related to "media." Therein, the problem of surveying the fields of cultural and media theory and analysis is to present their "ramifications" and "extensions" – the dimensions of their "rhizome." This book represents such an attempt in the context of CMS at Aalborg.

WORKS CITED

Bourdieu, Pierre. 1992. *An invitation to reflexive sociology.* Oxford: Oxford University Press.

Button, Graham. 2001. *Ethnomethodology and the human sciences.* Oxford: Oxford University Press.

Castells, Manuel. 1996-98. *The information age: economy, society and culture.* 3 vols. Oxford: Blackwell.

Deleuze, Gilles and Félix Guattari. 1980/1987. *A thousand plateaus.* Trans. Brian Massumi. London: Athlone.

Deleuze, Gilles and Michel Foucault. 1972/1977. Intellectuals and power. In Michel Foucault, *Language, counter-memory, practice.* Ed. Sherry Simon and Donald F. Bouchard, 205-17. Ithaca, NY: Cornell University Press.

Derrida, Jacques. 1967/1995. *Of grammatology.* Trans. Gayatri Spivak. Baltimore: Johns Hopkins University Press.

Foucault, Michel. 1969/1977. What is an author? In *Language, counter-memory, practice.* Ed. Sherry Simon and Donald F. Bouchard, 113-38. Ithaca, NY: Cornell University Press.

Heidegger, Martin. 1927/1962. *Being and time.* Trans. Edward Robinson and John Macquarrie. San Francisco: Harper and Row.

Hunt, Lynn and Aletta Biersack. 1989. *The new cultural history.* Berkeley: University of California Press.

Huntington, Samuel. 1996. *Clash of civilizations and the remaking of the world order.* New York: Simon and Schuster.

Jørgensen, Marianne and Louise Phillipos. 2001. *Discourse analysis as theory and method.* London: Sage.

López, José and Gary Potter, 2001. *After postmodernism: an introduction to critical realism.* London: Athlone.

Lyotard, Jean-François. 1983/1988. *Differend: phrases in dispute.* Trans. Georges van den Abeele. Minneapolis: University of Minnesota Press.

McLuhan, Marshall. 1964/2002. *Understanding media: the extensions of man.* London: Routledge.

Ross, Norbert. 2004. *Culture and cognition: implications for theory and method.* Thousand Oaks, Cal.: Sage.

"WHAT DOES IT MEAN TO THEORIZE CULTURE?"

Theory, Culture and Society

Christian Jantzen
Department of Communication
Aalborg University

Introduction: The Poverty of Cultural Theory

In his novel *Bouvard et Pecuchet* (1881), Gustave Flaubert tells the story about two clerks who, in a typical nineteenth century fashion, attempt to compile an inventory of all the world's nonsense after having become prosperous. Unfortunately, the author died in 1880 before his two heroes could carry out their deed, so the novel ended up being published posthumously and unfinished. I cannot help thinking that cultural analysis would have benefited greatly from Bouvard and Pecuchet's endeavors. It would have been a work of titanic dimensions; the two gentlemen would have produced a grand *oeuvre* of *idées reçues* that should be extinct, but have nevertheless been passed down and handed over as the safe haven of lazy thought.

In fact, I see cultural analysis as founded on nonsense. A set of curious and antiquated ideas about human being and society makes it difficult to pinpoint the domain of cultural studies. Indeed, the subject matter of cultural studies is hardly ever precisely defined, and the methods that the discipline uses are often borrowed randomly from other disciplines. As a domain, culture is "everything"– "the whole way of life" (Benedict 1961), or "that complex whole" (Tylor 1903), as put in the tradition of cultural anthropology. For that reason, it apparently goes without saying that the subject matter under investigation ("a cultural product") should somehow be related to that whole. *How* to justify this relation seems less important. Instead, the cultural scientist eagerly engages with the *meanings* supposedly generated by the cultural product in relation to "that complex whole." Especially in its diluted versions of poststructuralism, the method mostly looks like a blend of free association and the Kula exchanges, which Malinowski (1922) found among the Trobiands in his own time – except that the mussel shells have been exchanged for French "post"-thinkers or Franco-American cultivators of "theory."

If one challenges the culturalist and asks him or her how the meaning of the cultural phenomenon is embedded in reality, he or she will typically point to a broader "socio-cultural framework" in which the phenomenon and its meaning(s) are entrenched, have emerged from, and/or refer to. However, it is exactly the terms "socio-cultural" (or "social and cultural") and "frame" (or "context") which, perhaps, make the word compound the haziest term within humanities today. What does "frame" mean? And what does "the social" stand for? Exactly at what level do we find "the cultural?" Which connection or relation does the dash in "the socio-cultural" or the nexus "and" in "the social and cultural" imply? The fact that these questions are left unanswered does not seem detrimental to the popularity of the term. In my opinion, this indicates that we are not really dealing with an analytical concept, but rather with a metaphysical *Letztbegründung*. So why, one might mockingly ask, are we not talking about the "culto-social" instead?

The poverty of cultural theory consists precisely in the fact that it abstains from systematic investigations into the causal or dialectical relation between phenomenon and reality, and instead hypostatizes the fact that such a relation exists. Thus, cultural analyses take it for granted that human acts, human artifacts and the meanings that we invest in them somehow reflect a deeper meaning. Such analyses, whose purpose is to inform us about that 'deeper meaning' are, in short, based on the implicit theoretical assumption that there is a system of shared presumptions, which supposedly structure everyday-life and its discourses. This assumption, originating from sociology and anthropology, functions as an implicit cultural theory in the humanities: i.e., as a widespread, mainstream conception that is taken for granted in many actual analyses. Its popularity is not least due to the Birmingham School of Cultural Studies, whose concepts of culture stress the shared social meanings and collective ways of making sense of the world.[1]

In the following I argue that this "implicit cultural theory" is wrong. I will suggest that one cannot presume that there are shared presumptions, which structure actions and their meanings. Furthermore, culture should be clearly distinguished from "the social" as well as from "society." "The social" and

---

1 The founding father of Cultural Studies, Raymond Williams, explicitly defined culture in a culturalist manner, e.g. "as a constitutive social process, creating specific and different 'ways of life'" (Williams 1977: 19). Stuart Hall, who blended Williams' ideas with French (post)structuralism defines culture in close relationship to society: as "the actual grounded terrain of practices, representations, languages and customs of any specific society" (1996: 439). For a further critique of these modern culturalist positions, see also my reading (Jantzen 2004) of Jensen (1988), which is perhaps the most eloquent and balanced defense of culturalism in the Danish humanities.

"the cultural" work at different levels, which, at least in a scientific context, should be held out from one another. My own argument is based on three assumptions, or axioms, if you will, which I present in the following.

FIRST AXIOM: TEXT AS THE SUBJECT MATTER OF THE HUMAN SCIENCES

As a result of the parceling out of universal science into main fields and, later, increasingly specialized subfields that has taken place since the seventeenth century, it has become a common feature of the human sciences that they examine "text" and "textuality." The research tradition that I am a part of – semiotics – defines "text" as a finite structure of signification. A text depends on the coherence of its elements, which, exactly *qua* structural coherence, distinguish this text from other texts and other objects. Each text has a border against other objects, i.e., it has a limited extension of the text. The elements may consist of the same or of different types of signs: they can be linguistic, visual, auditive, tactile, etc... Since the 1970s, there has been discussion about "the extended text concept" in order to encapsulate artifacts, which are characterized by non-linguistic signs or are composed of elements from different types of signs. Thus, the extended text concept, at least in principle, embraces all artifacts, if they are viewed in the light of signification.

Inasmuch as signs constitute texts, Morris' (1938) heuristic model of the three semiotic levels is right at hand for understanding the nature of a text. Morris thinks that signs are characterized by syntactic, semantic and pragmatic aspects. While syntax ensures the coherence of the text and marks its outer limits, semantics ensures the systematic relation between form and content that guarantees the text's reference to a text-external reality. Pragmatics is essentially the text's effect on its users.

The "implicit cultural theory" as described in the introduction has some obvious problems with textuality. "Culture" is perceived as the text's structure (syntax), the text's meaning (semantics) or the context in which the text emerges or to which it refers, respectively. The confusion is carried even further when the limited artifact (the text's syntax), its broader meaning (the text's semantic) and its context are all referred to as "culture." When "culture" is "everything" it is, logically speaking, nothing at all – or just a big mish-mash. In relation to my second axiom, I therefore limit culture to the *effect* of the text (not its meaning). This means that culture is neither an innate quality of the text nor a determining factor prior to the text. It is neither text nor context. Culture is a specific consequence in and of the text. Culture is not something that exists out there independent of our acts and thoughts. Instead it is something that we do or bring about while engaging in social life.

SECOND AXIOM: THE SUBJECT MATTER OF CULTURAL ANALYSIS IS SITUATIONS

Since the term "cultural analysis" found its way into Danish universities in the beginning of the 1980s as a consequence of the emerging interest in "popular culture," all sorts of artifacts, ideas and habits have been subjected to cultural analysis. This has led to some times sensational conclusions (or statements), nonetheless, the methods and purposes of the analyses have been remarkably lacking in stringency and reliability – i.e., repetition and control. It has simply been very difficult to find out what exactly the individual analysis actually analyzes (for example, a small detail is taken to be symptomatic of the whole *Zeitgeist*), how the analysis is justified empirically (data), which considerations the choice of methods is based up on, and by which paths the analyst reaches her conclusions and if and how these conclusions might be generalized.

Of course, we all need to find our own academic spaces, and each person probably remains blessed in his or her own beliefs. For my part, I think that it is crucial for cultural analysis in the humanities to ground its practice in the textual sciences. This is to say that cultural analysis must find a "text" to analyze, as opposed to ethnographic and other social science types of cultural studies, who epistemologically are grounded in a "context" based approach. The point of departure for a text based cultural analysis is, thus, a limited and cohesive structure of signification. The kind of cultural analysis that I am interested in takes its point of departure in *interactions* (cf. Jantzen & Frimann Trads 2004). Interactions have the following features:

- They have a beginning and an end – i.e., they are limited and defined
- They have a course or a succession of actions from a beginning to an end, and this course typically shows a certain regularity – a i.e. they are cohesive
- They begin, evolve and end with reference to an external intention: that is, they have meaning

Interactions have syntax – i.e., consistency and coherence. They also have semantics because they refer to situations. By its special way of evolving, the interaction invests the *situation* with a specific meaning. Furthermore, the interaction has an effect: in its course it creates, maintains and changes the *relation* between the inter-actors. The inter-actors can be two or more people, two or more artifacts or people and artifacts. Thus, we can add the following features to the list:

- Interactions are always social: they depend upon the interplay between two or more actors and they affect the actors' future relation to one another;
- Interactions are always situated: they begin because one or more actors have specific intentions; they end when a specific goal (which is not necessarily identical with the initial intention) is achieved by one or more of the actors, and the actual course is dependent on the actors' sensitivities to the situation.

To that extent, I am interested in how people are able to buy bread and gasoline, go to restaurants, watch TV, get married, mate in brothels and many other things. Throughout these interactions, we talk and do various things in relation to other people and the artifacts at hand (utensils, TV-apparatuses, engagement rings, "toys"). All of it is, in one way or another, social in the Weberian sense: intentional actions oriented towards other intentionalities (Weber 1922: 1). The relations that are instigated or maintained are also social: formations of power and dominance, families, friendships, generation gaps and respect for trade conditions take place in such relations. In line with micro-sociology, it is my assumption that interactions and relations create society rather than vice-versa. Interaction leads, with Simmel's words, to *Vergesellschaftung* (1983). Or, to push the point even further, society is a routinized way of having relations to many other actors. On the one hand, society is highly complex because numerous interactions are aggregated at this higher level of abstraction. On the other hand, society is, in line with Tarde (1962), relatively simple because concrete situations at this level are boiled down – are anonymized and objectified – to almost binary oppositions between class, gender, generation, ethnicity, and other groups.

The point of departure for cultural analysis is interactions, which we can analyze as "text." Like relations, interactions are social. They constitute *and* affirm the social bond – but they are *not* culture. But what about situations? Situations can be understood abstractly as metatextual interpretations of interactions, which, in the same abstract manner, can be regarded as a bunch of chitchat and other biophysical processes. The metatextual interpretation frames these processes in such a way that they seem defined, coherent and goal-oriented. As Bateson (1972a) suggests, we might conceive of this frame as a higher level of abstraction than interaction: the frame is a message (it defines the situation) about the message (the interaction).

To offer a sleazy example: from a superficial point of view, the words that the customer and the prostitute exchange in a brothel and the acts in which they engage are not necessarily any different than the bio-physical processes or the interactions that take place in the conjugal bed. However, the mere fact that both actors are conscious of the specific situation of the interaction (the brothel), enables the customer to demand certain favors which he would never dream of asking from his spouse. Also, he does not need to concern himself with the question "was it really good for her too?" In return, the customer is expected "to get the job done" – and, of course, to pay in advance for the favors. If we look at the text's syntax, the actors' sensitivities to the situation ensure that the interaction runs smoothly, that is, in a way defined by the situation. Beginning and end are adapted to the situation (for example, shorter foreplay, no intimacy afterwards), certain elements are lacking (for example, kissing) whereas other elements are added (for example "exotic cocktails"). As a metatextual frame, the definition of the situation answers the question: "what's going on?" This answer is a hypothesis. As long as the interaction runs smoothly, there is no reason to adjust this hypothesis. In that case, the expectations – of the event as well as of its course and its possible outcomes – are contained in the frame. Thus, the frame can be seen as a mental model containing information about:

- The overall theme, meaning and intention of the interaction (semantics)
- The regular course of the interaction with a beginning and an end (syntax)
- The relation's distribution of roles between the actors (the pragmatics of the interaction)

Throughout the interaction this information is continuously tested in the form of hypotheses. These are, if necessary, adjusted along the way in order to match the events of the interaction or to open up other reasons for being together. Consequently, the individual actor modifies his or her behavior in order to test a new hypothesis. If the customer in the brothel begins to see the prostitute as a girlfriend, the original hypothesis is adjusted (for example, the distribution of roles). Such a situation would probably limit the realm of interaction in bed and lead to other, often mistaken, expectations towards the emotional engagement of the prostitute.

The point is that actual interactions emerge as "text" out of mental models of the text's structure (syntax), theme (semantics) and distribution of roles (pragmatics). These models or metatextual frames are not culture either – they are in line with my third axiom, cognitive frames or scripts based on universal ways of information processing and on individually based experiences. In that sense, they outline the potentiality of the interaction in the shape of hypotheses that are tested and adjusted. The actual course of the interaction realizes a concrete situation, and this course very often diverges from the initial definition of the situation (the hypothesis) and from the actors' sensitivities to the situation (abilities). In that case, an adjustment of or an addition to the frame takes place because new information has to be incorporated into the present scripts. Culture is the interpretation of this new information, and it takes the shape of a better social understanding understood as the individual's enhanced knowledge of her surroundings and as more sophisticated or elaborated hypotheses about what's going on? What is expected of me? Or what does it mean for my social roles? Culture is something being done: it emerges out of the gap between the initial definition of the situation and its actual realization. It is a *surplus* of the existing metatext, and it influences the future social roles of the actors. Thus, culture is related to Bateson's concept of information (1972b), according to which information is the difference that makes a difference. Culture is, in other words, an interpretation of the significance of "this doing" for the individual in social life. This implies that culture is *not* the *cause* of social interactions but rather the interpretation of the effect of these actions. As implied by the third axiom, this interpretation is *not collective*.

THE THIRD AXIOM: "ONE MAN, ONE BRAIN"

Cultural theory and analysis should take its point of departure in the quite ordinary fact that every human being is endowed with his or her own brain and, thus, as an organism, has his or her own specific way of processing information from the environment. Neurologically, "normal" brains function similarly, regardless of the skull in which they happen to be located. The foundation of information processing is, thus, universal, common and human. The information that is processed (used or reworked), however, is different from one situation to the next, and the impressions that individual actors receive in specific interactions are tied to their bodily placement in space and to the mental abilities which they can put to use in a given situation. Mentally, we have each our own perspective on interactions, and we form our own, individual experiences – understood as cognitive adjustments – of the situation.

First of all, this means that there is no ontological distinction between cognition and culture. They pertain to the same sphere of reality – namely, to the mental processes that take place in interaction. While cognition is the common denominator of these processes – of acquisition, storage, transformation, use and communication of information – culture is an *aspect* of cognition. Culture pertains to the situatedness of the mental processes in in-

teraction with others – individuals as well as artifacts. It stands for the interpreted and evaluated activity, which emerges as soon as the consequences of
the interaction and the relation are evaluated: when hypotheses are adjusted
– expanded, narrowed down, refined, specified etc… Such adjustments take
place in order to evaluate the *social effect* of the interaction. It is the individual's own success in accomplishing his or her purpose as well as other actors'
contributions to the situation that are interpreted and evaluated. This evaluation takes place in order to optimize the behavior of the actor in such a way
that she is better adjusted to the situation in the future.

Secondly, if we follow the idea of "One Man One Brain," we must discard
the information model presumed by the "implicit cultural theory." This
model assumes that culture is some kind of shared hard disc to which actors
are connected and from which they acquire their information. The individual actor is *not* a data terminal in a far-reaching cultural intranet, where the
codes are predetermined by the system, the software is programmed in advance, and information is stored in a collective database. Even though this
specific metaphor was hardly in vogue at the time when the "implicit cultural theory" was formulated more than a hundred years ago, the founding fathers of cultural theory, nevertheless, foreshadowed it. Despite their differences, both Durkheim (1933) and the theoreticians in the culturalist Boas-
tradition (for example Kroeber 1917) talked about society and/or culture as
a super-organism, which determined actions, and to which individuals were
either functionally (Durkheim) or mentally (Boas) attached (cf. Jantzen
1997: 46). This model is dominant for defining the subject matter of cultural research in mainstream Danish and international academics. It is, as I will
show in the next section, wrong.

THE CULTURAL FALLACY
"Implicit cultural theory" is rooted in a number of traditions from structural functionalism in the French sociological tradition (the Durkheim-tra-
dition) and British social anthropology (Radcliffe-Brown and those who followed him) to American cultural anthropology (the Boasians), who, in turn,
were deeply influenced by the German idealism of Herder (1784-1791).[2] The
imperial idea of this implicit theory is that culture is a deep structure or pattern regulating everyday life. This idea is based on the following assumptions:

---

2   As pointed out by Williams (1977: 17), Herder is also essential to the genealogy of
     the relativistic concept of culture in the Birmingham tradition of cultural studies.

- Culture is a system of ideas (values, *Weltanschauungen* and other mental processes) or behavior (habits, customs and other material practices) or of ideas and behavior. This system is often perceived as coherent and consistent.
- The system is *shared*: that is, it is collective.
- The system is *presupposed to have an existence in and by itself*. As such, it is *determining* for the actions of the individual.

Logically speaking, this "implicit cultural theory" is built on naïve but, nevertheless, widespread folkloristic explanations, which associate the manifest levels (observable behavior, measurable attitudes) with a hidden level (which is presupposed to be the system), whereupon the manifest is causally explained by the hidden.

It is, for example, manifest:

- a. "that NN goes to church (as many others)" and
- b. "that NN participates in certain rituals in the church (along with many others)"

Hidden – but nevertheless obvious – is the following:

- c. "That NN has a faith."

Here, the argument is that:

"NN goes to church and participates in certain rituals *because* NN has a faith."

The causal argument runs as follows:

1. "Faith (cause) determines behavior (result, effect)

and further that

2. "Because the result (behavior) is collective, it is fair to assume that the cause (faith) is collective too.

"Faith" is a system of values, "culture." We cannot see it, but as analysts we already know that it must be there. Therefore, it is not – or rather does not seem to be – difficult to make out. Hence, it also seems unproblematic to set up the hypothesis that both cause (hidden) and effect (observable) have the same collective characteristics.

In fact, on this point, lay-people are often less naïve than the analyst, because they know that the argumentation is flawed: faith, which supposedly motivates the churchgoer, does not necessarily play a large role in the churchgoer's life. However, perhaps exactly because the hidden was so obvious in advance, the professional analyst often takes the opposite stance. Inasmuch as the cultural analyst claims "that a group behaves in a certain way *because* it *has* (or is subjected to) a certain culture," the manifest is analyzed according to the hidden, which is theoretically presumed as:

- determining
- shared and presumed
- systematic

The tautology is completed when the analyst ends by "proving" or "showing" that the manifest is conditioned by the hidden, which has a systematic, shared, presumed and determining quality.

"The system", "culture", is, thus, the factotum of cultural analysis. What should have been explained ("the system," "culture") really remains a mere assumption on which the analysis and interpretation of a specific cultural phenomenon rests. The whole argument is grounded in a naïve and unprofitable causality. Naïve, because there might be entirely different reasons for the particular behavior: for example, non-believers go to church too, for burials, marriages or baptisms. Unprofitable, because presuming such determinism actually obscures investigations in to cultural change. If manifest acts are causally determined by a deeper, cultural structure, we can only explain changes in the manifest level by way of changes in the deeper level. But why should this deeper level change? According to the metaphors of culturalism, these changes can only be explained by means of analogy, as a virus- and hacker attack on the computer system, or as a consequence of an external and dominating influence (cultural imperialism, for example). However, postwar ethnology that explores popular culture in the modern, western world (Bausinger 1961) demonstrated long ago how cultural change takes place at the manifest level, that is, at the level of everyday events and occurrences, rather than at a deeper level (cf., for example, Voskuil 1973).

But what about the implicit presumption that culture, as a shared system, is a collective phenomenon? It is only by starting from this folklorist presumption that anybody can assume that people need to believe the same things, simply because they have the same routines (for example, going to church) and rituals (for example, singing psalms or communion). People can individually believe this and that, even though they perform the same collective acts. In other words, there is no logical connection between the collectively observable – what we can observe the community do or what the community can observe its own members doing – and a deep, cultural level, from which the manifestations spring or by which they are determined. The fact that manifest behavior is shared does not mean that the hidden level is shared as well. In fact, the hidden level is often individual and might contain evaluations of and motivations for the situation that lie outside the grasp and control of the community.

My point is this: a group's collective behavior does not necessarily signify a shared culture. There might be numerous individual reasons for the same behavior, and the same behavior might have numerous different conse-quences. In short, in our analysis we cannot presume that culture is shared. On the contrary, the driving questions of the analysis should be *whether* and *to what extent* "culture" is shared at all, in *what* the shared and the sharing consists, and *how* it emerges.

When we can neither presume that the system is shared, nor that it is a de-termining factor, it makes little sense – at least in the context of textual analysis – to hold on to the idea of "culture" as a more or less coherent whole: as a system. In that sense, we have to reformulate the concept of cul-ture.

CULTURE AS CONSEQUENCE

If we follow the micro-sociological assumption that society consists of routinizations of a myriad of everyday interactions, the actors' undertakings must be seen as a contribution to the creation, maintenance and change of society. As a genuine contribution to the constitution of society, an actor's undertakings are not preprogrammed by a determining system. Collectivity cannot be presumed, neither qualitatively nor quantitatively.

On the other hand, actors do not act in a social vacuum. First, it is a bio-logical fact that human beings, as soon as they are born, are dependent on others and seek interaction with others. Human beings are born social, inso-far as they are genetically predisposed toward attracting the attention of oth-ers: as ethology has shown, human beings and other animals are born with an innate ability to appeal to the other's care (Lorenz 1981). In an abstract sense, the same can be said for the artifacts that participate in interactions. They are dependent for their social survival upon other actors using them, and they are designed to attract the attention of others. Moreover, what ac-cording to evolutionary psychologists and biological anthropologists sets human beings apart from all other species, including other primates, is the fact that humans not only have innate social behavior but also seem genetically predisposed to understanding other individuals as intentional beings, that is, as beings with goals and means of their own. This ability explains a unique feature in human beings: imitative learning. Whereas chimpanzees are perfectly able to mimic the behavior of older and more experienced tribe members, humans can also interpret the goals and rationality behind this behavior and learn from this interpretation (Tomasello 1999).[3]

Secondly, interaction takes place in a world that is infra-structurally (buildings, roads, transportation etc.), institutionally (organizations, political institutions, money systems, etc...) and judicially (law, legal rules, etc.) pre-given. This world – society – is a product of the fact that interactions have routinized relations. Routinization has resulted in materializations (for example, infrastructures and artifacts), objectifications (money as the standard equivalence) and codifications (law). Such routinizations limit the realm of action: if you cross the road without paying attention, you run the risk of being run down. At the same time, routinization, to a large extent, reduces complexity. This means that we do not have to consider and plan all our actions in detail. We can, without too much ado, go from point A to point B, because the road is already there and the vehicle is at our disposal.

Socialization, however, is not the only thing that reduces complexity. Because of our cognitive abilities, we are mentally programmed to sort out and process information from our surroundings, and we can easily bring our actions into accord with this information. We have a number of metatextual frames, schemas or scripts in store that we can use to decode what the situation is about, what others' intentions are, what we can expect of their behavior and what is demanded of us. These frames are used in our situated interactions with others. They guide our actions and are, in that sense, the third reason why our actions are socially informed. Our actions are aimed at making an impact on our surroundings – in terms of recognition and distinction, of integration and differentiation – and they are based on a know-how of what is going on in the interaction (a sensitivity to the situation).

The actors' undertakings in relation to one another constitute interaction. Interaction takes place in a social realm, which, from a micro-sociological perspective, is a result of previous acts and their routinizations. Interaction

---

3   In this respect cognitive science has recently presented the evolutionary arguments in favor of both Tarde's (1962) "laws of imitation" and Weber's (1922) understanding of "social action."

is motivated by a biological urge *and* ability to form social bonds and to build up communities. It evolves due to the participants' cognitive abilities to act socially in given situations. These abilities are partly neuro-physiologically determined, partly determined by individual experience. Knowledge about how to interact comes from interacting, whereas the way in which the information is organized is due to the structure of the brain. The form is universal (neurological) and is valid for everybody, whereas the content is particular, inasmuch as no one shares the exact same experiences. In this regard, our cognitive abilities can be characterized as a routinization of the information process – a routinization of modes of understanding, evaluating and using information. In the same way as metatextual frames, schemas and scripts routinize cognition, interactions become routinized as habit. In this respect, society as well as cognition are consequences *of* and prerequisites *for* interactions: the former at the social and relational level, the latter at the mental and situated level.

In continuation of my proposal to conceive of culture as the interpretation of new information in relation to established schemas, we can now define culture as the mental consequences of acts. These acts have a social aim, the point however is that the interpretation – and thereby the formation of schemas – is an individual event.

INDIVIDUAL AND COMMUNITY

Culture is "something being done." Culture is a result of the gap between the actor's sensitivity to the situation prior to an interaction and the adjustments after the interaction. These adjustments involve changes in the schemas or elaborations on the metatextual frame. Culture thus is the individual's explanation and interpretation of the social meaning of these adjustments. Insofar as adjustment of schemas is the same as learning, culture is closely associated with situated learning processes. These processes stem from individual experiences of social settings, and culture is, as such, the evaluation of the processes that takes place in order to pave the way for new social settings. Culture is not "out there" – a phenomenon beyond the horizon of the individual. Culture is "in here."

Rather than a shared condition *for* actions, culture is the individual result *of* actions. We should, therefore, reverse the causal relations of the "implicit cultural theory" and, instead, say that "*Because* NN goes to church and participates in particular rituals, NN becomes a believer." In this sentence, "to go to church" is understood as the action and "to believe" as the result of that action.

At an elementary level, by participating in the sacrament you become part of a Christian community. Without the communion and without collective participation in the sacrament, there is no Christian community. For those who participate in the liturgy of a religious community for the first time, both the rituals and their meaning are new and unknown: this person simply lacks the script and the metatextual frame for understanding what is going on, and for what is expected of others and of the person him- or herself. The fact that others apparently participate with ease in the liturgy and that they are, therefore, more initiated, compels the novice to adjust her behavior to them. The purpose of this adjustment is to avoid being an outsider, which is accomplished by aping the insiders.

It requires skills to become part of a community. By participating in a number of liturgies, the actor gains a fuller and more profound understanding of what the situation requires. He or she gets to know her role, and begins to recognize the basics in others' contributions as well as the significance of the ritual. Faith becomes incarnated, and the outsider turns into a member of the community. Culture is the process through which actors acquire a full understanding of the patterns of interaction. Firstly, this process implies a process in which hypotheses are formed, elaborated or discarded, adjusted or reformulated. Secondly, this process is guided by observing what others do and by interpreting the possible reasons why they behave in this manner. This learning process is accomplished when the actor masters the situation. The ritual has become routine, and the actor has gotten the faith under her skin. Partaking in other religious communities might, in turn, expand the schemas, just like existential crises might lead to a reevaluation of the significance of the community – at that point a new cultural process might begin.

Generally, then, we might conclude the following:

> "*Because* a certain group behaves collectively in a recognizable
> manner, (*therefore*) it becomes a collectivity or community."

Acts generate communities; culture does not generate acts. Culture is the consequence of practices. As a consequence, culture is not the product (the essence) of the act, but an evaluation of the act. Or rather, culture is an interpretation, which invests behavior with inter-subjective meaning – that is, culture is perceived (treated and negotiated) as an act. Culture is not a product: the novice does not physically change as a direct result of the initiation, rather he or she is perceived, evaluated and judged (treated and negotiated) differently, both by herself and by the other participants. Confirmation is culture exactly because the ritual allows for a reevaluation of the role of the confirmee within the community. Subsequently, this role and the acts that are now permitted (participation in the communion) quickly become routine.

We can conclude two things from the above analysis. First, recognition plays a crucial role for interactions and for the formation of social relations. The actors strive to model events according to the kinds of situations and relations that they already know. The known is fundamental for forming hypotheses, and recognition amounts to testing these hypotheses in real life. Therein, the unexpected is recognized as a deviance from the known, and may lead either to an eradication of the unexpected or to the formation of a new and expanded model – "a difference that makes a difference" (Bateson 1972b) – that integrates the unexpected so it fits future expectations. In interaction, the community emerges out of recognition. When the actors can fine-tune, or recognize, their behaviors to one another, they are essentially in concord: the actors become visible to one another. The urge to become visible and recognizable to the other means that learning a behavior and participating in and interpreting and evaluating activities often happen through imitation. Furthermore, establishing relations to a large extent depends on symmetry, insofar as the participants have to imitate each other's styles in order for the interaction to be mutually recognizable.

Secondly, however, one might say that signification amounts to culture-specific versions of universal cognitive competences. This specificity is in its turn entrenched in intra-psychological generalizations– interpretations, evaluations – of the individuals own experiences with particular situations. *Because* these situations resemble those experienced by other individuals and because the interpreting and evaluating activity is learned through imitating other individuals, *(therefore)* our experiences and behaviors often resemble one another and are recognizable in others and for others. Because we rarely are complete strangers and never completely identical to one another, social life or society develops in a continuous tension between mutual recognition and misunderstanding. No interaction runs exactly like the other, and our sensitivities to the situation have to be adjusted from time to time in order to match the present situation. Thus, culture is a dynamic process.

CODA: THE TASK OF CULTURAL THEORY

Any cultural theory should deal with these three issues:

1. The relation between individual and community
2. The relation between "culture" and "nature" on the one hand and "culture" and "society" on the other.'
3. Cultural change

This article has especially focused on the relation between "culture" and "society" – concepts that are tend to be regarded as synonymous by mainstream cultural theories. Terms such as "socio-cultural context" or "the social and cultural framework" are symptomatic of this conceptual blurriness. According to these theories, culture is a collective phenomenon insofar as it is the shared foundation for our acts within the framework of the community. "Culture" typically stands for a sphere particular to humankind and sharply distinguished from the sphere of nature. "Culture" is conceived as the sphere of consciousness and consists of symbolic forms, historical narratives, manifold traditions and eye-catching ritual. Nature on the other hand is matter without consciousness: the world of atoms and electrons, of regularity without will or intention. This type of theory has had difficulties explaining cultural change as a dynamic factor inherent to culture itself. This is due to the fact that our *idées reçues* are derived from cultural anthropology, whose primary aim was to explain how traditional societies (or "cultures") were able to maintain and hand down their social foundations relatively unchanged throughout generations. Cultural change was perceived as a defect, which inflicted culture from the outside. When this anthropological concept of culture was utilized on modern cultures, which are characterized by an extensive inner dynamic, the problem of change became obvious. The solution has typically been to explain away cultural change as a consequence of social change. The popularity of (post)modern theories within mainstream cultural research is symptomatic of this pattern of explanation, which by the way only serves to blur the distinction between "culture" and "society" even more.

The problem with the "implicit cultural theory" is not just that it is wrong. By its inability to focus on the relation between "culture" and "nature" it is about to detach a large part of the humanities from the scientific world, where neuroscience is setting the agenda. In fact, neuroscience is redefining fundamental concepts of philosophy as we speak: the self, consciousness and free will (Churchland 2002). While this goes on, cultural research roams the humanities with its *idées reçues* – ideas that soon only will be valued as curiosities or relics from the past.

For my part, however, I see no reason why we should give up on cultural research or the humanities. Neuroscience does not deny the relevance of a textually based approach. On the contrary, it allows for new insights into "text" and offers new models of explanation that are certainly worthwhile pursuing. Furthermore, it offers the possibility of expanding cultural research in different and more fruitful ways than hitherto. For by conceiving culture in terms of cognitive and information science, the concept can, in a fertile way, be connected to micro-sociology and interactionism.

In this paper, I have tried to unfold this perspective by defining culture as an aspect of cognition. Cognition, among other things, makes it possible for us to understand situations and to act appropriately in our interactions with others. It gives us a metatextual framework that we can use and elaborate in concrete interactions. In this sense, culture is the evaluation of the suitability of the frame in relation to the actual course of the interaction. Culture is an interpretation of which metatextual adjustments are necessary for the actor's future social relations. The bonds that are forged between actors (individuals and artifacts) in interaction are "social." "Culture", on the other hand, is our cognitive ability to interpret information from our surroundings and adjust our future expectations as a consequence of this information. These interpretations may be materialized as symbolic artifacts in the public sphere which in turn are open to interpretations by other actors as the expression of shared imaginations.

My point is as follows: "shared imaginations" do not exist in and of themselves. On the contrary, there are individual imaginings about communal life and collectivity. These individual imaginings may to a large extent resemble those of other individuals. The stress here is on "to a large extent": among individuals there is an identical neuro-physiological structure of imagining, but our own imaginations are marked by private experiences in the surrounding world. These surroundings are natural, social (understood as interactions) *and* societal (understood as routinized relations). "Culture" is the way in which actors attempt to generalize these private experiences in order to create mutual understanding with others. Because no interactions are completely alike and because all sharing may be subject to randomness, the actors' sensitivities to the situation have to be adjusted on a regular basis. Thus, the cultural process of interpretation is an ongoing one.

As I have pointed out elsewhere (Jantzen 2004), it is time to overcome Dilthey's (1959) separation of the human and the natural sciences, inasmuch as culture essentially stems from the natural foundations of human life. However, this requires that we are able and willing to transgress our disciplinary biases and the ideas that have been handed down to us.

Translated from Danish by Maren Lytje

Works Cited

Bateson, Gregory (1972a): "A theory of play and fantasy," in: *Steps towards an ecology of mind*, New York (Ballantine).

Bateson, Gregory (1972b): Towards a theory of alcoholism. The cybernetics of "self," in: *Steps towards an ecology of mind*, New York (Ballantine).

Bausinger, Hermann (1961): *Volkskultur in der technischen Welt*, Stuttgart (W. Kohlhammer).

Benedict, Ruth (1961): *Patterns of culture*, Boston (Houghton Mifflin) (original 1934).

Churchland, Patricia Smith (2002): *Brain-Wise. Studies in neurophilosophy*, Cambridge, MA, (MIT Press).

Dilthey, Wilhelm (1959): *Einleitung in die Geisteswissenschaft*, in: Gesammelte Schriften, Bd. 1, Stuttgart (B.G. Teubner) (original 1883).

Durkheim, Émil (1933): *The division of labor in society*, London (MacMillan) (original 1893).

Flaubert, Gustave (1881); *Bouvard et Pecuchet, Dictionnaire des idées reçues*, Paris (A. Lemerre).

Hall, Stuart (1996): "Gramsci's Relevance for the Study of Race and Ethnicity," in: D. Morley & D.K. Chen (eds.) *Stuart Hall*, London (Routledge).

Herder, Johan Gottfried (1965): *Ideen zur Geschichte der Menschheit*, Berlin & Weimar (Aufbau Verlag) (original 1784-1791).

Jantzen, Christian (1997): *Fra evolution til strukturation – rids af nogle kulturteoretiske positioner*, Aalborg (Aalborg Universitet), onlinepublication: http://www.kommunikation.aau.dk/publikationer/online.html.

Jantzen, Christian (2004): "Tertium datur. Kampen om kulturbegrebet," in: Karen Klitgaard Povlsen & Anne Scott Sørensen (red.) *Kulturkamp og kulturkritik*, Århus (Klim).

Jantzen, Christian & Søren Frimann Trads (2004): "På tanken," in: Christian Jantzen (red.) *Situationer*, Aalborg (Aalborg Universitetsforlag) (in press),

Jensen, Johan Fjord (1988): "Det dobbelte kulturbegreb – den dobbelte bevidsthed," in: H. Hauge & H. Horstbøll (eds.) *Kulturbegrebets kulturhistorie*, Århus (Aarhus Universitetsforlag).

Kroeber, Alfred L. (1917): "The superorganic," in: *American Anthropologist*, Vol. 19.

Lorenz, Konrad (1981): *The foundations of ethology*, Berlin (Springer).

Malinowski, Bronislaw (1922): *Argonauts of the Western Pacific*, London (Routledge & Kegan Paul).

Morris, Charles (1938): *Foundations of the theory of signs*, Chicago (Chicago University Press.).

Simmel, Georg (1983): "Das Gebiet der Soziologie," in: *Schriften zur Soziologie*, Frankfurt a/M (Suhrkamp).

Tarde, Gabriel (1962): *The laws of imitation*, Gloucester, MA (Peter Smith) (original 1890).

Tomasello, Michael (1999): *The cultural origins of human cognition*, Cambridge, MA (Harvard University Press).

Tylor, Edward B. (1903): *Primitive culture: Researches into the development of mythology, philosophy, religion, language, art and custom,* London (John Murray) (original 1871).

Voskuil, J.J. (1973): "Die Diffussion des Weihnachtsbaumes in den Niederlanden," in: *Rheinisch-Westfälische Zeitschrift für Volkskunde,* Vol. 20.

Williams, Raymond (1977): *Marxism and Literature,* Oxford (Oxford University Press).

Weber, Max (1922): *Wirtschaft und Gesellschaft. Grundriss der verstehende Soziologie,* Tübingen (J.C.B. Mohr).

THE "HISTORICAL APPROACH" TO CULTURAL THEORY
Toward a Historical Phenomenology of Culture

Ben Dorfman
Department of Languages and Intercultural Studies
Aalborg University

By 2004, the travails of cultural theory are difficult to follow. The reasons for this are multiple: the interdisciplinary origins of cultural studies (e.g., from literature, philosophy, philology, linguistics, sociology and history), the frequent institutional resistance to cultural studies' interdisciplinary methodology and the ensuing lack of surety as to precisely where cultural studies belongs in the academy are all examples of factors contributing to the confusion over what it means to "theorize culture." However, it may be that the leading difficulty in coming to grips with cultural theory are the broad disagreements on the nature of its object: "culture." The use of quotation marks here is indicative. Whereas "culture" could once be evoked with relative assuredness as a matter of "spirit," "consciousness" or an overarching set of historical characteristics for groups and individuals, today such definitions seem anachronistic. Indeed, while the neo-Marxist/neo-poststructuralist "Birmingham School" made a play for dominance in the game of defining culture over the 1970s, '80s and '90s, it found itself on a field in which various stripes of sociological, anthropological and discursive-analytical approaches were competitors. Moreover, it was often the case that the lines between these approaches were unclear. Thus, as of yet, the idea of culture remains open and fluid. This provides the challenge of the stabilization of the idea of culture as perhaps the central task for the student of culture.

Now, it should be noted that, in 2004, "stabilization" is a tricky word. After the so-called "postmodern challenge," the idea that definitions should be firm and reflect anything but one's subjectivity is difficult terrain.[1] However, I

---

1   This is perhaps best expressed in Foucault's assertion (1977/1980) that one speaks not as a "bearer of universal values," but rather as a "person occupying a specific position" linked to the "general functioning of the apparatus of truth" (132).

would simply assert that to seek to firm up terminology is not necessarily to disband subjectivity in favor of objectivity. Rather, it might represent an exploration of the terrain on which subjectivity is formed – the constitutive relations of the semiotic field on which subjectivities function, and the realization of the "orders of knowledge" that gives discourse its specific possibilities.[2]

Therein, as concerns the stabilization of the idea of culture, the student of culture might recognize three possibilities. The first of these we might term the "phenomenological approach." That is to say that, asserting culture as an objectively existing "entity," or concrete "thing" that might be made an object of investigation, the student of culture might attempt to find what I would call an "existential-generative" connection between culture and its terminological and ideological invocations. In other words, one might ask whether or not culture *itself* offers any clues as to what it is. Can an objectively existing "entity" of culture tell us something about the uses of the term that have been *applied* to that entity? Or, to put it another way, is it possible to account for the debates in cultural theory *by way of*, or *through*, culture "itself?" There would be fruitful possibilities in such an approach. Primarily, it would offer the firmest sense of what culture *is* as we would gain a sense of a connection between a concrete *object* of culture, or an object that *is* culture, and the historical invocations of *term* "culture." However, we can also recognize that such an approach would pose its problems: without a firm sense of the object in question before hand – i.e., culture – one would be engaged in a frustrating search across multiple dimensions of contemporary and historical society for an object that he or she would not, in fact, be *allowing* themselves to find. In other words, to search for an object without a definition of what one is searching for is to engage in a search that will inevitably result in confusion and failure.

The second approach available to the student of culture as regards the stabilization of the idea of culture, then, is what we might call the "contemporary consensus" approach. Under the terms of this approach, the student of culture might accept the fact that definitions of culture change over time, and thus set his or her task as determining whether or not, despite *claimed* points of disputation, there is *actually* more agreed upon within the range of

---

2   The idea of an "order of knowledge" borrows from Foucault's (1971/1972) notion of "orders of discourse" and "discursive formations": "the conditions of existence…coexistence, maintenance, modification and disappearance" of "statements" (31, 38).

contemporary cultural theories than is usually thought.[3] In such an approach, the presumption is that the constitutive issues for culture lay in the now, and that that the "now" of cultural theory represents the historical culmination of the idea of culture. That is to say that the assertion here would be that contemporary cultural theory should enjoy pride of place over *past* cultural theories because contemporary theory has already "dealt with" past cultural theory. And, indeed, in operating on this presumption, despite a temporally truncated view, the "contemporary consensus" approach recognizes the disputed nature of the field of cultural theory – its point of analysis becomes contemporary *debates* over culture. As with the "phenomenological" approach" the rewards here could also be noticeable. If one considers the problem of defining culture as in fact a problem of *definitions* – as opposed to objects – then it is among definitions that one must work. However, the keen reader will realize that there are limitations here too. What, in fact, is one attempting to define in seeking to reconcile different contemporary visions of "culture?" In pursuing terminology, one could ask: is one ever working *solely* on that terrain? Or, in attempting to stabilize the *idea* of culture, are we actually after more – namely, the object of culture *itself*, or that which the *term* "culture" is supposed to describe?

The third approach available to the student of culture in terms of stabilizing the idea of culture is thus what I would call the "historical approach." This approach toes the line between the "phenomenological" approach and "contemporary consensus" approaches because as it posits neither a historically fixed definition of culture nor an unchangeable cultural "object." Rather, what the "historical approach" offers is a consistency to *ideas* on culture that in fact *relies* on their differentiation over time. This involves two ideas. First, history relies on differentiation. In other words, an object that exists in historical time never remains the same object – a historical object always represents a differentiated form of itself at one time than it did at another.[4] Nonetheless, this differentiation also gives us the ability to recognize objects as what they are in a manner that overcomes differentia-

---

3   We will be talking about the nature of those definitions shortly.
4   This is related to the classic concept of historicism. Robert Burns (2000) points to Friedrich Meinecke's well-known definition of the essence of historicism – generally taken as the driving force in nineteenth century historical thought – as "the substation of a process of *individualizing* observation for a *generalizaing* view of human forces in history [without excluding]…altogether any attempt to find general laws and types in human life" (57).

tion: that an object at one moment is *not* itself as it was in "another" form is made *possible* by way of its shared identity with itself over time.[5] In terms of ideas of culture, what this means is that the "historical approach" advocates a return backward into time on the hunt for the *term* culture. However, in moving beyond the pale of the present, the historical approach escapes the transitoriness of the "contemporary consensus" approach. That is to say that while the "historical approach" does not find a "real" cultural "object," it nonetheless opens a greater spectrum of *claimed* cultural "objects" than does the "contemporary consensus" approach by way of including more historical moments than just the present, and one's *not* giving pride of place to contemporary definitions of culture. And, perhaps most provocatively, we gain here the possibility of generating what we might term a "historical phenomenology" of the idea of culture. In other words, a "historical approach" to cultural theory gives us a sense of the dynamics of the *change* of ideas of culture over time, as well as a sense of the dynamics of change in relation to the idea of culture based on the establishment of *connections* between how "culture" *has been* used and how it is used *today*. This gives us a sense of culture as a phenomenon, but in avoidance of a recourse to a cultural "object" or "reality" – in the classic manner of Husserl's (1929/1995) "epoche" it "inhibit[s] every co-objective of objective positing produced in unreflective consciousness, and therewith [inhibits] every judgment drawing on the world as it 'exists'...straightforwardly [for the observer]" (17). Clearly, this does neither solve all of the problems of the "contemporary consensus" approach, nor those of the more "purely" phenomenological approach (the first of our three approaches to culture). The "historical approach" to cultural theory still leaves us lacking a "cultural object," or historical "reality" of culture that extends beyond the boundaries of terminology or ideas. Additionally, the "historical approach" does not stabilize the definition of "culture" *before* the move to investigation, thus not allowing us to *identify* such an "object" of culture. However, the historical approach nonetheless gives us a broader sense of the terminology of "culture" and reveals a range of consistencies across historical time such that, after a

---

5   I see this as also related to classic conceptions of historicism. We might note that there are two parts to Meinecke's definition of historicism – the "general" and the "particular." The notion of differentiation draws from emphases on the particular. The assertion of a trans-temporally shared identity draws on the emphases on generality.

certain point, one has to wonder whether it is worth interrogating into a difference between "reality" on one hand and historical "terminologies" or "ideas" on the other. This is the basis for the idea that culture might have a "historical phenomenology."

Over the next several pages, then, I will ask the following questions. How have ideas of culture changed over time? In other words, what are the definitions of culture from the past that might be different from definitions we have today? However, what are the *dynamics* of change involved in the concept of culture? In other words, *why* have concepts of culture changed, irregardless of their specific cotemporary formulations, or the specific reasons driving us into our historical interrogations of culture? From there, however, I will also ask whether or not we can establish a *historical* consensus – as opposed to "contemporary" consensus – regarding culture. In other words, can we gain a sense of an object that we are in search of by way of the term "culture" over the pale of historical time through finding points of commonality with the *historical* debate on culture, or the debate on culture over time? Lastly, however, we might inquire as to whether or not we can gain such a sense of culture in a way that allows "historical consensus" to give way to historical *phenomenology*, or a mode of understanding culture that, given culture as property within the human domain, posits the *history of ideas* on culture as what we might call culture "itself", or the "object" of "culture" as such.

I. CULTURE OVER TIME

In terms of addressing the idea of how culture has been used over time (question 1 from above), I would suggest that can identify six approaches to culture. I will list these numerically, with an accompanying list of some of their major proponents. [6]

1. Culture-as-consciousness:	Kant, Hegel
2. Culture-as-apparatus of domination: [7]	Marx, Gramsci, Horkheimer and Adorno, Althusser, Foucault, Deleuze, Lyotard, the "Birmingham School"

---

6   I ask that readers accept this list on a purely heuristic basis, rather than under the terms of "completeness."

7   I borrow this terminology from During (1999, 4).

3. Culture-as-social experience:	Durkheim, Weber, Simmel (classic sociology)
4. Culture-as-action:	Ethnomethodology, Conversation Analysis (e.g., Garfinkel, Tannen)
5. Culture-as-behavior:	Malinowski, Boas, Geertz (anthropology)
6. Culture-as-history:	Heidegger, Gadamer, Ricoeur

Clearly, the above list involves some controversial mixing of traditions that might neither automatically place themselves together, nor would immediately characterize their understanding of culture with the precise the labels I have used. Therein, I will restate the list, however, this time with a definition for each approach as well as a justification for the labels assigned to each position.

1. Culture-as-consciousness
"Culture-as-consciousness" suggests that culture has to do with the processes of mind and reason and their development over time. The justification for this label is that "culture-as-consciousness" suggests consciousness as not only the generating force of culture, but also what we might call the "content" of culture, or its main artifact.

2. Culture-as-apparatus of domination
"Culture-as-apparatus of domination" is the idea that culture has to do with the imposition of mindsets and behaviors on social subjects, if not, in fact, the creation of social subjectivity by way of such impositions. The justification for this label is that culture-as-apparatus of domination's major proponents see culture as related to social, political and economic power and, more specifically, social, political and economic power as integral to the creation of knowledge.

3. Culture-as-social experience
"Culture-as-social experience" suggests that culture has to do with the mental life formed as a result of existing in sets of social relationships. The justification for this label is that "culture-as-social experience's" major proponents see culture as demanding social interactivity, but with the recognition that social activity results in more than simply further social actions – i.e., "mental" life.

4. Culture-as-action

"Culture-as-action" is the idea that culture is no more or less than the precise and exact things we do in social interaction. Here, less room is left for the idea of a "mental life" than is done in the "culture-as-social experience" model. Rather, the assumption is that though "mental life" may be present, it is generally acted out.

5. Culture-as-behavior

"Culture-as-behavior" is the idea that culture has to do with the fact that mental life, or at least mental structures, are *reflected* in human behavior. What differentiates "culture-as-behavior" from "culture-as-social experience" is that "culture-as-behavior" puts culture de facto *at* the level of behavior such that when one is watching behavior, one is watching culture. Therein, behavior, rather than mental life, *becomes* culture.

6. Culture-as-history

"Culture-as-history" is the idea that culture has to do with states of historical being at all levels at which historical being might be conceived: social, economic, political, artistic/creative, intellectual, etc… The justification for this label is that "culture-as-history's" major proponents all see culture as a product of the fundamental fact of our existence through time.

I will make several comments regarding these six approaches. First, we might recognize the singularity of the first approach: "culture-as-consciousness." In part, this is because of its age – as I have posed it, it is the only school without a representative in the twentieth century. However, the "culture-as-consciousness" approach's singularity is also a matter of the fact that it suggests that culture is a matter of the mind alone. In other words, though certainly distinct philosophers, Kant and Hegel both essentially asserted that culture was a matter of the mind interacting with *itself*. In Hegel, this was a matter of the thesis/antithesis/synthesis triad. "The Spirit of this world is…permeated by *self*-consciousness," wrote Hegel (1807/1977), yet "the self only knows itself as a *transcended self*" (297, 299) – the mind recognizes itself (thesis), knows itself (antithesis) and thus achieves a new level of consciousness (synthesis). In Kant (1781/1998), the mind interacted with itself by way of what he called the "synthetic *a priori*" (10-12). In other words, the mind had "categories" by which it processed knowledge. However, that we could process the mind *itself* meant that it had an objective existence that the subjectivity of the categories could not deny. Therein, there was a synthesis between subjective knowledge and objective "reality" that was the basis for knowledge itself that we might call "true." In the cases of both Hegel and Kant, "culture" [*Bildung*] designated the development of this knowledge. "Culture" was education, and improvement of the individual mind.[8]

The closest relation to the "culture-as-consciousness" approach, then, is approach number six: "culture-as-history." The similarities come on two levels. First, the "culture-as-consciousness" and "culture-as-history" approaches both make what we might call "existential" claims about the nature of culture. In other words, culture-as-consciousness suggests the de facto incidentality of the world outside the mind: consciousness and the powers of reasoned reflection are existence themselves and, thus, history themselves. Therein, culture exists inasmuch as history exists. Heidegger, Gadamer and Ricoeur, the major proponents of "culture-as-history," all supported this essential argument. Heidegger (1936/1971) asserted that the "governing expanse" of culture is the world of a "historical people" (42). Gadamer (1960/1998) phrased culture as a matter of historically received "tradition" (277), and Ricoeur (1983/1984) posited it as a matter of "mimesis" or an imitation of the communication of time itself (53-55). The *difference* between the "culture-as-consciousness" approach and the "culture-as-history" approach is that the proponents of culture-as-history did not necessarily see history as a matter of *consciousness*. In fact, a key point in all of their works, their point is precisely the opposite: rather than cognating history, we are simply *in* it. Heidegger (1962) suggested that that "entities within the world are historical as such, their history does not signify something 'external' which merely accompanies the 'inner' history of the 'soul'" (440). Gadamer (1960/1998) asserted that "to be historically means that knowledge of oneself can never be complete" (302). Ricoeur's (1983/1984) thesis was that "historical events do not differ radically from those framed by a plot" (208). In other words, for "culture-as-history," history was not something that we came to from the outside of which we could be "conscious", or know as an "objectivity." Rather, we *were* historical in our very nature, giving us a lack of distance and thus at least partly-obscured consciousness of that fact, be it by

---

8   Hegel (1807/1977), for example, posited that culture [*Bildung*] was "self-alienated Spirit" – the "external essence" of the world and its "free content of legal right" – culture was the development of the world out of consciousness (294). Kant (1784/1991) argued that "In the same way [that] trees in a forest, seeking to deprive each other of air and sunlight, compel each other to find these by upward growth…all culture and art…are fruits of his unsociability." Humankind, asserted Kant is compelled to "discipline itself" into progress and thus to "develop completely the germs which nature implanted" (54).

way of "being" (Heidegger), history itself (Gadamer) and "emplotment" (Ricoeur).

What this means is that, in terms of "schools of culture," we might accord approaches two through five – "culture-as-apparatus of domination," "culture-as-social experience," "culture-as-action" and "culture-as-behavior" – a high degree of similarity. To some extent, this is a controversial point. Certainly, the late nineteenth and early twentieth century sociology I am characterizing "culture-as-social-experience" (Durkheim, Weber, Simmel) was critical, for example, of Marxism (from "culture-as-apparatus of domination"), rejecting what it saw, for example, as the "ideological" or "political" nature of its analysis.[9] And, we might note, it was precisely ideological and political aims that *all* of the members of what I call the "culture-as-apparatus of domination" approach invoke as the central concerns of cultural analysis.[10] However, we should recognize that in all four cases – culture-as-apparatus of domination, culture-as-social experience, culture-as-action and culture-as-behavior – the distinctions from "culture-as-consciousness" and "culture-as-history" are sharp. That is to say that, for culture-as-consciousness and culture-as-history, culture was *naturalistic*. In both cases, culture *came* with human existence itself: either consciousness was the essence of human existence, and culture was a product of the development of consciousness, or historicity (the transformational quality of time) was the essence of human existence, and culture was a product of historicity. For culture-as-apparatus of domination, culture-as-social experience, culture-as-action and culture-as-behavior, however, culture was/is a *heurism*, or organizing device for sociological and anthropological behavior imposed *from the outside* – observable and *not* the object of a speculative philosophy on "mind" or "history", á la Kant, Hegel, Heidegger, Gadamer or Ricoeur. Marx (1845/1975), for example, described culture as "superstructural," or an "ideology" imposed over "real individuals, their activity and the material conditions of their life" – items that were "empirically verifiable" (31). Durkheim (1894/2001b) posited culture as a matter of sorting through "social phenomena" that present

---

9   Durkheim (1893/2001a), for example, characterized socialism as a "zealotry" oriented toward pursing the concept of a "futuristic" thinking to its "limits" (77, 94).

10   This is a very broad point. However, I would simply refer the reader to Marx (1845/1975), Hall (1991/1999), Foucault (1977/1980), Lyotard (1984/1992), Deleuze and Guattari (1972/1983, 340-82), Gramsci (2000, 275-99) and Adorno (2001) by way of example.

themselves as "distinct from consciously formed representations of them in the mind" – culture was not a matter of intrinsic, existential qualities but social actors (290). Weber perhaps presents the most complicated case. In his view, culture was causal to the specificity of our historical conditions; it was a "finite segment of the meaningless infinity of the world process, a segment on which human beings confer meaning and significance" (Weber 1904/1949, 81).[11] Nonetheless, the better cultural analyst sought a "concrete science of social reality", and the historical conditions of social formations being "*so* and not *otherwise*" (1904/1949, 72). In other words, culture was *attributed* as such "insofar as we relate it to value ideas," giving it its manifestation in "empirical reality" that might be traced (1904/1949, 76). Indeed, in perhaps the most radical formulations of the empricity of culture, Harold Garfinkel (1967/2001) argued that "cultural events" are made solely by their "members… only, entirely [and] exclusively in actual, singular, particular occasions through actual witnessed displays of common talk and conduct" (111), and Stuart Hall (1991/1999) of the Birmingham School proposed culture to be a matter of "the intertextuality of texts in their institutional positions, texts as sources of power [and] textuality as a site of representation and resistance" (105).[12] To that extent, "natural" cultural realities did not exist. Rather, what was at work were *constructions* of reality in which human beings existed, transformed "apparent" reality and, in the process, gained experiences and behaviors that might be *termed* cultural, but were not so in any existential or "pre-social" or "pre-interactive" sense. In general, it is such positions that represent the range of options for cultural theory at the start of the twenty-first century.

---

11   This is the basis, for example, of Weber's classic *The Protestant Ethic and the Spirit of Capitalism* (1904-5/2001).

12   Some would be surprised to see the Birmingham School, of which Hall is a leading proponent, as holding an "empirical" view of culture as its embrace of post-structuralism appears to destabilize notions of the empirical in humanistic investigation. However, not unlike Foucault in his post-structuralism, the Birmingham School places such a premium on the social situatedness of culture that the premium then becomes placed on the *observation* of "intertextuality" in its socio-political contexts. Foucault's (1971/1977) notion of a methodology that was "grey, meticulous and patiently documentary" is applicable here (139). The claim to contextualized sociological investigation, I would argue – sociological investigation that recognizes its own social nature – does not relieve sociological investigation of its empirical, "scientific" nature.

II. CULTURAL THEORY AND THE DYNAMICS OF CHANGE

In essence, we can establish some historical dividing lines that separate out the six approaches to cultural theory on a historical basis. Based on the years of activity of their major proponents – or at least those we have listed here – we might chart these as follows:

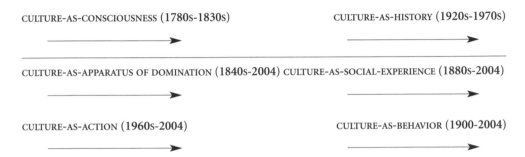

CULTURE-AS-CONSCIOUSNESS (1780s-1830s)   CULTURE-AS-HISTORY (1920s-1970s)

CULTURE-AS-APPARATUS OF DOMINATION (1840s-2004) CULTURE-AS-SOCIAL-EXPERIENCE (1880s-2004)

CULTURE-AS-ACTION (1960s-2004)   CULTURE-AS-BEHAVIOR (1900-2004)

The basis for the above divisions are two-fold. First, at the start of the twenty-first century, we have to recognize the death of "culture-as-consciousness" and "culture-as-history." In other words, although certainly not utterly unified in their approaches to culture, the "culture-as-apparatus of domination," "culture-as-social experience," "culture-as-action" and "culture-as-behavior" approaches have won the day. What is at work here is the victory of what we might call a "scientific epistemology." In other words, in general accordance with the tenets of natural science, the primacy of cultural research today is placed on the validity of observational results. The leading question for culture among the culture-as-apparatus of domination, culture-as-social experience, culture-as-action and culture-as-behavior models is what people *do* rather than what they *are*, or at least asserting that the existentiality of human existence – what people *are* – is a function first and foremost of their "doing." Therein, though not neatly reducible in terms of chronologies, we arrive at two senses of cultural theory: one "older" ("culture-as-consciousness" and "culture-as-history") due to its essential death on the field of cultural theory, and one "newer" (culture-as-apparatuses of domination, culture-as-social experience, culture-as-action and culture-as-behavior) due to its persistence into the twenty-first century.

The reasons for the victory of scientific epistemology, or what I referred to in the title of this section as "cultural theory and the dynamics of change", are difficult to identify. One of the most readily invoked rationales for this victory – one that is often invoked out of the culture-as-apparatuses of domination approach to cultural theory – is that the emergence of scientific epistemology as a dominant form of knowledge has to do with the emergence of the historical dominance of economic capitalism. The argument here is that, in relation to the industrial revolution, both Western and global society became increasingly organized around the demands of industrial production. These demanded factual information, or empirically verifiable information that could be put to use in industrial society. This was the case not only in terms of industrial production itself – i.e., how industrial production could be made more efficient and thus more profitable – but also in relation to industrial *producers*. In other words, how could human labor power integral to industrial production be kept healthy, educated and psychologically content such that it might *contribute* to the efficiency and increasing profitability of industrial production?[13]

Despite the power of the economic capitalism argument, however, it may not be *only* the case that the history of ideas *only* responds to economic forces. Rather, in a sense that might be described as related to the idea of "culture-as-consciousness" (although in a more Hegelian than Kantian fashion), it may be that the fact that ideas exist in time, or are historical, means that ideas respond to *themselves*. In other words, how is it that ideas enter into a conversancy with one another? What is the form of "theoretical" discourse when, in fact, conceived of as, in fact, *theoretical*, and *not* primarily economic?

I would make two proposals in response to these questions. First, ideas develop dialectically. In other words, what I am proposing is that, rather than fitting into *a priori* categories of validity, ideas function in relation to *one another*. In operating on the terrain of ideas, we are operating on the terrain of *differences*; one idea is *not* another and thus, for an idea to be formed as *distinct* from another, an idea must be formed, at least partially, *against* another idea. Herein, the history of ideas relies on negation. That is to say that the production of a history of ideas that includes distinction *among* ideas – which in fact *is* the history of ideas – involves the attempt at, or at least *conditions for*, the eradication and supercession of "older" ideas. The victory of the concepts of culture working under a "scientific epistemology" is an example of this.

---

13 Foucault (1975/1977), for example, writes that "as the machinery of production became larger and more complex, supervision became ever more necessary" and "elementary teaching" became increasingly standardized (174-5). See also, for example, Horkheimer (2001); Gramsci (2000); Lyotard (1984/1992); Hobsbawm (1962/1996, 168-308).

However, my second proposal on the nature of theoretical discourse as responding to itself and not "external" factors is that the act of historical negation, or the *conditions of negation* of "older" ideas by newer ideas, also involves what I would call "historical sustenance." That is to say that negation is also a mode of validation. We might understand this as follows: to negate "older" ideas of culture means recognizing their importance on a historical basis. Here, I would simply indicate my support for certain ideas implicit in the culture-as-history approach. History is a baseline – it is a condition for existence, intellectual and otherwise, that we do not get to escape. Indeed, even the move to escape history, or posit something *as* "genuinely new," works in reference to the "old." Therein, the "old" is never completely lost, even as it must be overcome, subdued and in fact relegated to the past for it to gain its status as "old" or "historical."

Therein, in terms of cultural theory and the dynamics of change, we might suggest the following. First, there are "external," or "non-intellectual" factors that might be taken to explain the historical victory of scientific epistemology. The rise of capital economy would be primary among these. However, we need to be sensitive to the nature of theoretical discourse as well. This is not only in terms of its relations with economics and the social relations and/or political that might accompany economic relations, but in terms of the fact that "theory," or ideas, may have a history *themselves*, or a history "on their own terms" – a history, one might say, that does not exist anywhere except on the "pure" terrain of ideas.

III. THE HISTORICAL CONSENSUS

At this point, we are ready to reap the first level of the results of what I have called the "historical approach" to cultural theory. That is to ask into a larger *claimed* set of objects of culture, especially given the idea that we might find among them not only points of opposition, but, in a dialectical fashion, oppositions that also reveal the artifacts of "historical sustenance," or those ideas that come to be *sustained* in the space of cultural theory *by way of* their historical negation.

In essence, I would pose the following question in that regard: in deploying a "scientific epistemology," or an epistemology based on observation and the validity of observational science, what is it that the "culture-as-apparatus of domination," "culture-as-social experience," "culture-as-action" and "culture-as-behavior" approaches seek to explain? In other words, what is it that they get at that is *cultural*, as opposed to concerned with apparatuses of domination, social experience, human action or human behaviors? To formulate it yet another way, at what point do apparatuses of domination, social experience, human action and human behavior *become cultural,* as opposed to simply apparatuses of domination, social experiences, human action or human behavior?

The answer comes by way of the historical negation, or the fact that "new" ideas of culture must, in fact, "overcome" and "subdue" "older" ideas of culture or at least exist in the conditions that would *allow* for such negations yet, under those conditions, *validate* "older" ideas of culture as providing the conditions of existence for "newer" ideas of culture. The point is this: new ideas about culture only become *about culture* by entering into a relationship with "older" ideas about culture and claiming to refine them, disprove them and exceed them on a historical basis. This can be seen in the history of cultural theory. Marx, for example, claimed to overcome Hegel and, to a lesser extent, Kant. As Marx (1845/1975) put it, the tradition of philosophy focusing *solely* on consciousness was slave to "phantoms formed in the brain" (36). Thus cultural study should set out from "real premises": the "empirically verifiable…material life process" that would, in fact, *explain* the realm of "ideology" on which he thought the culture-as-consciousness model functioned (36-37). To move to another figure in the culture-as-apparatus of domination tradition, we might note that Foucault (1977/1980) also claimed that one had to dispose of "transcendental" ideas such as "consciousness" and establish a form of inquiry that can account for the "constitution of knowledges, discourses and domains of objects *without* making reference to a transcendental subject" (117, my italics).[14]

And, indeed, although identifiable as different approaches, the culture-as-social-experience approach, culture-as-action approach and culture-as-behavior approach emanate from the same epistemological premises. Durkheim (1894/2001b), for example, asserted that relying on what he saw as "objective" social phenomena rather than "images formed in the brain" kept the cultural analyst on the terrain of "reality" rather than an "intellectual ideal" (302-303). Weber (1904/1949) suggested that we needed to keep

---

14 It should be clear here that, although both Marx and Foucault maintained extensive critiques of the metaphysical, Foucault saw Marx as practicing a variety of metaphysics himself – the dialectic, wrote Foucault (1977/1980) whether materialist like Marx or ideological as in Hegel, "is a way of evading the always open and hazardous reality of conflict" and reducing history to an "empty sameness" (114-15, 117). Thus, while leveling certain similar epistemological critiques, Marx and Foucualt can also be viewed as advocating substantively different epistemological positions.

track of "coexistently emerging and disappearing events" that were "outside" (objective, observable) as much as "within ourselves" ("mental") (72). Garfinkel (1967/2001) suggests that the premium was on the "phenomena of rationality" in which conduct occurs – the "description" (observability) of which he sees sociology as primarily concerned (104). Malinowski ("culture-as-behavior," 1927/2001) offered that an encounter with culture in "*statu nascendi*," as he put it, or a primordial evolution of "Spirit" or "mind," was impossible. What *was* available to us were the "facts" of culture, "already accomplished" (144). Indeed, it is only in the "culture-as-history" approach that we find sympathy with the idea of culture-as-consciousness. Heidegger (1927/1962), for example, asserted that what is "primarily historical" is "Dasein" – the essential entity which "each of us is himself" and precedes the "definite realm" of "entities themselves" (27, 130, 433). Gadamer (1960/1998) asserted that "whoever has a historical sense knows what is possible for an age and what it not" – similar to the assertion one might posit for culture-as-consciousness that whoever would know consciousness would know what is possible for culture (17).[15]

Nonetheless, the question of historical consensus demands that we look carefully at these statements, especially in the cases of "culture-as apparatus of domination," "culture-as-social experience", "culture-as-action" and "culture-as-behavior." In other words, is it the case that in the "culture-as-apparatuses of domination" approach, "culture-as-social experience" approach, "culture-as-action" approach and "culture-as-behavior" approach, we *really* gain a reconfiguration of the idea of culture? Indeed, in terms of what we have called the "object" of culture, or the *claimed* "objectively" existing "reality" we *call* culture, are there any differences in "newer" approaches to culture? Or, is it simply the *explanation* of that entity that is different, or the levels of *evidence for* its existence that might give us *access* to it that have changed?

Here, I would suggest that the answer to the above question is "yes" – it is simply the *explanation* of the cultural "entity" that are different, or the levels of *evidence for* its existence that might give us *access* to it that have changed. That is to say that when Marx claims that "empirically verifiable…material life" explains the realm of "ideology," it is not only the material world that he seeks to explain, but "ideology" or "mental life" *them-*

---

15 This assertion is based on the notion that a coextensiveness, or coincidentality of consciousness and culture suggests that detailed investigations of consciousness are *also* detailed investigations of culture, and thus an outlining of the dynamics of culture as much as consciousness.

selves. This is a matter of his own analysis – ideology and "mental life" *come from*, or *emerge* out of, the interaction of the human and material world. Our alienation from the material objects we produce, argued Marx, means that we begin "with the results of the process of development ready to hand [accomplished]" and gives the social order an "immutable" meaning at the level of "mind" (Marx 1867/1967, 80).[16] Similarly, when Foucault asserts that the analytical premium should be placed on a specific constitution of "knowledges, discourses and domains of inquiry," *without* reference to a "transcendental subject," one of the "knowledges, discourses and domains of inquiry" he provided explanation for himself *were* those of the "transcendental subject." In other words, although he posited the human sciences as *not* an analysis of what "man is by nature," it was the *attribution* of a constant "nature" to man that was one of the driving forces behind his epistemological and discursive inquiries (Foucault 1966/1994, 353). Finally, when Durkheim claimed that we needed to focus on "objective" social phenomena, Weber asked for the formation of a "concrete" science of "social reality," Malinowski claims culture as a "fact already accomplished" or Garfinkel asserts that "cultural phenomena" are made "entirely [and] exclusively in actual, singular, particular occasions through actual witnessed displays of common talk and conduct," we gained precisely an acknowledgement of those things that their ideas on culture are intended to negate. To know about "objective" social phenomenon, in Durkheim's vocabulary, "socially reality" in a scientifically "concrete form" (Weber) or the "witnessed displays" of "common talk and conduct" (Garfinkle) was to gain insight into the "intellectual ideal," as Durkheim phrased it, "coexistently emerging and disappearing events *within* ourselves" (Weber) and identities that were previously thought hidden (Garfinkle). In other words, the apparent or observable gives us *access to* or is the *same* as the "hidden," or the life of the "mind." In this sense, then, despite claims to have abandoned the idea, culture *does* have something to do with consciousness, and the travails of what might be considered a "primordial mind" through history. I call this the "historical," as opposed to "centemporary," consensus on culture.

---

16 This is supported by Marx's statement in *The German Ideology* (1845/1975) that "men can be distinguished from animals by consciousness, by religion or anything else you like" (31). In other words, Marx may reveal here that an "intangible" consciousness may be the ultimate repository of material experience, and that the point of "empirically verifying" material experience may be to *explain* changes in that "intangible" mental domain.

IV. TOWARD A HISTORICAL PHENOMENOLOGY OF CULTURE

In the introductory remarks to this paper, I mentioned that not only might we be able to establish a "historical consensus" concerning ideas of culture, or a sense of convergence concerning both contemporary and "past" concepts of culture, but that we might also be able to build a "historical phenomenology" of concepts of culture – a point of connection between the dynamics of change of ideas of culture and the specific connections between "older" and "newer" ideas on the topic. Indeed, the specific connections have been established by way of the "historical consensus": the connection between "older" and "newer" ideas of culture is that they *have* a connection. In other words, there are not "new" ideas on culture without "old" ideas and, in fact, for newer concepts of culture to be *about* culture, they must enter into a dialogue, or conversancy, with older conceptions of the term.

Despite its seeming common sense nature, there is drama to this idea. That is to say that, though a disputed area under the rubric of historicity, the field of cultural theory all of a sudden gains a stabilization and, in fact, becomes *less* disputed. In other words, while disagreement may exist as to what culture *is*, we are presented with a solution to that disagreement. *Culture is the historical roots of its discourses. It is those things that contemporary attempts to define culture attempt to negate but, in fact, must sustain in order to in fact stand as "contemporary" or "newer" discourses on culture.* This, in fact, is "culture-as-consciousness" and, perhaps to a lesser extent, "culture-as-history." That is to say that at the same time that we have clearly exceeded "culture-as-consciousness" and "culture-as-history" as ideas on culture over historical time, we simultaneously remain within their purview in the *act* of historical succession. This presents us with the *raison d'etre* for cultural studies: to get at an ephemeral realm of consciousness and historical existence that has to do with the unique properties of the human and its travails through time. The space of contemporary or "new" cultural thought does not represent a negation of this legacy. Rather, in attempts to make such a negation of specific manifestations of that legacy (i.e., culture-as-consciousness or culture-as-history), it represents a decided historical continuation of that legacy by way of its engagement with it.

Now, here we have to take care – as mentioned in the introduction in relation to the "phenomenological" approach to stabilizing the idea of culture (approach number 1), finding an "object" of culture is impossible. That is to simply say that culture is a name game: one thing becomes cultural and another thing does not, and the generating force behind the attribution of the cultural is not things themselves, but *us*. In other words, nothing has the status of the cultural in a "metaphysical" sense – without the attribution of the *idea* of culture, there *is* no culture. This, however, becomes the basis for what I am calling a "historical phenomenology" of culture: that attribution of "the cultural" has happened over time and *continues* to happen over time. The determinations of our actions and consciousness happen both within a constantly emerging past as well as in reference to a past which already *is* past. The past, then, comes to have play in the present – it makes itself known every time we "advance" historically and not only *claim* to do so, but *in fact* do so. In other words, history relies on progress and change. However, progress and change are in fact structured by a "dead" past – a past which comes alive again each time new presents are constituted. In this context then, what the historical approach to cultural theory tells us is that the history of cultural theory becomes its present and is the context that gives us the space and dimensions for our very understanding of the idea. A historical *phenomenology* of culture shows us the reflexivity of cultural theory's present away from itself and to its past, yet then back to itself again. This generates cultural theory as a phenomenon and presents its origin as in relation to itself – i.e., cultural theory as concerned with itself as a phenomenon. However, this is a relation completely conditioned by the fact that things are in time and thus, phenomenologically, always relate to themselves as *historical* phenomena.

To this extent, then, a historical phenomenology of culture might be defined as maintaining four elements:

1. The primacy of ideas.

As mentioned, "external" factors to the history of ideas on culture, such as capitalist economics, cannot be ignored. Nonetheless, the history of ideas on culture does not become the history of ideas on culture *without* ideas. As such, ideas become the prime investigatory target in a historical phenomenology of culture: how do ideas on culture relate to one another *as* ideas?

2. A emphasis on the role of negation in history.

Once ideas are delimited as the terrain on which one is working, the question becomes their fate. That ideas have a history in the first place gives us a clue in this regard: ideas must be overcome, superseded and undone by other ideas. For the idea of culture to have a history, older ideas of culture must be overcome, superseded and undone. This relegation to the past is tantamount to a destruction (negation) – an explosion of relevance to one's current place and time.

3. An emphasis on the act of intellectual sustenance in history.

By intellectual sustenance, I mean the sustenance of essential characteristics of historical entities. On the surface, this appears to contradict the importance of the role of negation in history as it suggests that negation is less than complete, or less than negating. However, even such a statement is indicative: to negate a concept, one must engage that concept, identify it – usually more than once – and, in doing so, make it intellectually present, or at-hand.[17] To that extent, a historical phenomenology of culture identifies the sustenance of ideas of culture *within* their negation, and views this as fundamental to the historical condition, or the condition of being historical.

4. An emphasis on the fact that the historical condition of things provides their existential possibilities, and thus the essence of what they are.

Here, history is defined as both transcending time as well as standing prior to it – ideas of time may be historically conditioned, and history is more than simple temporality. Ideas of culture rest mainly on their content as ideas, and their return to and interplay with themselves *as* ideas of culture, or that which they are by way of content. The conditions of this interplay are negation and sustenance, making the history of ideas of culture the ultimate touchstone and *only* site of transformation for ideas of culture. History becomes a baseline for ideas of culture – a domain that cannot be transgressed once one comes onto the terrain of culture.

In one the classic statements on phenomenology, Husserl (1929/1995) asserted that phenomenology concerns itself with the "consciousness-of" or "appearance-of things" (15). A historical phenomenology of culture extends this to our "consciousness-of" or the "appearance-of" "culture." It further asserts that this appearance is tantamount to the history of ideas on culture.

V. CONCLUSION

That the travails of cultural theory are difficult to follow by 2004 is neither necessarily problematic nor surprising. It is not problematic, one might say, because those complications are historical themselves – they arise out of the

---

17   The vocabulary draws from Heidegger's (1927/1962) ideas of the "present-at hand" and "ready-to-hand," whereby the fundamental question for things was both simple mode of its presence (present-at hand) and a more complicated or "deeper" layer of its ontological condition and purpose (ready-to-hand) (110).

history of cultural theory unfolding out of itself and, insofar as one accepts that being within history at least gives us a start for a governing logic, this "problemesis" (quality of being a problem) is less than surprising. The history of cultural theory unfolding out of itself is a process that leads to the *multiplication* of cultural theory and its diversification over time. Cultural theory's unfolding sets itself up as a problem as reflection upon itself *as a* problematic is intrinsic to its activity as cultural theories relate to and orient themselves toward other cultural theories. This stands as an effective acknowledgement that approaches to stabilizing the idea of culture are themselves products of cultural theory's historicity. For the student of culture, this creates a densely populated theoretical terrain regarding culture on the theoretical level.

Nonetheless, navigation of this terrain is possible. This is precisely by way of the fact that cultural theory *is* historical. This constitutes the basis of what I am calling the "historical approach" to cultural theory: looking across the range of time for ideas on culture. There are two elements involved in this exercise. First, as mentioned in the introduction, it transcends or exceeds attempts to find culture "itself." Such a discovery is impossible as such a thing would exist *only* in attachment to, if not *by way of*, a history of *ideas* on culture. Secondly, however, we gain a *de facto* sense of culture "itself," at least in terms of an essential essence to the *idea* of culture by, in fact, looking *beyond* the present of the term and *comprehending* its historical diversification. In this paper, I have referred to this as a "historical consensus" regarding the idea of culture. As presented here, that consensus essentially amounts to the idea that "anachronistic," or "older," conceptions of culture as "consciousness" or "history" hold a great deal of sway. Again, this is by way of the historical negation: to conceive of culture means to conceive of its history and sustain of that history even in the apparent *absence* of consciousness of doing so. That is what it means to be *of* history. Today, and to my mind, unfortunately, an education in cultural studies often means *not* becoming educated in "older" concepts of culture, e.g., "culture-as-consciousness" or "culture-as-history" in deference to the supposed scientificity of "culture-as-apparatus of domination," "culture-as-social experience", "culture-as-action" or "culture-as-behavior." Nonetheless, in such a situation, the student of culture in fact gains a *variety* of education in "culture-as-consciousness" and "culture-as-history" as the traces of "culture-as-consciousness" and "culture-as-history" are left in the intellectual milieu of ideas of culture in the present, i.e., "culture-as-apparatuses of domination", "culture-as-social-experience", "culture-as-action" and "culture-as-behavior." The possibilities of the discourses of these more "contemporary" definitions of culture are structured by their historically anachronistic counterparts and in many cases, I would argue, can be shown to share objects of analytical concern (e.g., consciousness and the historical).

It is this situation that gives way to what I am terming a "historical phenomenology" of culture. As is consistent with the "historical approach" to cultural theory, this idea is structured around the idea that culture "in itself" is *not* – at least not anymore than we imagine it, or make it an element of the "order of discourse." That, however, begs the point. We *do* imagine culture, and it *is* an element of our "order of discourse." Within our orders of discourse, "culture" deserves no priority; indeed, as Foucault (1966/1994, 217-21, 367-73) suggested, it might be that "history" *itself* is the term we prioritize most, at least as concerns the intellectual history of the nineteenth and twentieth centuries. Therein, a historical phenomenology of culture does not suggest a connection between the invocation of the term culture and an objectively existing entity of culture, or "object" of culture. Nonetheless, it *does* make a distinction between reality and our orders of discourse. We *will* toward culture – we bring culture into being as "projected by thought" (Nietzsche 1888/1968, 483). To that extent, a historical *phenomenology* of culture has no naturalistic or "objective" existence either. Rather, a historical phenomenology of culture becomes the exculpation of the order of discourse of *itself*. And, to this extent, it dismisses a belief in will as the "cause" of culture.[18] We do not make culture because we desire it, nor is there a predetermined direction for either culture as it is acted in its schematics *or* the intellectual history of the *idea* of culture. There is rather only the *being* of the idea of culture in relation to itself over time. Interposed against the distribution of this idea over the pale of what we might call "society" – groups individuals, institutions and relations between these elements – this *becomes* culture; it is the *phenomenon* of culture on a historical basis.

In conclusion, then, I would state that in the context of a historical phenomenology of culture, we see that what were characterized in the introduction as the "broad disagreements" on the nature of cultural theory's object are indicative. Ultimately, they tell us that, with culture, we are involved with history of an idea and, in fact, *as* an idea, culture *is* an idea and makes itself present as such. In other words, it is something other than an artifact of another component of historical life, e.g., the economy, society, behavior or the "political."

---

18   As with the notion of culture as "projected by thought," this also borrows from Nietzsche (1888/1968, 483).

WORKS CITED

Adorno, Theodor. 2001. *The culture industry*. Ed. J.M. Bernstein. London: Routledge.

Burns, Robert. 2000. Classical Historicism. In *Philosophies of History*, ed. Robert Burns and Hugh Rayment-Pickard, 56-71. Oxford: Blackwell.

Deleuze, Gilles and Félix Guattari. 1972/1983. *Anti-oedipus: capitalism and schizophrenia*. Trans. Robert Hurley, Helen Lane and Mark Seem. Minneapolis: University of Minnesota Press.

During, Simon. 1999. Introduction. In *The cultural studies reader*, ed. Simon During, 1-28. London: Routledge.

Durkheim, Emil. 1893/2001a. Definition of socialism. In *Mainstream and critical social theory, vol. 2*, ed. Jeffrey Alexander, 77-94.

____. 1894/2001b. Rules for the observation of social facts. In *Mainstream and critical social theory, vol.*, ed. Jeffrey C. Alexander, 290-309. London: Sage, 2001.

Foucault, Michel. 1966/1994. *The order of things*. Trans. Alan Sheridan. New York: Vintage.

____. 1971/1972. *The archeology of knowledge*. Trans. Alan Sheridan. New York: Pantheon.

____. 1971/1977. Nietzsche, Genealogy, History. In *Language, counter-memory, practice*, ed. Sherry Simon and Donald Bouchard, 139-64. Ithaca, NY: Cornell University Press.

____. 1975/1977. *Discipline and punish*. Trans. Alan Sheridan. New York: Vintage.

____. 1977/1980. Truth and power. In *Power/Knowledge*, ed. Colin Gordon, 109-33. New York: Pantheon.

Gadamer, Hans-Georg. 1960/1998. *Truth and method*. Trans. Joel Weisenheimer. New York: Continuum.

Garfinkel, Harold. 1967/2001. Passing and the managed achievement of sex status in an "intersexed person." In *Mainstream and critical social theory, vol. 7*, ed. Jeffrey Alexander, 61-117. London: Sage.

Gramsci, Antonio. 2000. *The Antonio Gramsci reader: selected writings, 1916-35*, ed. David Forgacs. New York: New York University Press.

Hall, Stuart. 1991/1999. Cultural studies and its theoretical legacies. In *The cultural studies reader*, ed. Simon During, 98-109. London: Routledge.

Hegel, G.W.F. 1807/1977. *Phenomenology of spirit*. Trans. A.V. Miller. New York: Oxford University Press.

Heidegger, Martin. 1927/1962. *Being and time*. Trans. Edward Robinson and John Macquarrie. San Francisco: Harper and Row.

____. 1936/1974. The origin of the work of art. In *Poetry, language, thought*, trans. Albert Hofstadter, 15-88. New York: Harper and Row.

Hobsbawm, Eric. 1962/1996. *The age of revolution*. New York: Vintage.

Husserl, Edmund. 1929/1995. Phenomenology. In *The continental philosophy reader*, ed. Richard Kearney and Mara Rainwater, 15-22. London: Routledge.

Kant, Immanuel. 1781/1998. *Critique of pure reason.* Trans. J.M.D. Meiklejohn. Whitefish, MT: Kessinger Publishing.

___. 1784/2000. Progress in history. In *Philosophies of history*, ed. Robert Burns and Hugh-Rayment Pickard, 52-6. Oxford: Blackwell.

Lyotard, Jean-François. 1984/1992. Ticket for a new stage. In *The postmodern explained*, trans. Julian Pefanis and Morgan Thomas, 81-6. Minneapolis: University of Minnesota Press.

Malinowski, Bronislow. 1927/2001. *Sex and repression in savage society.* London: Routledge.

Marx, Karl. 1845/1975. *The german ideology.* In *Karl Marx and Friedrich Engels: collected works, vol. 5.* London: Lawrence and Wishart.

___. 1867/1967. *Capital, vol. 1.* Trans. Samuel Moore. New York: International Publishers.

Nietzsche, Friedrich. 1888/1968. *Twilight of the idols.* In *The portable Nietzsche*, ed. Walter Kaufmann, 463-564. New York: Penguin.

Ricoeur, Paul. 1983/1984. *Time and narrative, vol. 1.* Trans. Kathleen McLaughlin and David Pellauer. Chicago. University of Chicago Press.

Weber, Max. 1904/1949. Objectivity in social science and social policy. In *The methodology of the social sciences.* Ed. Edward Shils and Henry Finch, 50-112. New York: Free Press.

___. 1904-5/2001. *The protestant ethic and the spirit of capitalism.* Trans. Talcott Parsons. London: Routledge.

THEORIZING CULTURE, OR ECHO AND CIVILIZATION

Tadeusz Rachwal
Division of British Culture and Literature
University of Bielsko-Biała

For the world enjoys itself, and in itself all things that are…
The world itself can have no loves or any want (being content
with itself) unless it be of discourse. Such is the nymph Echo, a
thing not substantial, but only a voice… But it is well devised
that of all our words and voices Echo alone should be chosen for
the world's wife, for that is the true philosophy which echoes
most faithfully the voices of the world itself, and is written as it
were at the world's own dictation, being nothing else than the
image and reflection thereof, to which it adds nothing of its
own, but only iterates and gives it back. (Francis Bacon, De
dignitate et augmentis scientarum, II, xiii)

In Greek, *Theorein* meant "to look at," "to view" or "to speculate." Its nominal version could refer to "a sight" or "a spectacle." The word thus also seems to be related to theatre, to the idea of spectacle which in turn derives its various senses from mirrors, from mirroring and reflecting hidden in the word "speculum." Interestingly, the word "speculum" also referred to "surgical instrument of various forms, used for dilating orifices of the body so as to facilitate examination or operations" (cf. *OED*). Theorizing, from this perspective, seems to be a quite complex process of both looking at and looking into, of viewing a spectacle with the simultaneous desire to see what is hidden behind the stage, to peep into what is visible so as to examine its inside, its hidden mechanisms. Given that the prefix *Theo-* has clear references to the divine, we can see that a clear explication of what it could possibly mean to "theorize" is quite an unpromising task.

The word "culture" is not an easy one either. One of the "founders" of cultural studies, Raymond Williams, writes that it is one of "the two or three most complicated words in the English language" (Williams 1983: 87). Let us begin with one, now slightly forgotten, sense of the word "culture," that of tending crops and animals, an agricultural sense associated with the cultivation of land and the production of food.

When the English poet, Alexander Pope, wrote in the 18th century that "My Garden like my Life, seems to me every Year to want Correction and require alteration" (Sherburn 1956: IV, 40), he definitely proposed some views of culture by way of problematizing the relationship between man and nature, and between the natural and the artificial – the relationship which thinking is part and parcel of any cultural studies. 18th century culture is already elevated to the sphere of aesthetics, to the cultivation of beautiful scenery which is also the sphere of one's harmoniously organized life. The culture as production of food gives way to the culture of elevated taste for which the former is no longer cultural. Pope, as it were, works on his life, shapes it and reshapes in the form of the English garden, in the form of a leisurely space in which the only work done is that of an artist figuring as the gardener of life. To be cultural begins to mean to be cultivated without the necessity of growing such ugly things as potatoes, for example. If, as Terry Eagleton notes, "labour is a form of intercourse with nature which produces culture; but because of the conditions under which this labour takes place, that culture is internally split into violence and contradiction" (Eagleton 2000: 110), then what Pope seems to be communicating in his statement is that there are at least two kinds of intercourse with nature – an economic one in which labour is an unwelcome and imposed activity, and the landscaping one in which man and nature only execute what is "wanted" by both the garden and the life.

Pope's metaphorical comparison of his life to his garden at Twickenham is already a theorization, a speculation on the possible similarities between two seemingly different "sights" – a life and a garden – which, from a certain perspective, perhaps from that of the speculum, become similar within and governed by certain rules which are invisible from the outside, or on the surface. The spectacle of Pope's life and the spectacle of his garden, when carefully looked at and into, are in his eyes governed by the laws of nature which naturally produce a culture. If we add that, for Pope, nature was simultaneously "the source, and end, and test of Art" (see his *An Essay on Criticism*), we can say that his theory is a speculation on the nature of art which, from his perspective, should be natural. Since, as Williams notices, it is exactly in the 18th century that the words *culture* and *cultivation* "acquired definite class associations" (Williams 1983: 88), Pope's theory can be read as a middle-class biased vision of being cultivated, of the art of shaping both life and its contexts "naturally," in such a way that culture is but extension of human nature which itself is an extension of nature. There are those who are natural, who follow and cultivate their nature, and those who are not, the unnatural ones who produce things as artificial as themselves.

The true gardeners of life are only those whose art is so perfect that it is invisible in what it creates. As Joseph Spence (a professor of poetry at Oxford in the 18th century, and follower of Pope's ideas) wrote to one of his friends, advising him on the design of his garden: "Wherever art appears, the garden-er has failed in his execution" (Hunt and Willis 1975: 268). Such a theoriza-tion of culture is also in obvious ways a political gesture which establishes a hegemony of one vision of reality over another, which, through aesthetiza-tion of the social, brings aesthetics very close to ethics. What is mine, my gar-den, reflects what I am, my life. What looks unnatural and artificial must ei-ther undergo a naturalization, or has to be excluded from the territory of the appropriate. Pope's theory in obvious ways excludes both those who are too poor to give an expression to their lives, and those who are too rich, perhaps the aristocracy, whose lifestyle is pure artifice and exaggeration. When Joseph Spence writes that "what is, is the great guide as to what ought to be" (Hunt and Willis 1975: 265), he is implicitly stating that what is, is not enough. Read along with his simultaneous warning against the artifice, this theory suspends "man" within the sphere which is slightly above "what is," and below what is too artificial, between the rough and the overdone, be-tween the production of the necessities of life (agriculture) for which there is no space in the garden of life, and the "unnecessities" of the failed art of the too leisured class, whose degeneracy is expressed by the excess of ornamen-tation which, in turn, testifies to pride and the lack of modesty. The position of the middle is also the ethical position of being virtuous and modest. Alexander Pope was the owner of a garden with a Palladian villa. He also built there a grotto which he frequently admired in his poems. In one of them (*On His Grotto at Twickenham*), Pope boasts at his own modesty and invites there only those who are like himself, who live modestly, which mod-esty he, I do not think ironically, perceives as being poor:

> Let such, such only tread this sacred floor,
> Who dare to love their country, and be poor.

I have begun with an excursion to the 18th century so as to give an example of a clearly prescriptive cultural theory which confines the scope of its gaze to the sphere of what is perceived as proper and excludes from its considerations huge areas of the social, and not only social, reality. Though it is difficult to use the term reality with any certainty after Jean Baudrillard's claim that the reality which is now accessible to us can only be a simulacrum, a copy without the original, I think that what is inevitably involved in theorizing culture is a certain nostalgia for reality, a disbelief that where we live and what we live is a technological extension of something which lacks any authenticity. In the case of Alexander Pope, this nostalgia surfaces as an attempt to conceal technology altogether, to conceal the threat of the industrial revolution going on outside Pope's garden by way of derealizing it, by withdrawing the gaze from the city to the country, with a garden as the ideal medium expressing identity. This derealization is achieved, in Pope, through aestheticization, through the conflation of the beautiful with reality, thus implying that technology, figuring as art, is unreal, because it is fake and, say, ugly.

Slavoj Žizěk, using Jacques Lacan's terms, claims that what separates the beautiful from the ugly is "the very gap that separates reality from the Real: what constitutes reality is the minimum of idealization the subject needs in order to be able to sustain the horror of the Real" (Žizěk 1997: 66). This minimum of idealization is also a minimum of aestheticization, of translation of the horror of the inexpressible into expressible. What Žizěk does not quite articulate, however, is that what makes the Real horrible is exactly the idealization, that the Real can become inarticulate only from the perspective of the idealized, of what has been mediated through language and conceptualization. The Real is only thinkable as it were "backwards," at a distance created through the mediation language.

Commenting on the French Philosopher Henri Bergson, Marshall Mc Luhan wrote that:

> ... language is a human technology that ... does for intelligence
> what the wheel does for the feet and the body. Speech acts to
> separate man from man, and mankind from the cosmic uncon-
> scious. As an extension or uttering (outering) of all our senses at
> once, language has always been held to be man's richest art
> form, that which distinguishes him from the animal creation
> (McLuhan 1965: 79-80).

The cosmic unconscious seems to be the equivalent of the Real here; the sphere from which the use of language has separated us and to which there seems to be no return. McLuhan's famous claim that "medium is the message" is a remainder that thinking about culture we always already think about media, a remainder that culture begins with the use of a technology of expression. The realization of this, as he put it, might be shocking:

> In a culture like ours, long accustomed to splitting and dividing
> all things as a means of control, it is sometimes a bit of a shock to
> be reminded that, in operational and practical fact, the medium
> is the message (McLuhan 1965: 7).

Our culture is an "outering" culture which through the extensions of the body develops what he calls "an analytic technology of fragmentation" (McLuhan 1965: 124). The Polish sociologist, Zygmunt Bauman, finds a similar technology at work in Claude Levi-Strauss's division of societies into anthropophagic and anthropoemic:

> Claude Levi-Strauss suggested that one of the crucial differences between our, modern, type of society and other, simpler societies is that they are 'anthropophagic', while we are 'anthropoemic': they *eat* their enemies while we *vomit* ours. Our way of dealing with the Other (and thus, obliquely, of producing and reproducing our own identity) is to segregate, separate, dump onto rubbish hip, flush down into the sewer of oblivion (Bauman 1992: 131).

If in McLuhan we are dealing with a medial emission, Bauman transforms this emission into a "vomission," thus adding a strongly critical edge to his vision of the contemporary culture. What seems to be a link between the two theorists is again a nostalgia for the loss of a more originary world, a world in which media do not completely cut us off from the Other, a world in which we can commune with it, regardless of its being untranslatable into recognizably digestive entities.

Claiming that medium is the message and seeing media as extensions of the body, McLuhan still believes in a certain continuity with the origin. Language is a technology which does fragment and idealize the Real, but it simultaneously, as an extension, contains at least some memory of it. We have lost the primordial unity with the Other, but this unity is traceable through media/messages which are only a stage in the prospective reconstruction of the unity of the global village of the future, which reconstruction is possible thanks to electricity, the medium which in McLuhan as it were plugs us back into the newly unified world. Electric technology, he writes,

> ... ends the old dichotomies between culture and technology, between art and commerce, and between work and leisure. Whereas in the mechanical age of fragmentation leisure had been the absence of work, or mere idleness, the reverse is true in the electric age. (McLuhan 1965: 346)

The mechanical age of fragmentation will thus transform itself, or extend, into a global network which will make it possible for us "to *react to the world as a whole*" (McLuhan 1965: 348). With the disappearance of the distinction between labor and leisure we will become "nomadic as never before" (McLuhan 1965: 358) as the idea of place as something mechanically con-structed and stable will be unconceivable.

Alexander Pope, as we have seen, constructed his horticultural world by way of naturalizing art, by attempting at making technology invisible. McLuhan, we might say, technologizes nature and thus reproduces a fullness of human participation in the world which is a replica of the natural man, of the tribal man to whose figure he frequently refers in his writings. Unlike civilized man, McLuhan's "tribal man had freely extended the form of his body to include the universe" (McLuhan 1965: 124). With the coming of electricity, the electric man does the same, though the universe is now a copy, a virtual reality which makes the dream of electronic replication of everything, dreamt for example by the fractal geometry, come true. If Pope's project was prescriptive, McLuhan's one seems to be strongly predictive. With Bauman things are slightly more complicated.

Though Bauman refers to Levi-Strauss's nostalgia for cannibals, for a "sim-pler society" in which "the essentially equivocal relationship that obtains be-tween self and other" (Bauman 1992: 132) is expressed, no return to whole-ness is promised here. For him medium is not the message, but the message's discontinuous other which serves the purpose of fortifying the message, of leaving it "intactly" permanent. If cannibalism "figures forth a radical idea of kinship" (Bauman 1992: 132), modernity promises no kinship between the medium and the message. The relationship between them is that of subordi-nation, of subordination to the stability of the identity of the message which "vomits" the indigestible fragments of the message as the Other, and attempts to dispose of them as nonexistent. It is also a relationship of quasi-mutual hostility in which identity "externalizes" the other as threatening, as hostile to its permanence, thus necessarily positing identity as hostile to the Other. Per-manence has thus become a task, "a paramount task ... and so it makes cul-ture, that huge and never stopping factory of permanence" (4).

If we turn to Jacques Derrida for a bit, we can notice that, quite surprising-ly, hostility and hospitality are somehow related, not only etymologically. Though seemingly opposite terms, they do not belong to mutually exclusive areas and somehow aporetically support each other (cf. Derrida and Dufour-mantelle 2002). In Bauman, modernity is constituted exactly as a blindness to hospitality for the Other. Modernity is the art of seeing stability as the only mode of identity's existence, a mode in which the Other cannot be hosted. For Freud, one of the harbingers of modernity, the whole edifice of civilization has been erected against what he terms "hostile impulses" which he ascribes to those who, naturally, prefer leisure to labor. "Thus civilisation," he writes,

> has to be defended against the individual, and its regulations, in-
> stitutions and commands are directed to that task. They aim not
> only at effecting a certain distribution of wealth but at main-
> taining that distribution; indeed, they have to protect everything
> that contributes to the conquest of nature and the production of
> wealth against men's hostile impulses (Freud 1961b: 7).

The hostile impulses threat the stability of the distribution of wealth, the permanence of wealth for which, perhaps paradoxically, most people do not care: "For masses are lazy and unintelligent; they have no love for instinctual renunciation, and they are not to be convinced by argument of its inevitability; and the individuals composing them support one another in giving free rein to their indiscipline" (Freud 1961b: 9).

Freud divides people into two antagonistic categories which are posited as natural. The first category, the masses, naturally dislikes labour, while the second category, perhaps one with Freud himself on the top of the list, loves the "instinctual renunciation" and the culture whose construction is founded upon it. The masses are also rendered as constantly plotting against culture. They nothing but "combine" how to be undisciplined, to constantly have sex, for example, and eat bananas. They are slaves to their own laziness and in order to break free from it they have to realize that, say, *Arbeit Macht Frei,* and to thus get back to the "path of happiness":

> And yet, as a path to happiness, work is not highly prized by
> men. They do not strive after it as they do for other possibilities
> of satisfaction. The great majority of people only work under
> the stress of necessity, and this natural human aversion to work
> raises most difficult social problems (Freud 1961a: 27).

Freud, of course, did not suspect that the path to happiness might lead through Auschwitz, yet the very idea of leaders of culture solving the "difficult social problems" is clearly at hand here. As he quite explicitly claimed, "It is only through the influence of individuals who can set an example and whom masses recognize as their leaders (*Führers*) that they can be induced to perform the work and undergo renunciations on which the existence of civilization depends" (Freud 1961b: 9-10).

Where Pope's prescriptive culture was a model offered to the few modest ones, for Freud those few should lead the masses out of the dullness of their natural instincts to their equally natural repression, to the renunciation of their lack of love for work and culture, and to the elimination of the hostile otherness. What he perceives as the task, as happiness, is a culture without the repressive violence of renunciation, a culture in which repression has been, perhaps paradoxically, though positively, repressed.

According to Richard Rorty, theories provide new contexts, and they are "to be evaluated by their efficiency in effecting changes, not (as the logocentrists believed) by their adequacy to the object" (Rorty 1999: 220). Yet even those theories which claim "adequacy to the object" are also theories which may effect changes, as what is at stake in them is always an attempt at proving the existence of a norm which is constantly undermined by human discourse. Pope, Freud, and also McLuhan's theories are about a finality; seemingly describing what is, they describe what ought to be.

Bauman realizes that culture is "emission" of articulation which silences huge areas of this emission as the hostile Other. Already some time, ago Jacques Derrida articulated in *Writing and Difference* that articulation is inevitably violent, with the violence protecting a certain silence of peace (cf. Derrida 1978: 148). Elsewhere he finds such an "economy of war" inescapable, because inscription infinitely articulates the horizon of silence, the horizon of what Derrida, more recently, calls "paradise." Such a paradise is thinkable as a space without violence, but only given the Other becomes unthinkable. Derrida does not embrace that paradise, seeing in it a space devoid of responsibility, a space in which it is no longer possible to respond to difference (cf. Szydłowska 2003: 171). The economy of war is inevitable, though wars were, and are, waged against that economy, in the name of paradises devoid of writing and difference, of the uncanny instability which inevitably makes culture, and ourselves, equivocal: "the violence of writing, the violence of founding, of in-stating, of producing, of judging or knowing is a violence that both manifests and dissimulates itself, a space of necessary equivocation" (Grosz 1999: 12).

Jean Baudrillard begins his *America* with a caution: "*Objects in this mirror may be closer than they appear!*" (Baudrillard 1988: mellemrum 1). Rephrasing this caution, one might say that objects in the mirror of theories look different than they appear. In *Simulacra and Simulation* he argues that the "postmodern" culture is made up of signs that no longer have a relation to reality:

> Abstraction today is no longer that of the map, the double, the mirror or the concept. Simulation is no longer that of a territory, a referential being or a substance. It is the generation by models of a real without origin or reality: a hyperreal. The territory no longer precedes the map, nor survives it. Henceforth, it

is the map that precedes the territory – precession of simulacra –
it is the map that engenders the territory. (Baudrillard 1998:
166)

Theory is no longer the mirror of reality, but in a sense its echo. Medium has
been deprived of any message, and our culture is a production of signs about
signs about signs in which even the word "our" seems to have lost any definite reference. If map can be an image of theory, then, in fact, it is theory that
engenders its objects which are their own, somehow spectral, images.

With Baudrillard, reality becomes its own specter, a haunting presence-
absence of reality which translates the cultural space into an echo. In Latin,
John Hollander notices, the word *imago,* or sometimes *imago vocis,* was used
for *echo.* In this sense *echo* "precedes, rather than tropes, our primarily visual use of the word *imago*" punktum mangler (Hollander 1981: 11). In the
epigram above, Bacon glorifies Echo for her faithfulness to the original of
the world, for her ability to repeat without admixing her own voice and thus
falsifying the message. Iteration is, like Echo, feminine, and the image of the
world produced by her is actually a gesture of incessant unveiling of her hus-
band, the world. Bacon's Echo, as it were, gives birth to the discursive world,
herself being limited to a bodiless matter, a thing not substantial.

Bacon's Echo is the faithful wife of the Greek god Pan in whose "milieu
she becomes a credential voice, associated with truth rather than with the
qualities of the other Echo, the spurned lover of the self-loving Narcissus"
(Hollander 1981: 11). This other Echo is divorced from the world and, very
much like Baudrillard's simulacra, repeats things without any origin. She
herself does not exist even as the source of repetition, and becomes deprived
of any material body. The Ovidian Echo is bodiless; she is unmarried to any
god or world and is thus limited to being a pure sound/image of nothing
which signifies nothing. Such "negative readings of Echo, come from associations of fragmentation of the anterior voice, the hollowness of her concavi-
ties of origin transferred to the progressive diminution of successive rever-
berations" (Hollander 1981: 11).

Thinking about culture in the context of the two Echoes again brings to
mind the question of the technological production of culture, the question
of why is the other reading of Echo posited as negative. The question is not
new, and Plato's allegory of the cave in which we perceive only shadows of
reality is but a rendering of the problem in visual terms. What, as it were,
motors culture is the already mentioned nostalgia for the lost authenticity
which it has been vainly tried to reconstruct for quite a long time. This nostalgia sometimes takes the form of suspicion that the authentic does not ex-

ist. And yet, through that very same suspicion the authentic becomes its haunting, echoing other. Shakespeare, for example, like Baudrillard, suspected that visions might be weaved out of a "baseless fabric," and thus are bound to be unfaithful to any authenticity that preceded them. This suspicion gives rise to the crisis of authenticity which, on the moral plane, is the crisis sincerity. The other Echo, the Ovidian one, has nobody to be faithful to, even herself, and thus has to bodilessly embody a certain betrayal, an insincerity.

Lionel Trilling looks for the beginnings of this crisis in the era of the Shakespearian Globalization of the theatre. "It is surely no accident," he writes, "that the idea of sincerity, of the own self and the difficulty of knowing and showing it, should have arisen to vex men's minds in the epoch that saw the sudden efflorescence of the theatre" (Trilling 1973: 10). What is born in the 16th century along with the modern theatre is the individual who compartmentalizes the previously smoother social space and becomes an actor who has to demonstrate his sincerity, to constantly reproduce it. "If he is an artist, the individual is likely to produce self-portraits; if he is Rembrandt, he paints threescore of them" (Trilling 1973: 25). Individuals thus become artists, the artisans of identity which gradually becomes, like Echo, a pure surface. "Down goes the audience, up comes the artist," writes Trilling, and quotes T.S. Eliot writing that "the progress of an artist is a continual self-sacrifice, a continual extinction of personality" (Trilling 1973: 7) Perhaps those still remaining "down" in the audience are other individuals, those against whom Freud wanted to protect civilization. Only those taking part in the spectacle, the active coiners of the new realities take part in its re-authentication. If there is nothing but art, then art is the origin of things, and the faithfulness of Bacon's "positive" Echo is replaced with the solidification of her voice, in whose production she does not partake. An individual is thus placed in the position of the god Pan, the creator of everything, and the uncreative voice of Echo disappears from the stage as an artless iteration of impermanence, a repetition of repetition, an echo of an echo that is distant from the originality of the construction.

Regardless of the "positive" or "negative" values passed on the two Echoes, they are both evidently confined to silence, to being voices twice unheard. Culture as we know it looms as a masculine construct which also lies hidden in the etymology of the word "sincerity." Being derived from the Latin *sincerus*, it first of all meant clean, or sound, or pure. Echoing this etymology there is another one, which Trilling calls a "merely fanciful etymology" which suggests that the word could also be derived from "*sine cera*, without wax" (Trilling 1973: 12). Perhaps it is this fanciful etymology to which

Shakespeare's fancy makes recourse when, in *The Rape of Lucrece*, he compares the feminine mind to wax:

> For men have marble, women waxen, minds,
> And therefore are they form'd as marble will;
> The weak oppress'd, the impression of strange kinds
> Is form'd in them by force, by fraud, or skill:
> Then call them not the authors of their ill,
> No more than wax shall be accounted evil
> Wherein is stamp'd the semblance of a devil.

Some kind of writing is always a culture's technology, and the art of writing, printing and impressing needs some kind of wax. Yet, it perceives most sincere authenticity only where the wax is missing, only where it is not there. Marble is the material from which palaces and monuments of culture can be erected but, more importantly, it is the material which has the power of inscription, of commemorating the erection. Wax has no signifying properties of its own and it can only be written upon with hard objects. Those objects leave on its surface traces which search for independent identities, which desire to "discorporate" themselves to become, exactly, *sine cera*, without any trace of the soft substance they had violated and in which they had been stamped. The cavities left in the wax by that stamping are, like Plato's cave, spaces of distorted repetitions, of echoes, of fragmented traces of messages which deformity posits a threat to their masculine origin.

Thinking about culture, theorizing it, one has to be sensitive to its power to exclude the Other, one of whose embodiments has been the feminine perceived as what Rosi Braidotti calls "devalued difference" which:

> remained a constant in Western thought; in philosophy especial-
> ly; "she" is forever associated to unholy, disorderly, subhuman,
> and unsightly phenomena. It is as if "she" carried within herself
> something that makes her prone to being an enemy of mankind,
> an outsider in her civilization, an "other." (Braidotti 1997: 64)

Shakespeare's Lucrece commits suicide in public, being unable to say who raped her. She is even unable to kill herself by herself: "He, he, fair lords, 'tis he / That guides this hand to give this wound to me." The public spectacle, the nominal version of the Greek *theorein*, seems to be over, but, as Freddie Mercury taught us, "the show must go on." Perhaps the world, as Francis Bacon told us in the beginning of this paper, still "enjoys itself, and in itself all things that are."

WORKS CITED

Baudrillard, Jean, *America*, transl. Chris Turner, London: Verso, 1988.

Baudrillard, Jean, "Simulacra and Simulations," in: *Selected Writings*, Stanford: Stanford University Press, 1998.

Bauman, Zygmunt, Mortality, *Immortality, and Other Life Strategies*, Polity Press: Oxford, 1992.

Braidotti, Rosi, "Mothers, Monsters, Machines," in: Katie Conboy, Nadia Medina, and Sarah Stanbury (eds.), *Writing on the Body. Female Embodiments and Feminist Theory*, New York: Columbia University Press, 1997.

Derrida, Jacques, *Writing and Difference*, transl. Alan Bass, Chicago: University of Chicago, 1978.

Derrida, Jacques and Dufourmantelle, Anne. *Of Hospitality*, transl. Rachel Bowlby, Palo Alto: Stanford University Press, 2002.

Derrida, Jacques, *Seminar at Ecoles des Hautes Etudes en Sciences Sociales*, Paris, 13 March 2002. Quoted in: Valeria Szyd?owska, *Nihilizm i dekonstrukcja*, Warszawa: IFiS, 2003.

Hunt, Dixon, John and Willis, Peter (eds.), *The Genius of the Place. The English Landscape Garden 1620-1820*, London: Paul Elek, 1975.

Eagleton, Terry, *The Idea of Culture*. Oxford: Blackwell, 2000.

Freud, Sigmund, *Civilization and Its Discontents*. New York: Norton, 1961a.

Freud, Sigmund, *The Future of an Illusion*. New York and London: Norton, 1961b.

Grosz, Elizabeth, "The Time of Violence; Deconstruction and Value," *College Literature*, Winter 1999, vol. 26, Issue 1.

Hollander, John, *The Figure of Echo. A Mode of Allusion in Milton and After*, Berkeley: University of California Press, 1981

McLuhan, Marshall, *Understanding Media: The Extensions of Man*, New York: McGraw-Hill, 1965.

Rorty, Richard, *Philosophy and Social Hope*, London: Penguin, 1999.

Sherburn, George, (ed.), *The Correspondence of Alexander Pope* (5 vols.), Oxford, 1956.

Szydłowska, Valeria, *Nihilizm i dekonstrukcja*, Warszawa: IFiS, 2003.

Trilling, Lionel, *Sincerity and Authenticity*, Cambridge Mass.: Harvard University Press, 1973.

Williams, Raymond, *Keywords*, London: Fontana Press, 1983.

Žižek, Slavoj, *The Plague of Fantasies*, London: Verso, 1997.

CULTURE, HISTORY, AND TEXT

Benjamin C. Sax
Department of History
University of Kansas

From a number of apparently independent sources within various academic disciplines, there has recently arisen a new (or renewed) concern with "culture" and the processes of "cultural formation."[1] This turn, however, has resulted neither in establishing common definitions or common problems in anthropology, sociology and literary studies nor in promoting a more comprehensive view of "culture" or the meaning of "culture." In addition, the study of "culture" has not, at least as of yet, replaced other discourses presently dominant in the social sciences and the humanities: the scientific discourse of society with its categories of "class," "race" and "gender" and the discourse of the "text" with its textual model of truth. As a result, the turn to "culture" has become a source of further confusion, conflict and contention, resulting in increased divisiveness among, and additional fracturing within, the disciplines.

More interestingly and perhaps more significantly, "culture" is not just an "object" of academic research and debate, and the issues raised by the ques-

---

1   As several scholars have recently suggested, "culture" is gradually replacing "text" and "society" as focal points for investigation in the humanities and social sciences. Within literary studies, the New Historicism examines the historical intersections of the production of texts and the construction of culture – sometimes at the expense of literary analysis itself. Among sociologists the analysis of cultural "configurations" after the manner of Norbert Elias has become a current area of scholarly interests. And cutting across disciplinary boundaries is the growing interest in material culture and the practices of everyday life in the fields of sociology and history.

For a discussion of the New Historicism in literary studies, see Louis Montrose, "Professing the Renaissance: The Poetics and Politics of Culture," *The New Historicism*, ed. H Aram Veeser (New York: Routledge, 1993), pp. 15-36. And for a general discussion of these issues, see John Czaplicka et. al. "Introduction: Cultural History and Cultural studies: Reflection on a Symposium" introduces a series of papers presented at the Center of European Studies at Harvard University in the spring of 1994 and published in *New German Critique* 65 (Spring-Summer, 1995), p. 3.

tion of "culture" will not be resolved by achieving a mere consensus of basic definitions and meanings.[2] "Culture" has also become a force in the politics and "culture wars" of both the academic and the ultra-academic worlds, as various "cultures," "sub-cultures," and "cultural groups" demand that their voices be heard and themselves empowered, politically and academically, on the simple grounds that they are in fact "cultures." The notion of "culture" then seems to be less a basis of a new consensus than a reversion to corrosive relativism and unrestrained demands for power.

The general turn to "culture" coincides with the proliferation of postmodern thought across the human sciences; and, indeed, on one level, postmodernism seems both to encourage and to provide the theoretical "grounding" for such a turn. Even a cursory glance at what appears to animate current interests in "culture" reveals less a renewed search for a formal definitions than a shared critical stance towards all such conceptions.[3] What has in recent

---

2   Jack Goody agrees with me that the problem of "culture" is not to be solved by reaching a consensus over definition or acceptance over various disciplinary boundaries. See Goody, "Culture and its Boundaries: A European View" in *Social Anthropology*, vol. 1, no. 1 (1993), p. 11.

3   To a large degree, the general move to the study of "culture" has arisen as a result of a lack of general agreement over the definition of "culture." Traditionally, anthropologists have employed "culture" in a global sense. Although in its broadest definition, "culture" demarcates a total way of life of a given people at a given time, the concept remains ambiguous, agonizingly ambiguous. Even today anthropologists continue to debate whether "culture" should consists of the symbolic level of human existence and the historical transmission of these symbols or whether it should include the non-symbolic, the material bases and behavior of a people. In *The Interpretation of Culture*, Clifford Geertz for instance defines it as "an historically transmitted pattern of meaning embodied in symbols, a system of inherited conceptions expressed in symbolic forms by means of which men communicate." Clifford Geertz, *The Interpretation of Culture: Selected Essays* (New York: Basic Books, 1973), p. 89. And in this definition, Geertz essentially agrees with such sociologists as Talcot Parsons and Edward Shils. Talcot Parsons, "Culture and the Social Sciences Revisited, " in L. Schneier and C.M. Bonjean (eds.), *The Idea of Culture in the Social Sciences* (Cambridge, Eng: University of Cambridge Press, 1973). Connected to these various attempts to grasp "culture" conceptually is the question of the "appropriate" methodology for the study of culture and the deployment of a "science" of "culture." The notion of a universal and abstract definition of culture implies, if not a single, universal and abstract methodological approach, then a single language "appropriate" to the "science" of culture.

Others social scientists, including Jack Goody, have quibbled with this defini-

years generally been referred to as the "Birmingham School" of cultural studies is a case in point. Although arising form independent sources, cultural studies in this sense legitimates the diversity of its interests and the plurality of its methods by reference to the postmodernist critique of "grand theory" and "master narratives."[4] To posit a "culture" as a totality of symbols and behaviors seems necessary to impose a determinist theory upon the human world. Cultures, it is argued, do not in fact form such totalities. At best such holistic notions are constructs, imposed upon the human reality for cognitive purposes. At worst, they provide a type of legitimization for the arbitrary use of power. "Totality" seems to be on the side of established power relations, employed to diminish conflict and to legitimate the unequal distribution of and access to power. From this critical perspective, all "cultures" appear to be constructed – and illegitimately so – from specific power relations which establish and re-enforce specific national identities and social divisions.[5] Students of this model of cultural studies have challenged the no-

tion, arguing that it unjustifiably separates the "symbolic" from the "non-symbolic;" but, even with such additions, these definitions of culture posit "culture" as some type of totality – a totality of material and non-material components, of thoughts and actions, or of symbolic and structural codes of a given people at a given time. Jack Goody, "Culture and its Boundaries: a European View," *Social Anthropology*, pp. 9–32.

There is a strong argument, current today, that only in the particularity of their manifestations can cultures be known. This seems to be Geertz's more recent position. See Clifford Geertz, *Local Knowledge: Further Essays in Interpretive Anthropology* (New York: Basic Books, 1983), pp. 167-234. Specific cultures set up specific boundaries or horizons, but these boundaries are porous or at least semi-porous, allowing influences from the outside to enter and reshape its meanings and values. Or, in Edward Said's terminology, cultures—both dominant and non-dominant—are "transformational." They are characterized by their "hybridity," by their two-way openness to influence and be influenced. Edward Said, *Culture and Imperialism* (New York: Routledge, 1995), pp. xxv, 58.

4   The recent challenges to empirical research raised by poststructuralism have also put into question all notions of totality. See Jean-François Lyotard, *The Postmodern Condition: A Report on Knowledge* (Minneapolis: University of Minnesota Press, 1984).

5   Power infuses the problem of who has the right to represent this totality and who has the power to include and exclude individuals and groups based upon this representation. This denial of totality and totalizing thinking confirms a basic postulate of poststructuralist criticism. Foucault is not alone in arguing that all discourses are innately political in the sense that they include and exclude, empower and disempower. Foucault, *Power/Knowledge* (New York: Pantheon, 1980), pp. 80-81; Jean-Francois Lyotard, *Toward the Postmodern*, ed. Robert Harvey and Mark S. Roberts (Atlantic Heights, N.J.: 1993), pp. 159-162.

tion of cultural totality by inverting the notions of "high" and "low," "dominant" and "subaltern," "representation" and "reality," as much as "culture" and "nation."[6] Cultural studies therefore endorse the notion that "reality" is a social construct and is thus open to a social critique.

If on the surface postmodernism supports the turn to polysemious notion of "culture," on another level it is highly critical of all such moves. More precisely, those groups of thinkers identified with poststructuralism have challenged all definitions of truth and attempts at stabilizing meaning which have come to dominate the human sciences, including the study of culture.[7] While Immanuel Levinas' notion of "the other" and Jacques Derrida's *différance* undercut all attempts to comprehend other peoples and other expe-

---

6   This conflictual model of culture is both explicitly and implicitly endorsed by a growing and seemingly all-pervasive interest in what is ambiguously referred to as "multiculturalism." Multiculturalism perhaps receives its clearest academic identity in Cultural studies. This "school" of cultural studies has grown out of the pioneering studies of Raymond William and received institutional form in the Centre for Contemporary Cultural studies of the University of Birmingham. See, Lawrence Grossberg, Cary Nelson and Paula A. Treichler, eds., *Cultural Studies*, (New York, 1992).

     The Birmingham School of Cultural studies speak both to the increasing awareness of diversities among cultures and to the interaction among various cultures. It also includes a critique of the relation of dominant to subaltern cultures. But there is an ambiguity inherent within the notion of Cultural studies, which is reflected in the wide range of subject matters and methodologies which variously and often confusingly employ both literary and social scientific modes of analyses. While challenging and redeploying such conventional notions as class, ethnicity, race, gender and sex as categories of meaning and objects of research, this same stance or rather the aggregate of stances that assume the title of Cultural studies remain unclear as to its own methods of research, objects of investigation, and modalities of thought. While rejecting the traditional Marxist base/ superstructure dyad, these studies have not developed a paradigm of their own. Within its heterogeneous theoretical positions, there is revealed only a shared commitment to decoding artifacts as products of hegemonic cultures. See, in particular, John Fiske, "Cultural studies and the Culture of Everyday Life" and Stuart Hall, "Cultural studies and its Theoretical Legacies" in *Cultural Studies*, pp. 154-173, 277-294.

7   The coincidence of these concerns over "culture" – with the growing critique of "modernism" by postmodernism in general but more specifically by the poststructuralism of Michel Foucault and Jacques Derrida – has both broadened the areas that have been put under question and deepened its critique of reality and truth. Based upon a linguistic model, structuralism first called into question the relation of language and reality. By the very structure of language, the critique of the notion

riences, the poststructuralist critique has come to center upon the notion of representation and the theory of truth based upon representations.[8] The problem of representation includes a questioning of the relation of subject to object (including the notion of the "object" of a field of research and the supposedly external and neutral notion of a inquiring "subject"), of self to other, of present to past. In *The Order of Things*, then, Foucault has demonstrated the paradoxes upon which the human sciences are founded, as "man" is posited as both the "subject" before which "representations" appear and the "object" of the study of these same "representations."[9] In fact, through his critique of representation (through what Foucault calls "the anthropological sleep" of the human sciences), the entire conception of knowledge and the ways in which knowledge is attained and technological employed – the entire "Enlightenment project," in other words, with its notion of science – have been seriously challenged.

The implications for the study of "culture" are clear. Foucault demonstrates the ways in which both "history" and "culture" allowed for the uncritical deployment of the human sciences in the nineteenth and twentieth centuries.[10] As a result, a number of foundational assumptions of "science," even when it is a theory of interpretation, remained unexamined. In addition to

of reference has undermined all attempts to capture reality in language and to all truth claims based upon representations. And perhaps even more telling than a critique of truth for an understanding of culture, poststructuralism has challenged the notion of meaning. Beyond Saussure's "difference" between sign and referent, Derrida has developed a notion of "differance," which by destabilizing the relation between signified and signifier indicates that signs are open to a limitless play of readings and an infinite construals of meaning. All means of restricting such play are illegitimate, the result either of uncriticized conventions or simply impositions of power.

8   But the deployment of these languages and logics of the sciences were based upon representations and a representational theory of truth. As a result, a number of foundational assumptions of "science, " even when it is a theory of interpretation, remained unexamined. The binary oppositions of self and other, of past and present, of culture and the languages in which we speak of "culture" were never fully understood. There remained a split then between the ways in which we speak about "culture" and the openness, diversity and polysemy both within a culture and among cultures. How is this reality experienced, the way in which a "world" opened, and how is the truth of this reality as a reality and this world as a world brought to language?

9   Michel Foucault, *The Order of Things: An Archaeology of the Human Sciences* (New York: Random House, 1973), pp. 236-249, 312-367.

10   Michel Foucault, *The Order of Things* (New York: Vintage, 1973), pp. 370-373.

questioning the truth claims of the human sciences, deconstruction has raised issues of the very nature of the language in which we claim to speak about the world and challenges the discourses we employ to legitimate its various practices and institutions.[11] As with similar questions confronted by gender studies and indeed by all claims to truth, poststructuralist thought has criticized all reversions to notions of "essence," "foundation" and "reference." "Culture," in other words, can neither be defined by designating a specific human "reality" nor define the truth upon which its knowledge is founded in terms of supposed representations of "culture."[12] As opposed to the social construction of "reality," Foucault and poststructuralism in general endorses what might be termed "a discursive construction of reality."

However one understands the impact of poststructuralist thought upon contemporary notions of "culture," though, the poststructuralist challenge has often been refreshing by raising issues hitherto unquestionably accepted.

---

11 Based upon a linguistic model, structuralism first called into question the relation of language and reality. By the very structure of language, the critique of the notion of reference has undermined all attempts to capture reality in language and to all truth claims based upon representations. And perhaps even more telling than a critique of truth for an understanding of culture, poststructuralism has challenged the notion of meaning. Beyond Saussure's "difference" between sign and referent, Derrida has developed a notion of *différance*, which by destabilizing the relation between signified and signifier indicates that signs are open to a limitless play of readings and an infinite construals of meaning. All means of restricting such play are illegitimate, the result either of uncriticized conventions or simply impositions of power. Even such notions as the text, the integrity of a text, and of a context cannot not be invoked to restrict the "dissemination" of meanings and possible meanings. Or, as Derrida claims, the notion of text should be so understood that the "world" itself is only an open and infinitely extendable text. By extension the idea that a culture provides a distinct horizon of meaning is also brought under question. Neither individual nor collective attributions of cultural meaning by participants within a culture nor the ascriptions of meaning by observers "outside" the given culture limit this play and stabilize meaning or structures of meaning.

12 In the face of these concerns, it is understandable that a number of scholars across the disciplines have called for the abandonment of the term "culture" altogether.

And yet, however appealing and refreshing this simple abandonment might initially appear, such a move neither comprehends the reasons for these conflicts nor understands the necessity behind the insistence – in the modern West – upon defining reality in terms of "culture." Even Jack Goody's suggestion that all such general categories should be understood merely as "signposts" and not as actual divisions within the human world – however practical it might initially seem – only swerves around and does not remove these obstacles. Goody, pp. 12-13, 29-30.

Moreover, in revealing what is dogmatic and ideological in our thinking, it is even necessary. But, as has recently become more evident, poststructuralism is less a thorough-going critique of current and/or conventional practices than currently perceived. It is less a reversal of Enlightenment thought than its last incarnation. Foucault's later thought not only makes such a relation explicit, it also indicates that Foucault cannot "legitimate" his own attempts at writing "histories" and even "cultural histories." In more subtle ways, deconstruction also reenacts the founding gesture of Enlightenment thought itself. Although critical of structuralist notions of a purely formal definition of "language" (*langue*), deconstruction still retains the "theory" of a closed, abstract system of signs. This post-structural notion of "language" functions as a universal – a universal anti-logic – against which all claims of reference and all claims to theoretical and practical legitimacy have to be measured and eventually found wanting. Against such a critique, there seems to be no appeal.[13]

In the face of this necessary critique of conventional notions of knowledge and in the wake of the critique of this critique, how are we to think of or even speak of "culture?" The poststructuralist critique has made us more aware than ever of the disjuncture between "words" and "things." Explicitly or implicitly, all recent discussions – both academic and non-academic – revolve around this disjuncture between the "reality" of culture and the truth of "culture."[14] "Culture" continues to indicate some "fundamental" sense of "reality" in the modern West and, if it does not provide the "meaning" of this

---

13 Against the holistic relational system of *langue* and "behind" this the infinite play of *différance*, Derrida sees all actual linguistic and cultural forms as arbitrary or conventional limitations. Contexts and cultures can then only be understood as "instantiations" of these "universals." Even Derrida's own forms of discourse are limitations of such universals; but his recognize this fact by pointing out the aporia of thinking and saying.

By writing specific histories, Foucault avoids making such universal claims but ends up not being able to justify his own use of language or his approach to writing history. He can only speak of a status of permanent critique. See *The Foucault Reader*, p. 42.

14 But what is the "reality" we designate by "culture"? However much we cannot do without a notion of "culture" to designate this "reality, " difficulties arise once we attempt to define either this term or this reality. For an interesting approach to this problem, see David K. Danow, "The World of Culture and the World of Life, " *Semiotica: Journal of the International Association for Semiotic Studies*, vol. 106, no.3/4 (1995), pp. 355-364.

"reality," then it points to the possible range that these meanings might take.[15] While all attempts at defining "culture" scientifically seemingly results in failure and the meaning of "culture" perpetually evades our grasp, the truth in the notion of "culture" might perhaps lie specifically in this failure and this evasiveness.[16] Somehow beyond the search for a unified definition on the one hand and the demand for the appreciation of the diversity of cultural voices on the other, "culture" seems to speak to the basic Western "experience" of "reality." This notion of "experience" draws out the tensions, if not contradictions, between the ways we experience "culture" – the "reality" of "culture" and the ways we tend to know and speak of "culture" – the "truth" of "culture."

While not positing this "experience" as foundational or as a ground for thinking about "culture," this experience of culture can be thought further. It is necessary – to expand upon Foucault's later thought – to understand how experience is "problematized" through the notion of culture, to what problem is "culture" the solution.[17] How is the "reality" of culture experienced? What is the way in which a "world" is opened through "culture?" And how is the truth of this reality as a reality and this world as a world brought to language? Such reflections are far removed from the problems of theory and

---

15   Perhaps we should conclude, as do the editors of a recent scholarly journal dedicated to the problem of culture that "this lack of precise definition [of concept of culture], should however be taken as a programmatic gesture rather than as a default to be remedied." "Cultural History/Cultural Studies" *New German Studies* 65 (Spring-Summer, 1995), p. 4.

16   For an interesting discussion of contemporary problems faced by anthropologists, see Anna Grimshaw and Keith Hart, "Anthropology and the Crisis of the Intellectuals" in *Critique of Anthropology* vol. 14, no. 3 (1994), pp. 227-261, 38.

Against the holistic relational system of *langue* and "behind" this the infinite play of *différance*, Derrida sees all actual linguistic and cultural forms as arbitrary or conventional limitations. Contexts and cultures can then only be understood as "instantiations" of these "universals." Even Derrida's own forms of discourse are limitations of such universals; but his recognize this fact by pointing out the aporia of thinking and saying.

By writing specific histories, Foucault avoids making such universal claims but ends up not being able to justify his own use of language or his approach to writing history. He can only speak of a status of permanent critique. See *The Foucault Reader*, p. 42.

17   Michel Foucault, *The Use of Pleasure*, pp. 11-24.

definition, even when they are understood on the epistemic level.[18] In this sense, the notion of "culture" seems to speak to the modern (and even the postmodern) experience of the world and the ways in which this "world" is open to language.

Can we find a way of revealing this reality and of speaking its truth? In the following essay, I would like to address this question and attempt to answer it from a perspective and through the lens of a discipline not usually engaged in poststructuralist criticism or in theoretical discussions of any type.[19] I turn to the ways in which "culture" has come to be defined in historical studies because, as I will contend, the historical approach to "culture" allows us a degree of reflexivity not available in other disciplines.[20] While some anthropologists have recently moved to a form of reflexivity of their academic project, and others have turned to an understanding of the need to think of "culture" and "history" together, certain modes of cultural history have wrestled

---

18   These problems are not necessarily overcome with a clearer definition of the term culture. The tensions between theories, and most often grand theories coming out of philosophy and social sciences, and actual written histories is not always bad or resolved through a clearer set of definitions; for there are limitation with the very use of theory and even of conceptual language. Because of its ties to the representational theory of truth social history maintains wedded to theory. This is true not only of Marx's concept of praxis but also of Braudel's notion of the *longue duree*. However much Braudel would like this notion be real, it remains a construct, a concept applied to "reality."

For a discussion of the questionable relation of theory to historical practice, see Lynn Hunt, "History Beyond Social Theory" in *The States of "Theory": History, Art, and Critical Discourse* ed. David Carroll (New York: Columbia University Press, 1990).

19   The general problem of historical knowledge in a postmodern world—and with an emphasis upon cultural history – is raised but not very deeply analyzed in Joyce Appleby, Lynn Hunt and Margaret Jacob, *Telling the Truth about History* (New York: Norton, 1994). Whatever else it may be, this work at least addresses some of the issues which most historians neither comprehend nor address.

20   Reflexive Anthology has taken a lead in addressing this issue; but it takes its thought along different lines than I follow. For how this reflexive move works in anthropology, see *Writing Culture: The Poetics and Politics of Ethnography* eds. James Clifford and George E. Marcus (Berkeley: University of California Press, 1986); James Clifford *The Predicament of Culture: Twentieth-Century Ethnography, Literature, and Art* (Cambridge, Ma.: Harvard University Press, 1988); Renato Rosaldo, *Culture and Truth: The Remaking of Social Analysis* (Boston: Beacon Press, 1989).

with these issues in relation to their own attempts to capture the truth of our own cultural-historical existence for some time and offer another approach to the problem of "culture."[21] But in speaking of historical studies and even of cultural historical studies, I do not intend to justify a specific academic discourse or even to propose a re-establishment or the overturning of academic boundaries. I am concerned with possible way in which we can develop a language or, more precisely, a "textuality" of culture.[22]

---

21   Marshall Sahlins is the leading anthropologist to confront the problem of history directly. He argues that anthropologists need to introduce a notion of historical time into the study of unchanging symbolic system and the interactions among cultures. See Sahlins, *Historical Metaphors and Mythical Realities* (Ann Arbor: University of Michigan Press, 1981); Sahlins, *Islands of History* (Chicago: University of Chicago Press, 1985); and Sahlins, "Goodbye to *Triste Tropes*: Ethnography in the Context of Modern World History," *Journal of Modern History* 65 (1993), pp. 1-25. For further discussions for a suggested integration of anthropology and history, see Bernard S. Cohen, *An Anthropologist among the Historians and Other Essays* (Chicago: University of Chicago Press, 1990) and John and Jean Comaroff, *Ethnography and the Historical Imagination* (Boulder: Westview Press, 1992).

  Although these interests speak to a common concern with cultural history between anthropologists and historians, in actual practice there is only limited communication across disciplines, let alone a shared set of problems, definitions, or projects. In part, the fact that these disciplines take independent orientations towards cultural history is explained by the ways in which each understands both culture and history. In the study of literature, ethnology, or multiculturalism, the notion of cultural history adds a historical dimension to an already circumscribed definition of culture. However defined, "culture" is to be looked at from a temporal perspective. In cultural history, on the other hand, the notion of culture is added to a basic historical understanding of the world. "Culture" had to be defined in order to provide an explicit object of study. Given these circumstances, one would think that cultural history should provide the lead in defining common problems across disciplinary boundaries.

22   Even such notions as the text, the integrity of a text and of a context cannot not be invoked to restrict the "dissemination" of meanings and possible meanings. Or, as Derrida claims, the notion of text should be so understood that the "world" itself is only an open and infinitely extendable text. By extension the idea that a culture provides a distinct horizon of meaning is also brought under question. Neither individual nor collective attributions of cultural meaning by participants within a culture nor the ascriptions of meaning by observers "outside" the given culture limit this play and stabilize meaning or structures of meaning. See Jacques Derrida, "Signature Event Context" in *Margins of Philosophy* (Chicago: University of Chicago Press, 1982), pp. 273-330.

I.

Explicitly or implicitly, all recent discussions on culture – both academic and non-academic – revolve around this disjuncture between the "reality" of culture and the truth of "culture." In fact, "culture" is one of, if not *the*, basic way in which we have come to comprehend "the human," both in under-standing our own modes of being and in identifying those of others. But what is the "reality" we designate by "culture?" However much we cannot do without a notion of "culture" to designate this "reality," difficulties arise once we attempt to define either this term or this reality.[23] Although in its broadest definition, "culture" demarcates a total way of life of a given people at a given time, the concept remains ambiguous, agonizingly ambiguous. Even today, anthropologists continue to debate whether "culture" should consists of the symbolic level of human existence and the historical trans-mission of these symbols or whether it should include the non-symbolic, the material bases and behavior of a people. Connected to these various at-tempts to grasp "culture" conceptually is the question of the "appropriate" methodology for the study of culture and the deployment of a "science" of "culture." The notion of a universal and abstract definition of culture im-plies, if not a single, universal and abstract methodological approach, than a single language "appropriate" to the "science" of culture.[24]

This move to universal definitions and general methodologies has today not gone unchallenged. In general, poststructuralism has raised issues of the very nature of the language in which we claim to speak about the world and challenges the discourses we employ to legitimate its various practices and institutions. "Culture" can neither be defined by designating a specific hu-man "reality" nor define the truth upon which its knowledge is founded in terms of representations.

This line of criticism has been expanded so that around the critique of representation there has evolved a serious questioning of the dominant forms of knowledge which are based upon such definitions of truth. Even a

---

23   For an interesting approach to this problem, see David K. Danow, "The World of Culture and the World of Life, " *Semiotica: Journal of the International Association for Semiotic Studies*, vol. 106, no. 3/4 (1995), pp. 355-364.

24   For a "semiotic" approach to the study of culture, see Yuri M. Lotman, *Universe of the Mind: A Semiotic Theory of Culture*, Ann Shukman, trans. (Bloomington: Indi-ana University Press, 1990). And for a discussion of Lotman and the Tartu Group, see Arthur Blaim, "Cultural Semiotics –The Uses of a Theory" in *Russian Literature* 36 (1994), pp. 243-254.

cursory glance at what appears to animate current interests in "culture" reveals less a renewed search for an abstract theoretical definition than a shared critical stance towards all such conceptions. There is a strong argument, current today, that only in the particularity of their manifestations or even only through a specific personal or group experience can cultures be known.[25] This does not imply that the term "culture" means anything anyone wishes to make of it in any given instance. Instead, the emphasis seems to be that, while we may debate the definition of "culture," the "reality" we are concerned with is comprehensible only through the variety of specific – materially and symbolically bounded – "cultures." "Culture" appears to be extremely mercurial, dispersing from a single and universal "Culture" into multiple and distinct actual forms of "cultures," only to ball up again into an apparently commonly human "substance."[26] Specific cultures set up specific boundaries or horizons, but these boundaries are porous or at least semi-porous, allowing influences from the outside to enter and reshape its meanings and values. Or, in Edward Said's terminology, cultures – both dominant and non-dominant – are "transformational;" they are characterized by their "hybridity," by their two-way openness to influence and be influenced. [27] Although open, "cultures" are nonetheless integral entities; they are not mere instantiations of a general "Culture."[28]

Beyond this questioning however, it is also evident that no consensus has

---

25 This seems to be Geertz's more recent position. See Clifford Geertz, *Local Knowledge: Further Essays in Interpretive Anthropology* (New York: Basic Books, 1983), pp. 167-234.

26 At times, Michel Foucault suggests that we speak of "culture" as a "substance, " the "substance" in which we have our existence. It is for Foucault "ethical substance"-employing Hegel's suggestive term. What is this substance? Hegel argues it is *Geist*, which can be understood in its historical unfolding and ultimately known through its own logic. This substance language – however felicitous the phrase "ethical substance" may be – obfuscates more than clarifies. Culture is not a substance – simple or compound – and it cannot be understood through the analogy of substance – material or spiritual. See, for instance, *The Use of Pleasure* (New York: Pantheon, 1985), pp. 26-32.

27 Edward Said, *Culture and Imperialism* (New York: Routledge, 1995), pp. xxv, 58.

28 The acknowledgement of such diversity and specificity however seems not only to disperse the study of culture into multiple and apparently infinite subdivisions – as "culture" now includes the experiences of various groups and even life-styles within the larger culture – but also to question the capacity of outsiders to comprehend the "truth" of these particular formations.

yet emerged either over a general experience of "culture" or over the meanings of specific "cultures." In the face of such difficulties even more radical solutions have been sought. Chris Jenks, for one, contends that "culture" points not to a site of shared meaning and social order but explicitly demarcates the area of conflict over basic meanings.[29] This conflictual model of culture is both explicitly and implicitly endorsed by a growing and seemingly all-pervasive interest in what is ambiguously referred to as "multiculturalism." Multiculturalism perhaps receives its clearest academic identity in cultural studies in both the broad and the narrow (Birmingham School) sense of the term.[30] Even if we follow the suggestions of cultural studies and venture to think of culture in terms of conflictual space, it still tantalizingly and frustratingly eludes our conceptual grasp.

These critiques are not limited to theoretical and epistemological problems. Across the academic disciplines the study of culture merges with the critique of cultural practices and their dominant discourses. As such, Foucault encourages the criticism not only of academic practices and disciplinary stagnation but also of the present organization of society, the structures of existing power relations, and the currently dominant representations of culture. In

---

29   Chris Jenks, *Culture* (New York: Routledge, 1993), pp. 157-158.

30   This school of cultural critics has grown out of the pioneering studies of Raymond Williams and has received institutional form in the Centre for Contemporary Cultural studies of the University of Birmingham. See, Lawrence Grossberg, Cary Nelson, and Paula A. Treichler, eds., *Cultural studies*, (New York, 1992).

These studies speak both to the increasing awareness of diversities among cultures and to the interaction among various cultures. It also includes a critique of the relation of dominant to subaltern cultures. But there is an ambiguity inherent within the notion of Cultural studies, which is reflected in the wide range of subject matters and methodologies which variously and often confusingly employ both literary and social scientific modes of analyses. While challenging and redeploying such conventional notions as class, ethnicity, race, gender and sex as categories of meaning and objects of research, this same stance or rather the aggregate of stances that assume the title of Cultural studies remain unclear as to its own methods of research, objects of investigation and modalities of thought. While rejecting the traditional Marxist base/ superstructure dyad, these studies have not developed a paradigm of their own. Within its heterogeneous theoretical positions, there is revealed only a shared commitment to decoding artifacts as products of hegemonic cultures. See, in particular, John Fiske, "Cultural Studies and the Culture of Everyday Life" and Stuart Hall, "Cultural studies and its Theoretical Legacies" in *Cultural Studies*, pp. 154-173; 277-294.

this light what is increasingly referred to as "reflexive anthropology" is highly instructive. This type of anthropology emphasizes the need to move beyond an explanation of how the concept of culture functions in the study of other peoples to a rigorous analysis of the development and deployment of "culture" in contemporary academic, political and social formations of the West. Reflexive anthropology raises intriguing questions concerning the interplay between totality and diversity, identity and difference, meaning and power within our contemporary cultural practices. It poses again the problem of whether the notion of culture itself can ever be merely a descriptive and not an evaluative concept. As such, it transgresses and then subverts such foundational categories as "self" and "other," "same" and "difference," "modernity" and "pre-modernity" within a general critique of Eurocentrism.[31]

Cultural studies, again in both the narrow and broad sense, extend this line of criticism. Both explicitly and implicitly, cultural studies legitimates its diversity of interests and methods by reference to the postmodernist critique of "grand theory" and "master narratives." It relates, in other words, the problems of cultural totality and cultural diversity to questions of power and politics. To posit a "culture" as a totality of symbols and behaviors seems necessary to impose a determinist theory upon the human world. Cultures, it is argued, do not in fact form such totalities. At best such holistic notions are constructs, imposed upon the human reality for cognitive purposes. At worst, they provide a type of legitimization for the arbitrary use of power. "Totality" seems to be on the side of established power relations, employed to diminish conflict and to legitimate the unequal distribution of and access to power. From this critical perspective, all "cultures" appear to be constructed from specific power relations, which establish and re-enforce specific national identities and social divisions. Students of cultural studies have challenged the notion of cultural totality by inverting the notions of "high" and "low," "dominant" and "subaltern," "representation" and "reality," as much as "culture" and "nation." Power infuses the problem of who has the right to represent this totality and who has the power to include and exclude individuals and groups based upon this representation. In other words, who has the authority to "represent" a culture, not just in terms of political power but also in terms of producers of "culture?" The critique of representation also precludes all conventional moves to search for a general, all-encompassing

---

31   For an interesting discussion of contemporary problems faced by anthropologists, see Anna Grimshaw and Keith Hart, "Anthropology and the Crisis of the Intellectuals" in *Critique of Anthropology*, vol. 14, no. 3 (1994), pp. 227-261.

definition of culture or a universal theory of reality however much such a resort to common logic is appealing and theoretically sanctioned.

Beyond questions of defining academic disciplines and even of criticizing these disciplines, there are larger issues at stake. The critique of conventional notions of "culture" is not limited to theoretical and epistemological problems.[32] Across the academic disciplines, the study of culture merges with the critique of cultural practices and their dominant discourses. Foucault encourages the criticism not only of academic practices and disciplinary stagnation but also of the present organization of society, the structures of existing power relations, and the currently dominant representations of culture. And Foucault is not alone in arguing that all discourses are innately political in the sense that they include and exclude, empower and disempower.[33] This is true as much of academic theory as of all overtly political discourses. What appears as a merely descriptive use of the term "culture" often becomes confused with evaluative claims and political intentions. All too easily the idea of a culture as a totality becomes entangled with the ambiguity inherent in the concepts of norm and normality. As a normative ideal, "culture" becomes entwined with "culture" as a descriptive term. The poststructuralists Jean-François Lyotard and Jacques Derrida are vehemently opposed to any and every idea of totalizing theory precisely because, according to them, it inevitably leads to totalitarianism.[34] They argue that, as with all linguistic

---

32   These concerns with representation are not just epistemological. They are also political. Dominick LaCapra has recently suggested that today's debates revolve around "the politics of representation." Dominick LaCapra, "Is Everyone a *Mentalité* Case? Transference and the "Culture" Concept" reprinted in *History and Criticism* (Ithaca: Cornell University Press, 1985), pp. 71-94.

33   Foucault, *Power/Knowledge* (New York: Pantheon, 1980), pp. 80-81; Jean-Francois Lyotard, *Toward the Postmodern*, ed. Robert Harvey and Mark S. Roberts (Atlantic Heights, N.J.: 1993), pp. 159-162.

34   While not directly concerned with either a theory or even a definition of culture, post-structuralism—especially as developed in the texts of Barthes, Foucault, Lyotard, and Derrida—is hypercritical of all concepts of totality as well as of the possibility of meaning. They have shown that the claim to find or construct a totality is an illegitimate means of establishing meaning. Whether located in texts, society, or culture, they have argued that all such notions are theoretical ideological and practically authoritarian. For instance, see Jean-Francois Lyotard, *The Postmodern Condition: A Report on Knowledge* and Jacques Derrida, "Signature, Sign, and Play in the Discourse of the Human Sciences" in *Writing and Difference* (Chicago: University of Chicago Press, 1978), pp. 278-293.

formations, the concepts of cultural and cultural totality neither describe nor probe "reality." Instead of understanding the diversity and differentiation that constitutes a culture, this notion of culture requires the suppression of all ambiguities and differing elements in order to establish at least an illusion of unity. It establishes a value to be achieved either in contrast to other cultures or in terms of valorizing only what "fits" into a larger national unity. In this sense, culture is prescriptive, providing an ideal, a goal, a desire, a sought-after identity. "Culture" then imposes meaning unto the world, which in the name of unity results in the most horrendous consequences. "Cultures" in this sense form totalities which preclude deviation, difference and freedom.

In the face of these concerns, it is understandable that a number of scholars across the disciplines have called for the abandonment of the term "culture" altogether.[35] And yet, however appealing and refreshing this simple abandonment might initially appear, such a move neither comprehends the reasons for these conflicts nor understands the necessity behind the insistence – in the modern West – upon defining reality in terms of "culture."[36] Even if beyond conceptual grasp, "culture" is not unthinkable. It does not form an aporia. We can pass through it and think it – but think it only in certain ways. The question of course remains: in what ways? There is a need to reflect further and more openly upon the ways in which the experience of culture is constituted and brought to language.

Although initially only complicating matters further, relating the ambiguous notion of "culture" to what is perhaps an equally ambiguous notion of "history" provides one possible starting point for such a reflection. Initially, the historical approach to culture and the cultural approach to history do not necessarily resolve any of the issues circulating in, through, above, and below the definition of "culture." In fact, taking such a historical approach in the face of recent debates only seems to complicate some issues and confuse others unnecessarily. Cultural studies in particular have identified historical research as the focus of all that is wrong with conventional scholarship with

---

35   Is "culture" simply so "clumpish" a term, as Geoffrey Eley has recently stated, that it should be entirely eliminated from scholarly discussion. Geoffrey Eley, "What is Cultural History" in *New German Critique* 65 (Spring-Summer, 1995), p. 23.

36   Even Jack Goody's suggestion that all such general categories should be understood merely as "signposts" and not as actual divisions within the human world—however practical it might initially seem – only swerves around and does not remove these obstacles. Goody, pp. 12-13, 29-30.

its mooring in the modern, Eurocentric world.[37] While the history of culture need not limit itself however to merely establishing developmental lines of continuity between the past and the present and thereby creating question-able forms of identity, it also seems to posit the even more questionable no-tion of superficial notions of knowledge and truth and at base uncritically serve ideological functions.

Beyond questions of defining academic disciplines and even of criticizing these disciplines, there are larger issues at stake. As Yuri Lotman reminds us, for example, "culture" and "history" are intimately connected; questions of having or existing within a culture seem to call forth questions of existing within time. I go further than Lotman, claiming that while in a general way cultural formations have their distinctive "experiences" of time, in the mod-ern West the "reality" of "culture" is interconnected to the meaning of exist-ing within historical time.[38] But as Lotman's ultimate failures to bring "cul-ture" and "history" together indicate, this connection cannot be approached through the assumption of even a sophisticated definition of culture within the traditional notions of historical knowledge. What specifically is "histori-cal time" then remains troublesome. Is it distinct from "natural" time and the "time" of internal time consciousness?[39] All that can be assumed is that the modern notion of culture is intimately connected to the experience of historical time, and perhaps more contentiously, the modern notion of his-torical time is not externally connected through chronology but intimately interwoven with the experience of culture itself.[40]

When cultural history involves an attempt to capture the cultural past of our own culture and its sense of time, it creates, for example, the possibility which the study of non-Western cultures advocated by reflexive anthropolo-

---

37   For a discussion of history and Cultural studies, see Carolyn Steedman, "Culture, Cultural Studies, and the Historians" in *Cultural studies*, pp. 613-622; and Tony Bennett, "Out in the Open: Reflections on the History and Practice of Cultural Studies" in *Cultural Studies*, vol. 10, no.1 (1996), pp. 133-153.

38   Yuri M. Lotman's works along these lines have not been fully appreciated. See, for instance, Lotman, *Universe of the Mind: A Semiotic Theory of Culture*, Ann Shuk-man trans. (Bloomington, IN: Indiana University Press, 1990), pp. 217-273.

39   For the most extensive discussion of current theories of time, see Paul Ricoeur, *Time and Narrative* 3 volumes, (Chicago: University of Chicago Press, 1983-85).

40   See Michel de Certeau, "History: Ethics, Science, and Fiction, " in Norma Haan et. al. *Social Science as Moral Inquiry* (New York: Columbia University Press, 1983), pp. 143-150.

gy does not. It raises questions beyond conventional notions of linear time of the specific nature of historical time, of continuity and breaks, of repetition and innovation within our own culture. Understood in this sense, cultural history creates the possibility of splaying out temporally both reflections upon the definitions of culture which we bring to our own experience of culture and the possibilities of speaking the truth about ourselves as cultural beings. Without positing either dubious lines of continuity within a single culture or a notion of cultural totality, the description of the past in terms of culture or the contest of cultural meanings establishes a distance to be established between the past and the present as well as between one culture and another. It calls not for the conceptual or theoretical grasp and thus cognitive control of other cultures through their reduction to our culturally conditioned forms of knowing but for a putting into question of our own cultural horizon as both a cognitive and existential boundary. Such a distance then opens the possibilities for a type of reflexivity on the level of culture itself which is called for but not achieved within the academic debates and culture wars of the present. Without falling back into a dubious notion of re-presenting the real of conventional historical studies, this reflection also puts into questions notions of the "past" as the "object" of a scientific project defined by a neutral "subject."

Related to this question of historical time is the way in which we have come to comprehend "culture" and the historical formations of "culture" as basic ways in which we come to define "the real." Beyond questions of definition and even in spite of them, the historical interpretation of culture allow us to step back from ourselves and our own ways of knowing – to bracket as it were the familiarity of our own cultural meanings and modes – and reflect upon "culture" and the ways in which "culture" has come to "define" reality in the modern West. In this way, we can examine the interplay between "same" and "other" as well as between "inside" and "outside" as they interact through historical time. It thus suggests ways of knowing "self" in terms of "otherness," and the constitution of "otherness" which is also ourselves. Through such a historical detour, we come to the purpose of all forms of knowing however apparently remote and unconnected to us: to know ourselves reflexively as cultural beings. The historical study of culture allows for a type of reflection upon the immediate an all-inclusive "reality" which "culture" supposedly reveals and to fulfill what historical studies have always claimed but failed to achieve – as the critiques of Roland Barthes and Michel de Certeau reveal – to speak the truth of this reality.[41] Understood in this sense, cultural history suggests way to write history as "the history of the present" in Foucault's sense.

II.

Paralleling and at points intersecting with this renewed interest in the study of culture in general, there has arisen within historical studies what has come to be called the "New Cultural History."[42] The New Cultural History is not only the way in which historians have responded to the general concerns raised in anthropology and "cultural studies;" it is also one of the chief means through which a limited number of historians have attempted to engage with the theoretical and critical issues raised by poststructuralism. Perhaps with the sole exception of the study of gender, the New Cultural History has become the main way by which historians have addressed the larger currents of contemporary thought and present-day critiques of conventional understanding of knowledge and truth.[43]

As with the recent move to the study of culture in general, the denomination "New Cultural History" designates less a common subject matter or a

----

41 Roland Barthes, "The Discourse of History" and "The Reality Effect" reproduced in *The Rustle of Language* (New York: Hill and Wang, 1984), pp. 127-148; Michel de Certeau, "History: Ethics, Science, and Fiction," pp. 123-152.

42 For an overview of the New Cultural History, see Appleby et al. *Telling the Truth*, pp. 217-223.

43 Robert Mandrou and Robert Muchembled, for instance, have taken up Lucien Febvre's challenge to write cultural history in terms of social psychology; and they have developed the notion of *mentalité* as the collective world view of the common people. Robert Mandrou, *Introduction to Modern France, 1500-1640: An Essay in Historical Psychology*, trans. R.E. Hallmark, (New York, 1975), and Robert Munchembled, *Popular Culture and Elite Culture in France, 1400-1750*, trans. Lydia Cochrane (Baton Rouge: Louisiana State University Press, 1985).

Natalie Davis and Robert Darnton have explicitly brought anthropological theory and models to bear upon the interpretation of specific moments in the cultural history of early modern Europe. Natalie Zemon Davis, *Society and Culture in Early Modern France* (Stanford, Calif., 1975). Robert Darnton, *The Great Cat Massacre and Other Episodes in French Cultural History* (New York, 1984).

And Roger Chartier, Lynn Hunt, as well as Davis have found in the recent developments in semiology a linguistic understanding of cultural formation. Roger Chartier, "Text, Symbol, and Frenchness," *Journal of Modern History* 57 (1985): 682-695; *Cultural History: Between Practices and Representations*, trans. Lydia Cochrane, (Ithaca, N.Y.: Cornell University Press, 1988); and *The Cultural Uses of Print*, trans. Lydia G. Cochrane, (Princeton, N.J.: Princeton University Press, 1987). Lynn Hunt, *Politics, Culture, and Class in the French Revolution* (Berkeley, 1984). Natalie Z. Davis, *Fiction in the Archives: Pardon Tales and Their Tellers in Sixteenth-Century France* (Stanford, CA.: Stanford University Press, 1987).

shared methodology than a rejection of traditional approaches to the history of culture. Implied in the notion of a "New" Cultural History, of course, is the idea of an older cultural history.[44] The new cultural historians identify this other form with older generations of *Annales* historians. From its origins in the inter-war years, the *Annalistes* were centrally concerned with "culture" in the sense of a "total history" of past existence. Lucien Febvre and Marc Bloch – the founding fathers of the *Annales* – spoke of the "history of civilization" as the study of the total way of life, of *histoire totale*.[45] To Fernand Braudel, we owe the generally accepted tripartite division of history into structural, conjunctural and event-filled levels, which have become in the classical *Annales* formulation the division into economic, social and cultural levels.[46] "Culture" or "civilization" in this structuralist approach was thereby relegated to the third level, the famous *troisieme niveau*. These divisions also established hierarchies in their geographic breadth an explanatory power. Dependent upon society and ultimately upon the economy, culture is an epiphenomenon of an epiphenomenon, an imitation of an imitation.

---

44   There is no generally agreed upon definition of the "old" cultural history; there are in practice two commonly accepted uses of the term. "Cultural history" is either vaguely applied to histories of the fine art, of literature, of philosophy, of tastes and in general of all those aspects of human life that lay outside of political/diplomatic and social/economic history. As such, although there are individual examples of excellent histories of painting and literature, cultural history as a whole remains an inchoate array of mixed objects of study and multiple methodologies, without clearly defined problems or common concerns.

45   Even the first generation of *Annales* historians understood themselves narrowly, insisting upon both the novelty of their approach to history and the specifically French origins of cultural history. See, for instance, Febvre's essays "A New Kind of History" and "*Civilization*: Evolution of a Word and a Group of Idea" in *A New Kind of History and Other Essays*, pp. 27-43, 219-257.

46.   While Fernand Braudel has developed the notion of "total history" in a more systematic fashion on both practical and theoretical levels than other *annalistes*, still there remain real difficulties with this notion. The locus of "culture" is displaced from the reality of a culture or even from its structures of meaning to the unity of the scientific enterprise itself. For Braudel this totality is legitimated through the unity of the social sciences. This position, of course, is subject to poststructuralist critiques of representation as the foundation for scientific knowledge. Fernand Braudel, *On History* (Chicago: University of Chicago Press, 1980), pp. 25-54. For a fuller discussion of the so-called "new cultural history," see the Introduction to this volume.

This distinction between "new" and "old" forms of cultural history is not just chronological. In addition to separating current historical practices from those developed in the first half of the twentieth century, the New Cultural History redefines the "field" of culture and how it should be studied. In one sense, the New Cultural History finds its unity in the rejection of such totalizing structures. Braudel, whose project has dominated second and third generation *Annales* scholars, ends up positing this totalizing structure on the side of the knowing subject. He projected a unity of all the human sciences within a total science, founded upon the underlying and unifying notion of the *longue durée*. This central notion of the *longue durée* then functions both as a "deep structure" of reality and an epistemological foundation for the human sciences. The implication of taking such a stance obviously confronts the problem of legitimating and hegemonizing tendencies of total theory. In addition to falling prey to the poststructuralist critique of scientific and specifically social scientific knowledge, Braudel's "total history" also succumbs to its specific criticism of structuralism – the claim that all meaning is established by position within a structure and all truth upon the "deep structure" of the *longue durée*.[47]

Instead of searching for such a totalizing theory and a structuralist definition of truth, the historians of the New Cultural History are united by the diversity of their approaches to a common set of problems.[48] They have thus re-opened the whole question of the relation of social structure and cultural meaning in new and creative ways. Their idea of culture is also non-totalizing. It accommodates discontinuities and even conflict both among and between various *mentalités*. "Culture" thereby becomes a more flexible set of interrelations and interpretations. Questions of the shared beliefs and values of dominant cultures and subcultures, of popular culture and elite culture, and the relations between them replace the assumption

---

47 For recent discussions among historians concerning the problem of representation and the representational foundation of truth, see Hayden White, *Metahistory* (Baltimore: Johns Hopkins Press, 1973); Sandee Cohen, *Historical Culture* (Berkeley: The University of California Press, 1986); and Michel de Certeau, *The Writing of History* (New York: Columbia University Press, 1988).

48 For a description and history of the New Cultural History, see Lynn Hunt, ed., *The New Cultural History* (Berkeley, 1989), especially the Introduction, pp. 1-22. For a history and interpretation of the *Annales* school, see Traian Stoianovich, *French Historical Method: The Annales Paradigm* (Ithaca, N.Y., 1976) and Francois Furet, "Beyond the *Annales*," *Journal of Modern History* 55 (1983), pp. 389-410.

and the confirmation of cultural totality. Roger Chartier has recently questioned whether there is a universal symbolic code within a given society at a given time which can account for all its activity.[49] He thereby challenges both the structuralist notion of total history and the foundational Marxist model of base and superstructure.[50] And the new cultural historians in general have concentrated upon specific sets of relationships and often unforeseen ties between social life and legitimating discourses or between national or religious ideologies and individual and group identities. Natalie Davis sees sixteenth- and seventeenth-century France not in the conventional categories "Renaissance" and "Reformation" and not even in the more recent and more empty formulations "early modern" and "age of transition." Instead, she perceives a competing set of movements and trends against which both specific groups and identifiable persons variously respond. The New Cultural History sees in culture not a global unity but a discreet number of conflictual relations among social groups, complex multiplicities of relations to power, and contending varieties of discourses. The play of meaning and social structure or of meaning and relations of power always depends upon the specificity of each case; and the truth of their research lies in this specificity.[51]

This rejection of totality in either its Braudelian or Marxist forms, however, has raised its own set of difficulties. Denying a unified notion of culture results less in a more complex and open understanding of culture than at first appears. Without either a common subject matter, a shared methodology, or a working definition of "culture," the New Cultural History tends to be an incoherent diversity of specific investigations. As a result, it all too often devolves into an unconnected number of specialized investigations and case studies. This line of criticism has been most forcefully expressed by proponents of the New Cultural History itself. Both François Furet and Robert Darnton, for instance, have criticized the notion of *mentalité* for lacking a

---

49 Chartier, "Text, Symbol, and Frenchness," *Journal of Modern History* 57 (1985): 682-695.

50 Clifford Geertz, *The Interpretation of Culture* (New York: Basic Books, 1973). Geertz has nuanced his initial position. See, for instance, the essay in *Local Knowledge: Further Essays in Interpretive Anthropology* (New York, 1983).

51 See Barbara B. Diefendorf and Carla Hesse ed., *Culture and Identity in Early Modern Europe (1500-1800): Essays in Honor of Natalie Zemon Davis* (Ann Arbor: University of Michigan Press, 1993).

precise definition and clear focus for research.[52] Lynn Hunt warns against "a cultural history defined topically [which] could degenerate into an endless search for new cultural practices to describe, whether carnivals, cat massacres, or impotence trials."[53] These studies may be individually fascinating but collectively they have exploded into an incoherent multiplicity of isolated studies, which result in no intellectual insights and threatens to fall back into antiquarianism. Its supposed methodological innovations address current theoretical and practical issues than provide an isolated series of images from the past.

What often salvages these studies from scholastic atomization and ultimate meaninglessness is their ties to contemporary social scientific and literary theories. Most often they understand their research in terms of adapting or testing these theories. But there are distinct limitations with such an approach to cultural history. Robert Darnton, for example looks to Clifford Geertz and not directly to the hermeneutical theories upon which Geertz bases his "interpretive anthropology." Lynn Hunt relies upon Hayden White's adaptation of structuralist linguistics instead of examining semiological theory itself.[54] Their studies neither address directly the hermeneutic poststructuralist and textual theories upon which contemporary anthropology and literary theory depend nor contribute a truth of its own to a historical understanding of culture. Cultural historical studies appear to be relegated to the minor task of elucidating counter examples to social scientific models and poststructuralist theories, as Certeau has argued for contemporary historical studies as a whole.[55] Worse still, in too many cases the "new cultural historians" have all too often employed theories without a recognition of either their full explanatory powers or the logical consequences of their basic assumptions. And, in others, they have made universal claims that

---

52 Francois Furet, "Beyond the *Annales,*" *Journal of Modern History* 55 (1983): 389-410; and Robert Darnton, "Intellectual and Cultural History," in *The Past Before Us: Contemporary Historical Writings in the United States,* ed. Michael Kammen (Ithaca, N.Y.: Cornell University Press, 1980).

53 Hunt, *New Cultural History,* p. 9.

54 The only exception seems to be Roger Chartier who looks directly to the works of Michel Foucault. But then again, Foucault is already a historian who himself does not always take into account the thought of other contemporary theorists.

55 Michel de Certeau, *The Writing of History,* trans. Tom Conley (New York: Columbia University Press, 1988), pp. 56-192.

undermine the specificity of their studies or have developed imaginative case studies that defy all attempts at larger or deeper meaning.

Not only has the New Cultural History adopted social scientific and literary theories without making independent contributions to current thinking, it has not even opened those questions which directly concern historical existence and the writing of history.[56] Problems of the interrelation of text and context, of language and discourse as well as of the relation of the past meaning to present truth have not been sufficiently worked out. Even within the restricted area of testing and adapting social scientific theories and literary models, the new cultural historians have not always been successful, as problems specifically revolving around existence within time are overlooked. In addition, not only has the definition of what constitutes "culture" and the interplay of various meanings receded into the background but also the specifically historical nature of the "object" of inquiry has been displaced to ones concerning methodology and research techniques. As such, it shows a limited horizon of technological knowledge and not the understanding of

---

56 The inability of historians to enter into contemporary discussions lies not only with the new cultural historians, of course. This situation has arisen because as a group historians have in the last few generations declared themselves professionally against theory in each and every form. Practicing historians are much more comfortable with description or with low level (and often merely) material causal explanations than with problems of interpretive methodology, theoretical concerns, or cultural criticism. With all their intentions of speaking to these issues, the new cultural historians reveal the limitations of this anti-theoretical heritage.

Because of the mistrust and misunderstanding of theory among practicing historians, cultural history like most other forms of history articulates itself mainly through a multiplicity of specific histories, monographic examinations and case studies. To ask specifically "What is the New Cultural History?" results merely in pointing to a number of individual works that claim to be cultural histories, ranging from grand programmatic statements to studies of world views and symbolic codes to the thick descriptions of specific incidents. The New Cultural History not only leaves basic assumptions unexamined and significant consequences unexplored but also undermines serious discussion of basic definitions and common problems. There is not so much a single type of New Cultural History, or a distinct number of competing definitions of cultural history, or even a lively multiplicity of approaches to a common set of concerns, than a simple state of confusion over the definition and purpose of cultural history. Related to this limited and confused definition of culture, is the ambiguous and often merely implied connections between what is called culture and what is posited as society. This confusion is compounded by the amorphous and therefore ambiguous definition and purpose of historical studies themselves.

a past world as a distinctly past culture or of the relation – defined by a specific notion of historical time – of this past to present truth.[57]

Without further reflection and without a critique of its own forms of knowledge, the New Cultural History all too easily falls back onto the dominant and largely outmoded discourse of academic history.[58] In renouncing Braudel's structuralist approach to history, the new cultural historians often fall back upon simple empirical definitions of "culture" through the representations of certain given functions or products. The historians of the New Cultural History often revert to the details of archival research and the legitimization of empirical data. As a result, their research depends upon the uncritical modes of presently dominant form of historical discourse. While naive empiricism thinks it discovers "culture," "society," "the economy" and other such general categories within the world they are investigating, the definitions and functions of such supposed entities is dependent upon a prior assumption of the deployment of conventional fields of positivity.

This can be most clearly seen in the ways the New Cultural History understands the relation of "culture" to "society." While the New Cultural History does not conceive of culture in terms of a totality of intellectual, artistic, political and social activities, it still posits a unity notion of "society." With all its ambiguity, this notion always seems easier to define than "culture." Beyond a set of class relations, the notion of society implies that the foundation of the human world lies upon concrete social groupings which supposedly determine all other – material and non-material – relations. Posited as either a "real" set of grouping and processes open to empirical analysis or a ideational terms made accessible through the positing of a unified methodology, "society" is the assumed ground upon which everything, including "culture," is thought or even thinkable.[59] "Society" in this sense becomes rei-

---

57   See Appleby, et al. on historical time, pp. 205.
58   This is clearly indicated in the ways in which Lynn Hunt points in *The New Cultural History* to *Telling the Truth about History* as providing the theoretical foundations for this type of history. *Telling the Truth* is more a manifesto of a position than an engagement with postmodernism.
59   Even when historians turn away from evidence as the full ground of historical truth and develop a notion of model-building after the manner of the social sciences, there still remains the problem of verification. Verification in this sense functions as a testing of the proposed model. But instead of positing a referential truth, model-building and model-testing relies upon the status of scientific knowledge and its claims to define and delimit reality. As such it falls under the ideology critique of all forms of scientific knowledge.

fied and, despite all contentions to the contrary, still functions as the "reality" upon which all truth claims are made. Although empirical, verification alone neither exhibits nor fails to exhibit the existence of an entity we call "society," "society" is nonetheless posited as an empirical totality, a totality which supposedly can be empirically verified.

Even today when the domain of cultural history is extended and redefined as a relation between elite and popular culture and the study of *mentalités*, "culture" is still abstracted from the totality of human existence and subordinated to "society" and its supposed history.[60] What should still be an open question – the relation of society to culture – and approached critically, is merely assumed as the dependence of the latter upon the former in historical practice. Problems of meaning then are too often simply reduced to questions of the social role or economic status of the "carriers" of this meaning. In other words, "culture" might be open to interpretation but "society" retains its position as an infrastructure, as the substrate of all reality.[61] However narrowly or broadly defined, "culture" still functions as an expression of "society" or of various social groups and relations.[62] However much "culture" in this sense is understood as an arena of the free play of meaning, the assumption that "social" facts convey their own meanings immediately

---

60 Similar problems are encountered in the "reflexive sociology" of Pierre Bourdieu. See Bourdieu, *An Invitation to Reflexive Anthropology* (Cambridge, Eng: Polity Press, 1992) and *The Field of Cultural Production* (Cambridge, Eng: Polity Press, 1993). See also the review of Bourdieu's work, Richard Jenkins, "Language, Culture and Sociology: Pierre Bourdieu in Context" in *History of the Human Sciences*, vol.7, no. 4 (1994), pp. 95-104.

61 Historians and sociologists like Bourdieu are not alone in understanding "culture" as a subset of "society." Even Geertz makes the distinction between social structure as "the ongoing process of interactive behavior" which lies at the basis of a groups' activities and culture as "the framework of beliefs, expressive symbols, and values in terms of which individuals define their feelings, and make their judgments." *The Interpretation of Culture*, pp. 143-169.

62 More than the notion of culture, the concept of society allows the new cultural historians to deploy its field of investigation objectively. However complex society might be, it is still an objects open to the type of investigation presented in the social sciences. With this social foundation for culture, it is understandable that the New Cultural History has either explicitly or implicitly adopted the methods, models and problems developed in the social sciences. As with most other areas of contemporary historical practice, the attempts to define the New Cultural History has remained within traditional social scientific frameworks of objective description and universal causation.

shows to what extent the New Cultural History endorses the theory of the social construction of reality.

Even with this move to a more traditional form of empiricism, the New Cultural History still posits a notion of history which is far less critical of the *Annales* paradigm than it initially appears. Even with its criticism of Braudel's notion of total structure, the New Cultural History continues to rely upon a number of questionable assumptions inherited from earlier generations of the *Annales* School. Inconsistencies therefore arise. While shifting current academic research from the more social scientific questions of the *longue durée* to questions of the third level and then undermining this level as a level, the question remains if the new cultural historians have found an alternative notion of truth to the *Annalistes'* notion of totality and structure. The retention of a general category "society" is linked to structural (though not necessarily structuralist) definition of reality.

The relations between "society" and "culture" raise questions not simply of categories and causal schema but also of the definition of truth and the knowledge based upon this truth. Even when the new cultural historians take an anti-explanatory approach and develop an interpretive stance in terms of symbolic codes, anthropological models and the like, the notion of

> The universality of method, for instance, demands the constitution of its objects within a unified field. Not only is "culture" subordinated to "society" as the "really real" but also "society" is knowable through science. "Society" is posited not only as a substance within which historical events and conflicts occur but as infrastructural concept, which as the basic category of human life remains constant through time. This quest for a universal method flattens all it studies into an object for research. As a result, there is also posited a false "equality" among all areas and problems the same for same method can be applied. Although defined as "object," "society" is constituted by method. Its supposed unity is actually only the unity imposed by a common method, a unity construed by science that grounds the truth claims of this research. Truth then becomes redefined in terms of verification of statements and correctness of method.
>
> The abstraction "society" allows culture to be defined as an object of study and thus open to scientific explanation. It also allows the deployment of a causal schema, fulfilling the methodological demand for explanation. This demand necessitates a hierarchal structuring of evidence. Not only is "society" causal it is also pan-causal, the cause of everything. Like the New Social History, the New Cultural History thereby endlessly repeats the idea that reality is "society," ceaselessly reiterates that society or any of its various components cause everything. Not questioning its grounds, historical research falls into dogmatism by endlessly recycling the findings of research within the same categories of knowledge and ultimately depending upon an operational definition of truth.

"society" however diversified still forms a temporal and spatial unity of the world and history founded upon a questionable epistemology. As with all current forms of historical discourse, the essential problem faced by the New Cultural History lies in its adherence to a representational theory of truth. The problem of representations – their truth and meaning – lies at the heart of the entire historical enterprise. Lynn Hunt rightly contends that "representation [is] a problem which historians can no longer avoid;" but she does not work out either the ways in which this contention undermines historical studies, including the studies of the new cultural historians, or what an alternatives to a representational theory of truth might be.[63]

This problem of representation is complex and works on a number of levels. In its most obvious form, representation functions as a type of truth claim. In this, the "new cultural historians" simply conform to the theories of reference and operational definitions of truth which dominate more traditional forms of academic history. In practice this involves the factual verification of its various statements. The claim to be "truthful to the past" sets into operation a set of procedures, which even when it takes on social scientific models and theories merely aims at finding archival referents in order to verify its claims. Behind such moves, there is the fundamental theoretical gesture characteristic of all appeals to representation, even when unacknowledged, to define reality in terms of "objectivity" – and "objectivity" in the strict sense of the representation of an object by a subject. In the light of contemporary critiques of representations, this position is no longer defensible. Without either a critique of representation or a new approach to the truth of culture, they therefore conform to a notion of empirical knowledge or a combination of empiricism within a set of structuralist assumptions which are all too uncritically accepted in historical practice.[64] With its notion of "society," the New Cultural History then has not so much done away with the notion of totality as displace it from a "spiritual" or "cultural" definition to a "social" one. It represents a shift away from what was more often an intention than an actualization to write a total history and a displacement of what was a form of social history to the third level of culture. But this shift was accomplished without a fundamental displacement or even examina-

---

63   Hunt, *New Cultural History*, p. 16.
64   For the ways in which historians who are even aware of the poststructuralist critique of representation still speak of representation, see Appleby et. al. pp., 214-215.

tion of the three-tiered model of history itself. Braudel's attempt to ground historical knowledge in a structuralist synthesis of all the social sciences based on the *longue durée* is perhaps the most extreme example of this definition of science and reveals its fundamentally epistemological and ultimately idealist presuppositions; but it is one shared by the new cultural historians.[65] Illegitimately, "society" provides a way to stabilize and thus limit the openness and ambiguity in the notion of "culture." Since neither "society" nor "culture" is a "fact" or a natural phenomenon, it is a construction and as such has its own affiliations to present power relations and prescriptive totalizing claims about the present.[66] In this way, the New Cultural History is threatened with the loss of the very insights it has achieved in the understanding of "culture."

It is understandable, then, that without a move to a form of reflexivity, of

---

65   In defining its identity in terms of its supposed break from the more structuralist tendencies of earlier generations of the *Annales* tradition, the New Cultural History also misperceives its own history. What is of particular interest in this shift to cultural history is that, unlike so many other "advances" within historical or any other academic practice, this move to a new paradigm has not been undertaken by those who oppose the reigning paradigm. This transformation of social into cultural history has been made by the *Annales* historians themselves. This lineage to the *Annales* School and its uncritical adoption of Braudel's three-tiered definition of history explains why the New Cultural History still remains within the general definition of historical knowledge assumed by the founding generations of this school.

The New Cultural History also accepts this account of its own history uncritically. It does not questioning the epistemological foundations of historical knowledge itself. The new cultural historians envision their enterprise in terms of its "cutting-edge" status. And this form of self-understanding speaks of an implied progressive history of knowledge. This hidden interpretive schema further questions their notions of history, culture and cultural history. As such, it not only falls under the criticism of poststructuralism but also succumbs to ideology by claiming that reality is limited to contemporary, scientific definitions of knowledge and defined in terms of a progress of knowledge. This definition of knowledge covers over the ways in which knowledge is always a construct of particular social, political, historical factors. By not reflecting either upon the scientificality of its own assumptions or upon the ways in which this scientificality shapes their view of history, the New Cultural History denies the historicity of its own investigations.

66   Appleby, Hunt and Jacob are at least aware of some of the problems raised by postmodernism. But they are not capable of responding to them except in the form of a pledge to continue to undertake traditional forms of research in the face of them. See, for instance, *Telling the Truth*, pp. 202, 206.

a critique of its own categories, schema of explanation, and modes of truth, the new cultural historians – with all the supposed methodological sophistication of these approaches and the liveliness of the debates they have engendered among historians – have offered little to the current intellectual discussions which have so galvanized the human sciences.[67] The new cultural historians are not even aware of (let alone in control of) the intellectual currents that are transforming their own field. As Joan Scott – herself a historian – makes clear in relation to the history of gender, historians are generally unaware of (or, if aware then unconcerned with) such fundamental currents.[68] More pointedly, without thinking through the constitution of experience as an interplay between meaning and social structure in the past, the connection of past meaning to present truth, and the specific modality of historical time, the New Cultural History only conforms to the uncritical operational definitions of the dominant discourse of history. In the face of these debates, the New Cultural History still staunchly maintains a belief in "society" as a "basic stratum," which functions as an "essence" of reality and is "objectively" known through conventional forms of knowl-

---

67   The New Cultural History is particularly vulnerable to questions of its own relation to power. Even an overview of the notion of "objectivity" as it functions as the "truth" of historical knowledge – as argued by both Peter Novick and Sande Cohen – indicates that in addition to providing a merely operational definition of truth for this academic discipline it functions primarily in terms of restricting more thorough-going forms of criticism. In itself, historical knowledge constitutes a particular relation to power. Historical knowledge, in other words, functions ideologically. In large measure unbeknownst to its practitioners, it legitimates present social and political power relations. Michael Geyer and Konrad Jarausch among others have pointed out how current historical discourse has been constituted in and through the consensus politics of the cold war years. In order to provide a specific ideological justification for these relations, the post-war discourse of history sets the boundaries – in the invidious ways in which power functions – of both the range of possible answers and more devastatingly, the scope of possible questions deemed significant even to be asked.

See Michael Geyer and Konrad H. Jarausch, "The Future of the German Past: Transatlantic Reflections for the 1990s" in *Central European History*, vol. 22, no. 3/4 (1989), pp. 237-241. See also Kerwin Lee Klein, "In Search of Narrative Mastery: Postmodernism and the Peoples without History" in *History and Theory* vol. 34, no. 4 (1995), pp. 275-298.

68   Joan Scott, *Gender and the Politics of History* (New York, 1988), p. 41. Clifford Geertz makes a similar point in discussing the "blurring of genres," "Blurred Genres: The Refiguration of Social Thought," *Local Knowledge*, pp. 19-35.

edge. More significantly, it has not raised questions either of why we want a knowledge of the past or why we want such a knowledge in terms of a category of "society."

III.

The New Cultural History's failure to question its own "scientific" assumptions return us to the need for further reflection upon the truth of culture. Although truth as representation or even truth as structure has been recognized as inappropriate for cultural history, these definitions of truth have so thoroughly defined historical studies for over a century that it is difficult for historians to think of truth in any other terms. The truth upon which current historical discourse is founded occludes other approaches to questions of truth and meaning – the question of the meaning of the relation between the past and the present, for instance, or even of the truth of historical existence itself. This reflection however should not entail one more return to the modernist position of examining the epistemological foundations of historical knowledge as is most usually done.[67] With their universalist and ahistorical orientations, such traditional theoretical moves lead away from rather than toward the problem of culture and cultural meaning.

One possible alternative approach is to think through the notion of cultural history differently. The problems of the reality which is supposedly designated by "culture" and the ways in which we can speak of this reality in its truth have been understood in other ways by other groups of cultural historians. The concern with the relationship of history and culture accounts in part for the continuing and indeed increasing interest in the thought of Michel Foucault. Foucault explicitly deals with the questions of how meanings functions in actual situations, with how discourses (neither *langue* nor *parole* but *meaning*) interplays with power (and not just in a political or institutional sense), and with the historical formations of distinct discursive regimes. With his description of the "carceral" or his later notion of the "sexual society," he has shown how a particular cultural formation – a specific interplay of discourse and power – has arisen in, and defines, the modern West in its underlying experience of self and world.[68] In his later thought, Foucault seems to ascribe to neither a social nor a discursive constructionist theory of reality.

In his description of modern culture as a "carceral," for instance, Foucault argues that the inner resonances among various micro-powers form an un-

---

67   Foucault, *The History of Sexuality II*.

derstandable whole, a totality of a particular kind. But Foucualt's notion of totality remains implicit. It is too sketchy to function as a basis of cultural historical interpretation in general. His later and more comprehensive understanding of modernity as a "sexual society" in which not just the discourses of the human sciences or their relations to institutional practices in some sense coincide historically. More intriguingly, Foucault's thinking as it progresses from the conclusion of the first volume of *The History of Sexuality* to the remaining two volumes of this study indicates how he was able to include the very "constitution of the self" – a type of freedom within the very "depths" of our self-definition – with an inclusive notion of discursive and institutional practices. Here, at the end of his career, Foucault was able to incorporate into an integral whole both a more traditional theory of political power and Marxist notion of class, which in his earlier works he had struggled so diligently to displace. In spite of the fact that Foucault's name is often invoked to legitimate the empowerment of various groups, cultures and subcultures, Foucault himself strives for a type of interpretation of modernity based upon a complex, multidimensional, historically staggered, yet nonetheless integrated whole.

The evolution of Foucault's thinking along these lines is instructive. Instead of simply describing everything in terms of power or in indorsing various new forms of empowerment, Foucault raises the problem of meaning and the interpretation of meaning as a mode of truth. He no longer defines truth in terms of scientificality or even epistemic structures and not even as a relation of knowledge to power. In his last works, Foucault understands truth – "the games of truth" of his later writings – in terms of the historical

---

68   Even Foucault's notion of historical formations seems to confront a major stumbling block. Foucault alerts us to the fact that such concepts as "totality" need to be critically examined and as general theory rejected. What centrally concerns him – as it does Derrida and Lyotard – in the notion of totality is that form of "theory" which claims to explain everything through the positing of such an abstraction. Marxism and Freudianism are the chief targets of this line of attack. And as Foucault is well aware, "history" can be so deployed as to limit questions and buttress established beliefs and institutions. But it can also function genealogically, thereby providing the basis for a criticism of such beliefs and institutions. By acknowledging the inseparable relation between discourse and power as Foucault formulates it underscores the fact that all discourses have political implications. Foucault emphasizes the need for a constant critique of the power/knowledge dyad. See Foucault, *Power/Knowledge*, pp. 80-81.

"constitution of experience." "Beneath" the problem of the relation between power and discourse, Foucault posits another level, one of experience. In the *History of Sexuality* the search for an alternative to the modern form of sexuality leads Foucault to questions of the formation of the modern, sexual self and the ways in which institutional forms and bodies of knowledge are constituted upon it. Here, invoking Heideggerian language, he even speaks of a "historical ontology." Foucault understands not just series of specific types of selves but of an ontology of experience that is, however paradoxically, historically.[69] In this way, he raises questions of how truth is disclosed in the modern world in the first place. In this way he suggests that the notion of interpretive totality does not so easily fall prey to the questions of power relations or of social domination.

The movement of Foucault's later thought, in other words, points to an alternative way to understand the relation between totality and power. The more inclusive interpretation of "culture" opens even more creative and inclusive ways to comprehend the truth of culture as both the defining experience of our existence as individuals and structuring modalities of the larger and sustaining discourses, apparatuses, and relations of power which sustain this experience. Itself a construct, "culture" as such carries with it a recognition of its own affiliations to present power relations and prescriptive totalizing claims about the past. Without, however, developing such a notion further and with working through this notion of totality, this suggestive move on Foucault's part has generally been overlooked or relegated to merely an insightful aside. As a result, however provocative for further thought as his approach is, without thematizing these problems and with only a limited reflection upon the notion of "culture," Foucault's thinking along these lines itself remains confused and inconclusive.

However one interprets Foucault's later thought, it is in need of further reflection. Another form of cultural history, one which lies outside of the *Annales* tradition, is helpful here. Although recently renewed, the question of "culture," of course, has been, in one way or another, a major problem for the West for some time. Since the word was coined in the late eighteenth centu-

---

69   Foucault also speaks of the need to address the issue of "historical ontology" in "What is Enlightenment" and "On the Genealogy of Ethics: An Overview of Work in Progress" both reproduced in Paul Rabinow ed., *The Foucault Reader* (New York: Pantheon Books, 1984), pp. 45, 351. See also the interview in James Bernauer and David Rasmussen, *The Final Foucault* (Cambridge, MA: MIT Press, 1991), pp. 1-20.

ry, "culture" has replaced notions of Christendom and at least challenged understanding "the human" in terms of an overly rational contract theory of polity or an over abstract concept of society. This older form of cultural history – originating with Herder and fully realized in the works of Burckhardt and Huizinga – understands culture as some type of relative totality.[70] Relative and historically changing, this totality rather than "society" or "discourse" sets into play social relations and forms of meaning. Both Jakob Burckhardt's *The Civilization of the Renaissance in Italy* and Johan Huizinga's *The Autumn of the Middle Ages* project their cultural worlds as relative totalities and semiporous horizons.[71] These more traditional modes of cultural history pick up, in a sense, where Foucault leaves off.

Even before the rise of poststructuralist thought, there was a critique of culture as a totality. In 1960 Ernst Gombrich launched a major attack against this traditional concept of cultural history as based upon an illegitimate positing of holism. In his provocative *In Search of Cultural History*, he argues that culture history makes the illegitimate claim that to understand any single aspect of a culture necessitates comprehending it in relation to the ways in which it functions within a cultural whole. Defined in terms either of a national culture or of a cultural epoch, this type of history rests upon the dubious claim that the economy and society, morality and political activity, intellectual life and artistic production of a given people at a given time are in some way so interrelated that in order to understand any one of them entails comprehending the whole.[72] Faced with this seemingly impossible task of understanding such a whole, the cultural historian, according to Gom-

---

70   For a general discussion of the term culture and of cultural history see Lucien Febvre, *A New Kind of History*, trans. K. Folca (New York: Harper and Row, 1973); and Johan Huizinga, *Men and Ideas: History, the Middle Ages, the Renaissance*, trans. James S. Holmes and Hans van Marle (New York: Harper and Row, 1959). For a more detailed discussion of Burckhardt's position in relation to the history of cultural history, see Karl J. Weintraub, *Visions of Culture* (Chicago: University of Chicago Press, 1966); Wolfgang Hardtwig, *Geschichtsschribung zwischen Alteuropa und Moderner Welt: Jacob Burckhardt in seiner Zeit* (Göttingen: Vandenhoeck und Ruprecht, 1974); Felix Gilbert, *History: Politics or Culture?: Reflections on Ranke and Burckhardt* (Princeton, NJ: Princeton University Press, 1990).

71   In Karl Weintraub's formulation, the task of the cultural historian is to see "a culture not as a mere aggregate of traits but as forming an intricately interrelated pattern." Karl Weintraub, *Visions of Culture: Voltaire, Guizot, Burckhardt, Lamprecht, Huizinga, Ortega y Gasset* (Chicago, 1966), p. 2.

72   Goody is also critical of all such totalizing notions of culture, pp. 18-19.

brich, searches for a unifying point in a common *Weltanschauung*, a shared set of values, or a dominant psychological type.[73] Ultimately, Gombrich contends that this type of cultural history is determinist and progressive, based upon the highly dubious assumption of the spiritual and historical unity of experience.[74]

But such a reading of *The Civilization of the Renaissance in Italy* results in a gross misinterpretation, more appropriate to Hegelian (and in a "restricted economy") than Burckhardtian approaches to history. In this text as well as in *The World Historical Observations*, Burckhardt does not posit the notion that all cultures form harmoniously integrated wholes or could only be understood in such terms. In fact, he argues that only very few actually do. Burckhardt's understanding of "culture" both exhibits the ambiguity inherent in the term and attempts to limit the range of this ambiguity. For him, "culture" is more complex than a simple notion of a harmonious integration of parts into a whole leads one to believe. For Burckhardt culture works on a number of levels at the same time.

On a basic level, Burckhardt perceives "culture" in the sense of a *Kulturepoche*, as a temporally bounded field of forces, as the actualization of certain "potentials" (*Potenzen*). Initially, Burckhardt posits this notion of a cultural period in order that the relative significance of various historical forces could be identified and evaluated. The totality of a culture is what allows power to appear in the first place as the forces within a certain specific domain. There is thus no universal discourse of power or a science of social processes. This assumption of a totality need not be posited as an integrated unity either of symbols or of symbols and actions, as some commentators have attributed to them. Culture might be a site of conflict – political, social, religious contentions over meaning, symbols and power – as well as a site of integration and unity. Some type of whole, he contends, needs to be posited by the cultural historian in order that various characteristics of a period could be recognized and the interplay among them understood. As an inter-

---

73 Since totality is impossible to perceive or conceive in all its unity and diversity, cultural historians intellectually grasp a culture or "explain" its developments only by dividing up a culture into understandable components, isolating certain aspects of the cultural whole as "characteristic" of the whole, and selecting certain "mechanism" which supposedly organize and direct the whole. This is the trope of metonymy. The claims of national character as well as of Marxist "infrastructure" are often placed upon a scientific basis.

74 E.H. Gombrich, *In Search of Cultural History* (Oxford: Clarendon Press, 1969).

pretive device, the *Kulturepoche* therefore provides a framework for comprehending the forces which resulted in either the unity or the disunity of an
age.

The concept of a *Kulturepoche* also allows Burckhardt to define a type of
necessity not open to the social sciences. This is not a necessity in the way
that the metaphysical tradition has taught us to think of necessity as a universal determinant of action and thought. Rather, it is a specifically modern
sense of a historical necessity. Unlike Foucault who understands the historical field as the realm of contingency, Burckhardt sees it as defining a specific
type of necessity in the modern period. Against the defining forces of the
age, Burckhardt attempts to comprehend human freedom in both its individual and collective senses. It is not simply the points of resistance against
the power/discourse dyad in poststructuralist thought. Freedom for Burckhardt arises as the possibility of responding to the necessity of historical circumstances. It therefore opens the domain of history as an ethical domain.
But again not in terms of a universal set of abstract ethical categories. Ethics
too is historical, a response to a given historical situation. As the free response to these forces, Burckhardt understands "culture" in another sense.
Against the necessities of the *Kulturepoche*, peoples have the possibility of
creating their own forms of life, of freely forming their culture.

Burckhardt speaks of the "culture" of the Renaissance, for instance, in the
sense of *Bildung*. One reason he turned to the study of the Italian Renaissance was that from the various general "forces" which comprised the fourteenth and fifteenth century – the disparate political, social, moral and religious then prevalent – the Italians were able to fashion an integrated and
harmonious cultural whole. The *Kulturepoche*, then, is less a field of positivities which can be scientifically analyzed and definitive of historical research
than a historically determined set of conditions of possibility. These possibilities can be symbolized, given meaning, actively rejected or creatively
shaped through the free response of "cultures" in the narrower sense.[75]

---

75 What, according to Burckhardt, was the basis of such the unity of the culture (*Bildung*) of the Italian Renaissance? It was less, he argued, the result of a dominant
idea, a common *Weltanschauung*, or even a single personality type than it was the
result a conscious drive to bring together a new sense of reality through a
metaphor of the world as microcosm of the divine macrocosm. This metaphor
with all the ambiguities, slippages and polysemy inherent in metaphors provides a
unity to the various responses to the various, competing aspects of existence. Relations between religion and literary forms for example, or in a more specific in-

The problem with cultural history then lies not so much with the concept of totality itself as with how this notion is understood. There is an obvious difference between positing a cultural totality either as the unity of *Bildung* or as a determinist unity of *Kultur* and positing *Kultur* as the site of investigation of the real. Even when no such device is consciously employed, it seems questions of cultural meaning, of degrees of social prevalence, as well as of historical significance all depend upon some such notion of the real as a common background, as a background which allows more obvious "objects" and "processes" to emerge. It moves to bring to language the phenomenon of culture itself. In this sense, "culture" is the site of investigation not of pre-established definitions, concepts and processes. It is in Foucault's language, the site of problematization, of what we moderns discern as problems that have to be addressed in our comprehension of the real. In this way "culture" is not subordinated to "society." It is rather the site of a pre-linguistic or partially spoken experience of the real as we experience it.

And this is true of earlier notions of cultural history as of several more recent ones. As the medieval cultural historian Aaron Gurevich has recently shown, the supposedly sharp divisions that a number of historians of the Middle Ages have seen between popular and elite cultures has often been taken too far. For Gurevich they have overlooked the basic structures that made for a common medieval "world." For Gurevich the fundamental and historically specific definitions of space and time allowed this world to emerge in the first place. Such "worlds" constitute relative totalities unto themselves.[76] Or, to draw another example of how such relative totalities functions within a more explicitly "Marxist" formulation, Lucien Goldmann explores how the forms of economic activity in seventeenth-century France shaped the system of religious belief and was the way in which dramatic literature came to be defined. Understanding the "reality" of the past in our own categories of economic trends or social classes is beside the point or at least insufficient for an understanding the problem of past meaning. The relation between the ways a group of people understand economic activity opens up an understanding of their relation to politics and the arts – and not

---

stance, the interconnection between the social position of women and power politics exhibit a drive to unite all aspects of existence. The resulting culture – now understood as *Bildung* – was consciously developed as a whole and handed down to the West as a model of possible unity of modern culture.

76   Aaron Gurevich, *Categories of Medieval Culture*, trans. G.L. Campbell, (London: Routledge, 1985).

just substantially but formally and functionally.[77] Furthermore, while these interrelations might be limited to specific religious, social, or other groupings, they in no way undermine the existence of a common culture. Even when cultures are conceived in terms of contested symbolic codes and alternate forms of self-representation, the idea of division and contest is made only against some notion of a common background.

This notion of culture as a background entails a certain approach to the "method" of cultural history. Huizinga makes this "method" explicit. In "The Task of Cultural History," he argues that cultural history raises problems not of definition, theory, or epistemology. The question of "culture" calls for interpretation and not merely scientific verification. Cultural history is constructed upon the interconnected ideas of "context" and "event," which in themselves preclude all "objective" designations. There is in historical studies, Huizinga contends, simply no identifiable, isolatable objects as there are for instance in the physical and biological sciences. The cultural historian confronts only multiple and potentially limitless contexts and "turnings" of contexts which we call "events" on the cultural level. There is therefore no specific class of entities called either "cultural objects" or simply "past facts" – as there are no objects as "culture" or "the past" – which either can or cannot be captured conceptually.[78] Culture and events are always a set of relations, changing relations, which, nonetheless, have, if not a determining, at least a conditioning effect. The openness, contextual nature and eventful processes that comprises cultural history entails the understanding that culture can never be known with the certainty and conceptual transparency which the various social sciences seem to hold out. Culture can only be interpreted and interpreted not as with what passes as historical interpretation, i.e., variations upon causal explanations but as a process of comprehending the relations of parts and wholes. It often involves an alternate understanding of "fact" and "evidence" and the use of such evidence than is generally supposed. For cultural historians, historical facts are neither immediately present nor expressions of some deep structure. They are only possible pieces of evidence within possible interpretive schemes, possible meaningful alignments of "surface" phenomena.

---

77 Lucien Goldmann, *The Hidden God: A Study of Tragic Vision in the "Pensees" of Pascal and the Tragedies of Racine* trans. Philip Thody (London, 1976).
78 Johan Huizinga, "The Task of Cultural History" in *Men and Ideas: Essays on History, the Middle Ages, and Renaissance,* trans. James S. Holmes and Hans van Marle, (New York, 1959), pp. 17-76.

Cultural-historical modes of knowing must therefore develop an understanding of the process of evaluating various factors which comprise a culture and cultivates the arts of interpretation of their meanings.[79] This interpretive basis of cultural history entails certain assumptions. For such interpretive methods to functions, questions of meaning necessitate the explicit positing of a framework. Cultural interpretation demands such a framing device. The positing of such totality defines the meaning of parts only within the whole of a culture. Only within such a framing devise can the various "factors" or "forces" be recognized and evaluated. Only in some type of relation of parts to whole can significance and relative weight be comprehended.[80] This device constitutes more a hermeneutic principle than a scientific description of reality.[81] It does not depend upon a representational definition of the real since the real lies not simply in the factual verification of the sum total of its multiple "truthful" statements. By bringing to light what was partially or fully unknown in the past – namely a culture as some type of response to defining forces of the *Kulturepoche* – a cultural history reveals its specific truth. As such, cultural history is a form of interpretation, its truth an interpretive truth, which as Nietzsche makes explicit, might be the way we have truth in and of "modernity."

This openness to interpretations offered in these approaches to cultural history should be understood as a decided advantage over a notion of sociological explanation. Unlike the categories of society, race, or gender which tend all too quickly to be defined conceptually, located on the level of nature or neces-

---

79   Hunt dismisses interpreters who do not have a universalizable method. She condemns as idiosyncratic such powerful cultural visions as that of Geertz and Foucault. Hunt, "History Beyond Social Theory, " p. 99; and *The New Cultural History*, p. 8.
        Burckhardt, however, stresses the fact that all cultural history is a specific type of interpretation. In the Introduction of *The Civilization of the Renaissance in Italy*, he contends that each attempt to write the history of a culture is precisely that, only an attempt, an interpretation by a individual historian and from a single point of view. Cultural histories are only "essays" in interpretation.
80   In Karl Weintraub's formulation, the task of the cultural historian is to see "a culture not as a mere aggregate of traits but as forming an intricately interrelated pattern." Karl Weintraub, *Visions of Culture: Voltaire, Guizot, Burckhardt, Lamprecht, Huizinga, Ortega y Gasset* (Chicago, 1966), p. 2.
81   Norbert Elias developed his own theory of culture which itself has its relation to Neo-Kantian philosophy. See Benjo Maso, "Elias and the Neo-Kantians: Intellectual Backgrounds of the *Civilizing Process*" in *Theory, Culture, and Society*, vol. 12, no. 3 (1995), pp. 43-80 and the various responses to this article contained in the same issue.

sity, and "explained" scientifically, "culture" as such a relative totality never allows itself to be conceptually grasped and per definition closed. It would be wrong to assume, in other words, that "culture" is an empty category which merely needs to be filled in by research. "Culture" avoids the pitfalls of positing "society" as a foundational category since it is neither a basic "reality" nor causal of this and all other "levels" of this "reality." Like race and gender, "society" is itself a social construct and thus more mediated and less direct than the literary and other forms of evidence from past modes of consciousness which social historians in particular have dismissed as obscuring a direct conceptual grasp of the past. The claims to "objectivity," in this sense, obscures or even blocks access to the fluidity of past relations, as they limit the full deployment of the signifying system which circulates within a culture. And it undermines all understanding of these past meanings to present truth.[82]

Such a whole also function reflexively. *Kulturgeschichte* for Burckhardt does not eliminate causal explanation as it involves a complex understanding of causal relations within a cultural whole. Beyond this however, it subordinates this intention to another – the intention to uncover the larger significance of the historical formation and of its relation to us and our definitions of ourselves. Only with such a frame can questions of the meaning of past culture as a whole be understood in its meaning to the present frame of reference. Extracted from such totalities, the analyses of social or economic processes only reaffirm their reified categories, only generate vague and abstracted meaning of the past and reaffirm uncritical universal notions of truth and meaning of the present. As a result this stance to "reality," interpretive cultural history makes a more radical break from all scientific and implied scientific definitions of knowledge and truth. While not eliminating explanatory discourse or setting itself in a sterile opposition to it, interpretive cultural history subordinates it to the demands of interpretation. Burckhardt, in other words, does not just understand *Kulturgeschichte* in Paul Ricoeur's sense of a 'dialectic' between causal explanation and the meaning of individual historical agents, between *erklären* and *verstehen*.[83] The positing

---

82   The theory of interpretation as it has been developed within philosophic hermeneutics might provide a basis for the use of interpretation as the basis of cultural history. The position developed by Paul Ricoeur in *Time and Narrative* (3 volumes, [Chicago: University of Chicago Press, 1985-88]), if historicized I believe, could be extended to cultural hermeneutics.

83   Paul Ricoeur, "The Model of the Text: Meaningful Action Considered as a Text" in *From Text to Action: Essays in Hermeneutics, II* (Evanston, ILL: Northwestern University Press, 1991), pp. 144-167.

of a "cultural totality" is a tool in the ascertaining of this notion of meaning as well.[84]

This notion of *Kulturgeschichte* provides a means not just of conceiving of the past through a notion of totality but of understanding our own participation within a cultural horizon. Here again it is not a question of positing a simple fit among all aspects of our culture or of identifying a unifying principle, world view, or personality type. Rather, it is a way of opening a field as a horizon of identifying and evaluating various "forces" which comprise the field. It does not establish a cultural or historical identity as define a site for the questioning of all such claims to identity. In this way, a horizon provides not the basis of experience as the origin of an ontology but of the conditions of possibility of a historically specific constituted experience.

Cultures and the histories of cultures demand interpretation and the exploration of possible "realities" through the cultivation of the art of interpretation of various possible realities. "Culture," in this sense, functions as a transcendental concept, but unlike "society" it constantly reasserts itself as a construction. Precisely because it claims some type of totality which can never be conceptually grasped, the notion of culture constantly raises the question of totality and closure without however ever being able to reach a final conclusion. "Culture" is not just the collection of, or the "container" surrounding, all possible meanings. Rather, it appears to be the condition of the possibility that this world have meaning or is a world at all. In this sense culture functions merely as a heuristic device, or a Kantian regulative idea allowing an investigator with a methodological tool for interpretation.

The openness to interpretation is also an openness to the very definition of "culture." The lack of the precision of theory opens a possible site for the play of various interpretations. The very incompleteness of "culture" and its open-ended definitions permits the category to serve as a permanently available site of contested meanings. In this sense, interpretation functions both as a foundation of historical knowledge and a limit to its comprehension of "reality." It itself is a means of phenomenologizing its "object," of bringing "culture" – as a horizon or a condition of possibly – to light.[85]

---

84   Dominick LaCapra reconceives of cultural identity in terms of a modified psychoanalytic notion of transference. Dominick LaCapra, *History and Criticism* (Ithaca, N.Y.: Cornell University Press, 1985), pp. 71-94.

85   I do not mean this in the sense of Husserlian phenomenology or Heidegger's existential phenomenology. Rather, I mean simply as a bringing into view what is not obvious or can be made an object of a science such as a cultural whole or a world.

IV.

Beyond regulative devices, is there a reality to which "culture" responds? I would like to approach this difficult question indirectly and through a detour. By addressing the problem of how "culture" is comprehended textually, by inquiring after the textual status of cultural history in particular, I think we can approach this difficult question of the reality that is a culture. Reconceiving of cultural history along these lines also raises questions of the ways in which culture can be known and the ways in which its truth can be brought to language.

The interpretive form of cultural history most directly raises the problem of truth through the question of the construction of texts.[86] Today, "culture" and "cultural history" are less in need of theoretical definitions and universal methodologies than an awareness of the ways in which, beyond representation, they remain sites of textual production. Without falling back into a representational theory of truth then, the older forms of cultural history – unlike their current counterparts – allows us to rethink the relations of meaning and text, of textuality and world, of language and truth. The model of the text is part of a larger linguistic turn of contemporary thought. This form of cultural history, for instance, speaks to the current discussions of a fundamental paradigm shift within the human sciences. As Joan Scott has contended, the humanities and social sciences are experiencing "a moment of great epistemological turmoil that takes the form...of a shift from scientific to literary paradigms."[87] This shift and the modes of truth it brings forth are at present not very clearly articulated. The traditional and often uncritically accepted distinction between scientific modes of truth and literary genres are not as easy to prove as the New Cultural History assumes. The mere intention to find the facts or to verify a social or economic process is neither a guarantee to tell the truth or a renunciation of literary presentation. In this way, cultural history can be brought to bear upon current discussions of truth.[88]

Various discourses of poststructuralism have widened the gap between textual meaning and extra-textual truth. By concentrating attention upon

---

86   See Appleby et. al. pp. 224-5.

87   Joan Scott, *Gender and the Politics of History* (New York: 1988), p. 41.

88   As Chartier suggests (and only suggests) cultural history needs to work out the relation between symbolic codes and social action, between text and context. Chartier, "Texts, Symbols, and Frenchness," p. 690. Chartier expands upon this argument in *Forms and Meanings: Texts, Performances, and Audiences from Codex to Computer* (Philadelphia: University of Pennsylvanian Press, 1995).

texts and the textual construction of meaning, poststructuralism directs us to an investigation of the relationship between fiction and non-fiction.[89] Deconstruction in particular demonstrates how all such oppositions are basic to the ways in which we comprehend "reality," determine "truth" and decide among possible meanings are founded upon self-contradictory assumptions and an uncritical reading of syntax upon what is considered to be reality. Derrida denies that we are ever capable of defining truth through reference or even of stabilizing meaning through interpretation and instead insists upon the textual nature of all "reality." This "textuality" is open to many possible reading to the ever-recurring dissemination of its meanings. All attempts to contain and limit this infinite play is the result either of inadequate notions of the text or of the play of uncritical conventions of text or context.[90]

Once the limitations of deconstruction's own attempts to criticize all forms of meaning is challenged, however, and its own foundations in theory (with its own assumptions about language) and a counter-metaphysics (as in the ontology of *différance*) demonstrated, the force of its criticism becomes restricted to the conventional philosophic gesture of attempting to make language incontrovertibly ground itself from within itself. Yet the very limitations of this form of critique open new possibilities for understanding the relation of meaning and text. By undermining the distinctions between texts and contexts, deconstruction has exhibited the ways in which – through a general theory of "textuality" – texts can be read as worlds and worlds as texts. Against the intentions of deconstruction, this move not so much undermines historical interpretation as give it a new provenance.

Avoiding the difficulties of both conventional political and social history perpetuated by new cultural history on the one hand and the hypercritical stance and dead end positions of deconstruction on the other, cultural histo-

---

89   The use of a literary model should not be thought of in terms of literary history or the ways in which "literature" can be employed as historical evidence. Such moves misconceive of the level of the problem upon which language and text operate in relation to the construction of experience. There are also limited notions of "literary theory" and history, see for instance Peter Jelavich, "Contemporary Literary Theory: From Deconstruction Back to History" in *Central European History*, vol. 22, no. 3/4 (1989), pp. 360-380.

90   Although he shows the limits of all discourses to capture reality, Foucault still believes that he in some way can still speak of reality in his own texts. He never, it seems to me, legitimates his own claims to truth.

ry as I conceive of it offers another way to comprehending historical phenomena and understanding their meaning. Its central task of cultural history is more open, initially less certain of the terms and relations through which it can be comprehended. The central task of cultural history is to show, rather than explain, a past or present culture in the first place, to bring it before the eyes.[91]

Let me conclude by pointing to two specific examples of this type of cultural historical text. In their cultural histories, Jacob Burckhardt and Johan Huizinga do not "represent" these past cultures by describing various social, economic, and intellectual currents "objectively." They investigate the problem of defining a culture, not by defining it abstractly through the social scientific discourse of modern historical writing or falling back upon any variation upon an uncritical notion of reference. The "Renaissance," "the later Middle Ages," or any other *Kulturepoche*, in other words, is not an object – an entity standing over against a knowing subject. Their chronological definition, chief characteristics, and broad outlines are not initially known by the historian. They have to be investigated, known from their own shape and interrelation of forms before their structures of meaning can be known. To see this whole and to evaluate components of it within the whole involves "perceiving" this a culture as a whole.[92]

---

91 These questions of textual intention are therefore related to others. Although not accomodatable to a notion of representation, Burckhardt's and Huizinga's form of cultural history are clearly and even powerfully related to the ways in which they "envision" a cultural totality. And for much of the twentieth century, this fact has been a stumbling block to the appreciation of their works. Poststructuralism in particular has successfully undermined the representational theory of truth and their critique has often been taken as an attack upon all visual forms of knowledge.

See the recent *Modernity and the Hegemony of Vision* ed. David Michael Levin, (Berkeley, 1993). Instead of understanding representations to be theoretically and historically limited to the post-cartesian concept of the object, this critique too readily, I contend, extends the notion of objective representation to all uses of images. In this way, poststructuralism limits itself. It assumes the same set of assumptions as those they criticize. Only by agreeing that truth is opened through the way in which both modern science and philosophy define objectivity and representation, is the charge that truth is unavailable to us sustainable. Question of the tension between image and text, the visual and the linguistic, should not be avoided or repressed by highlighted and thought through.

92 And recently, a group of cultural historians have raised the question "whether disinterest in older varieties of cultural history is not in part occasioned by that tendency to disparage the visual" in general. John Czaplicka, et. al. "Introduction," p. 12.

The phenomenon of an entire culture does not immediately present itself; it is not something directly given. As a non-referential "object" or as a background, as Burckhardt does, this world is not initially visible. It has to be brought before the eye. In this sense, cultural history brings what is otherwise an unseen or only partially visible phenomenon to view. Culture is thus brought forth as a horizon of past meaning and, equally significant, as a boundary for historical research. The current critique of the visual, however, confuses the claims of empiricism and the epistemological legitimization of the natural sciences with a broader understanding of perception and the ways in which perception is related to language.[93] The form of presentation of cultural history is, therefore, integrally related to the process of interpreting the phenomenon. In fact visual thinking allows specific relations to emerge that a more linguistically based notion of knowledge often misconstrue or miss entirely.[94]

---

93   And further, it can be questioned if it is ever possible to have a sense of culture that is not at base visual? Whether it is a vision of some type of totality or of a symbolic image, activity, or feeling that captures something of this whole, vision is still important both for "comprehending" and conveying a notion of culture. As the very definition of metaphor and therefore of language itself implies, the relation between language and image is not so easily separated.

     For a general discussion of image and language, see W.J.T Mitchell, *Iconology: Image, Text, Ideology* (Chicago: University of Chicago Press, 1986) and Keith P. Moxey, *Visual Culture* (Ithaca, NY: Cornell University Press, 1994). For a discussion of how images condition our knowledge of history, including a discussion of Burckhardt and Huizinga, see Francis Haskell, *History an its Images: Art an the Interpretation of the Past* (New Haven, CN: Yale University Press, 1993).

94   And further, it can be questioned if it is ever possible to have a sense of culture that is not at base visual? Whether it is a vision of some type of totality or of a symbolic image, activity, or feeling that captures something of this whole, vision is still important both for "comprehending" and conveying a notion of culture. As the very definition of metaphor and therefore of language itself implies, the relation between language and image is not so easily separated.

     For a general discussion of image and language, see W.J.T Mitchell, *Iconology: Image, Text, Ideology* (Chicago: University of Chicago Press, 1986) and Keith P. Moxey, *Visual Culture* (Ithaca, NY: Cornell University Press, 1994). For a discussion of how images condition our knowledge of history, including a discussion of Burckhardt and Huizinga, see Francis Haskell, *History an its Images: Art an the Interpretation of the Past* (New Haven, CN: Yale University Press, 1993).

     Also the relation between a linguistic model of culture and the multiple voices of culture as has been suggested by several poststructuralists has not been worked out. What is a "discursive model of culture" is difficult to understand beyond the

A creative work is needed to bring to sight and to language what is not simply "observable" in the facts or in the literature of the past. We need the work itself to bring a *Kulturepoche* forth as a whole.[95] Only a "work of art," and a work of a specific imitative type, can capture these movements.[96] Burckhardt's interpretation of the Renaissance or Huizinga's interpretation of the culture of the later Middle Ages consists of presenting an image (*Bild*) of an entire culture. Phenomenonalizing a culture involves for cultural history the construction of a mimetic text, which is creative not just in the way it relates parts to whole but in the way it brings forth this whole as a whole.[97] As

intention to speak to multiple components. By itself voice is no more liberating than sight; commands come from the voice (including the commands of God) and sight is often employed to free individuals and cultures from the commands handed down by tradition.

The critique of perception, in other words, should not lead to a dismissal of a visually base form of cultural history. Instead, it should encourage a rethinking of the relation of image to meaning. Although the notion of totality clearly separates the modes of cultural history of Walter Benjamin and Aby Warburg from those of Burckhardt and Huizinga, they share a common concern with the visual. While the former thinkers look to the singular and the fragmentary and the latter to the general and the typical, the ocular and the imagistic links Benjamin's method to that of Warburg and that of both of them to those of Burckhardt and Huizinga. And this shared devotion to visual thinking is, I think, tied to the modern experience of the world. Despite so much current discussions to the contrary along these lines, perception need result neither in empiricism nor in the subordination of seeing to language. Not all forms of perception fall under the critiques of images and representations, of empiricism and science. And a visual model of cultural totality should not so readily be displaced for the sake of a purely linguistic or discursive model, as so much poststructuralist thought argues.

95   Ricoeur seems to be arguing the process of imitating "reality" through "artistic" means is not something to be dismissed out of hand. In fact the text's artistic and creative qualities are precisely those which allow it to reveal its truth.

96   Hunt gives up too much and does not work out the consequences of claiming that "history [is] a branch of aesthetics." *The New Cultural History*, p. 21.

97   For the most recent criticism of *The Civilization of the Renaissance* as an "aesthetic" rendering of the Italian Renaissance, see Peter Burke, "Introduction" to Jacob Burckhardt, *The Civilization of the Renaissance in Italy*, trans. S.G.C. Middlemore (London: Penguin Books, 1990) p. 4. Burke writes "Burckhardt saw history as an art. He regarded history as a form of imaginative literature, akin to poetry." See also on this point Jörn Rüsen, "Jacob Burckhardt: Political Standpoint and Historical Insight on the Border of Post-Modernism, " *History and Theory* XXIV, no. 3 (1985). Gilbert speaks of Burckhardt's "Renaissance stands by itself like a painting upon an easel" (Gilbert, p. 57).

a result, Burckhardt and Huizinga attempt to portray the entirety of a culture and to construct the cultural historical text as what might to be called
an "imitative text."[98]

What separates the cultural histories of Burckhardt and Huizinga from
those of Walter Benjamin and Aby Warburg, for instance, is the mimetic intention of the cultural historical text itself. What Benjamin and Warburg
miss in the older form of cultural history is that imitation itself – as opposed
to representation – bears the truth claim of Burckhardt and Huizinga's form
of cultural history. Burckhardt and Huizinga do not make universal claims;
rather they attempt to bring to language the truth of the experience of a particular culture as a specific, historically constituted, culture. Burckhardt and
Huizinga "imitate" the "object" – the image of a cultural epoch – through the
construction of a specific type of text. In differing ways, *The Civilization of
the Renaissance in Italy* and *The Waning of the Middle Ages* present us with an
understanding of cultural totalities through the texts of cultural history
themselves.

In *The Waning of the Middle Ages*, Huizinga presents an image of the fourteenth and fifteenth century northern European culture through the functioning of a historically distinct system of signs. Huizinga does not claim
that the reality of the pasts is only a projection of these signs; rather, he argues that these signs open the possible range of meanings which this reality
might designate. Unlike contemporary cultural criticism, he defines not an
abstract and merely virtual system of signs but an actual and functional production of meaning. Neither is Huizinga's vision of the later Middle Ages a
variation upon a Geertzian-type unified, atemporal set of symbols. Unlike
Geertz, Huizinga neither positions this symbolic code within an underlying
set of social relations nor understands this code ahistorically. Instead, he
places his vision of culture within historical time and discerns the reasons
for the decline of this symbolic system in terms of the overloading and eventual internal collapse of the meaning system we call the Middle Ages.[99]

Huizinga thus opens the possibility of a historical semiology, of a changing play of signs within time, and the evolution and destruction of distinct
sign systems. These sign systems open past worlds as worlds. And Huizinga

---

98   For recent discussions of mimesis, see Gunter Bebauer and Christoph Wulf, *Mimesis: Culture, Art, Society* Don Reneau, trans. (Berkeley: University of California
Press, 1995).

99   Johan Huizinga, *The Autumn of the Middle Ages*, Rodney J. Payton and Ulrich
Mammitzsch, trans., (Chicago: University of Chicago Press, 1996).

brings the same insights to his own attempts to write cultural history. Cultural history does not simply represent brute facts or even reveal social processes about the past. Rather, cultural history involves the creation of an image of past reality. It is an invention, a means of comprehending what perhaps can never be captured in a definition or reduced to the precision of a theory. He therefore understands "culture" and cultural history as inclusive of the relations between description and creation, between historical analysis and narrative exposition, between science and art. Without conflating fiction and truth, it needs ultimately to question the relation between language – understood as a historically specific use of language – and truth – understood as the interrelation between past meaning and present truth.[100]

In *The Civilization of the Renaissance in Italy*, Burckhardt presents an even more convincing example of textual imitation. He is concerned with the general conditions of a *Kulturepoche* and how from these conditions a unified culture emerged. Burckhardt does not posit that this unity is based upon a general theory or definition of culture or upon a notion of the necessary primacy of either politics, society, or religion within this unity. He presents through his own "image" of the cultural unity created by the Italians of the fourteenth and fifteenth centuries. This image allows Burckhardt to understand the interplay among these components within this specific historical epoch. Within the *Bild* of his cultural histories, Burckhardt identifies, for instance, the problem of literary genres and asks why certain genres developed and others declined. But not concerned with the internal history of these genres or even of literature; rather Burckhardt is concerned with the ways in which the development of the sonnet in Renaissance Italy was related to the emergence of the novella, biography, autobiography, as well as to a new individuated sense of personal identity, to new social attitudes and relations. He then shows how all these are related to the new independence of the Italian city-states and the break from medieval notions of Christian morality.

In constructing *The Civilization of the Renaissance in Italy*, Burckhardt follows a number of interconnecting threads that define the experience of the Renaissance in Italy. The idea of weaving dominates the imitative intention of the texts of cultural history. Through the recognition of the interweaving of these threads, the cultural historian creates an image of cultural totality. In part, the reason why Italian Renaissance culture formed a whole is that is itself a held a unified image of itself – on both the individual and collective levels – of a governing metaphor of the relation of the macrocosm to the mi-

---

100 Chartier, "Texts, Symbols, and Frenchness," p. 690.

crocosm. Pico's "Oration on the Dignity of Man" as text and as idea is the formative metaphor through which the entirety of *The Civilization of the Renaissance in Italy* is made.[101]

More than Huizinga's symbolic codes, Burckhardt's form of cultural history unites interpretive image with the textual imitation of the perpetual unity within constant change, which is culture. In a culture there are processes of interaction among some or even all forms of a culture. These processes produce intensifications and distillations that produce common practices and modes of discourse. The truth of *The Civilization of the Renaissance* lies not just in the interconnections, of the network of threads, which comprise a common Renaissance in Italy; for it also consists of the coming to consciousness of this process and the redefinition of its intention through this form of consciousness. The self-consciousness of the Renaissance itself contributed to its own formation and in many ways is the image that Burckhardt presents in *The Civilization of the Renaissance in Italy*.

In addition to the question of cultural interpretation, the problem of historical time is related to problem of textual production. With what is at base a synchronic depiction of the culture of the Italian Renaissance, Burckhardt confronts the textual problem of presenting change over time at the same time as a cultural whole. In addition, there is the Renaissance's own understanding of time. For Burckhardt the Renaissance "discovers" the modern sense of historical time. This involves more than a notion that the past is distinct from the present or even of a notion of the development from the past to the present. Modern historical time involves the continuity of traditions and established values and ways of acting, of the revivals of past traditions and the invention of new ones. More importantly, however, historical time is a worldly sense of time, one that finds it meaning within itself and does not measure itself in relation to a notion either of timelessness or of eternity.

Beyond the Renaissances's own notions of historical time, there is Burckhardt's understanding of time. As with all else that is interpreted within the horizon of a culture, the cultural historian does not complete his task by presenting the culture as a whole. By standing outside this horizon and understanding the "fate" of this culture, he also evaluates the culture. This evalua-

---

101 Burckhardt therefore employs a notion of synecdoche in the writing of this specific cultural historical text and not a functionalist variation upon metonymy as other employ in the writing of history. I do not agree with Hayden White in his argument that Burckhardt writes history under the trope of irony.

tion is not based upon a set of universal or supposed universal notions of human behavior or abstract definitions of culture. Instead, the evaluation is based upon what the cultural historian understands as the world – the historically specific set of "realities" and not reality in general – against which the culture reacts and creatively interprets through its "truths" and meaning, values, and institutions reacts. The world is also what escapes these meanings and values and can only be captured retrospectively by the historian.

This understanding of the relationship of culture and world brings forth what might be called the distinctly modern sense of historical time. As with the other "givens" of the *Kulturepoche* in *The Civilization of the Renaissance in Italy*, Burckhardt understands this modern sense of historical time as opening a range of possible reactions to it. It is a time sense involving coincidence of various factors and the freedom to act and create within this coincidence that is limited and to a large measure defines the world of modernity.

The emergence of sense of history is what Burckhardt thematizes in *The Civilization of the Renaissance in Italy*. Although he portrays the culture of the Renaissance as a movement through time, he is not simply stating that this culture simply occurred in time. Temporal change in one area, Burckhardt is arguing, leads to changes within the whole. Within a general sense of temporal flow, and even the disparate rate of flow within various aspects of experience, Burckhardt makes vertical slices, his famous *Durchschnitte*. Within historical time, he then reveals another movement, the coincidental movement that defines the interplay among the parts of the cultural whole.

The hermeneutic philosopher Paul Ricoeur has provided us with the most extensive reflection upon the process of textual production. In his magisterial *Time and Narrative* he argues that this process (emplotment) in both its historical and fiction forms overcome the aporias that plague all attempts to constitute a consistent philosophy of time. Practically and poetically (in the sense of *poesis*), narratives produce a specifically "historical time."[102] As opposed to natural and psychological time, historical time synthesizes agent and circumstance, intention and actualization, reception and meaning.[103]

With these questions of time, the problem of textual production becomes both sharpened and deepened. Through the structure of the text, the significance of *The Civilization of the Renaissance in Italy* is revealed as the coming into existence of this world and this-worldly sense of time. This is a histori-

---

102 Paul Ricoeur, *Time and Narrative III*, Kathleen Blamey and David Pellauer, trans. (Chicago: University of Chicago Press: 1988).

103 Ricoeur, *Time and Narrative III*, pp. 142-156.

cal sense that is not the universal notion of "history" as Ricoeur would have it. Temporality based upon the language of the world is neither superimposed upon the process of cultural formation nor subordinated to it.[104] Rather, temporality is coordinated, is integrated internally and necessarily, with cultural formation itself. The truth lies in the mimetic nature of the text itself as it brings forth a culture against the background of its world.

From this reading of *The Civilization of the Renaissance*, I would argue that, however far Ricoeur has taken the idea of textual production to the problem of historical truth, the concept of emplotment does not govern all modern forms of imitative texts. In cultural historical texts – as opposed to narrative histories – the world or the ways in which we understand the relation of world and time is the "object" of these texts. Historical time is less a question of emplotment in a text than a way in which it is a question of how this language creates a specific notion of time. These forms of historical understanding are dependent upon a world – that ways in which "reality" comes forth through language – and the relationship of a world to time – as a co-incidence of various forces, cultures and events – in a uniquely historical sense of time. Along these lines, I move from a philosophical hermeneutics to a cultural hermeneutics.

Since the late eighteenth century "culture" has become a major way in which individuals in the West have come to understand both themselves and others, however well or ill defined and inherently ambiguous this notion remains. Without falling into a reflection upon a general or even a regional ontology in which the specificity and the historical nature of any particular culture becomes lost, the notion of culture reveals how a common modern reality is experienced, how this experience is constituted, how we are given being in the modern world. Cultural history, then, has a much more extensive history than can be traced within the changing trends within contemporary historical studies or be understood in terms of recent developments within a single national tradition of historiography. Neither is the new interest in cultural history the result of changing trends across academic disciplines. The recurrence of interest in culture and its interest to a wide range of scholarly concerns points to larger currents.[105]

---

104 I do not mean by "temporality" Heidegger's existential; rather I employ it in an un-Heideggerian way as a general and thus abstract notion of time that is actualized only in a diversity of forms within historically specific worlds.

105 For a discussion of micro- and macro-history, see Carlo Ginzburg, *Clues, Myths, and the Historical Method* (Baltimore, MD: Johns Hopkins Press, 1989).

Prior to all the interpretations of cultural historians and all explanations of social causation, culture puts into question all postmodern notions, which all too quickly reduce definitions of "modernity" to problems of scientific claims and of grand narrative schemes. The ambiguity inherent in the term culture pushes to the limits what we know and how we know and exhibits the boundaries of our knowing and our being. The issue is not whether we accept or reject what we conceive of as the culture and the power relations of the West or whether we should continue to define "modernity" in terms of specific definitions of "science," "technology" and "nature."

The problem of understanding modern culture is perhaps more than a question of modes of interpretation and of competing understandings of truth, for culture seems to be definitive of the way we experience "reality" or better yet our existence is actualized in a very specific way. Modernity in this sense is defined not as a substance with a number of characteristics but by and through our notion of temporality, our modern experience of historical time. This time exhibits the fact that the past is never complete. As Ricoeur forcefully states, history consists of an "opening up of forgotten possibilities, aborted potentialities, repressed endeavors in the supposedly closed past. One of the functions of history in this respect is to lead us back to those moments of the past where the future was not yet decided, where the past was itself a space of experience open to a horizon of expectations."[106]

To posit a cultural whole does not arise from the demands of method, science, or a philosophy of history. It is not even demanded by any "aesthetic" intention to bring unity to the text. It does not mean that "modernity" or even the notion of "culture" is simply a construction of the text. The imitative text "discovers" modernity in the double sense of the term. It reveals "facts" and "processes" within the historical period and presents them in such a way that its meaning is uncovered by the very organization of the text. The interconnected space between the structure of the text and its "object" of representation, between the writing of cultural history and the idea of "culture," exhibits the interpretation of the cultural meaning of modernity. In other words, the creation of an imitative text allows a world to come forth,

---

106 Ricoeur, *Time and Narrative III*, p. 227.

allows relations to be comprehended and without which would be only partially or improperly conceivable.[107]

The issue is how we self-critically employ the notion of culture and how we open possibilities of actual finite forms of being through this general search for the truth of culture. It is the meaning and the truth of meaning which we know our world. It is the way we understand ourselves within a horizon of meaning and act and create within this horizon. And like the term culture, "history" itself has come to define the open and often totalizing ways that we come to understand the world as a world. The difficulty in defining the notion of culture, perhaps the inherent polyvocity implied in the term, arises from this wholeness and openness. And history, understood in terms of cultural history, then functions not as a form of identity but as the sight of both affirming and challenging all simple determinations of the meaning of our existence.

---

107 In *Weltgeschichtliche Betruchtungen*, Burckhardt opposed all such theories. While theorists claimed -and Hegel is his main example – to rise above history and to give it its themes and meaning, they actually succumbed to a nationalist and presentist view of history. Nationalism and presentism functioned as – in Burckhardt's well-chosen phrase – "optical illusions, " which occlude viewing the past as having meaning in any other ways than as either universally valid or as simply developments to our own contemporary form of existence (GW IV:181-196).

"What Does it Mean to Practice Cultural Analysis?"

DERRIDA, 911 AND CULTURAL ANALYSIS

Bent Sørensen
Department of Languages and Intercultural Studies
Aalborg University

PART 1: FORGIVING DERRIDA FOR DYING…

On the morning of September 11, 2001 my wife and I were asleep in our dingy B&B in midtown Manhattan. We were rudely awakened by a loud, heart-stopping thud as something fell out of the broom closet on the corridor directly outside our door. "What the fuck was that?" were the immortal words I saw fit to utter as the first of many inquiring, cursing and doubtful words spoken on that day.

Shortly after the interruption of our sleep, I had progressed to my morning shower – one of many ritual actions performed almost mechanically every morning. In preparation for our going up to Columbia University, my wife performed another ritual, recurring act: she switched on the TV, regularly tuned in to NY1, a local news station, chiefly of use because they bring an accurate weather report every ten minutes around the clock. We regularly commented on how having such a channel was a sign of the greater service-mindedness of New York as a city and the US as a civilisation (for lack of a better term). On the news that morning, it transpired, was one item, and one item only. No weather updates were forthcoming, either. My wife called me, trying to drown out the noise of the shower: "There is something wrong with one of the towers!" As I re-entered the bedroom, I saw on the screen that that indeed was a bit of an understatement.

I would like to say that my first thoughts were noble and gracious. Much like my first words that morning they were not. I rather think they were in rapid sequence: This is going to screw up the morning traffic… I hope there won't be a power outage and too much looting in the streets… Maybe we'd better stay at home today…

It has not been all that easy to forgive myself for these selfish and cynical thoughts, and I am not sure that I am ready to yet. But it gets worse. As the morning unravelled and NY1 and other news channels filled us in on what was actually happening, I found myself becoming more and more paralysed with anxiety. There was of course nothing we could do: there were planes in the air intent on hostile acts, seemingly directed at random against things

American, and there was no way we could dissociate ourselves from that despite the fact that none of us were American or particularly sympathetic to things American, with the possible exceptions of *Starbucks, Barnes & Noble* and *The Metropolitan Opera.*

My thoughts, as I now attempt to reconstruct them thirty months later, seemed to fluctuate between imagining scenarios of terror involving burning buildings and escape attempts through ash-filled streets (not very imaginative, since that was what the TV screen literally displayed); visions of poor, disenfranchised citizens taking advantage of the lack of available police and other representatives of law and order to loot, pillage and plunder every neighbourhood in sight, including our borderland territory between the Theatre District and Hell's Kitchen; and, worst of all perhaps, the lucid and absolutely certain knowledge that these events would be supplying material for volumes and volumes of papers in cultural studies for years to come. As it happened, only the latter thought was vindicated by actual events involving myself, and my fears and prejudices concerning my fellow New Yorkers were proven to be quite unfounded in their particulars.

Later in the day we decided to switch off the TV, which by now had started its pattern of repetitive showing of clips that had been too horrible to grasp the first few times we had viewed them, but which now seemed merely a nuisance in their lack of new information about what had happened or was about to happen. We decided to brave the streets instead.

Outside it was a crisp and rather nice day. The shops on Broadway were open, Starbucks was crowded and there was nothing much unusual going on on the sidewalks, except that people would frequently crane their necks and look towards the south. Nothing was actually visible in that direction, not even the plume of smoke that we had stared at on TV. The local buildings were simply blocking the view of anything untoward appearing down there. The sounds of New York were also familiar, the only noticeable difference being more sirens than usual. 8th Avenue saw a lot of emergency traffic even on a normal day with one of the NY Fire Department buildings being just a few blocks down the road, but that day all vehicles were southbound and it seemed they all sought out 8th Avenue.

We didn't talk to anyone, but it seemed that there were more instances of strangers having conversations than you'd normally see in shops and restaurants. This is not to say that such things did not occur every day in New York, because in fact one of the reasons we enjoyed the city so much was that one was never a stranger for very long there. The fruit vendor and the hot dog man knew your preferences after two visits, and after four he was likely to know your ethnicity, name and family history too. The staff of the Indian restaurant on the corner would recognize when you came in and ask if you wanted the usual goat Jalfreezi, even though you hadn't been there since last year. These facts never ceased to amaze us, and we should of course have known that such people wouldn't turn against us and rob us, just because some terrorists had rammed the World Trade Center towers with jet-planes. Still, I felt wary of people in the street that day, drained of confidence in other people's benevolence and kindness as I was.

In the evening we ate sushi at the corner of 8th Avenue and 51st Street. The service was slow because the chef hadn't come in that morning, but other than that it was business as usual. It wasn't until the following days that restaurants started closing down because supplies were hard to get onto Manhattan with the bridges and tunnels closed or tightly policed. The maid at the B&B didn't come in all that week and we were getting irritated at having to sleep in the same bed-sheets. The pettiness of this and many other irritations has not been thematised in any of the analyses of the post-911 events I've read; yet they were part and parcel of the response pattern across the city.

People were trying very hard to behave better than normal, and indeed it was observed in the weeks to come in most of the media how New Yorkers were no longer rude to one another in public. That they took it out on one another in private, as a whole city and a whole world slid into post traumatic stress, was evident from the programming which replaced the usual news, sports, weather cycle on stations such as NY1. More and more call-in shows appeared on the air, usually featuring people crying, expressing a sense of loss and bewilderment at the events and their significance, and often boiling over with repressed aggressions against the terrorists, Islam in general, and ultimately all their fellow human beings, including their nearest family and kin, who, unlike the terrorists, were within reach.

We were, to say the least, struck by the strangeness of such public displays of emotion. People cried at every possible turn: on the air, at concerts, in classes and at lectures, on the streets in front of the thousands of improvised memorials for the lost and dead loved ones. We felt out of place, because we didn't cry, because we were no longer hysterical. When Jacques Derrida came to NYU the following week to give classes there with Avital Ronell, and to Columbia to speak about death and forgiveness, we were appalled when the American students would read into his already prepared lectures and readings, emotions and comments related to the recent local events. When Derrida talked about forgiving the Holocaust, he was met with no critical questions by supposedly some of the most intelligent students at NYU. The only responses that day were strangely schizophrenic: One girl would giggle loudly, almost in a snorting fashion, every time Derrida referred to Kant by name. The one intelligible verbal response when Ronell asked the class for questions, was another girl stating: "I'm crying..." When asked to repeat what she had said (I suppose the response was so irregular that neither Derrida nor Ronell could quite believe what they had heard), she elaborated: "I'm crying – it's so emotional." I felt sick and angry at such a monumental missing of the point; Derrida had been trying to make: that forgiveness is only possible in the face of the unforgivable. If any relevance to the events of 911 were to be found in Derrida's painstakingly prepared and phi-lologically researched analysis (he certainly didn't make any overt parallels), it seemed to me that it would be that America would have to at some point collectively forgive the terrorists. No such point could, however, be voiced at that time, in New York, and barely has even at this late stage, any-where.

When Derrida gave a reading from his volume of eulogies to departed friends and associates a few days later in a jam-packed auditorium at Co-lumbia, there were not many questions about the pantheon of French, Ger-man and American friends and philosophers Derrida had written about in that book. One question, though, stands out vividly in my memory. A woman in her forties got up and confessed: "My mother died very recently. Can you say anything that can help me understand that event?" I was myself mortified. Possibly the greatest philosopher alive was reduced to the role of a radio-psychologist, being asked to give advice on coping and getting on with life. Derrida seemed to take it in his stride and his answer was no different than it would have been to an academic question, at least not in tone and *po-litesse*. The substance of the answer I have forgotten, and this actually trou-bles me more today than the fact that the question was posed, since forget-ting Derrida and remembering the trivia seems ethically wrong. Yet the im-age of Derrida cast as the wise white-haired father/philosopher/wizard fig-ure remains with me.

It's not that we ourselves didn't cry during those days. I was particularly tearful the evening after the attack when the news-hungry media pounced on a man who claimed that he had intercepted a call on a cell phone from someone trapped under the ruins of a building near the Towers. He claimed to be a fire fighter and appeared on TV, full of patriotic gusto and power. He swore that they would get their "brothers" out from under the rubble, even if it were to cost them their own lives. He yelled "God Bless America" at the top of his lungs and hurried off, apparently to do meaningful things in the res-cue business at hand. I was enormously moved by this apparition. A few hours later the TV stations quietly and briefly referred to the event as an apparent hoax. There had been no phone call, there were no "brothers" trapped, no one would be rescued... I've never been able to find out who the hoaxer was, nor what motivated his act. No one I've asked remembers the episode, no one seems to want to talk about its implications. The man must have been quite simply the ballsiest guy in New York at the time, so blatantly exposing people's deepest desires and fears, at no small risk to his own life and limbs once the hoax was exposed. The media were ashamed, or perhaps I should amend that to say that they ought to have been ashamed of being exposed as being so eager to get live meat to display on people's TV screens. Somebody bought the hoax hook, line and sinker and deserved to get fired as a result. The satisfaction of this glimpse behind the façade of the news-frenzy left me beaming through my recently dried up tears.

Derrida was in fact one of the few French intellectuals who dared come to New York that month, or actually the whole of the next year. Countless events that were to have featured European university people got cancelled over the next few weeks. The whole atmosphere of intellectual interaction and cultural interchange suffered incalculably in the aftermath of 911. The Met went from Mozart to "God Bless America" as a hastily compiled tribute to "Our Heroes" was put together. I cried at that too. I blame Thomas Hampson, whose baritone lent itself particularly well to "Let Us Gather By The River," which he featured both at the Met, and more appropriately at the memorial service at the Riverside Church, where we regularly attended services. Things became very American during those first few days and weeks, but they also became increasingly Gothic. One night when the Met had reverted to its regular programme of Mozart and Verdi, we ate at a burger restaurant on the other side of Lincoln Square before the performance. The food there sent me straight to the bathroom, and I was concerned about attending the upcoming four hours of opera with an upset stomach. As I paid the bill, the cashier remarked without preamble: "What a horrible smell," which needless to say rather embarrassed me further. I confess that I was relieved when she continued: "It's the smell of death. I can sense it in the air tonight." For a disorienting moment I had thought she was speaking to me as an individual person, but of course I realised that I was just incidentally being addressed, and that she just needed to vocalise the widespread Gothic phantasm that the 3,000 dead bodies under the Towers were infecting the swankier up-town neighbourhood of 66th Street with a miasma of death and decay. Those phantasms were shortly thereafter fuelled further when someone started sending anthrax spores through the mail to several TV stations in New York, and to politicians in Washington. The Gothic atmosphere of that November in New York has not yet received any serious academic interest, but must be seen as an essential part of the events and climate leading up to the activities of retribution which are still ongoing on the part of the US government and military.

In the months to follow the events of 911 continued to haunt me through TV screens, dreams, discussions and conversations with friends and strangers (a sure-fire conversation freshener was to tell the story of where we were on that day, a fact we exploited shamelessly many times), but most eerily through the presence of the spectre of Jacques Derrida on the margins of my life. Recently, when I started this essay, I told my wife half-jokingly that I was about to write my memoirs of Derrida, which seemed appropriate now that friends had informed us that he was in the last stages of terminal pancreatic cancer. Her response surprised me: "But you have no relationship with Derrida!" I reflected on what might cause her to state such an opinion: it is true that I generally hold the opinion that philosophy is less interesting than literature, and it is clear that the discourse of most French philosophers tends to affect my blood pressure negatively, but to go so far as to imply that I had *no* relationship with "Frere Jacques," as I usually refer to Derrida as (outside the class room), was hard to swallow. But I am getting ahead of myself here.

Derrida's presence had on several occasions been quite palpable in our lives both before New York, and after we returned to tranquil Denmark at the end of the year 2001. He was an honoured guest at a conference earlier that year in Kolding, where Roy Sellars, a self-avowed "Derrida groupie," had gathered forty scholars for a two-day event wholly dedicated to "Glossing *Glas*," as the conference was titled.

Here, I first heard Derrida "speak as a woman," as one fellow conference participant commented on Derrida's tendency toward the falsetto when making a particularly exquisite point of dialectic subtlety, yet infinite self-evidence. During the final session of the symposium Derrida answered a number of questions posed to him in advance by the organisers. In the course of explaining the dualities of *Glas*, this extraordinary book on Hegel and Genet, the mother and disgust, fetishism and the death penalty, and other juxtapositions far too numerous to recount, Derrida spoke about the heteroglossia he had felt impelled to practice ever since his first attempt to write the two columns of *Glas*. He said: "I have always been since then compelled to write in more than one voice. I have a number of texts which are unavoidably haunted by a multiplicity of places and voices, and marked – and the sexual difference is essential – by always at least one feminine voice. I can quote a number of texts, for instance *La verité en painture*, and all the time all these characters and signatures involved one or more than one feminine voice."

This claim struck me as wonderfully paradoxical. The previous day Derrida had responded to some of the many papers in honour of him and his quasi-Talmudic text, but the conference as a whole had been somewhat marred by the poor acoustics of the Hall at Koldinghus Castle where the event took place. Most of us had trouble hearing everything, but for Derrida himself it must have been nearly impossible to distinguish anything, since he was at the time already rather deaf. This was not particularly apparent to anybody until the moment when Sarah Wood brought up the name of Derrida's old friend and debating partner Paul de Man (for insight into their relationship, see Mark Tansey's witty painting "Derrida Queries de Man," which pla(y)giarises classic Sherlock Holmes illustrations, and casts Derrida and de Man as Holmes and Moriarty above the Reichenbach Falls – an image I now use as my screen saver), and Derrida was quite incapable of catching the reference. Sarah Wood repeated the familiar name three or four times at increasing volume, until the hall resounded with those quasi-French syllables. Everyone but Derrida had by now understood Wood's invocation. Finally she gave up communicating to Derrida what her point had been, and the conference lumbered on. Derrida who spoke routinely in "one or more feminine voices" was incapable of hearing one of the few female voices present at the conference, undone by inadequacies in technology and acoustics no doubt, but perhaps also by the praxis of Wood's voice.

Such somewhat facile observations were to come back to haunt myself at a later stage, but rather amused me at the time. I was reminded of an analysis I had written of Derrida at another conference speaking about being spoken about, "as if dead" (not "deaf"). The proceedings had later appeared under the title *Applying: To Derrida*, and one contribution in particular had explored the playful multiplicity of meanings to be teased out of that title. I quote a modest portion of the article in question: "Applied Derrida. Derrida applied. Apply Derrida. Derrida, apply. The application of Derrida. Apply Derrida sparingly, liberally, gently, regularly (to the affected parts). A brief application of Derrida soon brought about considerable improvements."[1] This example of Derrida-fetishism was in itself disturbing, but easily topped by the ensuing twisting of Derrida's proper name into a verb: the introduction to the whole book actually suggested a possible synonymity between the two elements of the conference title, so that "applying" became the same as "to Derrida," in the sense of the latter word becoming some new verb desig-

---

1   Bennington in Brannigan, et. al., 1996

nating a new activity synonymous with application. In fact the editors suggested such a verb and gave all its conjugations[2]. This "Derridaing" was then an applying in all the senses given in the above, which, however, negated all the previous readings by making them tautologies: to apply is to Derrida is to apply... Geoffrey Bennington was the author of the first quoted exercise in wordplay, and he was also present at "Glossing *Glas*," where he had in fact excelled in stating the painfully obvious in a rarefied complex of convoluted sentences and half-finished mumblings. One could only conclude that Bennington in print was rather more applicable than oral Bennington, but ultimately both Benningtons seemed direly in need of a good Derridaing.

The affable, but somewhat deaf Derrida of the "Glossing *Glas*" conference was a different entity than the post-911 Derrida I had met in New York. In September there was no need to laugh at his aural blind spots, no need to lay the blame for fetishistic worship of his persona at his own feet. The tables were turned by the terrorist intervention into all our lives, and Derrida who spoke as a woman, yet could not hear one speak, was now instead becoming a Gandalf-like focal point for people's sorrow and desire to mourn their dead and the passing of innocence they experienced inside themselves, and which extraverted itself as a desire in everybody to also have experienced the loss of a near and dear one in the tragic event of the World Trade Center collapse – and thus to "share" (a particularly American desire). The persona of this new Derrida (marshalling as it does the archetype of the white haired wise man, counsellor, or wizard – hence my naming this persona after Tolkien's character of Gandalf, which seems to function in this way for many young people) was not to be ridiculed, but rather associated itself inextricably with sorrow, loss and mourning, also in my own psyche.

Not surprisingly, therefore, the old Derrida came back to haunt me in the months after our return to Denmark. His voice, feminine or not, had in fact quite literally been entrusted to me to transcribe by Roy Sellars, a task to which I had foolishly acquiesced shortly after the symposium in Kolding. While in New York I had done none of the work of transcribing Derrida's lecture, being as it were replenished almost daily by new Derrida impressions of a far more pertinent nature. Unwittingly to myself the miasma of 911 intervened in my perception of Derrida and made it traumatic to return to the fetish of the old Derrida which manifested itself as a present object in the shape of a large number of poor quality cassette tapes waiting for

---

2   Brannigan, et. al. (eds.), 1996: xvi

me to listen to and transcribe. As the months after 911 unfolded I was finding myself in an unintelligible crisis, and this crisis of non-productivity was obviously a result of post-traumatic stress. I had not thought at the time that the stress would affect me other than to an extent where an ironic distance would protect me from its evil influence. I was wrong, as I should have known from the post-ironic emotionality I had felt in the presence of the fake fire-fighter, Thomas Hampson, and the Gandalfian Derrida persona.

The specific locus of my traumatic response was to be found in the unapproachable status of the pile of cassette tapes with Derrida on them. I stalled and lied and negotiated extension of deadlines for the transcripts to the best of my considerable ability. At the end of eight months I was forced to acknowledge defeat. I had to resign from the task as recorder of Derrida's words, and in this ignoble moment I felt that "the terrorists had truly won." (This phrase had by then become a stale joke in Leno and Letterman monologues…) Yet from the jaws of that defeat I managed to snatch a small victory. With the help of my wife I confronted the mouth of Derrida, and recorded seventeen pages of his final presentation, a portion of which I have quoted above. The tapes were atrocious, the discourse of Derrida not always inspiring, nor eloquent, yet the accomplishment of the work was reward in itself, and marked the beginning of a return from trauma for me. The Gandalfian Derrida mystique receded and ironic positions again surfaced from under emotional detritus and became almost as tenable as before.

For months after that I thought no more about Derrida than any academic engaged in teaching literary theory needs must do on the rare occasion that an issue arises in the class room where a bit of applied Derrida will hit just the right spot. I also went back to New York on several occasions and felt the spirit returning to the city again. The cab drivers seemed to have recovered completely in the spring of 2002, at least to the extent that they were as homicidal as ever towards wayward pedestrians. We did not visit the so-called "Ground Zero" on any of our visits to New York post-911, nor did we go there in the immediate aftermath. It seemed pointless and voyeuristic to do so then, as it does now. This may be a repression of the final core of traumatic conflict, but I doubt it. I rather believe now that exorcising Derrida will suffice to heal me completely and that I am in the midst of doing just that. Just as the miasmatic influence of 911 infested many of us who were present that day, and remains in us until spoken out, the influence of Derrida on my thinking and writing needs to be exorcised before the trauma associated with his name can be worked out.

Our later dealings with Derrida have been more sporadic, but no less guilt accompanied. In 2003 my wife and I spent three months in Portugal, researching and writing. I am in fact writing this very passage in Lisbon, where I have returned to give a paper written during my 2003 stay. While we were in Lisbon Derrida came to nearby Coimbra to speak on sovereignty. We didn't go. The recent Derrida movie played one night in Lisbon. We didn't go. The Coimbra event was held entirely in French; the Derrida movie featured interviews reportedly carried out in abysmal French. Thus a convenient alibi presented itself in the form of my Francophobia, and this justified to myself our absence from these Derridean appliances. When news then reached us in roundabout fashions from Avital Ronell (who confessed that she had moved temporarily to France to be near her "Master," and to perform "Californian healing rituals" upon him), and more final sounding bulletins from Mark C. Taylor, that Derrida was dying and might never appear at another conference, we were of course instantly guilt ridden and remorseful that we had not gone to see him in Coimbra. What if we had indeed missed the "Last Chance to See," as William Burroughs once billed one of his lecture tours? Were we not at least partially culpable in bringing about the death of Derrida? Were we not now facing the unbearable onus of forgiving Derrida for dying – for dying on us? All the derision of Derridaing once more returned spectrally to haunt our dreams.

The most noticeable effect on me was my tendency to mention Derrida's name in almost every class and supervision session I have conducted all year. This reflected an urge to come to terms with the several Derridean voices, and urging others to apply him seemed to soothe my own conflicted non-relationship (as my wife would have it) with him. If I myself could never properly read Derrida and apply him, perhaps my best and brightest students could apply to my approval by doing it – in their own names for sure, but counter-signed by me.

A few days ago another missive from Avital Ronell reached us, practically exonerating us from guilt of speeding along Derrida's demise. Apparently he is in recovery and thinking about returning to New York to teach in October 2004. A new guilt, now over mourning his passing prematurely presents its spectre to me as I write, so it seems the miasmatic influence calls upon a continued Derridaing before the exorcism is complete. Perhaps it will end in Zaragoza, where Derrida will be the guest of honour at the European Society for the Study of English conference in September 2004, if he lives… – and if I make it there….

PART 2: SPECTRES OF DERRIDA AND 911: TRAUMA, CONFESSION
AND FORGIVING

The preceding meditations on violence, trauma, guilt and shame should be read as an example of creative non-fiction. It stands where it stands, because I was requested to write an essay on what it means to practice cultural analysis. When I started thinking about how to answer that deceptively open-ended and straightforward sounding question, I realised that of the many traditional paths none would reach the goal of saying something pertinent and original enough to please my editor and me. What was called for here was a narrative, as indeed the essay form is rightfully famed for bringing forth, but a non-straightforward, wandering narrative it would have to be. This realisation allowed me to tap into the latest trend in academic writing, narrative scholarship, where the analyst tells a story to make a point of scholarly import. What's more, the first-person voice customarily used in narrative scholarship was exactly what the editor almost insisted on in his setting of the task, and therefore the personal approach was a given. A third reason for supplying a personal account as my own "object text" was simply that by doing so, I would solve the tricky problem of finding an exemplary text as my springboard, yet not a text that had already been done to death (no pun intended) – and also not a text that would be too esoteric and unknown to resonate with my potential readers. Therefore, dear reader, I wrote it (I am, of course, mock-quoting that great mock-Gothic novel, *Jane Eyre*).

The fourth and clinching reason was that this strategy allowed me to foreground a meta-dimension, in the form of a self-awareness, or more properly put, a self-consciousness in the text, which would permit me to tap into my main research areas, postmodern poetics, theories and metafictional practices. This meta-dimension also allows me, or rather mandates me, to insist that the relationship between the preceding essay and the present expository portion is not as straightforward as the reader might wish to think. The personal essay part is not merely the object text which the present portion analyses in order to show how analysis is done. Rather, the first part of the piece is in its own fashion as much of a cultural analysis as the expository part; and indeed the expository part is as much creative non-fiction as the essay part, since it is thoroughly imbricated in the themes and styles of the first part, and thus blatantly complicit in the same genre conventions as its object text. Indeed this serves to foreground the point that all essays – personal and critical – are creative in their construction of a speaker, a speaking position and a reader spoken to. This insight is often glossed over, because of the apparent objectivity and factual codification of critical work. My insistence on the importance of the self-conscious application is a meta-effect I have chosen in order to highlight what is often repressed in academic discourse: The imaginative and world constructing urge behind all writing.

The imbrication on the stylistic level between the two parts also mirrors another imbrication which needs to be commented on, and which the essay part in its own vocabulary has already revealed, namely the complex relationship between theory and analysis (or practice and application as the essay called it). This relationship in my opinion is such that there can be no analysis which is not always already a contribution to theory, by dint of the analysis situating itself outside that which it analyses, and by looking at its object obliquely. This process is theory applied to cultural analysis, and thus theory always peeps out of analysis itself.

The form of the preceding essay is typical of that of the so-called personal essay – filled with asides, digressions, whimsy, apparently random associations, chronological instabilities manifested in flashbacks and -forwards from an ontologically unstable now plane (the more dates are manifested to fix the chronology, the more uncertain the speaker's temporal location becomes), as well as ontological flickerings (I am here borrowing a particularly resonant phrase from Brian McHale[3]) caused by the alternation between first person singular and first person plural pronouns: "I" and "we." The tone is equally, if not more, in flux between apparently sincere evaluation and occasionally remorseful reflections, and wholly sarcastic, almost slanderous, characterizations of several of the real-life characters referred to and analysed in the piece. The focal character, "Jacques Derrida," is particularly prone to this fluctuating valorisation – as witnessed by the extremes of his being derided as a vain old chauvinist, while only a few breaths earlier being called the greatest living philosopher in the world. The derision Derrida is being exposed to is of course partly motivated by the same punning energy Derrida's own deconstructive philosophy and language is famous for subjecting both his own writing and his own name to, as well as the texts of other writers. It can therefore be seen as a writing back to Derrida, an oblique attempt at punishing Derrida for his sins of spurious etymological practices, free association and false causality – or as an awkward backhanded homage to Derrida's freshening up of the language in which we can now discourse about sovereignty, capital punishment and forgiveness without recourse to cheap sentimentality and emotion. (In the immediately preceding passage

---

3   McHale, 1984, p. 32 *et legio.*

we already see how the ironic tone of the essay migrates into the post-essay exposition and destabilises its purportedly privileged enunciation position; supposedly *post-festum, post hoc,* yet *in actu esse* as *ad hoc* as the essay *per se*). The wit and wittiness of the essay is constantly countered by its mocking and self-deprecatory tone, and this clash seems designed to set the reader in a position of experiencing syzygy, or the yoking together of two antithetical elements.

Along with its focal character, "Derrida," the essay also deals with a focal event, the violence of 911, and particularly the post-traumatic aftermath of 911, as observed and discussed through the lens of my own personal (in the sense of my persona's) experience thereof. The essay suggests that a Gothic atmosphere was produced by 911, and that in the manner of Edgar Allan Poe's unnamed narrator in *The Fall of the House of Usher* the narrator of the essay part became infected by the Master of the House's *malaise* as well as by the atmosphere of the House itself (as indeed in Poe and in life Master and House were/are one and the same). In this allegory Derrida is the Master Usher himself, and the House that fell is the Trade Center towers. The Fall transforms and disembodies House and Master, but the narrator flees and remains embodied as he lives to tell – but is nonetheless transformed into the carrier of Usher's *malaise* virally spreading its madness to the readers of his text. Unlike in Poe's story we in the essay portion follow the narrator struggling through guilt, shame and other features of post-traumatic stress, towards a tenuous healing through language, which however is expressed in such slippery ironic positions that we never know where the speaker is in the process of the dissemination of the talking cure's word hoard.

Throughout the account the essay meanderingly sets forth, the spectre of Derrida as Master, yet not always, and only, the narrator's Master, continues to haunt the text and its narration. The spectrality of "Derrida" is strangely undercut by, yet also highlighted by the 'real' Derrida's perceived position as dying, yet undead; perceptive, yet deaf; feminine, yet aurally phallocentric; himself, yet othered as an icon transformed by an eager audience into an array of fetishistic appliances and figures of the imagination. This sequence can be read as pay-back for Derrida's own spectral treatment and hauntings of the scenes of death of so many of his friends and fellow critical intellectuals. His persistent writing "on the death of" may in some way have invited this mixture of derision and derridaing of his own persona as the embodiment of the epitaphic voice in philosophy.

Since, ultimately, there is no theme in the essay portion which has not been dealt with extensively in Derrida's own writing, be it haunting and spectrality, violence, trauma, guilt and shame, confession and forgiveness, or

practice, application and theory, it is arguable that the entire piece is circumscribed by Derrida's thinking and that Derrida countersigns the essay both
in content, style and method. Even such terminology is of course completely
Derridean, which renders the essay a specimen of meta-deconstructive discourse, struggling against the circumfession of deconstruction, yet failing to
emerge uncircumcised by its method and language. Only in the aporia created by its mediation between irony and post-ironic sincerity and therefore finally unreadable enunciation position is the essay able to sign itself into its
own space, forgive Derrida for (not) dying, and (possibly) forgive itself for
its self-indulgence.

PART 3: "WHAT DOES IT MEAN TO PRACTICE CULTURAL ANALYSIS?"

In conclusion: the two texts I have written: "Forgiving Derrida for Dying"
– a personal essay, and "Spectres of Derrida: Trauma, Confession and Forgiveness," a deconstructive analysis of the personal essay, and therefore
equally essayistic and personal, combine to form the essay: "What Does It
Mean to Practice Cultural Analysis?" The question embodied in the last of
the three titles is answered by the two first parts and by the totality of them
and this conclusion.

The answers are meta-answers, exhibiting acute self-consciousness about
the contiguity and situatedness of any answer to such a question. The imbri-
cations of topic and analysis, analysis and theory, theory and method,
method and topic come full circle through the slippery medium of the
piece's language which itself circles around the aporia of haunting and spectrality. The text is in some sense, as Henry James said about his own short
novel about ghosts, hauntings and phantasmagoric events, *The Turn of the
Screw*, about exactly nothing.

All cultural analysis creates and manifests such aporias. The objects of
cultural analysis are decontextualised, reified and fetishised by the analytical
language. If, on the other hand, the analyst attempts to write subjectively and
injects him or herself into the text, the contagion of the spectral process migrates via the personal tone into the analyst's personal life and may spread
virally in a feedback loop from and to his or her words and life. This spectrality often mars the life of the cultural analyst to an extent where all events
are seen as fodder for yet more cultural analysis, and this cultural analysis
eventually ends up being the analyst's own talking, writing, reading cure, as
he or she tries to become his/her own analyst/analysand.

Therefore: what it means to practice cultural analysis is to become accul-
turated, to be culturally analysed, to become haunted by the spectres of cul-
turality, to be dispossessed of your personal identity in the process of being

infected by a cultural one, to become a cultural text, readable by other potential victims of cultural analysis. The cure is also the malaise itself: to talk, write and act culturally and ultimately to be willing to forgive culture (and even forgive oneself) and to beg others' cultural pardon.

Bibliography/Works Cited

Bennington, Geoffrey (in Brannigan et al., eds.): "X."

Brannigan, John, Robbins, Ruth and Wolfreys, Julian (eds.): *Applying: To Derrida*, Palgrave Macmillan, London (1996).

Brontë, Charlotte: *Jane Eyre*, Signet Classics, New York (1960).

De Man, Paul: *Blindness and Insight: Essays in the Rhetoric of Contemporary Criticism*, University of Minnesota Press, Minneapolis (1985).

Derrida, Jacques: *Glas*, University of Nebraska Press, Lincoln (1986).

—-: *The Truth in Painting*, University of Chicago Press, Chicago (1987).

—-: *Memoires for Paul de Man*, Columbia University Press, New York (1989).

—-: *Specters of Marx: State of the Debt, the Work of Mourning and the New International*, Routledge, London (1994).

Derrida, Jacques: *The Work of Mourning*, University of Chicago Press, Chicago (2003).

Glossing *Glas* website: http://www.ko.sdu.dk/conf/glas/.

James, Henry: *The Turn of the Screw*, Norton Critical Editions, London (1999).

McHale, Brian: *Postmodernist Fiction*, Routledge, London, 1984.

Poe, Edgar Allan: *The Fall of the House of Usher and Other Writings*, Penguin, London (1986).

Ronell, Avital: *Stupidity*, University of Illinois Press, Urbana-Champaign (2001).

Tansey, Mark: "Derrida Queries de Man," http://www.artchive.com/artchive/T/tansey/derrida.jpg.html.

Taylor, Mark C.: *Deconstruction in Context: Literature and Philosophy*, University of Chicago Press, Chicago (1986).

Tolkien, J.R.R.: *Lord of the Rings*, Harper & Collins, New York (1953/1991).

THE BETTER STORY

Life of Pi and Cultural Text Studies

Lene Yding Pedersen
Department of Languages and Intercultural Studies
Aalborg University

On my way home from a recent Irish Studies conference, I overheard a conversation on the train between two conference participants who were worried about the very "theoretical" approach a few of the papers had had. As my paper was most likely to be among those "theoretical" ones, I paid a little more attention to the conversation than was actually polite. The conference's theme had been "Liminal Borderlands: Ireland Past, Present, Future," and I had presented a paper on Irish novelist John Banville's novel *Shroud* and focused on how this novel "theoretically" deals with cultural history and historical knowledge.[1] It seemed that these two participants found "theory" an unnecessary aspect of "Irish Studies." I thought about the session my paper had appeared in. The first presenter in that session had made a distinction between "contextualized" readings of John Banville and "decontextualized" readings of him, where "contextualized" seemed to mean "within the context of Irish society and politics" and where "decontextualized" seemed to mean anything else. According to this presenter, Banville had mostly been read within the decontextualized framework, whereas the purpose of his paper was to point of the "Irish themes" in Banville, basically to show that Banville is a much more "Irish" novelist than he is usually considered to be. He went on to talk about autobiographical aspects of one of Banville's novels, *The Newton Letter*, and a series of violent public events in Ireland in the late seventies that he saw as main themes in the novel. In my own "decontextualized" reading of *Shroud*, I spoke much more about Paul

---

1   The Fourth Biannual Conference of NISN. Dalarna University College, Falun, Sweden. 22-24 April 2004. My paper was entitled "Revealing/Re-veiling the Past: John Banville's *Shroud*." The paper will be published as an article in *Nordic Irish Studies*, vol. 4 (forthcoming 2004).

de Man than about Banville, a lot more about Europe than Ireland, and a lot more about "theories" of history than "actual" history (which I argued was really being questioned both novels). Discouragingly, the first presenter got quite a few more questions than I did.

The conversation on the train and the attempt to "retrieve" a novelist like Banville into an "Irish context" made me think about the status of such a thing as "Irish Studies" and the status of literature within such a framework. It also made me think of what it is we do when we "do cultural studies" and when we "do literary studies," and what the relevance is of literary studies for cultural studies and vice versa. And it made me think of what we mean by "text" and "context" as those terms seem to belong to "literary studies" and "cultural studies" respectively. In these contexts, then, it seems to me that there are others ways of practicing "contextualized" readings of "texts" than those relying on a simple correspondence between the social and political conditions of the text's production or between the text and its author. This makes it seem relevant to practise and reflect on what we could appropriately call "cultural text studies." My use of the term "cultural text studies" follows a turn within parts of literary studies that has happened since the 1980s and 1990s. This turn has moved literary studies towards cultural studies. In Antony Easthope's 1991 book entitled *Literary Into Cultural Studies,* we see how this turn manifests itself. Here, Easthope attempts to establish a new paradigm for literary studies, mainly by reconstructing the literary object by incorporating into it "popular culture," but also by reconsidering the approach to the "literary object." My use of the term "cultural text studies" relies on both of these aspects. It is "*cultural text* studies" in the sense that the object of study is cultural text rather than traditionally defined literary text. In other words cultural text studies relies on a more broadly defined notion of text. Yet it is "cultural *text studies*" in the sense that the approach to text studies is "cultural" as opposed to, say, formalist. Roughly speaking, the first understanding of the term emphasizes the object, whereas the second emphasizes the (theoretical and methodological) approach to a given text.

Now, the first meaning of the term "cultural text studies" implies that we must include into cultural text studies other kinds of texts than are usually found in literary studies (for example "popular culture"). Yet it also implies

---

2   Antony Easthope, *Literary into Cultural Studies* (London and New York: Routledge, 1991).

that even when we talk about "traditional" literary objects such as poems or novels, it is not only the poem or novel *itself* that constitutes the text but rather the poem or novel as a text-in-context. What we study is text-in-context, which is to say that the context of the text-in-context is textual. This is why it is "cultural *text* studies" and not simply "cultural studies." Cultural text studies at the same time emphasizes the textual aspect of cultural studies and the cultural aspect of text studies.

The second meaning of the term "cultural text studies" implies that we view the "textual object" within a certain theoretical and methodological framework. Even with a broadly defined notion of text (the first meaning of the term) we could still keep it within a traditionally defined "literary studies" framework: it is unproblematic to provide a formalist (or "internal") analysis of a political speech or a close reading of pop song, for example (and it sometimes makes very good sense to do a thing like that). Yet "*cultural* text studies" emphasizes a different approach to text studies than a formalist or new critical approach, and it is set within a fundamentally different theoretical and methodological framework. Cultural text studies, as I see it, theoretically rests on theoretical notions that belong to both literary and cultural theory.[3]

What may be gained from reconceptualizing the literary object and by reconsidering the approach to it that the turn in Easthope's book illustrates? First, the turn shows that literary studies is part of cultural studies. This is both in the sense that literary studies must take into account cultural studies and in the sense that cultural studies must recognize the functions of literature and other texts. Second, it indicates that there exists a space worth examining where literary studies (its objects, theories and methods) overlaps with cultural studies (its objects, theories and methods). It is within this space that we find cultural text studies situated. To illustrate how cultural text studies may be practised, I will address the novel *Life of Pi*, written by Yann Martel in 2001, and I will try to demonstrate how it works as a "cultural text." I choose this novel for a few reasons. First, it is an up-to-date example of many of the central points of cultural text studies as I see them. As such the novel functions as a "model example" in this essay. From this, it follows that the more general points I make on account of this novel would

---

3   We find some of these notions on Julian Wolfrey's 2004 book, appropriately titled *Critical Keywords in Literary and Cultural Theory*. Julian Wolfrey, *Critical Keywords in Literary and Cultural Theory* (New York: Palgrave Macmillan, 2004).

be justifiable for other examples of contemporary cultural texts as well. I am aware of the risk of (over)generalizing on a too weak basis, but I still think that the strengths of a model example outdo its weaknesses. Additionally, I will show in the following, *Life of Pi* is a cultural text of significant importance, and thus a kind of text that students of contemporary culture should be aware of. Finally, since I have used the novel in my own university teaching, I have hands-on experience with how it works as a cultural text. In so far as this essay presents some of my thoughts about what we "do" when we "do cultural studies," this third point becomes relevant as the discussion of this novel allows for a thinking about a "doing" that has actually been done.

The novel opens with an "author's note," which begins like this:

> *This book was born as I was hungry. Let me explain. In the spring of 1996, my second book, a novel, came out in Canada. It didn't fare well. Reviewers were puzzled, or damned it with faint praise. Then readers ignored it. Despite my best efforts at playing the clown or the trapeze artist, the media circus made no difference. The book did not move. Books lined the shelves of bookstores like kids standing in a row to play baseball or soccer, and mine was the gangly, unathletic kid that no one wanted on their team. It vanished quickly and quietly.*
>
> *The fiasco did not affect me too much. I had already moved on to another story, a novel set in Portugal in 1939. Only I was feeling restless. And I had a little money.*
>
> *So I flew to Bombay. This is not so illogical if you realize three things: that a stint in India will beat the restlessness out of any living creature; that a little money can go a long way there; and that a novel set in Portugal in 1939 may have very little to do with Portugal in 1939.*[4]

In this "author's note," Martel lines up a whole list of agents surrounding his previous book who all appear to have been partly "responsible" for the failure of the book: it was *not* recognized and it did *not* make a difference. All these agents (the author himself, the publishers, the reviewers, the readers,

---

4   Yann Martel, *Life of Pi* (Edinburgh: Canongate, 2003), ix.

the media circus and the booksellers) are agents within what Pierre Bourdieu calls "the literary field."[5]

What we see in this passage is that Martel openly recognizes and acknowledges that he and his book were part of such a field of production. This
means that as a writer he positions himself within this field, realizing the
rules of the game and trying to follow them. Despite this, his novel failed,
and it failed in two ways: its value was not recognized by reviewers or read-

---

5   The main reason for bringing up Bourdieu in relation to cultural text studies is
that he has proved himself "a major theoretical voice in the critical study of cultural practices" since the early 1970s as he has developed some very fruitful theoretical concepts for dealing with cultural production. Another critic puts it this
way, "Bourdieu's sociology has been labelled, with only a little exaggeration, "not
only the best, but . . . the only game in town." Whereas it is debatable whether
Bourdieu really *is* the only game in town, it is incontestable that his theory has
been very influential within at least those parts of cultural studies interested in literature as cultural text. He is by now so "consecrated" (to use on of his central
terms) that little or no justification seems to be needed when a scholar turns to his
theories for an explanatory framework for discussing cultural production: see for
example the way Graham Huggan introduces Bourdieu in his *The Postcolonial
Exotic: Marketing the Margins*. Here Huggan briefly introduces "Pierre Bourdieu's
influential notion of cultural capital" and points to the usefulness of Bourdieu's
model for his own object of study ("how post-colonial writers/thinkers operate
within an overarching, if historically shifting, field of cultural production") while
referring in a footnote to two detailed critiques of Bourdieu. This is actually an important observation in relation to the question of what it is we do when we "do
cultural studies." I do not think it is the place here to outline Bourdieu's theoretical
heritage in any details (others have done that very well already). What we *do* have
to realize, however, is that any theoretical and methodological approach leaves in
the dark as much as it illuminates, and we have to be aware of the focus that our investigation has. When using Bourdieu as a theoretical framework for discussing a
novel, this implies that we come to emphasize much more a radical contextualization of the novel than the novel "itself;" we come to deal not only with different
agents in the literary field (such as authors and readers) but also with the structure
of the field itself; and we come to deal with the relationship between cultural practices and broader social processes. These implications of using Bourdieu are all
valuable for cultural text studies as I have tried to define it here. I therefore agree
with Johnson in his description of Bourdieu's "fruitful alternative": [Bourdieu]
provides an analytical model which reintroduces, through the concept of *habitus*, a
notion of the agent – which structuralism had excluded from social analysis –
without falling into the idealism of Romantic conceptions of the artist as creator
(or *subject*) which still informs much literary and art criticism today. At the same

ers, and it did not sell very many copies. Thus it failed according to two different kinds of logics where one relates to what Bourdieu calls *symbolic capital* and where the other relates to *economic capital*. In general, Bourdieu sees the literary field as an upside-down economic world whose fundamental law is the theory of art for art's sake (rather than for economic profit), and whose economy is based on a particular form of belief that requires symbolic capital rather than economic capital.[6] Symbolic capital has to do with prestige and authority and with the consecration of value. This means that when we talk about a work of art as an object, it is a commodity like any other commodity (a thing that can be sold according to the logics of the economic field), yet it is also – and this is quite important – a *symbolic* object. "The work of art is an object which exists as such only by virtue of the (col-

time, with the concept of *field*, he grounds the agent's action in objective social relations, without succumbing to the mechanistic determinism of many forms of sociological and "Marxian" analysis. See Bourdieu, "The Field of Cultural Production, or: The Economic World Reversed," "The Production of Belief: Contribution to an Economy of Symbolic Goods," and "The Market of Symbolic Goods," in Pierre Bourdieu. *The Field of Cultural Production*. Ed. and intr. by Randal Johnson (United States: Columbia University Press: 1993), 2, 35; Randal Johnson, "*Editor's Introduction*: Pierre Bourdieu on Art, Literature and Culture," 1; Bridget Fowler, *Pierre Bourdieu and Cultural Theory: Critical Investigations* (London: Sage Publications, 1997), 2; Graham Huggan, *The Postcolonial Exotic: Marketing the Margins* (London and New York: Routledge, 2001), 4-5.

It is also worth noting that Randal Johnson's introduction from *The Field of Cultural Production*, for example, situates Bourdieu within the field of cultural theory and contrasts his underlying idea of the "objectivity of the subjective" to Saussurean semiology, structural anthropology, and Althusserian Marxism. He outlines the theoretical background for Bordieu's central concepts of *habitus, field*, and *agent* and relates them to Cassirer's notion of a *relational* mode of thought. Furthermore he explains Bourdieu's notions of *symbolic capital* and *cultural capital* which he sees as showing similarities between Bourdieu's model and "depth hermeneutics." In Richard Shusterman's edition *Bourdieu: A Critical Reader* (Great Britain: Blackwell Publishers Ltd., 1999) Bourdieu is read in a philosophical context through critical assessment of his "philosophical" theories by philosophers from diverse philosophical perspectives including both Anglo-American philosophy and twentieth-century Continental philosophy. Much of the argument in this book relies on the notion of Bourdieu as a "metaphilosopher" rather than a sociologist or anthropologist. Bridget Fowler's book *Pierre Bourdieu and Cultural Theory: Critical Investigations* (London: Sage Publications, 1997) emphasizes Bourdieu's sociology of culture with special reference to Bourdieu's analysis of literature and painting. Fowler situates Bourdieu's cultural theory from a sociological perspective.

6   Bourdieu, 35.

lective) belief which knows and acknowledges it as a work of art," as Bourdieu phrases it.[7] Bourdieu sees works of art as *manifestations* of the field as a
whole, which also means that "[t]here is no other criterion of membership
of a field than the objective fact of producing effects within it."[8] So, Martel's
previous novel failed both because it simply did not sell well, and because it
produced no effect within the literary field as its value was not consecrated.
It is quite clear that when Martel talks about his previous novel, he talks
about something larger than "the novel itself." He talks about the processes
of production, dissemination and consumption that surround it. Martel's
reflection on the fiasco of his previous novel leads up to his meditations on
how *Life of Pi* came into being. Together with his need for recognition Martel repeatedly emphasizes his need for money. Despite his reassuring us that
"the fiasco did not affect me too much" the money issue (or the need for economic capital) keeps coming up. (Whereas we hear that money was one of
the reasons for going to India, Martel does not say if the writing of *Life of Pi*
was a way to improve his financial situation.) The following part of the author's note incorporates the story of how the author gave up on his novel
about Portugal in 1939, but as "[he] still had a little money," he travelled to
the south of India where he got his story for *Life of Pi* by being introduced to
the fictitious Piscine Patel (Pi), now living in Martel's native Toronto, Canada.[9] Finally (and here Martel again recognizes his own position within the
literary field), Martel thanks a series of (real as well as fictitious) people,
among them the Brazilian author Mr. Moacyr Scliar (whom I shall get back
to in just a moment) and the Canada Council for the Arts "without whose
grant I could not have brought together this story that has nothing to do
with Portugal in 1939."[10] All in all, the author's note calls attention to the
agents of the literary field, the importance of value and recognition and the
economic capital is needed for literature to be produced in the first place.

The fate of *Life of Pi* has turned out completely different from the fate of
Martel's previous novel. It certainly has not ended up like the kid no one
wants on their team, and in the following I will suggest some of the reasons
why. As it says in capital letters on the cover of my 2003 paperback edition,
bought from Amazon.com, it is the winner of The Man Booker Prize 2002.
The Man Booker Prize is a prestigious literary award. The winning of this lit-

---

7   Bourdieu, 35.
8   Bourdieu, 42.
9   Martel, ix.
10   Ibid., xiv.

erary award really made the media circus move. First because the organizers of the award mistakenly announced the novel's victory on their website a week before it was supposed to have been decided, and later as it was "revealed" that Martel had "stolen" the plot of the novel from a Brazilian novel from 1981, *Max e os Felinos* (translated into English in 1990 as *Max and the Cats*). After the award, *Life of Pi* has been widely translated and it is currently the number one bestseller of its publisher Canongate, as it also says on the cover – and also in capital letters. Canongate was voted Publisher of the Year partly on the strength of *Life of Pi* winning the Man Booker Prize. By the end of 2003 the novel was fifth in the Guardian's "fastsellers" list having sold 775,499 copies of its UK's publisher's edition, that is, excluding sales in other languages and US/Canadian editions generated by publishers there. (The paperback edition came out in May 2003.)[11] Including its translations the novel had sold close to two million copies by September 2003.[12] It is out in close to 40 countries and territories, representing over 30 languages.[13]

The dissemination and consumption of the novel have, in other words, increased tremendously with the award, and its effect is spreading in ever-widening circles. The publisher Canongate (in collaboration with Martel, who has recorded voice-overs for two of the scenes) has produced an "online promo" – which is a blend of animation, film and game (supposed to "do for the novel what the pop-video did for singles") – and whose purpose it is to "widen the recognition and appeal of books beyond the traditional book buying public."[14] What is perhaps even more important, the novel has been optioned for film by Fox 2000, a division of 20th Century Fox, apparently to be adapted by Dean Georgais and directed by M. Night Shyamalan (whose debut film *The Sixth Sense* starring Bruce Willis was 1999's second biggest money-maker and whose *Signs* starring Mel Gibson was also a success.)[15]

---

11   *The Guardian Unlimited*, 27 December 2003. <http://books.guardian.co.uk/ news/ table/0,6109,1110584,00.html > (26 may 2004).

12   *Politiken*, 6 September 2003.

13   "The Silence and the Glory." *The Guardian*, 6 September 2003. <http:// books.guardian.co.uk/bookerprize2002/story/0,12350,1036223,00.html > (26 may 2004).

14   "Life of Pi interactive movie back online." <http://www.canongate.net/ main. taf?_n=6> (26 may 2004).

15   *News India-Times*, 24 October 2003.
     <http://desitalk.newsindia-times.com/2003/10/24/cinema-48-top.html> (26 may 2004).

Shyamalan "reportedly connected with the project because the protagonist, Pi, hails from his birthplace – Pondicherry, Tamil-Nadu province in India."[16] The film will probably be released in 2005. Only time will tell if the film itself will be awarded (as *The English Patient* did – another Booker prize winner very successfully adapted for the big screen), but with the choice of Hollywood stars as writer and producer, the odds look quite good… Finally, Scliar's novel, which was first published in English by Ballentine Books in 1990, was published again in 2003 by Plume, and as Martel says when asked about the "scandal" and the similarities between his and Scliar's books, "He's actually done well with this scandal. He's had some offers from foreign publishers. He even joked in the Brazilian press that if you want to get published abroad you should orchestrate a plagiarism scandal."[17] In another newspaper article Scliar is quoted for having been hurt because Brazilian culture was being treated disrespectfully, "I consider Brazilian literature to be of the first magnitude, and I would like our culture to be judged on its own merits." Furthermore Scliar said that he considered the idea his "intellectual property." [18] In the end Sliar decided not to take legal actions against Martel. In an interview with Sabine Sielke Martel tones down the issue of plagiarism (which he could not justifiably be accused of as he had not read Scliar's novella), and instead suggested that the reason for the "scandal" brought up by Brazilian media was caused by the politically bad relationship between Brazil and Canada.[19]

It is obvious that the Man Booker prize has been extremely important for the cultural position of *Life of Pi* and its author. It shows how the processes of production, dissemination and consumption of literature are not only matters of literary quality and the author's genius. This is not to say that *Life*

---

16   *Hollywood.com News & Views*, 9 October 2003.
     <http://www.hollywood.com/news/detail/article/1730236> (26 may 2004).
17   "Piece of Pi." *Montreal Mirror*, 19-25 December 2002.
     < http://www.montrealmirror.com/ARCHIVES/2002/121902/books.html> (26 may 2004).
18   "Booker winner in plagiarism row," *The Guardian Unlimited*, 8 November 2002.
     <http://www.guardian.co.uk/international/story/0,3604,836088,00.html> (26 may 2004).
19   As these two paragraphs have shown, we are really engaged in radical contextualization here, but I think that if we are to account for the structure of the cultural field in relation to *Life of Pi* we have to take into account all these agents and positions.

of Pi is not a high quality novel (I certainly think it is) or that Martel is not an excellent writer (I certainly think he is), but if we want to explain how literature functions as cultural text, we need to recognize the material conditions of production and consumption of literature as well as the influence of publishers and (academic) institutions on the selection, distribution and evaluation of literature. In other words, we have to take into consideration the way in which novels exist as consumer products. Yet this is not all there is to it, and this is where Bourdieu's notion of the literary field and its reliance on symbolic capital enters the picture and proves its relevance for cultural text studies. Recognition, and thus value, in the literary field is not measured by economic success – sometimes economic success is even considered a problem within this field (as economic profit grows, discredit increases). As Bourdieu says this is because of the idea of disinterestedness that underlies the logic of this field: a writer of fiction is simply not *supposed* to produce his novels *for the market* – that is discredited within this field, or at least the most autonomous parts of the field.[20] Instead what does count is "prestige" or "authority" generated by the field itself. To gain such prestige and authority an agent within the field (such as the author of a novel) must accumulate specifically cultural capital,[21] and to do that he needs to recognize "the games of distinction" and the interrelations and interactions of the field "of which the work is only a silent trace."[22]

In a comment in *The Guardian Unlimited* Martel comments on the relationship between his role as a writer and the winning of the Man Booker Prize:

> Every serious writer hopes to see this faith recognized in some
> way at some time, whether in the form of a good review, an invi-
> tation to a festival – or a prize. I don't write to be reviewed well,
> to go to the So-and-So Literary Festival or to win Prize X, and I
> doubt any writer does, but the reviews, the invitations, the prizes
> are tokens of a faith that art matters. Alas, that faith is some-
> times hard, very hard, to keep alive.[23]

---

20 Bourdieu, 39.
21 Bourdieu, 82-83.
22 Bourdieu, 109.
23 "The Silence and the Glory." *The Guardian*, 6 September 2003. <http://books.guardian.co.uk/bookerprize2002/story/0,12350,1036223,00.html> (26 may 2004).

While playing the game of "art for art's sake," Martel again recognizes the importance of being in Bourdieu's words, "consecrated" in the literary field. "Serious writers" do this. Later in the same comment Martel affirms that whereas the prize has meant nothing for him as a person, it has meant "a whole lot" for him as a writer. About the money Martel simply states in an interview with Sabine Sielke that it is "nice" and that "[i]t makes for a more comfortable life."[24] Again we see how this corresponds with the logic of the literary field and the idea of the "pure artist." I am certainly not saying here that Martel *just pretends* to be disinterested (I would have no reason or basis for saying so); all I am saying is that the way he positions himself after getting the Man Booker Prize follows the logic of the literary field.

From Bourdieu's point of view a literary work gains its value and recognition through complex interplay between the agents of the cultural field. Literature is a kind of communication, but we would be deceived if we thought of it is this way: Author → work of art → reader (which Johnson refers to as "the idealism of Romantic conceptions of the artist as creator"), where the author – inspired by divine inspiration or his own talent – produces a work of art, and where this work of art is seen as a kind of self-contained object (perhaps recognized as part of literary history) read by a reader for pleasure, entertainment or education, and whose meaning can be extracted and explained in the light of the author's biography or the historical context of its production (what Bourdieu calls "external analysis").[25] Rather literature is part of a much more complex cultural field, where a novel will have to be recognized both as a purchasable, consumable commodity *and* as "symbolic goods." The value of a novel is consecrated by a complex interplay between the agents of the literary field and its logic, and by the relationship between the logic of the literary field and the commercial context of the novel. As we see in Martel's comment in *The Guardian* and in the "author's note," a writer of novels has to position himself within the literary field, that is, vis-à-vis other positions within that field. For *Life of Pi* these positions include publishers, critics, the institutions of literary prizes,

---

24   Sabine Sielke, "The Empathetic Imagination': An interview with Yann Martel." *Canadian Literature*, iss. 177 (Summer 2003).

25   This "Romantic notion of the artist" has been dismantled from all corners of contemporary literary theory, and though the dismantling has taken different directions and led to different "results," the Romantic notion of the artist is hard to find in literary theory, whereas it is a hard to kill concept in literary criticism, as my discussion of the "Martel scandal" illustrates.

the "media circus," other postcolonial writers, Hollywood, the international book market, and readers around the world, some of which I have discussed here.

> In short, what "makes reputation" is not, as provincial Rastignacs naïvely think, that or that "influential" person, this or that institution, review, magazine, academy, coterie, dealer or publisher; it is not even the whole set of what are sometimes called "personalities of the world of arts and letters;" it is the field of production, understood as the system of objective relations between these agents or institutions and as the site of the struggle for the monopoly of the power to consecrate, in which the value of works of art and belief in that value are continuously generated."[26]

What we are talking about here are, above all, the *relations* between agents within the field.

Within the literary field, it is not only the writer who must position himself, but also the other agents such as publishers and institutions. This becomes evident if we look closer at the Man Booker Prize.[27] The Man Booker Prize positions itself as "[o]ne of the world's most prestigious awards, and one of incomparable influence, it continues to be the pinnacle of ambition for every fiction writer. It has the power to transform the fortunes of authors, and even publishers' and "[t]he winner of the Man Booker Prize receives £50,000 and both the winner and the shortlisted authors are guaranteed a worldwide readership plus a dramatic increase in book sales."[28] This prize openly acknowledges its effect on the economic situation of writers and publishers alike, and it presents itself as an "influential" institution. It also emphasizes how its judges are chosen in order to secure "the total inde-

---

26 Bourdieu, 78.
27 In his thorough analysis of the cultural atmosphere in Britain since the late 1970s, Todd presents a survey of the Booker Prize and its winners up to 1995. This analysis rests on an impressive handling of statistic material and sales figures. Richard Todd, *Consuming Fictions* (Great Britain: Bloomsbury, 1996). For more on the Booker Prize, including an outline of its donor's past, see also chapter 4 of Graham Huggan's *The Postcolonial Exotic: Marketing the Margins* (London and New York: Routledge, 2001), 105-123.
28 The information about the Man Booker Prize is quoted from the Man Booker Prize's official website. <www.bookerprize.co.uk> (26 May 2004).

pendence and balance that lies at the heart of the choices made. It is that which gives the Man Booker Prize its very special distinction among literary prizes the world over." This means that the prize situates itself as a very influential yet "independent" agent within the literary field, and it emphasizes its own distinctiveness. The idea seems to be that whereas it is unaffected by other agents within the field (or outside it), its own effect on the field and its other agents is enormous. Yet if we look a little closer at how the prize works, we see that this is not really so, and that Bourdieu may well be right when he says that it is the *field* that generates the value of works of art and the belief in that value, not one "influential" institution.

As Huggan emphasizes, the Booker is now a meticulously staged media event.[29] Furthermore the procedures leading up to the shortlisting of authors display the relations between different agents within the field. United Kingdom publishers may each enter up to two novels. In addition to this, any title by an author who has previously won the Booker or Man Booker prize or who has been shortlisted in the last ten years may be submitted. Each publisher may also add a further list of up to five titles, of which the judges are requited to call in no less than eight and no more than twelve. This means that the first part of the evaluation is made by the publishers (and their criteria for what would count as "the very best of contemporary fiction" – whatever that is – may differ from the apparently "independent" jury). Ironically, *Life of Pi* was rejected by at least five larger publishers (including Penguin and Chatto & Windus) before it was accepted by the much smaller publisher Canongate. These publishers may now look back upon their rejection with regret, but as Dan Franklin of Jonathan Cape says, *Life of Pi* was much less likely to have been entered for the Man Booker Prize if it had been published by a top publisher due to the rule that limits each publisher to only two entries. Canongate may simply have had fewer suitable authors than some of the larger publishers. Furthermore, the authority of these larger publishers is a "credit-based value,"[30] in so far as their authority rely on the writers belonging to their stable: "If you have a lot of established authors and they find out you haven't entered their books you will soon discover you no longer have them," as Franklin says.[31] And then the publishers would lose some of their achieved

---

29   Huggan, 108.
30   Bourdieu, 78.
31   "Top Publishers rejected Booker winner." *The Guardian Unlimited*, 24 October 2002.
       <http://www.guardian.co.uk/uk_news/story/0,3604,817904,00.html> (26 May 2004).

authority. So it is a question of how much symbolic capital a publisher is will-ing to risk by entering a "young" writer instead of an already consecrated writer. By the same logic, Canongate's symbolic capital increases by them having a Man Booker Prize winner among their writers. And by the same log-ic Martel's next novel will already have some value in the field, "simply" by be-ing written by a previous Booker Prize winner.

So the publishers and their positions within the literary field function in relation to the positions of authors and novels, and a change in an agent's position means a change in the structure of the field as such. We also see this in the demands that the publishers are required to meet when submitting a title: "With the submitting of a title the publisher agrees to contribute £3000 towards general publicity if the book reaches the shortlist" and "to spend not less than £1,000 on direct, paid for media advertising of the winning book, including a winning poster or show card, within three months of the an-nouncement of the award," and the publisher is asked "to agree to the pro-duction of a promotional CD, featuring readings from the openings of the six shortlisted novels." This means both that the publisher is an active agent in the process of producing public recognition of the Booker (both the prize itself and its winner) and that the "media circus" (to the use words from the "author's note" in *Life of Pi*) must be taken into account. Before the names of the shortlisted novels appear to the reading public, a lot of "cultural produc-tion" has already taken place. With Bourdieu we can say that economic capi-tal is needed to produce cultural goods, but unless it is converted to symbol-ic capital, there is no basis for profit – either in the case of "distinction" prof-it or "economic" profit.

The distinctiveness of prizes within the cultural field is almost always em-phasized. In the music industry, for instance, there are prizes that position themselves as "independent" prizes, thereby signalling that they are not, or do not want to be, recognized as related to other (mainly commercial) posi-tions within the same field. An example from my own Danish context is the music award "Steppeulven" (established 2003), which is a representative case of such an alternative (in this case to Danish Music Awards). On Steppeul-ven's website it says that the organization behind it wants to "celebrate the best of Danish music on its own terms" and that they "naturally hope for the attention of the public and the media, but "Steppeulven" will never develop into a TV-transmitted media event."[32] Such "alternative" positioning recog-

---

32   Steppeulven's homepage. <http://www.steppeulv.dk/fdm.htm> (26 May 2004).

nizes "the ultimate values of 'disinterestedness',"[33] but as the quotes show, there is no way in which it can work without its cultural field, and unless it is recognized. Both the Man Booker Prize and "Steppeulven" position themselves within a cultural field *in relation to* the other agents in the field. It is always as a question of "being different," and this is most discernible in relation to newcomers in the field (like "Steppeulven" – The Booker Prize has been in the business for 35 years and has long since been consecrated). "To 'make one's name' [*faire date*] means making one's *mark*, achieving recognition (in both senses) of one's *difference* from other producers, especially the most consecrated of them; at the same time, it means *creating a new position* beyond the positions presently occupied, *ahead* of them, in the *avant-garde*."[34]

As I have tried to illustrate here, a lot of cultural production has already taken place before a novel (especially when it is by a "young" writer) reaches its reading public. And of course it does not stop here as my discussion of *Life of Pi*'s effect on its author, publisher and other agents has indicated. Bourdieu suggests that there are three competing principles of legitimacy within the structure of the field of cultural production. First, there is the recognition "granted by the set of producers who produce for other producers, their competitors, i.e., by the autonomous self-sufficient world of 'art for art's sake,' meaning art for artists." Second, there is the consecration "bestowed by the dominant fractions of the dominant class and by private tribunals, such as *salons*, or public, state-guaranteed ones, such as academies…" Third, there is the consecration "bestowed by the choice of ordinary consumers, the "mass audience."[35] Let us now consider Bourdieu's second principle in the light of *Life of Pi* and how I have used it to "do cultural studies."

Life of Pi was required reading for a seminar I taught in the English programme at Aalborg University in the spring of 2000 called "Languages of Storytelling in the New Millennium." The novel went on the reading list for the course actually before I had finished (or even begun) reading it myself. Now, this may not be as irresponsible as it sounds. I came across the title of the novel in a review in a Danish newspaper (I had never heard of the writer Yann Martel before), which reviewed the novel on account of it get-

---

33   Bourdieu, 79.
34   Bourdieu, 106.
35   Bourdieu, 50-51.

ting the Man Booker Prize. This newspaper is an acknowledged agent within the field of cultural production in Denmark, and it has the authority to review "good" and "serious" literature. I knew that the Booker is a prestigious prize and that there is often a great fuss over who gets the prize and on account of what, so I thought that no matter what the novel was really about, and no matter what "literary quality" it may have, the very fact that it had gotten the Booker was enough for me to include it on my reading list: if it got the Booker, then there must be something *in* or *about* the novel that made the judges of that institution choose it (as the prize awards "the very best of contemporary fiction"). Then I heard about the "scandal" that Martel had "stolen" the plot, and that really settled it. What if one of the languages of storytelling in the new millennium simply is to repeat already existing stories? Then we would at last get rid of the author who was claimed dead in literary theory decades ago, but who still lives on in the greater part of the literary field … (Obviously Martel's "borrowing" of Scliar's plot was *not* the reason he got the prize which, literary theory notwithstanding, insists on the authenticity and originality of literary works and authors). In one way or the other, all the fuss over the novel convinced me that it would be relevant for my course.

So it went on my reading list. I ordered it at the University Bookshop (whom we can include among the agents of the literary field), who ordered it from its British publisher. The students bought the book (and thereby increased its sales figures) and, what is perhaps even more important for the consecration of the novel, some of them ended up writing semester projects about it. Consequently they began reading reviews and articles about the novel from newspapers and journals. In a month or so they will have produced their own academic work on the novel. Of course I am not the only one to have used the novel in teaching: the novel has ended up in quite number of a university courses. I have seen in on the syllabus for English 101 Courses, Recent Anglophone Canadian Fiction courses, World Literature courses, and a course in philosophy and religion in literature, to mention but a few. It has also entered the syllabus of high school courses. And an abundance of papers, articles and projects about the novel can be expected to appear, and they will then contribute to the recognition of the novel. In this way the recognition of the value of the novel is further generated by its reception within the educational system. The educational systems, the publishers, the academic world, and the media in this way collaboratively produce and reproduce the value within the literary field of this novel. One could argue that at this point in the process of generating value, it is not so much a question of market and money, but more a question of generating and regenerating symbolic capital, which is what is required for a book to be acknowledged and recognized.[36]

The novel, by the way, is about a sixteen year old boy, Pi, who – on his way from India to Canada in the 1970s together with his family and the animals of the family's zoo – survives a shipwreck, ends up in a lifeboat with a zebra, a hyena, an orang-utan, and a Bengal tiger. After some days only Pi and the tiger (called Richard Parker) are left. Together they survive two hundred twenty-seven days on the Pacific Ocean before they make it ashore in Mexico. I say "by the way" because so far my discussion of the novel could have been a discussion of any novel or indeed any work of art and how works of art are circulated, recognized and perceived, and it is mainly because of the radical contextualization of the novel that Bourdieu's approach invites that I have been able to postpone a presentation of the plot of the novel until now. In the remaining part of this essay I will think about what *difference* it makes that *Life of Pi* is a novel and what it is about *this* novel that gives it its value. This will again bring me back to the relevance of literature within cultural studies.

The novel is organized around and plays off against each another two paradigms of human understanding: a scientific paradigm and a religious paradigm. The scientific paradigm is described in terms of its facts, logic, reason and empiricism, and the religious paradigm is described in terms of its reliance on belief, mystery and love. Quite appropriately we learn on the first page of the first chapter of the novel that Pi's majors were zoology and religious studies. As appropriate is Pi's statement two pages later that "Sometimes I got my majors mixed up."[37] Throughout the novel the boundaries between these two paradigms and apparent oppositions are transgressed, questioned and deconstructed. What is most important in this context is the idea of "strange facts." "Strange facts" are situated between the two underlying paradigms, relying on characteristics of both. We find examples of strange facts even in the first part of the novel, which is set in a familiar world working according to a familiar logic: this is India in the 1970s, a historical, factual and political world. Among other strange facts, we here hear of the many examples of animals coming to surprising living arrangements. Strange as they may be, these facts are acceptable as facts. We also hear of Pi's education into

---

36 There is much to be said about the whole issue of canon-formation, but that would be beyond the scope of this essay, though I realize that canon-formation is highly relevant for cultural text studies.

37 Martel, 5.

the three major religions Hinduism, Christianity, and Islam and the "strange facts" that they rely on. In Part Two, set in the unfamiliar or defamiliarized world of the lifeboat in the Pacific Ocean, itself a "strange fact," the idea of strange facts becomes more and more important. Quite early on we hear this:

> Of greater significance to me was the strange fact that Richard Parker had not killed it. In the normal course of things he should have killed the zebra. That's what predators do: they kill prey. In the present circumstances, where Richard Parker would be under tremendous mental strain, fear should have brought out an exceptional level of aggression. The zebra should have been properly butchered.[38]

Later on we hear of another strange fact as Pi meets another man on another lifeboat, and finally there is the strange island that Pi comes to. In the course of Part Two the strange facts become stranger and stranger and less and less factual and with the island it seems that factuality is almost completely gone, and Pi's observation about it is "based on intuition rather than hard evidence."[39]

"Strange facts" thus come to form a third paradigm of understanding underpinning the novel. The novel to a large extend explores this paradigm as it continuously tests how strange facts can get and still be accepted as facts. This becomes quite obvious in Part Three of the novel. This part overtly interrogates and reflects on the two (or three) underlying paradigms in novel. In relation to this, it examines the status of storytelling in the novel and the function of storytelling in a broader context. Consequently the third part of the novel returns to some of the questions raised in the "author's note." The interrogation of the novel's underlying paradigms happens through a dialogue between Pi and two Japanese from the Maritime Department in the Japanese Ministry of Transport, Mr. Tomohiro Okamoto and Mr. Atsuro Chiba. This dialogue takes place at the Benito Juárez Infirmary in Tomatlán, Mexico, where Pi ended up after his more than two hundred days at sea. In the story Mr. Tomohiro and Mr. Chiba's job is to find out how the ship sank (for insurance matters), but they also have the narrative function of examining Pi's story critically. Mr. Okamoto and Mr. Chiba pick apart Pi's story looking for "flaws" in its details to see if the story holds up. (Do bananas float? Is Pi's island botanically possi-

---

38   Martel, 109.
39   Martel, 271.

ble? How likely is it that two lifeboats would meet in the Pacific Ocean? How do you determine meerkat bones?) They find that the story does *not* hold up. Their *disbelief* in the story is a result of them being "reasonable," which means that belief (here in Pi's story) is subordinated to the science paradigm of the story: it is not accepted unless it is supported by this paradigm. Pi reacts strongly against Mr. Okamoto and Mr. Chiba's judgement of the story:

> "If you stumble at mere believability, what are you living for? Is-
> n't love hard to believe?"
> "Mr. Patel – "
> "Don't you bully me with your politeness! Love is hard to be-
> lieve, ask any lover. Life is hard to believe, ask any scientist. God
> is hard to believe, ask any believer. What is your problem with
> hard to believe?"
> "We're just being reasonable"
> "So am I! I applied my reason at every moment. Reason is excel-
> lent for getting food, clothing and shelter. Reason is the very best
> tool kit. Nothing beats reason for keeping tigers away. But be ex-
> cessively reasonable and you risk throwing out the universe with
> the bathwater."[40]

Yet Mr. Okamoto and Mr. Chiba keep insisting that Pi's story is *extremely* hard to believe, which it is within the logical framework they apply. Pi then wants to know if they did not *like* his story. To Mr. Okamoto and Mr. Chiba this is a quite different question from did they *believe* his story. This suggests that within the framework Mr. Okamoto and Mr. Chiba represent, stories have a function to please and be memorable, but they have little to do with *reality*. The are inventions, not "straight facts" as this part of the dialogue nicely illustrates:

> "So you want another story?"
> "Uhh . . . no. We would like to know what really happened."
> "Doesn't the telling of something always become a story?"
> "Uhh . . . perhaps in English. In Japanese a story would have an
> element of *invention* in it. We don't want any invention. We want
> the 'straight facts', as you say in English."
> "Isn't telling about something – using words, English or Japan-

---

40   Martel, 297-298.

ese – already something of an invention? Isn't just looking upon
this world already something of an invention?"
"Uhh . . . "
"The world isn't just the way it is. It is how we understand it, no?
And in understanding something, we bring something to it, no?
Doesn't that make life a story?"
"Ha! Ha! Ha! You are very intelligent, Mr. Patel."
Mr. Chiba: "**What is he talking about?**"
"**I have no idea.**"
Pi Patel: "You want words that reflect reality?"
"Yes."
"Words that do not contradict reality?"
"Exactly."
"But tigers don't contradict reality."
"Oh, please, no more tigers."
"I know what you want. You want a story that won't surprise
you. That will confirm what you already know. That won't make
you see higher or further or differently. You want a flat story. An
immobile story. You want dry, yeastless factuality."
. . .
"Here's another story."[41]

In this part of the dialogue we see two conflicting views on stories and what
their status is vis-à-vis "reality." Mr. Okamoto and Mr. Chiba represent a
view where language can represent reality "as it really is," and they believe in
a one-to-one correspondence between words and reality. To them this is not
the language of storytelling. Pi, on the other hand, represents a view that
challenges the representational notion of language and any essential difference between the language of storytelling and other kinds of language. Instead Pi's view suggests that "reality" to a large extent is an effect of how we
see it, present it and understand it. And to understand something, Pi suggests, we make a story of it.[42] In Pi's view, the difference is not between "in-

---

41 Martel, 302-303.
42 Pi's view here essentially represents poststructuralist thought about the non-
mimetic nature of language as well as the notion of narrative as a mode of understanding that we find in the many variants of contemporary narratology. Etymologically "to narrate" derives from *gnarus:* knowing or skilled (*Oxford English Dictionary*) as narratologists have pointed out.

vention" and "straight facts" but between "flat," predictable stories and stories that will make us see higher or further or differently.

Pi then tells another story – this time without the animals. This story is a brief, horrible story (as also Mr. Okamoto and Mr. Chiba comment) of how Pi survived together with three other people – his mother, a cook and a Chinese sailor. The cook killed the sailor and Pi's mother before Pi eventually killed him. Pi survived partly by eating the cook. This is a much more unpleasant but much more likely story, and it is based on the same "facts" in the novel as the story with the animals is; namely that the ship sank and Pi survived two hundred twenty-seven days before arriving on the coast of Mexico. As Pi puts it, "neither [of the stories] makes a factual difference to you."[43] Pi calls attention to the impossibility of deciding which story is true and which is not. He also emphasizes that for the facts in the novel they are equally valid, or invalid, "in both stories the ship sinks, my entire family dies, and I suffer." Pi then asks the crucial question in the novel, "*Which is the better story?*" Pi is very relieved when Mr. Okamoto and Mr. Chiba choose the story with the animals. The story with the animals challenges the scientific and rationalist paradigm, whereas the story without the animals makes sense within it.

The novel openly prefers the story with the animals and the paradigm of understanding it relies on. This echoes the statement about art and literature made in the "author's note." Pi and Martel seem to suggest that literature offers itself as a rescue from "worthless dreams and believing in nothing." Accordingly, literature has a function that differs significantly from the one we see represented in Mr. Okamoto and Mr. Chiba's conception of stories. In our society, Martel explicitly suggests, we should support our artists: without them and their cultural products, we will end up with "dry, yeastless factuality." From this point of view the novel reads like a kind of "poetic manifesto." Both the author's note and the third part of the novel bring forward the idea that literature can make us see "higher, further and differently." This places art and the artist in a special position vis-à-vis their context (cultural, historical, political and economic) here at the beginning of the twenty-first century. Yet this idea of art and the artist sounds almost like Percy Bysshe Shelley's "Defence of Poetry" (1821, published 1840), which also operates with the "two classes of mental action, which are called reason and imagination" to which poetry is related, and which is famous for its statements that "the

---

43   Martel, 317.

most unfailing herald, companion, and follower of the awakening of a great
people to work a beneficial change in opinion or institution, is poetry," and
that poets are "the unacknowledged legislators of the world." For Pi (and
Martel) "the better story" comes to share many of the features of the religious paradigm in the novel, and since this paradigm has been under heavy
attack over the past couples of centuries, it seems as if Martel suggests that
we look to literature for a philosophy of life and for a kind of filling in of the
(partly emptied) position of religion in contemporary Western culture. Martel criticizes the emphasis on factuality and rationality that he sees as identifying contemporary Western culture. By being "excessively reasonable," we
risk "throwing out the universe with the bathwater" as Pi phrases it in his
discussion with Mr. Okamoto and Mr. Chiba.

Fictions like *Life of Pi* have great potential regarding the willing suspen-
sion of disbelief – those famous five words of another Romantic poet – and
Pi repeatedly emphasizes that the point of his story is not to stumble at
mere believability. So fictions and stories are needed, and they have a cultural function that becomes vital in the novel and in the "author's note."
They are *worth* something (they can prevent us from ending up having
worthless dreams). This value of fiction and storytelling is not economic
value, but – as Martel presents it – a far more important symbolic value ex-
ceeding the rational and economic framework of our everyday life. In (yet
another) post-Booker interview Martel describes how he had composed the
story so that it would get more and more difficult to believe in its "strange
facts," despite the novel's realism.[44] Hereby he had wanted to test the reader's concept of reality. "Rational readers" would give up; some would try to
find "reasonable" explanations to the most fantastic episodes; and some
would buy the story with the animals though this requires a belief in belief,
mystery and love. In the third part of the novel it is then up to the reader to
choose between the two stories, as it is to Mr. Okamoto and Mr. Chiba.
When I read the novel for the first time, I was terrified by the alternative
story in Part Three. (I suppose that would make me a "non-rational reader,"
or perhaps a "post-romantic reader.") It says at the end of Part One (the
page before the ship sinks) that "*This story has a happy ending.*" This can of
course refer to the plot in the sense that Pi survives, but to me the happy
ending of the novel is above all that the "better story" is not replaced by the
"other story." The closing chapter of the novel is Mr. Okamato's report to

---

44   "Zoorealisme," *Information*, 8 September 2003.

the Oika Shipping Company with regards to insurance claims, and it ends with the following paragraph:

> As an aside, story of sole survivor, Mr. Piscine Molitor Patel, Indian citizen, is an astounding story of courage and endurance in the face of extraordinary difficult and tragic circumstances. In the experience of this investigator, his story is unparalleled in the history of shipwrecks. Very few castaways can claim to have survived so long at sea as Mr. Patel, and none in the company of an adult Bengal tiger. [45]

The animals have the last word in the novel.

To conclude: The novel's underlying conception of literature as well as its scepticism towards rationality and "dry yeastless factualty" go back at least to the Romanticists as epitomized by Shelley. At the same time the novel acknowledges the different logics it necessarily must deal with – both within the literary field and within its economic contexts. I think that both aspects and logics must be taken into account when we look at the novel as a cultural text and when we try to determine the relevance of literary studies for cultural studies and vice versa. Over the past decade or two a change seems to have happened both within the literary field itself and between the literary field and its economic context – a change which moderates the sharp division between the underlying logics of the economic world and the art world respectively. This may have to do with the three kinds of consecration that Boudieu operates with. I am not sure that they are *competing* principles anymore. A novel is not necessarily discredited just because it sells well (and succeeds according to the economic logic), and bestsellers can be consecrated by the educational systems as well. This also relates to the reconceptualization (broadening) of the literary object that cultural text studies relies on. Furthermore, the market of symbolic goods is not as exclusive as it has been before. Texts are more easily accessible because of information technology. Poetry, for example, is now available on the internet, so the potential audience need no longer find a bookshop and buy a book of poems. This is what the promo for *Life of Pi* makes use of. Reviews and articles and other secondary material are also available and from many different places in the world (witness the many electronic references in this essay. I can hardly begin to

---

45   Martel, 319.

imagine how I would have found just the materials and information about *Life of Pi* that I have used in my discussion here fifteen years ago). This, I think, has changed the structure of the literary field as a whole.

I would like to end this essay with a few reflections on some of the other cultural changes that have happened since Bourdieu wrote his essays in the mid 1980s and which my discussion of "the better story" has pointed towards. These reflections – like Pi's island – are based on intuition rather than hard evidence. Apart from that they may have very little to do with *Life of Pi*.

The value of "the better story" that Martel emphasizes is not only found within the literary field, and symbolic capital is no longer (if it ever were) only a valid capital with regards to the arts. Martel has emphasized that facts are only the foundation for how we build our lives. If we think of goods that may appear less "symbolic" (in Bourdieu's sense) than art, for example kitchens or cars, we see how they are tied up in stories. For example, in Denmark we may no longer buy "just" a kitchen for our home, but a "sociable kitchen" or in Danish "SAMTALEKØKKEN®."[46] This word entered the Danish language in 2000, and it refers to the kind of kitchen that gives room for experience, "quality time," and social life. With the kitchen we at the same time buy all the stories that go with it, which is something that the producers of kitchens are well aware of and use in their advertising. When we buy organic food, it is not only because it is better quality, but also because we like to see ourselves and think of ourselves in terms of the stories that go with organic food.[47] And if some people would not even dream of buying a Citroën Berlingo (an MPV – first used to refer to a particular kind of family car seating six or more in 1999 according to the *Oxford English Dictionary*), it is mainly because the car signals a *life style* that they do not identify with – there is nothing *wrong* with the car *as a car*.[48] These people may identify much more with a SUV (yet to be included in the *Oxford English Dictionary*), though they only need a car to get them from home and to work. All this, I think, has to do with the function of stories, and the stories we tell about ourselves and the world. It is again a question of positioning.

Then there is the notion of symbolic capital. Even companies that pro-

---

46   The word "samtalekøkken" is a registrered trademark of the Danish kitchen producer *Kvik*.

47   Words like "quality time" and "organic food" are also fairly new words which have only been around for two to three decades.

48   Citroën is a French make of car.

duce goods aimed at the market and for economic profit, and which should in theory not have to worry about symbolic capital, now have "ethical accounts" as a supplement to the financial accounts. The idea of ethical accounts became important by the mid 1990s. In 1997 Shell's business principles came to include a commitment to support human rights and to contribute to sustainable development (Shell was among the first international companies to do this).[49] The company's environmental and social performance is reported annually in the HSE-reports (health, safety and environment) that have appeared since 1998. These reports are accessible to the public, which is no surprise as they have an important branding function (if nobody knew about them, they would not be as valuable). To make money *by all means* is not really credited in contemporary society, though of course making money is still the point for the company. To make money *and* be a "responsible" company (ecologically and ethically, for example) is an effective way of branding.[50] The whole issue of branding relies on both the economic logic and the symbolic logic and on storytelling and "the better story." The logics of branding and the importance of stories also underlie the apparently strange phenomenon of producers of goods who do not want to sell as many products as possible. Why sell limited editions of CDs or DVDs instead of selling as many as possible? And why is it that the producers of Marlboro Classics clothes or of Police sunglasses go out to buy up parties of their goods if a department store has bought a lot of goods to sell to as many people as possible?[51] And why is it that Bang & Olufsen only sell their televisions in certain Bang & Olufsen stores, even if they could probably sell more if they were available everywhere?[52] The answer has to do with the fact that *if*

---

49   Shell is a Dutch/British company. In 1907 the Dutch Royal Dutch Petroleum Company merged with the British Shell Transport and Trading Company p.l.c . and the Royal Dutch/Shell Group was formed.

50   Another indication of the importance of "responsibility" for business practice can be seen from the fact that you can now get an MSc in Responsibility and Business Practice (for example at University of Bath in Britain).

51   Marlboro Classics is a fashion brand licensed by the Italian Marzotto Group. Marlboro is a cigarette brand from Philip Morris, the world's largest tobacco company. Police sunglasses are produced by American Eastern States Eyewear, and the collection of "hip, aggressive eyewear" is now represented worldwide by soccer star David Beckham who – as a fashion and style icon – becomes spokesperson for the brand and the life style it wants to signal.

52   Bang & Olufsen is a Danish company that produces design hi-fi products such as music systems, televisions and telephones that are sold worldwide.

these goods became public property, the stories that they rely on (which all have that in common that they emphasize *difference* from "ordinary" goods of the same kinds) would fall apart – they simply have as their basis that these are goods that only a limited group of people can own. So to sell as many as possible of these products would undermine their existence. The mechanisms of some of the distribution and value of these kinds of goods show some of the logics of the literary field, and they cannot all be explained within the economic framework. Furthermore they show how we use both goods and stories (and the interrelations between them) to frame our own lives. Of course I am not saying that the logic of the economic world is *reversed* (as Bourdieu says it is in the literary field), but even if the logic of the literary field and the emphasis on symbolic capital are only "tools" within the economic world, they are so central for the value of some kinds of goods that we have to take it into account if we want to understand how they work in contemporary culture.

Thus, we may be moving towards a kind of "dream society" where products of many different kinds are used to create or support our lives, or more correctly, the stories we tell ourselves – and others – about our lives.[53] Certain kinds of goods can generate more "dream value" than others: by wearing, eating, driving in or living in certain objects implying certain stories, we tell ourselves and others who we are/like to be. Buying certain products is not so much a question of showing that one has the economic means to do so but rather to show how we see ourselves as *differing* from others. And products with the ability to generate dream value are not necessarily expensive – sometimes it is more importance that they are rare or even unique. It is a question of "the better story" behind the product. This way of thinking owes something to the idea of "commodification" emphasized in much postmodern thinking. By puzzling together various stories (different or alike) one can compose one's own *unique* story (This is of course not to say that you can freely chose whatever life story you like). Rolf Jensen pushes it to extremes when he says, "[t]he tangible product will be a byproduct." Maybe best illustrated if one pictures meeting a friend who has been shopping, hap-

---

53 *The Dream Society* is the title of Rolf Jensen's 1999 book, which I risk mentioning, investing whatever little symbolic capital I may have within the academic world. Jensen was director of Copenhagen Institute for Futures Studies from 1988. He left the institute in 2001, founding his own enterprise and naming it "Dream Company, Inc." *The Dream Society* has been translated from Danish into seven other languages: English, Dutch, Japanese, Korean, Mandarin, Estonian and Russian.

pily exclaiming "I bought the loveliest story about loyalty and then this watch came along with it.'[54] Producers of goods (symbolic and other) are very aware of this, and I think that students of culture should be as well.

One of the critical keywords in Wolfrey's book is "narrative," and there is of course much more to be said on the issue of the cultural function of narrative, the idea of a "dream society," and the relationship between them. (A way to start would be to read Baudrillard and consider his idea of the hyperreal.) All I have tried to do here is to point to a few examples where it seems to me that Pi is very right when he says that stories are *worth* something in the sense that they prevent us from having worthless dreams. When thinking about the field of cultural production, we should perhaps also think in terms of a kind of "dream capital" intrinsically related to the functions of stories in contemporary Western culture.

---

54   Dream Company, Inc.
     <http://www.dreamcompany.dk/en/contribution/books/dreamsociety.php> (26 May 2004).

Discourse Analysis as a Non-Method of Cultural Research

Anders Horsbøl
Department of Communication
Aalborg University

Introduction

In this article I will offer a short presentation of discourse analysis as cultural analysis. "Discourse" is an ambiguous and controversial term, and, accordingly, discourse analysis has not gone in one but rather several directions with roots and applications in various disciplines such as linguistics, communication theory, history (of ideas) and sociology. I do not intend to give an account of or make a sketch for the history of these different directions. Rather, I seek to present one version of discourse analysis – a version which is especially influenced by Norman Fairclough's critical discourse analysis, although nonetheless differing in some respects from Fairclough's model. When I refer to *the* discourse analysis below, it is not meant in a totalizing manner, but is, rather, a simple consequence of textual economy.

The article has four parts. The first part is a short, epistemological prelude, which sketches the epistemological orientation of discourse analysis and its fundamentally dialectical position. In the second part, I present a set of key concepts, which, according to my interpretation, is foundational for the theoretical universe of discourse analysis. In the third part I, then, introduce two currents in discourse analysis which seem particularly promising. Finally, in the fourth part I return to the epistemological status of discourse analysis in order to discuss questions of method and critique. Thus, while the first part of the article shows *why* discourse analysis is cultural analysis, the subsequent parts are about *how* this is the case.

The Epistemological Orientation of Discourse Analysis

Which questions does discourse analysis answer? How can we define the knowledge interest of discourse analysis if not tautologically as "the analysis of discourses?" Discourse analysis, I offer, investigates *meaning in social practices*. Thus, discourse analysis is not interested in what the world might have looked like prior to collective signifying systems or formations of meaning, and discourse analysis is not interested in psychological phenomena. Or, following the ideas of the sociologist Niklas Luhmann's,[55] discourse analysis deals neither with biological nor with psychological but with social systems. Of course, the social world implies and/or has a necessary prerequisite biological life and consciousness; however, it is not reducible to either and can be studied in its own right.

This insight is not particular to discourse analysis, but rather places it within a larger cultural-analytical and sociological framework. Discourse analysis investigates culture – it investigates the webs of significance that people spin and have spun around themselves, and it investigates how knowledge-about-the-world, social relations and social identities inform and are informed by inter-human practices. Even though this interest is not peculiar to discourse analysis, it is, nevertheless, important to hold on to it as the overall aim. If the conceptual specialization of discourse analysis does not, in the end, add any insights into the formation of social meaning, it loses its significance.

Structure and Action: Discourse analysis investigates social constructions *qua* social constructions. This constructivism implies a structure- as well as an action-dimension. Structure, here, pertains to the frames and resources available to the formation of meaning which, in discourse analysis, is often labeled "conditions of possibility." This is the *langue*-dimension or the systemic dimension of discourse analysis. Here, the basic idea is that meaning emerges from a reservoir of signification, which both limits and allows for its formation. Discourse analysis tries to shed light on this realm of signification, which is not a cause of but a condition for the actual formation of meaning.

Action pertains to the actual formation of meaning, which takes place in concrete practices. Here, the stress is on meaning as an actualization or an instantiation. The basic idea here is the non-deterministic conception that the formation of meaning can never be deduced from the pre-given realm of signification: even though the formation of meaning does not create meaning (*ex nihilo*), it does not simply reproduce meaning either. One could also call this action dimension the *parole*-dimension of discourse analysis, though *parole*, here, is neither arbitrary nor structurally imprinted.

These two dimensions are not independent. On the contrary, there is a

---

55   See Luhmann (1984).

mutual and conditional relationship between structure and action, which Fairclough terms "dialectical." The signifying structures are fundamental to the formations of meaning, which, in their turn, leave sediments of new signification, which, again, function as resources for future formations of meaning, and so on. This position is not some kind of soft middle ground between structuralism and postmodernism, but a concerted effort to understand the social formation of meaning in terms of situated action. However, the question remains as to how this general theoretical position can be conceptualized in a way that allows for cultural *analyses*. The following deals with that question.

THE KEY CONCEPTS OF DISCOURSE ANALYSIS

Discourse analysis is distinguished from other kinds of cultural analysis in its view on how social meaning and signification are organized. Here, I sum up this view in four key concepts – "discourse," "genre," "order of discourse" and "text" – according to four discourse analytical perspectives on how social meaning and signification are organized.

Discourse:[56] I understand discourse, first of all, as a unit or a "bundle" of signification.[57] Thus, discourse analysis does not regard a statement or a point of view as isolated, but tries to assign it to a larger context. This context is the discourse which the statement not only belongs to but also presupposes if it is to make sense at all. The discourse is the horizon within which each statement acquires its meaning.

A discourse consists of statements, which do not simply describe but also produce and form reality. In that sense, a discourse is a *construction* of reality. Furthermore, discourses are *social* phenomena; there are no private discourses; discourses are not related to individuals but to communication. Discourses are also historical phenomena, which change over time: they come into being, develop, transform, multiply and disappear.

---

56 A similar interpretation of discourse can be found in Horsbøl (2003; 2004).

57 The bundle metaphor is borrowed from Reisig/Wodak 2000. Other discourse metaphors are "frame of reference" (Burr 1995); a *pattern* in language (Phillips/ Jørgensen 1999), a system of dispersion between a number of statements (Foucault 1969); A *speech process* or a *meaningfulness* (Andersen 1999);, a *structured totality* (Laclau 1993); a *river* of text and speech through time (Jäger 1999) and *arrangement* of significations (Keller 1997), and *ensemble* of ideas and concepts (Hajer 1995) and a *perspective* on the social field (Fairclough 1995a).

We find discourses in the *plural*, also synchronically. Like hermeneutics, discourse analysis suggests that the formation of meaning always takes place in a pre-given signifying field. Discourse, however, is a more local phenomenon than the hermeneutic horizon of understanding. A discourse is not a global horizon of understanding that defines a whole culture, but a unity of meaning among others which disseminates into (and constitutes) different social fields or engages in fights over defining the borderline between different fields.

Discourse as an *analytical* concept is used by Fairclough, and by discourse analysis in general, in the rather vague sense of "the language used in representing a given social practice from a particular point of view" (Fairclough 1995b: 56), and discourses are "ways of signifying experience from a particular point of view. (Fairclough 1995a: 132).[58] In Foucault, from whom Fairclough borrows the concept, we find a more elaborate definition: a discourse is the formation of *objects, subjects, concepts and strategies*:[59] Firstly, discourse is an objectification – discourse forms its own objects of knowledge, and the formation of these objects is logically prior to their modifications. Secondly, a discourse allows subject positions: that is, it assigns the location from which one can legitimately and meaningfully speak within a given discourse. In that sense, the discourse marks out a field of social relations and identities, not by establishing relations between pre-given subjects, but by establishing the subjects themselves. Thirdly, a discourse is a network or a *conceptual field of associations*. This should not be understood as a system of rules and regulations analogous to philosophical systems; the discourse does not start out from fundamental assumptions (about the human life, ethics, society, and etc.), but takes its point of non-departure in actual statements as they unfold in discursive practices. Therefore, the unity of the discourse is both *relational* and *productive*; the discourse establishes the link between objects, subjects and concepts, and it allows for new (links between) objects, subjects and concepts to emerge. Finally, a discourse is situated in an *interdiscursive field*, which is just as fundamental to the discourse as the formation of objects, subjects and concepts. A discourse does not emerge *qua* dis-

---

58 Fairclough also operates with a double discourse concept which might give rise to some confusion – as, for example, Frandsen (1996) points out – but which is essentially clear enough: "Discourse" (with capital D) means that language and the user of language are regarded as social practice while "a discourse" refers to the specific signifying perspective. Here, he refers to the latter meaning.
59 My explanation here is primarily based on Foucault (1969).

course only to subsequently enter into an interdiscursive field. It is always already positioned in relation to other discourses. Though the interdiscursive field might function as "the outside," it is an outside, which is co-determinant for the discourse itself. The discourse does not exist prior to its orientation toward what it is not.

Operationalization of the Concept of Discourse: The Foucauldian notion of discourse is still quite abstract, and it is difficult to transform it into an analytical concept. We find a more operational version of the Foucauldian concept in Åkerstrøm Andersen (1994), who defines discourse as a presentation of three "speech-orders" namely, a descriptive, a narrative and an argumentative order, respectively.

"*The descriptive order* organizes the way in which we perceive objects, their qualities and relations in discourse" (Åkerstrøm 1994: 15). This is the *what* of the discourse, which investigates how phenomena are produced, classified and coupled. *The narrative order* pertains to discourse as the realm of action: "The narrative order forms a number of subject positions that individuals and collectives can occupy, whereby they are enabled to act *as if* they were rational or had a free will (ibid.: 16). Åkerstrøm Andersen mentions five differences which specify the formation of subject positions: "outside/inside" (who is allowed access to discourse in the first place), "up/down" (how are the positions distributed within the discourse according to responsibility, competence and status), "past/future" (how does the subject span a realm of experience and a horizon of expectation), "subject/object" (who is placed as active subject and who is the object that the subject works upon) and "helper/opponent" (from whom and how can the subject expect opposition and support).[60] "*The argumentative order* organizes the way in which the discourse couples predicates when one reasons" (ibid.: 18). The argumentative order constitutes a frame for the formulation and approval of valid arguments and correspondingly for the rejection of arguments, e.g., for being unscientific. Hence, it lays down a framework for what kinds of arguments and conflicts are possible within the discourse. In that sense, a discourse does not imply consensus but rather a realm for meaningful conflict.

I would add a fourth order to the other three, which we might call the *interrogative order*. This order comprises the questions and problems that can

---

60   The first three differences are picked up from the German historian of ideas Koselleck, the last two from Greimas.

legitimately and meaningfully be raised within a given discourse. Unlike the descriptive order, the interrogative order is not about "facts" and how they may be classified, but about which questions are relevant to ask and which problems are central to a debate. And unlike the argumentative order, the interrogative order is not about what can be accepted as a valid argument, but about what it makes sense to argue for. The focus here is on discourse as a horizon of questioning within which problems become visible and develop.

A Complementary Concept – Genre: Discourse is a useful concept for describing the cultural organization of signification. As regards specific cultures it offers the possibility of describing how social actions are constituted as meaningful and within which signifying systems they are allowed to play out. Comparatively, this offers the possibility of describing differences between (sub)cultures according to what kinds of discourses they are influenced by. Moreover, on a diachronic basis, it offers the possibility of describing cultural change as the displacement, development and transformation of discourses.

I think, however, that the purpose of discourse analysis – to investigate meaning in social practices – would be better served if we couple the concept of discourse with the notion of *genre*. In fact, it is difficult to account for how discursive signification enters into practice, if we only take recourse to the concept of discourse. Here, the concept of genre might function as a kind of hyphen between discourse and practice. In fact, the discourses' organization of signification is realized as the social formation of meaning by means of the social forms that the genres make available.

Therefore, I suggest that we look at signification as organized not simply in discourses but also in genres understood as *forms of discursive practice*. The idea of genre draws on other theoretical contexts than the Foucauldian notion of discourse such as microsociology, anthropology, literary theory, rhetoric and text linguistics.[61] The focus here is on specific text- and interaction formats rather than on discursive signifying universes.

Like discourses, genres make social forms available such that the formation of meaning can take place. However, while a discourse is a signifying universe, which marks out concepts, subjects and problems, a genre organizes

---

61   In applied linguistics –discourse analysis in one sense of the term cf. Fairclough's double discourse concept – John Swales has made important contributions to establishing "genre analysis" as a branch of research (Swales 1996).

social actions into coherent activities. A genre is a *sequential form* that organizes a coherent sequence of speech-acts in time and/or space. Genre is
closely related to the notion of 'language games' (Wittgenstein 1984/1952)
and 'activity type' (Levinson 1992), understood as a category, which designates the total structure of an activity, its individual communicative characteristics and its language register according to an understanding of what the
purpose of the activity is.[62]

Like discourse, genre is a condition of possibility for social action – any
social action must take place in relation to one or more genres in order to
make sense (cf. Bakhtin 1986). And, like discourse, genre should be understood in a constructionist rather than a functional sense; a genre does not
simply realize the intention prior to it, it is not just fulfilling the intention; it
also sets the goal. Or, in Carolyn Miller's words:

> What we learn when we learn a genre is not just a pattern of
> forms or even a method of achieving our own ends. We learn,
> more importantly, what ends we may have. (Cited from Swales
> 1996: 44).

Following Fairclough, I suggest that we conceive of discourse and genre as
relatively autonomous phenomena[63] – autonomous because the same discourse can be articulated along with several different genres and vice-versa.
For example, a liberal political discourse can both appear in the genre "press
release" and the genre "political interview," just like the genre "political interview" can be articulated both within socialist and liberal discourses. And the
autonomy is relative inasmuch as the genre is not an abstract form independent of the discourse,[64] but rather, by virtue of its communicative purpose, is more or less connected to specific discourses. Thus, in a political interview, we might find scientific or conversational elements, however, if
these elements become dominant, the communicative purpose – and there-

---

62   The purpose is defined as genre-constituing in, for example, Swales (1996), Eg-
     gins/Martin (1997) and Miller (2001). "A genre comprises a class of communica-
     tive events, the members of which share some set of communicative purpose"
     (Swales 1996: 58).
63   In Fairclough (2003), the double perspective on discourse and genre has become a
     triple perspective with discourse, genre and style as key concepts.
64   As we might say is the case for text type. For the relation between genre and text
     type see Vestergaard (1999).

by the genre – shifts and becomes a scientific discussion or a chit-chat (or a mixture of both).

This double perspective on discourse and genre is presented in figure 1, which seeks to illustrate that discourse analysis investigates the formation of knowledge-about-the-world, social relations and identities *via* the key concepts discourse and genre. Also, it illustrates how the notions of genre and discourse have implications for knowledge-about-the-world as well as social relations and identities[65]

Figure 1

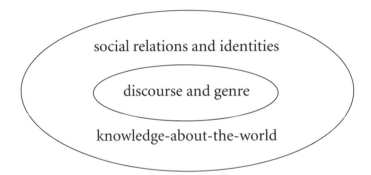

The Order of Discourse: So much for the complementary concepts discourse and genre. With Fairclough's notion of the order of discourse, we can use this double perspective at a level of abstraction above the individual discourse and genre.

An order of discourse is a configuration of discourses and genres within a social field such as media, sports, law, religion, politics, science and economics (according to distinctions which, from a sociological point of view, is characteristic of modern societies).[66] Within most social fields there is not just one discourse or one genre but several – which are not arbitrarily dispersed but configured in different supra and sub relations. These relations must, furthermore, be conceived as *tensional relations*, that is, as relations which do have certain permanence, but which are, nevertheless, under con-

---

65 Formulated in terms of systematic functional linguistics the genre is not specifically connected to the interpersonal metafunction of language practice, but also to the ideational. Similarly, the discourse pertains to the ideational as well as to the interpersonal metafunction.

stant communicative "negotiation." The relation between different orders of discourse is, similarly, only relatively stabile; thus, two of Fairclough's most essential time-diagnostic concepts – "marketization" and "conversationalization" – refer to the fact that discourses from the market and the intimate sphere, respectively, are gaining terrain in other orders of discourse. "Order of discourse" is a useful concept, partly because it offers the possibility of talking about both plurality and order when cultural arenas are investigated, and partly because it opens up for coupling discourse analysis to sociological entities such as institutions, organizations and fields.

Text: One analytical difficulty about discourses, genres and orders of discourse is that they are not immediately observable. They are abstract organizations of signification, not palpable things. Therefore, if discourse analysis is to be more than discourse speculation, we have to study discourses, genres and orders of discourse in *texts*. Thus, one must investigate discourses and genres via the formation of meaning in texts; discourses according to their presence and place in texts and genres according to the organizational principles that appear in texts. Here, I understand text as a part of or a product of a social practice; i.e., text is an *instantiation of meaning* in which (various) discursive practices are textualized into a coherent whole. A text is not a container for discursive elements, but an *organization* of them based on culture-specific genres. This textual organization cuts across the organization that characterizes discourse and genre (and order of discourse), insofar as the discursive and generic signifying resources are transformed into *situated* meaning.

In order for the texts to be open to investigation, they need to be available as objects. Some texts already are, whereas others need to be "objectified", that is, need to be adapted to research purposes, for example, through photos, tape recordings or transcriptions – an objectification which transfers the

---

66 Chouliaraki/Fairclough (1999) link the order of discourse to Bourdieu's field category: "We have already indicated a relationship between Bourdieu's category "field" and the CDA category of "order of discourse." An order of discourse is a socially constructed articulation of discursive practices (including both genres and discourses) which constitutes the discursive facet of the social order of a social field, such as politics, media or education. We can say that an order of discourse is the specifically decoursal organizational logic of a field – a field seen specifically in terms of its discursive practices" (ibid.: 114). See also Jørgensen/Phillips (1999) for a discussion of the analytical use of the concept.

text from one medium to another. In order to study a text it is, in that sense, often necessary to disconnect it from practice only to reinsert it analytically into practice afterwards. Discourse analysis is not interested in texts as objectified and independent units, but in texts *qua* practices.

Two Tracks of Discourse Analysis: Based on the above key concepts we can now specify the content of the structure- and action dimensions of discourse analysis mentioned previously, cf. Figure 2:

Figure 2

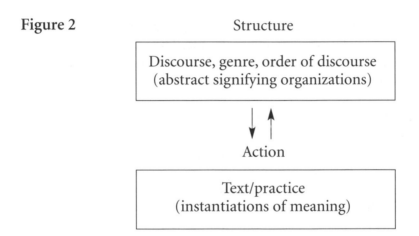

The structure dimension is filled out by discourse, genre and order of discourse understood as abstract signifying organizations, which are the resources for concrete formations of meaning. The "action-dimension" is filled out by text/practice understood as an instantiation of meaning which draws on generic and discursive resources.

The model encourages a division of discourse analysis into two tracks: a *"condition of possibility"* track and an *instantiation track*. On the condition of possibility track, focus is on the signifying resources available for the formation of meaning. Here, the emphasis is on investigating discourses, genres and/or orders of discourse as such; for example, one might to investigate how a specific discourse emerges, develops and is exported from one field to another. In the instantiation analysis, focus is on how the signifying resources are used in practice, that is, how different discourses and genres are actualized and articulated in a coherent text or a course of texts. This division reflects essential differences between prominent research directions in discourse analysis. While Foucault- and Laclau-inspired discourse analysis finds itself on the condition of possibility track, critical discourse analysis and discourse psychology primarily follow the instantiation track. Despite the differences, it is important to maintain the dialectical relationship between the structure and the action dimension. In principle, the two tracks are not parallel, but condition one another – condition of possibility analysis depends on the instantiation analysis and vice-versa. An instantiation analysis of the actual formation of meaning cannot avoid leaning on an understanding, however implicit, of which discourses exist prior to the instantiation and are drawn upon in it. Similarly, a condition of possibility analysis must be grounded on a number of instantiations of the discourse under investigation. Surely, concrete discourse analysis is subject to prioritization between the one track or the other. However, prioritizing is a simple matter of research resources and is not due to any theoretical gap between the two tracks. I would, therefore, like to encourage a more coordinated division of labor between the two tracks than is the case today; perhaps it has served a purpose for the different branches of discourse analysis to create some gaps in order to mark out their own territories, however, that phase should be over by now.

Discourse Analysis and Textual Analysis: It is not exactly uncontroversial to state that not only the instantiation track but also the condition of possibility track, in principle, involves textual analysis. In Foucauldian discourse analysis, for example, one often runs into forceful rejections of the idea that discourse analysis should have anything to do with textual analysis, mainly because of Foucault's own reservations toward textual analysis. I think, however, that this is based on a misunderstanding of what textual analysis is, or, to put it in slightly more sympathetic terms, it draws a border between discourse analysis and textual analysis that is only valid for a specific variant of textual analysis, namely the variant that seeks to uncover a deeper or latent level of signification beneath the surface of the text. In that case, textual analysis is perceived as a kind of code breaking, which seeks to understand what the text really says beneath what it apparently says. It is true that this variant of textual analysis is opposed to the surface orientation of discourse analysis. Discourse analysis does not operate with distinctions such as surface-depth, manifest-latent or hidden-visible; it does not seek to break the codes of the text, but takes the text quite literally.

This does not mean, however, that discourse analysis needs to distance itself from textual analysis as such. Textual analysis is perhaps more important for the instantiation track than for the condition of possibility track, however, textual analysis is not irrelevant to the latter. First of all a structural analysis cannot disregard the text as an organization of discursive elements. It is

not irrelevant to the continuous development of discourses how these elements are textualized, for example, whether they are accepted, problematized or negated. Secondly, it is a prevalent problem in many discourse
analyses that criteria for referring statements to specific discourse are unclear. Here, categories used in textual analysis can add to a clarification of
these criteria and sharpen the analysis.

The question of the *status* of textual analysis in discourse analysis is not to
be confused with the question of the *level of detail* of the analysis. Discourse
analyses vary significantly as regards the scope of the total textual corpus
that they investigate and thereby also as regards the level of detail of the textual analysis. Again, however, this is a matter of practical prioritization
rather than of whether textual analysis makes sense within discourse analysis
or not.

FUTURE ORIENTATIONS
In recent years, discourse analysis has undergone a dramatic development.
Here, I would like to emphasize two currents, which seem to me particularly
promising: the "transformative" and the "multimodal" current, respectively.

Transformativity: There have been several precursors to a "transformative
turn" in discourse analysis, this is to say, a turn away from investigating individual discourses and/or discursive practices toward investigating movements and transformations of discursive material from one context to another. The notion of *recontextualization* (see, for example, Chouliaraki/Fair-
clough 1999) can be used as a wider term for different types of such transformations: In this way, *re-semiotization* (Iedema 2001) designates a recontextualization which involves transportation from one medium or one semiotic mode to another, for example, from speech to writing. A *genre chain*
(Fairclough 2003) consists of a number of routinized recontextualizations,
where the transformations follow a relatively defined and predictable generic route, for example, from ministerial notes to press releases, press meetings,
news broadcasting and commentaries. And *intertextual chains* (Solin 2001)
consist of a set of texts that are related to one another in a single, chronological sequence without necessarily being a genre chain.[67]

These types of transformations designate different ways in which mean-

---

67   Fairclough (1992) uses the term "intertextual chains" for what he later calls "genre
     chains."

ing is formed within discursive practices when coupled with the formation of meaning within other practices. Like the "order of discourse," the notion of transformation pertains to relations between practices, however, whereas the "order of discourse" refers to a relatively stabile configuration of practices, the notion of transformation focuses on a diachronal course of different practices, a course that might comprise different orders of discourse.[68] This offers the possibility of (yet) another double glance at the formation of meaning: partly as textualization of discourses and genres in discursive practice and partly as recontextualization of these textualizations in yet other discursive practices. In the former instance, the crucial difference is between the signifying *structure* and the *formation* of meaning, and in the latter between the *formation* of meaning and the *transformation* of meaning.

The notion of transformation opens up a new way of looking at classical media and communication theories. In my opinion, we get a more complex picture of a large part of mass-mediated communication if we regard it as a course of recontextualizing practices, rather than as a "sender-text-recipient" model according to which a sender sends a media-text with a well-defined intention, which is decoded by an actively interpreting recipient. The notion of transformation also offers the possibility of taking into account the – justified – critique of discourse analysis for only dealing peripherally with issues of the production, distribution and consumption of texts. And, importantly, the notion of transformation retains the emphasis on *social meaning* characteristic of discourse analysis. If one, for example, imagines that an organization (a political party, a private company, a lobby) puts a text into circulation in public, the notion of transformation encourages us firstly to investigate "the sender" as the *organizational practices*, which lead to the production of the text, for example, meetings in different departments, and potential contacts with external communication bureaus (cf. figure 3). These practices, of course, produce a final text, but they can also be objectified (cf. the previous section on "Text") and become objects for textual analysis. Secondly, the notion of transformation allows us to look at the "reception" not as a psychological phenomenon, but rather as a recontextualization of the discursive material from one field to another, in this case from the public

---

68 This idea can also be applied to discourse analysis itself; discourse analysis is a practice, which recontextualizes texts from other orders of discourses within the scientific order of discourse. And, of course, this recontextualization might also be an object of discourse analysis.

sphere to the practices of the intimate sphere, for example through conversations over dinner or arguments in front of the TV. Finally, the notion of transformation allows us to understand the media-text as a part of a public practice, which gains its social meaning by drawing on given genres and discourses and by re-thematizing topics from previous public debates. To sum up: "the communicative situation" can be understood as a number of recontextualizations of discursive material that occurs across different social fields/orders of discourse – organizations, the mediated public sphere, the intimate sphere (cf. the horizontal arrows of the figure) – and within the individual fields, in an organizational context, for example, as evaluations or market research (cf. the vertical arrows).[69] The model can be expanded to other social fields, for example in order to describe how a media event is followed by a political or juridical afterplay, is integrated as a case study in the classroom, or is used as a model to be followed in other organizations.

FIGURE 3

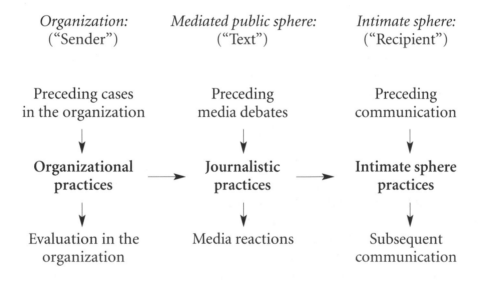

Organization: ("Sender")	Mediated public sphere: ("Text")	Intimate sphere: ("Recipient")
Preceding cases in the organization	Preceding media debates	Preceding communication
Organizational practices	Journalistic practices	Intimate sphere practices
Evaluation in the organization	Media reactions	Subsequent communication

---

69   This model can be seen as an alternative to the related but non-transformative understanding which is presented by Schrøder (2002) in an attempt to integrate reception analysis and CDA-inspired discourse analysis.

Multimodality and Materiality: The other current of discourse analysis that I would like to emphasize here is the orientation toward materiality and multimodality. *Materiality* refers to the fact that texts are given in a material form (newspaper, screen, runic stone) in which it is inscribed in a certain way (with smaller or larger letters, with this or that type of script). The materials and the inscriptions have different degrees of permanence, freshness and status, which are not external to the formation of meaning, but contribute to the social meaning of the text (Scollon/Scollon 2003). Strangely enough, this "materialization" of the concept of text may have the effect that the analyst directs his or her attention toward the many everyday texts that are normally not perceived as prototypical, and which are rarely made objects of textual analysis, such as plastic bags, monuments or milk cartons.

Multimodality refers to the fact that a significant part of the formation of meaning occurs in interplay between different semiotic modes, for example, verbal language, diagrams, music and pictures.[70] This is not simply the case with new, colorful multimedia texts but also with "dry" scientific articles (Lemke 1998) and with a host of everyday texts in general. Developing theoretical and analytical approaches for investigating multimodal formations of meaning is a great challenge to discourse analysis – a challenge which, ideally, promotes both interdisciplinary exchanges between experts from different signifying systems (linguists, creative writers, designers, architects, musicians, filmmakers, experts on perfumes etc…) and encourages the development of a meta-language that is usable across those systems. For discourse analysis, the multimodal turn implies that discourses can be realized in many different modes. For example, a picture or a building can realize an empirical discourse just as well as a speech. In that sense, the descriptive, narrative, argumentative and interrogative "speech-orders" of discourse must be understood at a level of abstraction above the (verbal) language. In that way, discourse is only metaphorically a language phenomenon, cf. "body language," " visual language," "sign language," etc… The "statements" of the discourse can be verbal expressions as well as photographs, diagrams and music.[71] Similarly, a genre is an organizational principle, which comprises multiple semiotic modes. In that sense, gesture and

---

70 As regards the development of theories of multimodality Kress/van Leeuwen have been particularly influential.

71 Which is, in fact, Foucault's (1969) point as well.

architectonic design, for example, pass as signifying elements in many genres. Finally, the multimodal turn points toward a broad concept of text according to which text is not simply a way of organizing (verbal) language, but also as a way of organizing other semiotic modes – not least their co-organization.

METHOD AND CRITIQUE

So much for the theoretical universe and potentials of discourse analysis. On a final note, I would like to take a broader view of discourse analysis as a scientific discursive practice and of how discourse analysis relates to the discursive constructions that it investigates. The former pertains to discourse analysis as a non-method, the latter to discourse analysis as critique.

Discourse Analysis and Method: In the above, I argued that discourse analysis is a type of cultural analysis. This is not to say, however, that discourse analysis is an actual method. Discourse analysis, as I have presented it in this paper, is incomplete, not simply due to shortcomings in my explanations, but exactly because it is not a *method*. Discourse analysis investigates culture, but it is not a method for investigating culture. It is, rather, a general view with a set of relatively plastic key concepts that can be used within different fields and can develop into concrete methods by being coined with other approaches. This coining goes "downwards" toward textual analytical concepts and "upwards" toward macrosociological theories. In Faircloughian discourse analysis, it is crucial to join textual analysis with an analysis of socio-cultural issues, cf. the notorious box model containing the elements text, discursive practice and social practice (Fairclough 1992 and 1995a). To me, this means that discourse analysis is essentially interdisciplinary and that it couples careful (multimodal) textual analysis with socio-cultural knowledge. The kind of discourse analysis described above is, so to speak, the medium in which this coupling or translation takes place. The kinds of analytical grids and knowledge that discourse analysis should employ, however, depends on the concrete case. With the actual discourse analysis, therefore, comes the development of a concrete analytical strategy, which has a not insignificant amount of scientific creativity to it. In this sense, discourse analysis is not a method which can simply be applied to this or that field, but, a point of departure for methodological thinking.

"Critical" Discourse Analysis?: It is at this point perhaps appropriate to take a step back from my introductory definition of the knowledge interest of discourse analysis and ask why we are actually interested in "meaning in social practices?" There is no philological interest behind this, just like discourse analysis does not occupy itself with privileged texts, which lay claim to special aesthetic interest. I will suggest three answers:

1. Discourse analysis is carried by a basic (philosophical) curiosity about the social realms in which we dwell and which we influence.

2. Discourse analysis has a critical edge. Discourse analysis is mindful of power because power is perceived as integral to social life. Power as such cannot be eliminated – if we try we often end up with totalitarian systems – but the concrete forms of power can be subject to critique, and they can be changed. And some forms of power are simply to prefer to others. Thus, discourse analysis offers a critical distance by regarding constructions of knowledge-about-the-word, social relations and identities as both immanent to power and as culturally changeable. In particular, the strength of discourse analysis lies in the fact that it points toward forms of power which seem so obvious that they have become almost invisible, and that it criticizes seemingly irresistible slogans by pointing to the realms of articulation and interaction that they help establish. The critical mind, however, must realize that the critical component of discourse analysis is also up for grasp; it does not have a privileged subject position, but realizes and advances the critical potential of everyday language. Furthermore, in order to be relevant, the critique of discourse analysis must be related to the societal situation/condition of critique and it needs to look for those areas that have been neglected or underestimated hitherto. We are better served without a critique that simply mimics another. Finally, critique needs to be critical of its own institutionalization and the kinds of power that it entails.[72] However, this does not change the fact that the critical voice is important. We live in a world where extensive resources go into planning and designing communication, and where many people make their living by representing and promoting given views. Discourse analysis ought to be a critical counterweight to this rhetorical rearmament.

3. Discourse analysis has a constructive potential. Critical thinking also implies an endeavor to cross borders for the thinkable and open up new realms for thought and action. Although discourse analysis is not an instructive enterprise, the "border crossing" endeavor could be taken a bit further. Similar-

---

72   As Billig (2000) has pointed out.

ly, a part of the analytical energy and subtlety of discourse analysis could – as suggested by Martin/Rose (2003) – be applied to texts and practices that are not solely to be criticized but also to be learned from.

Translated from Danish by Maren Lytje

Works Cited

Bakhtin, M. 1986: *Speech Genres and Other Late Essays.* (Edited by Emerson, C. and Holquist, M.). Austin, Texas: University of Texas Press.

Billig, M. 2000: Towards a critique of the critical. In: *Discourse & Society*, 11, 3.

Burr, V. 1995: *An Introduction to Social Constructionism.* London: Routledge.

Chouliaraki, L./Fairclough, N. 1999: *Discourse in Late Modernity. Rethinking Critical Discourse Analysis.* Edinburgh University Press.

Eggins, S./Martin, J.R. 1997: Genre and Register of Discourse. In: van Dijk, T.A. 1997 (ed): *Discourse as Structure and Process. Discourse Studies: A Multidisciplinary Introduction. Volume I.* London: Sage.

Fairclough, N. 1992: *Discours and Social Change.* Cambridge: Polity Press.

Fairclough, N.1995a: *Critical Discourse Analysis.* London: Longman.

Fairclough, N. 1995b: *Media Discourse.* London: Edward Arnold.

Fairclough, N. 2003: *Analysing Discourse: Textual Analysis for Social Research.* London: Routledge.

Fink, H. 2003: Universitetsfagenes etik. In: Fink, H./Kjærgaard, P.C./Kragh, H./Kristensen, J.E.: *Universitet og videnskab. Universitetets idéhistorie, videnskabsteori og etik.* København: Hans Reitzels Forlag.

Foucault, M. 1969: *L'archéologie du savoir.* Paris: Gallimard.

Foucault, M. 1994 (1976): *Viljen til viden. Seksualitetens historie I.* København: Det lille forlag.

Frandsen, F. 1996: Forskning i mediesprog – teorier, modeller og analyser. I Frandsen (ed.): *Medierne og sproget.* Aalborg Universitetsforlag.

Gadamer, H.G. 1962: *Wahrheit und Methode.* Tübingen: Mohr.

Hajer, M.A. 1995: *The Politics of Environmental Discourse. Ecological Modernization and the Policy Process.* Oxford: Clarendon Press.

Horsbøl, A.: 2003: Præsidenter kunne være anderledes. In: *Dansk Sociologi*, nr. 1/14.

Horsbøl, A.: 2004 (in press): *Diskursiveringer af politisk anderledeshed. En diskursanalytisk undersøgelse af offentlig meningsdannelse ud fra et debatforløb i de østrigske medier.* Ph.d.-afhandling. Institut for Sprog og Internationale Kulturstudier, AAU.

Iedema, R. 2001: Resemiotiation. In: *Semiotica* 137 1/4.

Jørgensen, M.W./Phillips, L. 1999: *Diskursanalyse som teori og metode.* Roskilde Universitetsforlag/Samfundslitteratur.

Jäger, S. 1993: *Kritische Diskursanalyse.* Duisburger Institut für Sprach- und Sozialforschung.

Keller, R.1997: Diskursanalyse. I: Hitzler, R. (ed.): *Sozialwissenschaftliche Herme-neutik.* UTB.

Kress, G./van Leeuwen, T. 2001: *Multimodal Discourse: the Modes and Media of Con-temporary Communication.* London: Edward Arnold.

Laclau, E. 1993: Discourse. In: Goodin, R.E./Pettit, P. (eds.): *A Companion to Con-temporary Political Philosophy.* Oxford: Blackwell.

Lemke, J. 1998: "Multiplying meaning. Visual and verbal semiotics in scientific text. In: Martin, J.R./Veel, R. (eds): *Reading Science. Critical and functional perspectives on discourses of science.* London: Routledge.

Levinson, S.C. 1992: Activity types and language. In: Drew. P./Heritage, J.: *Talk at Work. Interaction in Institutional Settings.* Cambridge UP.

Luhmann, N. 1984: *Soziale Systeme.* Frankfurt am Main: Suhrkamp Verlag.

Martin, J.R./Rose, D. 2003: *Working with Discourse: meaning beyond the clause.* Lon-don: Continuum.

Reisigl, M./Wodak, R. 2000: *Discourse & Discrimination.* London: Routledge.

Scollon, R./Scollon, S.W. 2003: *Discourses in Place: Language in the Material World.* London: Routledge.

Schrøder, K. 2002: Virksomhedsreklame – hen imod et diskurs-etnografisk per-spektiv." In: Petersen, H./Lund, A.K.: *Den kommunikerende organisation.* Køben-havn: Samfundslitteratur.

Solin, A. 2001: *Tracing Texts. Intertextuality in Environmental Discourse.* Helsinki: PIC Monographs 2.

Swales, J. 1996: *Genre analysis: English in Academic and Research Settings.* Cam-bridge UP.

Vestergaard, T. 1999: That's not News: Persuasive and Expository Genres in the Press. I: Trosborg (ed.): *Analyzing Professional Genres.* Amsterdam/Philadelphia: John Benjamins Publishing Company.

Wittgenstein, L. 1984 (1952): *Philosophische Untersuchungen.* Frankfurt a.M.: Suhrkamp.

Åkerstrøm Andersen, N. 1994: *Institutionel historie : en introduktion til diskurs- og institutionsanalyse.* København: Center for Offentlig Organisation og Styring.

Åkerstrøm Andersen, N. 1999: *Diskursive Analysestrategier.* København: Nyt fra Samfundsvidenskaberne.

DO ARTIFACTS HAVE MEANINGS?
On the Attribution of Meaning to Technical Artifacts

Mikael Vetner
Department of Communication
Aalborg University

Do the technological artifacts of our everyday life possess meaning? The fact that the automobile, the bicycle, the mobile phone and the personal computer have become highly valued and meaningful artifacts certainly has to do with the fact that they serve valuable purposes. The automobile and the bicycle facilitate our transportation and we use mobile phones and personal computers in our working and personal life when we communicate, entertain ourselves, and so on. These artifacts are valuable and meaningful since we employ them and because they subsequently serve us in our various endeavours. In this way, the meanings that accompany these artifacts typically have to do with that they have been designed in certain ways and consequently are imbued with intended meanings and functions, which are exposed, once they are marketed and put into use. The telephone, for example, was originally designed to deliver short to the point messages between businessmen and was therefore marketed as a rational tool for the entrepreneurial gentleman (Fischer 1992). The same was more or less the case with the mobile phone, which too at first was marketed as a means to instantly deliver concise messages. The intention and functionality of these technologies were clear and already constituted during the process of design and production.[1] Thus, due to their purposive constitution the meaning of such artifacts are closely related to their *telos*.[2]

An interesting question arises, however, when artifacts get so to say a *life*

---

[1] Madeline Akrich and Bruno Latour defines this intended functionality as *prescriptions* and points out that it has to do with: "What a device allows or forbids from the actors – humans and nonhuman – that it anticipates; it is the morality of a setting both negative (what it prescribes) and positive (what it permits)" (Akrich 1992: 261).

[2] By *telos* I mean the purpose or the ultimate object or aim of a given technological artefact. The telos of a technological artefact is—as I shall demonstrate below—not installed in the technology a priori; on the contrary it comes about via the social processes involved in the design and production of the artefact.

of their own. That is when they acquire meanings that transcend their originally intended meanings, functionality and telos. As Claude S. Fischer elaborates on in *America Calling* (Fischer 1992) the telephone might have been
marketed as a tool for the busy businessman but soon became popular
among women for small talk and social conversations. With increasingly
busy phone lines, AT&T at first tried to put a stop to the chitchat, but soon
realized that this unintended usage of the telephone had become a huge success and consequently included the possibility for making social relations in
their advertising campaigns. This means that the telephone underwent a semantic transformation in the social world. The physical artifact was not as
such changed, but due to the social appropriation the horizon of meaning
around it was altered (Fischer 1992). Put in another way, the intended functionality was more or less the same, but the meanings attributed to the telephone were transformed due to the user's telephony.

When introduced in a given socio-cultural context artifacts are more or
less bound to be interpreted and translated accordingly to the specific historical, political, cultural, economical etc... logics of the respective society.
This entails that different social groups associate various meanings with a
given artifact. So deliberately or inadvertently, consciously or unconsciously,
meaning is to some degree attributed to the various technological artifacts
of our society via our social exchange; be it that they for instance are liberatory, oppressive, efficient, entertaining, useful or that they are synonymous
with the future or economical growth. In such processes, different people
and groups unavoidably possess various and disproportionate degrees of
power and displays different levels of responsiveness. The market, advertising agencies and so on are consequently crucial social agents but not necessarily the single dominant force, when artifacts are saturated with meanings.
On the contrary, it is realistic to suggest that the users (and other interested
parties) by way of their everyday social exchange also shape or construe patterns of meaning and knowledge around the technological artifacts that are
part of their social arena.[3] From this viewpoint people are not solely impact-

---

3   This issue is discussed in a range of accounts. See for instance Keith Grint and
    Steve Woolgar in *The Machine at Work*. Here technologies are described in the fol-
    lowing manner: "Technologies, in other words, are not transparent; their character
    is not given; and they do not contain an essence independent of the nexus of social
    actions of which they are part. They do not 'by themselves' tell us what they are and
    what they are capable of. Instead, capabilities – what, for example, a machine will
    do – are attributed to the machine by humans. Our knowledge of technology is in
    this sense essentially social" (Grint 1997: 10).

ed and determined by the force of technological artifacts; on the contrary it seems likely that they, along with a great number of other social groups, manipulate the social world, instead of just being manipulated. And it is exactly this activity that I wish to address in this article. Thereby, I aim at demonstrating that a foci-shift from the producers (inventors, engineers, and manufacturers) to the users of the various artifacts will show that everyday people also have a say in the process of generating meaning and understanding of the technological artifacts that play such important roles in our social lives. And as such my primary interest is to discuss how this attributing of meaning can be understood, described and analysed.

THE SOCIAL MEANING OF CARS, ELECTRICITY, LEGO AND MOBILE PHONES

The social meaning[4] of artifacts is constituted in a multitude of ways by means of disparate social groups' interaction, habits, behaviour, ideas, socio-historical background etc... When an artifact is introduced in a given context, it is a possibility that it will be infused with new meanings or that its existing meanings will be elaborated on thus becoming coextensive with the social groups and the cultural logics. In this section, I will—by way of existing and new examples—introduce to different artifacts, which each in their own way have been saturated with new meanings.[5] The purpose of these illustrations is primarily to establish a point of reference for the further discussion but also to point out the differences in the ways such social meanings are configured, and consequently what we must be aware of when analysing such phenomena.

Cars

The first example can be found in Ronald Kline and Trevor Pinch's article *Users as Agents of Technological Change* (Kline 1996), and concerns the social construction of the automobile and the social meanings attributed to the automobile in rural America. Kline and Pinch describe that the automobile as

---

4   When I invoke the terms *meaning* and *social meaning* I am advocating a social semiotics approach. Meanings are thus perceived to come about via our social exchange and agency in society.

5   I could have used a variety of other examples, for instance Kenneth Lipartito's account of the picturephone (Lipartito 2003). Another example could have been Andrew Feenberg's description of the unexpected use of the French videotext system, the Minitel (Feenberg 1995). The examples have however primarily been selected to show the differences in how the constitution of meaning comes about.

having a historically spectacular impact on rural American life. As such, automobiles were early on named as 'devil wagons' by farmers since they disturbed the farm life, for instance because that the noise disturbed the livestock, upset the horses that pulled the buggies while the reckless driven autos in general made the country roads an unsafe place. These initial experiences lead to a series of protests by the farmers, who found that the noisy and dangerous automobile pestered the otherwise peaceful country life. Furthermore, the automobile was seen as a factor which undermined the local cultural milieu since they, e.g., made it possible for the farmers to go to other churches on Sundays or drive their children to better schools in other counties. The protests even amounted to the sabotaging of the country roads and in more radical cases to attacks on the drivers and their automobiles.[6] The "anticar" movement and the meanings generated here were evidently very intense and concise but also short-lived and disappeared when the manufacturers produced cars that met much of the public criticism and perhaps more importantly when the automobile was promoted in influential papers such as the *Wallace's Farmer* and the *Rural New Yorker* (Kline 1996: 772f). This means that the newly constituted meaning of the automobile as a hazardous devil wagon did not stabilize.

> Did this meaning of the car for this social group lead to a radical interpretative flexibility? The answer must be yes. By attempting to destroy cars directly and make roads impassable to cars, this social group was trying to affect perhaps in the most dramatic, direct way possible the development of the artifact. If they had succeeded the car might have taken a very different form—it would have been a short distance city vehicle only (Kline 1996: 772).

But at the same time these early events show that it is indeed possible to alter or change the meanings of such an artifact. And just a couple of decades later the social meaning of the automobile was in fact changed with more lasting and tangible effects. Following the promotional campaigns for the automobile the users started to embed new meanings into the automobile. In connection to this Kline and Pinch write:

> [...] it is clear that one social group initially had more influence than any other in terms of giving meaning to the artifact: the

---

6   Similar reactions surfaced in relation to the bicycle, where stones were thrown at the riders and sticks were thrust into the wheels. See for instance Bijker (1987: 32.)

> manufacturers. Because they produced the car, the automobile
> manufacturers exerted great influence on the form the technolo-
> gy initially took. [...] Furthermore, although manufacturers
> may have ascribed a particular meaning to the artifact they were
> not able to control how the artifact was used once it got into the
> hands of the users. Users precisely as users can embed new
> meanings into the technology (Kline 1996: 775).

Once the automobile gained a stronger foothold in the public opinion and, especially among farmers, it was "reshaped" to fit the farmer's own ends. As such some of the more enterprising farmers started to block up the rear axle and run belts over the wheels and around wheels on water pumps, washing machines, cream separators, corn grinders etc... In this way, the automobile became a stationary source of power. The automobile was in this manner used as both a domestic tool and as a farm tool in addition to its intended functions as a means of transportation. New meanings were attributed to the automobile or their intended meanings were reconfigured by a specific social group of users, namely the farmers who came up with new ways to use the automobile and consequently it became domesticated in ways unintended by the manufacturers.

To the urban user the car meant transport. For the rural users we have identified, the car, as well as being a form of transport, could be a farm tool, a stationary source of power, part of a domestic technology, or perhaps all of these (Kline 1996: 777).

These meanings were further stabilized due to the technological change they brought about. Because later on, in 1917 and years immediately following, these new meanings and new forms of usage were developed even further and kits were made to take the power directly off the crankshaft or even to convert the automobile into a tractor. Following the changes in the meaning of the automobile, farm equipment manufacturers, gasoline-engine firms etc... produced a range of accessories, which assisted the work on the farm and thus contributed to the sedimentation of the meanings of the automobile. The newly constituted social meanings of the automobile as for instance a farm tool or a stationary power source were however relatively local in that they primarily were limited to the countryside, whilst other and more conventional meanings could be found in the cities. But these meanings, however, became destabilized once again when stationary gasoline engines and electricity became common and when the automobile manufacturers started their own lines of trucks and tractors and, as a result, discouraged the conversion of the automobiles.

> [...] the interpretative flexibility we have described for the car
> disappeared by the early 1950s. Closure [in the meaning of the
> car] had occurred (once again) and farm people had stopped us-
> ing their autos for grinding their grain, plowing their fields, or
> carrying their produce to town. Instead, they had begun to buy
> tractors and pickup trucks in large numbers—new artifacts that
> manufacturers developed partly in response to these novel inter-
> pretations of the car. The users, so easily overlooked in writing
> the story of technology, had made their mark. (Kline 1996: 795).

This example clearly illustrates that a crucial circumstance in the attribution of meaning to technological artifacts evidently is the social agency of specific groups of people. We have thus seen that a range of new meanings appeared in a relatively clearly defined social milieu, where a specific group of social agents where the decisive force in constitution the new meanings. At the same time we have seen that the new meanings were closely related to the patterns of usage and the ways of conduct that governed the farmers everyday life; as such these new meanings came about alongside a series of exact technological changes.

Electricity

The second example I wish to include concerns the social meaning of electricity in America. Among other things this example illustrate that the new meanings, which surface in relation to a technology, not necessarily are clearly defined but that they just as well can be vague and almost indefinable while still being expressive. In *Electrifying America: The Social Meanings of a New Technology* (Nye 1990), David Nye describe how the American public between 1880 and 1940 encountered, experienced and employed electricity and thus came to live with this new technology.[7] Electricity was more or less from the first time it was "turned on" permeated with a variety of social meanings. Nye explains that it in the early days bordered on the supernatural since the new forms of lighting and illumination it made possible seemed to defy the natural order of night and day. Citing Ezra Pound it is made clear that electricity had given man almost godlike powers:

---

7   David Nye's book *Electrifying America* (Nye 1990) is very wide-ranging and I do not claim to give an in-depth description of his account; the purpose of incorporating this example is solely to demonstrate some of Nye's principal arguments.

> It is then [in the evening] that the great buildings [in New York]
> lose reality and take on their magical powers. They are immate-
> rial; that is to say one sees but the lighted windows. Squares after
> squares of flame, set and cut into the aether. Here is our poetry,
> for we have pulled down the stars to our will (Ezra Pound in
> Nye 1990: 74).

Nye furthermore uses the World Fairs as an example on how electricity was put into use. Here electricity and electrical machines were a useful and impressing way of displaying what modern man had achieved and was capable of doing. At these fairs "visions of a fully electrified world emerged" with dazzling displays, spectacular illuminations and new or revised means of transportation. At the fairs the visitor, once removed from the everyday routines, could catch a glimpse of the larger direction of society and culture and consequently American progress. The fairs were as such an idealized space – unlike the surrounding society – which propagated how the future would possibly turn out.

> "Electricity buildings" were among the largest, most central, and
> most popular halls at these fairs; they helped to impose a mid-
> dle-class progressive order on the world, and they helped give
> the visitor an explanatory blueprint of social experience. As a
> whole each fair offered a coherent set of symbols that linked
> past, present, and future, providing a vision of order during a
> convulsive period characterized by political corruption, violent
> strikes, rapid industrialization, and enormous immigration
> from Southern Europe (Nye 1990: 33).

At the same time electricity of course had a number of more substantial but equally obvious advantages. First of all, the introduction of electrical lighting in private homes, department stores, factories etc… was advantageous for everybody since the electrical lighting did not imply a consumption of oxygen, a production of heat and smoke and the danger of fire just as the previous forms of lighting did, whether it was gas mantles, oil lamps, candles or torches. Electrical lighting could not leak out, fill the room and explode; when a light bulb broke, it needed only be replaced. Second, electricity powered a great deal of the industrial machines and the new domestic appliances, such as electrical irons, toasters, percolators, fans etc…, which came in the wake of electricity.

Electricity was accordingly seen early on as a modern necessity that powered our machines, supplied us with new means of transportation and illuminated our ways, homes and workplaces. At the same time, electricity was also interpreted as a technology, which epitomized modern man's progress. Consequently, electricity was instilled with a wide horizon of social meanings, ranging from the ethereal or mythical to the more concrete meanings coming of the everyday social exchange in the factory or in the home. The experiences gained from these heterogeneous encounters resulted in a range of new meanings, which did not reside in the technology or in the electrical engineering in advance. Whether it was that electricity was "the nerve force of the modern city," that it improved and increased productivity in the factory or that it liberated the housewife, it is clear that the run-ins with electricity brought about a number of social meanings.

The patterns of social meaning which Nye describes, arguably appears more global, but certainly also less specific, than those constituted around the automobile in rural America. The lack of specificity has to do with the fact that electricity was introduced almost all over the country,[8] which means that there were a huge number of different social groups that took part in the attribution of meaning to electricity and to the different electrical appliances. But, at the same time, the number and diversity of the social groups involved in constituting these meanings also means that the new horizons of meaning generated and spread out all over the country. Like so disparate political, commercial and private groups played a part in constructing a multi-faceted horizon of social meanings. And finally we can see that broader and perhaps more culturally entrenched dimensions, such as religion and domestic life, also can play a substantial role, which the next example clearly shows.

---

8   There was however differences in how fast electricity were implemented in America. In the 1920s more than two-thirds of northern European farmers had electric power, while only 10 percent of the American farmers did (Nye 1990: 287), which testifies that the political system played a substantial part in the technological development and implementation.

Lego Bionicle

In January 2001, the Danish toy manufacturer Lego introduced a new brand of toys called *Lego Bionicle*.[9] The toys were a new range within the line of the popular building blocks, but were somewhat different from the original blocks in that they were accompanied by a distinct story line of heroes, villains and magic. The heroes and villains of the story line is the main theme and can be bought as small figures, just as it is possible to buy trading cards, books, board games, video and computer games and even special Nike Bionicle shoes. The new range became a big success for Lego as it soon became popular in Europe, the United States and in Asia. The main theme in the Bionicle game-world is six heroes or *Toa*, who struggle to bring peace to an imaginary tropical island called *Mata Nui*. The heroes are sworn to liberate its inhabitants, the *Tohunga*, from *Makuta*, an evil, shadowy beast.

But just months after the launch of the *Bionicle* range, Lego was presented with a claim from a lawyer, acting for a number of Maori tribes in New Zealand, stating that Lego did not have any rights using Polynesian names in the *Bionicle* toys; some of the words in mention, *Mata Nui* and *Tohunga*, both sacred words to the Maori, said to be used in a culturally degrading or violating manner. The claim was made since the Maori wanted to protect their cultural and intellectual heritage, and because reciprocity of respect and caring between the Maori and their creator gods is central to their relationship in order to make sure that the gods would ensure that the needs of the people were satisfied. Allegedly acting to take care of this relationship, the Maori tribes represented by lawyer Maui Solomon, sued the Lego Corporation.

> These names and concepts are derived from Maori and Polynesian traditional knowledge [...] The story line bears a remarkable resemblance to the traditional stories of the peoples from Rapa Nui (Easter Island) who are closely related to the Maori peoples. It is ... a violation of the cultural and intellectual property rights of the Maori, Hawaiian and Rapa Nui peoples. (Solomon in Osborn 2001).

---

9   The Lego Bionicle toys may not be included in an "archetypical" definition of technology, if such a definition exists. But I have however chosen to use this example since it first of all demonstrates the diversity in how such meanings evolve and secondly because it – just as it was the case in the electricity example – displays the diversity in the technological artifacts we encounter and have to decide our attitudes towards.

The conflict between Lego and the Maoris got a great deal of media attention, but eventually ended in an agreement and a code of conduct between the two parties, when Lego promised to stop any future commercial use of specific parts of Maori mythology and certain names.[10] The agreement even included that Lego and the Maori could work together and produce toys based on Maori knowledge and design.

The Maori tribes involved did not constitute a large social group, but because of the media interest[11] the lawsuit against Lego and subsequently the Maori cause attracted a great deal of attention. As such, it seems reasonable to suggest that the actions taken by the Maori lead to the attribution of a specific pattern of social or socio-cultural meanings to the Lego *Bionicle* range of toys and in addition that the media manifested or helped set up these meanings. Because of the Maori "revolt" the *Bionicle* toys were infused with meanings, which read that Lego and the *Bionicle* toy line were plagiarizing an ancient culture and religion. These meanings could thus indicate that the Lego toys were ethically inappropriate since they violated a people's cultural and religious values. The new meanings were in all probability not anticipated by Lego but were in a way the consequence of certain processes of design involved in creating the Bionicle range; that is, for instance, the choice of incorporating Polynesian language and mythology.

Whether this new social meaning affected the children's play with the Bionicle toys or the parents' inclination to buy them is hard to say, but the actions taken by the Maori did in some ways alter the intended horizon of meaning, which Lego had attributed to the toys. The new meanings did however not evolve due to the concrete appropriation or domestication of the toys by the Maori, but came about because of the enunciation of specific religious and cultural values. Therefore it can also be said that the new social meanings even can be seen as helping along Lego's attempt of establishing a mythical or fantastic universe around the Bionicle story line. But given that most children probably did not concern themselves with the impending lawsuit, which eventually was called off; this may not have been the case. The conflict between Lego and the Maori did however have actual consequences

10   The Maori lawsuit was eventually abandoned since Lego legally was entitled to use the names and register them as trademarks. The code of conduct established between Lego and the Maori was a set of ethical guidelines, which Lego promised to work by in the future.

11   The media attention was naturally quite significant in Denmark, as Lego is a Danish corporation.

since it ended in the passing of a code of conduct or a set of ethical guidelines, which Lego took upon them selves to work by in the future. As such, the new social meanings although not becoming stable, caused a technological change, as the design principles for future toys were changed. But even though the meanings did not become stable, the example shows that social institutions, such as religion and the law, just as social agents, can be a factor, which may influence the social construction of meaning.

Mobile Phones and Text Messaging

The final example I wish to include concerning the meaning of artifacts is related to mobile phones and more precisely to text messaging. The mobile phone is like its "ancestor," the stationary telephone, obviously first and foremost designed and used to make phone calls. The first commercial portable cellular phone, the Motorola DynaTAC 8000X, was introduced in 1983, costing just below $4000 and weighing in around 28 ounces (Motorola www1 and www2). The phones were an almost immediate success, despite their high cost and unmistakable inelegance and were praised for providing the owner with an unprecedented freedom, which the stationary phone could not provide. Almost a decade later, in December 1992, the first text message was sent from Sema, a British technology company, to Vodafone, a large British wireless carrier. Transmitted through the GSM network's signalling channel, text messaging was initially designed for sending service notifications and alerts, such as notifications to the subscribers of waiting voicemail messages and was later on developed even further, so it was possible to send text messages from one mobile phone to another.[12] Until the late 1990s, however, customer uptake was rather stagnant, since a large part of the wireless carriers had precluded themselves from opening their text messaging systems to interoperability, that is, to send messages from one carrier to another. This however became an absolute necessity caused by several circumstances: first of all it was necessary due to the high prices per minute and second of all an opening to interoperability was needed because of a huge increase in the number of young users, who had started buying prepaid calling plans. This development entailed an enormous growth in the number of

---

12 There are to distinct types of text messaging: the first, Mobile Terminated SMS, is messages sent from a server, software applications etc... and is received by a mobile phone. The second, Mobile Originated SMS, is messages sent from mobile phones to servers, software applications or other mobile phones.

sent text messages during the late 1990s and in the beginning of the twenty-first century.

The text messaging service, which as mentioned above originally was introduced with a view to sending short to the point messages, soon became object for actual communication. In some countries local and national contests in who were the quickest to write text messages were even held, and the producers of the phones started producing so called chat-boards and installing intelligent dictionaries (with predictive text input) in the phones to ease the otherwise fairly difficult typing. Instead of just being concise service messages, text messaging quickly became a significant part of the mobile phone communication culture. Several statistics illustrate the enormous increase in the number of sent text messages: an example could be Denmark, a country with around 5.3 million inhabitants and several wireless carriers. Here the number of sent text messages in the first six months of 2001 was 619 million; two years later, in the first half of 2003, this number had increased to 1.5 billion sent text messages (National IT and Telecom Agency www).

In contrast to the manufacturer's initial expectations, a relatively insignificant feature of the mobile phone became immensely popular during a very short period of time. And it seems more than reasonable to advocate that this development to a great extend took place due to the user's specific and frequent usage of the text messaging feature on their mobile phones. This development was of course only possible because the technology made it possible, but was not foreseen by the manufacturers of the mobile phones or by the original designers of the text messaging system. That text messaging would eventually turn out as an absolute success happened because of the appropriation of the users, who thus became agents of technological change as well as agents of the change in the horizon of meaning surrounding mobile phones. Because due to the popularity of text messaging the manufacturers started, as mentioned earlier, producing mobile phones with predictive text input, chat boards, mobile phones with special keyboards (such as the Nokia 5510 or the Nokia 6800 series) etc... and the text messaging culture also in turn spun of substantial changes in the advertising of wireless communication. But moreover text messaging became a distinct means of communication especially among young people, and does in this manner connote an ease-of-use, convenience, and discreteness not to mention that it is perceived as a fun and cheap way of communicating. The new social meaning of the mobile phone, which concerned an alternative way of communicating, thus evolved because of the patterns of appropriation by the users and developed into a distinct culture of communication (See also Wilska

2003). But at the same time this example illustrates that it is important to look into where the new meanings surface and again, which social groups that plays a role in the constitution of the new meaning.

The Attribution of Social Meaning

In the above mentioned examples, it appears clear that the social meaning that has been attributed to the four different technological artifacts came about in several different ways. At the same time, however, they all have as a common trait that these meanings were not originally intended. The surfaces of emergence are thus different since they appear in different social contexts, in different societies, at different periods of time and in different discursive formations.[13] In the case of the automobile at the start of the twentieth century, the social meaning, which were ascribed to it, mainly saw the light of day because innovative farmers sought to draw power from the automobile engine to power other machines. Later on, this resourcefulness led to special commercialised kits that made it possible to convert cars into semi-stationary sources of power or even into tractors. In this way the early automobile – at least in rural America – was physically reconfigured and at the same time new social meaning was ascribed to it as it for instance became a farm tool and a mediator of energy in the household.

Regarding the case of electricity, the social meanings, which appeared here were at times almost mythical and by large also vague and indefinable, as it, e.g., was perceived as a sign of progress as well as a revolution of domestic life. Electricity was, in short, transformative and desirable; it changed and reinforced society and American culture and did not seem to have any dark sides.

> Without any specific argument, the spectator was given to understand that progress, democracy, electrification and America were an indissoluble whole (Nye 1990: 61).

---

13   By discursive formation, I mean the regularities that exist between a range of statements, concepts, ideas, positions etc... As such the discursive formation can be described as a discursive framework, where statements, ideas etc... do not exist in isolation, but are parts of a set of structures that makes the statements, ideas, etc... make sense within the given period of time and in the given social context. See also Foucault (1972).

The new social meanings of electricity originated due to the experiences in the public social arena, where its reality and meaning were socially constructed a new by a vast heterogeneous configuration of social groups over a relatively long period of time.

The social meaning that surfaced just months after the launch of the Lego *Bionicle* toy range in 2001 was, on the other hand, the result of a two distinct social groups: the Maori and the media. Shortly after Lego introduced the Bionicle toys, they were met with a claim from the Maori that they were plagiarizing, degrading and even violating the Maori's cultural and intellectual heritage by using sacred words from the Polynesian language. This statement was further spread when various media carried the story and as a result contributed to the sedimentation of the new meaning of the *Bionicle* toys. These meanings did not evolve during processes of appropriation or domestication, but came about when the artifacts entered a specific socio-cultural context with fixed religious values; entering these settings the toys were perceived as related to the entire religious settings of the Maori society.

Lastly, the social meaning that emerged around mobile phones and text messaging grew out of the rapidly increasing consumption of an otherwise rather insignificant service feature. These patterns of consumption, especially among young people – led to new ways of perceiving the mobile phone and to changes in the concerned technologies. Because of the development of text messaging, mobile phones were seen as an alternative means of communications, which was not just limited to traditional – although mobile – telephony but also represented a relatively easy, cheap, discrete and less restrained way of communicating. Text messages can be written and read when the users fell like doing so, not just when the phone rings.

The examples I have drawn upon until this point illustrate that many of the artifacts of our everyday life do indeed have an interpretative flexibility or, to put in another way, it is a definite possibility that they may be interpreted or decoded in unintended or unforeseen ways depending on the social context in which they enter. These alterations may for instance end up

---

14 *Interpretative flexibility* is a term used in the Social Construction of Technology (SCOT) method (see also footnote 15) and has to do with that social groups may associate various incongruent meanings with technological artefacts, which leads to an interpretative flexibility appearing in relation to the design of a given artefact. See for instance Bijker (1987).

causing technological changes to the given artifact, reinforcing the meanings, which originally were installed in them during the process of design and production or dissuade people from using them as they may have been constructed as dangerous, incorrect, irresponsible or plain wrong. On the other hand, the new socially constructed meanings may encourage people to use the concerned artifact as it is construed as a correct, suitable, rational and efficient tool. Along these lines it is clear that such patterns of meaning as well as the manifestations and surfacing of social meanings see the light of day in a vast variety of ways, making it almost impossible to predict, steer or prevent their emergence.

But at the same time it also appears clear that the core phenomena, that is the attributing of meaning to artifacts is a somewhat uncovered subject. The surfacing of these meanings are evidently caused by different relevant social groups, but it is not clear how we are to perceive this development, which processes it includes and which variables that are important when we are trying to assess the construction of meaning. In what follows I will elaborate on the appearance or development of socially shaped meanings. The approach comprises a Foucault-inspired discourse analysis, which is meant to extend some of the analytical heuristics suggested by the "Social Construction of Technology" approach.[15] By utilizing this view I intend to dig deeper into how the attribution of social meanings can be understood, analysed and described. Furthermore, this account is aimed at illustrating the mechanisms of an artifact's interpretative flexibility – the conditions and variables we must assess when we are discussing and analysing how technological artifacts are perceived, received, domesticated and used in the social world. In short I aim at elaborating on a discussion of why given technological artifacts are perceived in specific ways in the social arena and how these meanings come about.

---

15   *The Social Construction of Technology* (SCOT) approach was developed in the 1980s by Trevor Pinch and Wiebe Bijker and is largely influenced by the Empirical Programme of Relativism (EPOR) (see Collins 1981 and footnote 21); and the Sociology of Scientific Knowledge (see for instance Collins 1985, Knorr-Cetina 1981 and 1983), which developed and elaborated on Thomas Kuhn's concept of paradigm (Kuhn 1962) in empirical studies and historical analyses to argue that scientific facts are socially constructed. SCOT thus rejects technological determinism and focuses on how social forces influence the design and production of technologies.

A Foucauldian Perspective

If it is possible that technological artifacts can be attributed with other meanings than those instilled in them during the various processes of design and production I will now outline how such an attribution might take place. By way of this outline I will discuss more distinct rules of formation, than those thus far covered. In order to assist the discussion let us return to the example of the automobile in rural America at the start of the twentieth century. When the farmers, who recently had invested in an automobile, realized that their new investment could be transformed or reconfigured into a semi-stationary power source or even a tractor, the discovery was manifested in several ways: the farmers wrote about how to make these reconfigurations in papers such as the *Wallace's Farmer* and the *Rural New Yorker;* they used their newly reconfigured power stations; and later on, they bought the special commercialised kits for transforming the automobiles into tractors or the like. So after having tried to resist the automobile early on, the farmers started weaving it into their existing socio-cultural patterns by adapting it in new ways. This means that the possibility for transforming automobiles into something *more*, that is, for instance a domestic tool for the farmer who perhaps could not afford to buy a new stationary power sources or who needed a power supply, was enunciated in several ways: from the more local daily use, the approval and endorsement of the kits to the more widespread press coverage. This enunciation entailed or was by large synonymous with the social construction of a new social meaning. Because of the regularity in the statements concerning the new ways of utilizing the automobile, a new horizon of meaning was being formed. The automobile, which until that point primarily had been perceived as a means of transportation, could now also be interpreted as a tool for the independent farmer to modernize his or her rural environment, which at that time still largely was without electricity (see footnote 8). Along these lines the new meanings unsurprisingly evolved in a dialectic relationship with the distinct technological changes that were being made to the automobile. But it was manifested and made visible to the general public due to the specific identity and persistence in the concerned statements.

In this way a vital point in the attribution of meaning to artifacts are the various new statements and patterns of behaviour made in relation to the concerned artifact. These statements and patterns of behaviour, although different in form, dispersed in time and in different geographical settings, and, regarding that the automobile could be used in other ways than as a means of transportation, formed a distinct group since they referred to the same object, but enunciated it in a specific new way. As such this example as well as the others – again unsurprisingly – shows that the attribution of new social meanings to artifacts happen by way of our social interaction and exchange, that is via our different statements and thus via our discursive practices and formations. But at the same time it leaves us without any clear idea of the rules or constraints to which the appearance of these new meanings is subject. The question I will address is therefore which factors that have steered the emergence and existence of these new meanings, and how we can assess these factors. I will seek to categorize and describe the heterogeneous and scattered statements; and I will try to illustrate what systems that govern their existence and how the statements relate to each other. My question consequently entails three necessary steps or analytical measures,[16] which are based on the observations I made in relation to the above four examples. These three steps are directly inspired by Michel Foucault's discourse analysis and by the analytical heuristics proposed by the Social Construction of Technology (SCOT).

1. First of all we must map the surfaces of emergence of these new social meanings. We must show how and where they differ from each other and from the existing or originally prescribed meanings. And we must demonstrate the specific rationality and codes utilized in the designation of new meanings to an artifact even though it is given that these surfaces will differ depending on the different social settings, the different periods of time and the different cultural milieus.

In relation to the Lego *Bionicle* case, the surface of emergence was clearly constituted by the religious Maori community, who evidently was the immediate relevant social group. As such the rationality behind defining the *Bionicle* toy range as a toy, which conflicted with a people's religious background, was that the Maoris wished to respect and protect the relationship to their gods. For that reason the specific codes utilized in the construction of a new meaning to Lego Bionicle were religious as well as judicial and had little or nothing to do with children's play, adventures, role playing etc., which were some of the Bionicle toy's initial codes or rules of enunciation.

The mapping of the surfaces of emergence include descriptions of the rel-

---

16 See also Michel Foucault's discussion on the formation of objects in *The Archaeology of Knowledge* (Foucault 1972). The three steps I describe here is in fact inspired by Michel Foucault's account on the formation of objects.

evant social groups,[17] which the SCOT approach points out as the key start-ing point for making social constructivist studies of technological systems (Bijker 1992). But moreover, these mappings must include the different forms of delineation and specification that the relevant social groups utilize in their way of enclosing the domain of which they speak. By focusing on these codes or discursive strategies[18] it is possible to illustrate the ways that social groups attribute more or less—according to their degree of stability, accuracy and coherence—distinct new meanings to artifacts as they are manifesting these meanings as describable, observable and endowed with specific consequences. The respective artifacts remain the points of crystal-lization or the nodal points from which the various meanings emanate; however, when the artifacts enter a new social domain or a new context it is possible that new nodal points or existing horizons of meaning conflict with the initial patterns of meaning whereby new meanings may come into exis-tence. This entails that the mapping of the surfaces of emergence conse-quently lead to a display of the existence of the given artifacts interpretative flexibility, or that such a plasticity has been activated once again.

2. Second of all, we must describe the authorities of delimitation. At a given time a closure[19] happens once again to the meaning-potential of the respec-

---

17 I do not wish to go into an in-depth discussions on how such relevant social groups are comprised; but it is obvious that they can be compiled by a vast variety of people, such as users, advertising agencies, journalists, scientists, NGO's etc... The SCOT approach, which is the primary inspiration for my use of the term, de-scribes the relevant social groups in the following way: "The use of the concept of a relevant social group is quite straightforward. The phrase is used to denote insti-tutions and organizations (such as military or some specific industrial company), as well as organized or unorganised groups of individuals. The key requirement is that all members of a certain social group share the same set of meanings, attached to a specific artifact" (Bijker 1987: 30). But at the same time Bijker acknowledges that there is no specific formula for the identification of the social groups.

18 By *discursive strategies* I mean the certain organizations of concepts, certain forms of enunciation, certain groupings of objects or the specific themes, which are ap-plied by one or more social groups.

19 The concept of *closure* is a SCOT term and is described as the process by which dif-ferent disagreeing social groups reach a consensus on how a specific technology must be designed, produced and what problems etc... it has to solve. Closure con-sequently means that the interpretative flexibility that exists in relation to e.g. the design of a given technology within a number of relevant social groups becomes inflexible. (See also Bijker 1992 and 1987 and footnote 21.)

tive technological artifact. In this way the plasticity of the new meaning or the reopened interpretative flexibility becomes inflexible. This process implies that different social institutions and groups play an important role, as they are recognized as authorities by the public opinion. These groups are characterized by having an extensive body of knowledge, ideas, habits and practices, which rule or define their perception and appropriation of the concerned artifact. Regarding the new meanings of the automobile that surfaced in rural America, it is obvious that a group of enterprising farmers were the primary dominant force in constituting the automobile as for instance a stationary source of power. With the introduction of the automobile in a rural countryside, largely lacking electrical power, this new technological artifact soon became an object of change. The change happened because the farmers wanted more efficient ways of ploughing, separating the cream or pumping water among other things. Or, put in another way, the farmers wanted and needed a way of easing their strenuous life. In this way the farmers had a specific body of knowledge, a series of practices and were situated in a particular societal setting, which made it obvious for them to make certain alterations to the automobiles. Their specific needs, knowledge and rationalities thus transformed the conventional perception of the automobile. Due to their actions, initiative and letters and articles in various papers, the group of farmers became an authority by demonstrating the new meanings of the automobile to other farmers, other social groups and of course to the automobile manufacturers.

Another example of the authorities of delimitation concerns text messaging, where the users undoubtedly were the most significant authority of delimitation even though they did not constitute a clearly definable whole. By the specific – and extremely widespread – patterns of usage the text messaging users were a crucial authority, because of their sheer number and distinct behaviour, which demonstrated their need for or inclination for using an alternative means of communication. In this way the increasing usage of text messaging manifested the altered or extended social meaning of the mobile phone to other potential users as well as to the manufacturers of the mobile phones and to the wireless carriers.

In relation to the design of technological artifacts the SCOT approach introduces the concept of technological frames, which is employed to depict the interactions between the relevant social groups that shape or design technological artifacts. These frames comprise the group's shared interpretations of possible problems, solutions, ways of employment, goals and so forth. The technological frames are continually shaped and reshaped; developed and stabilized by the social group as they structure the internal common assent of the group (Bijker 1987 and 1992). The concept of technological frames seems to be congruent with the extensive body of knowledge, values, practices, etc... which provide the foundation for the actions of the authorities of delimitation. But at the same time it is however necessary to stress that the technological frames primarily is used as a metaphor for the "concepts and techniques employed by a community in its problem solving" (Bijker 1987: 168).[20] For that reason, it seems apparent that the technological frames first and foremost are related to the process of design and production; or in other words the processes whereby the technological artifacts are endowed with their primary intention, functionality or *telos*. But, as it is illustrated in the Lego *Bionicle* example as well as in the electricity example, the designation of new meanings do not necessarily concern problem solving or other rational strategies typically encompassed in the design of technological artifacts. On the contrary, it is possible that the new social meanings ascribed to technological artifacts originate because of a variety – and not necessarily rational – reasons, such as e.g. habitual behaviour. This is naturally dependent on the artifacts in question, and in many cases it is given that the new social meanings imbued on a technological artifact will in fact be rational. This may for instance have been the case when the Internet in the public discourse in Denmark was described as an economical propellant (See, e.g., Forskningsministeriet 1999); whether this statement was purely rational is debateable as it surely was symbolically as well as rational. But this does however mean that the analysis of social meanings imbued on technological artifacts do not solely encompass unambiguous causal connections, but rather the result of complex interactions between different contextual variables. Therefore I would like to complement SCOT's concept of technological frames with the concept of *the institutionalised frameset*. This concept is aimed at highlighting the attention towards the "wider socio-cultural" context such as it is advised in SCOT and in the Empirical Programme of Rel-

---

20   In the same article Wiebe Bijker later on elaborates on the definition of the technological frames when he describes them as the actor's "goals, problem-solving strategies, experimental skills, theoretical training, and so on" (Bijker 1987: 174).

ativism (EPOR), [21] which is the ideological base for SCOT.[22] But when SCOT and EPOR speak of a wider socio-cultural milieu, the field of study more or less becomes everything. The fact that the socio-cultural context is a crucial influence and that it is necessary to relate the discussion and analysis to the wider socio-cultural setting is a definite truism. The predominant approach to culture (see e.g. Jantzen 1997) typically comes of the anthropological tradition of cultural analysis (see for instance Margaret Mead (Mead 1923) or Ruth Benedict (Benedict 1959)) and is typically concerned with defining culture as *a whole way of life* such as it roughly has been done since Edward Tylor (Tylor 1958) and even Johan Gottfried Herder (Herder 1965). But by advocating such a definition, culture and the socio-cultural context just seem to become a convenient label, which can be used to describe a great deal of the many often intangible factors that influence or determine the constitution of scientific knowledge or the construction of technological artifacts among other things. But at the same time, this context or milieu is an extremely difficult entity to assess analytically since it includes everything from our moral, laws, customs, institutions and art to our beliefs, codes, tools and so on. Therefore, I propose the concept of the institutionalised frameset, with which I aim at containing the relevant social institutions that characterize, regulate and determine the social exchange, which are related to or appears around the surfaces of emergence of the new social meanings. The social institutions are as such objective facts and are at the same time social constructions and clear

---

21   Wiebe Bijker identifies three stages in EPOR's dealing with the social construction of scientific knowledge: in the first stage the interpretative flexibility of scientific findings and knowledge is illustrated; the second stage contains the social mechanisms that limit the interpretative flexibility or brings it to a closure; and in the third stage the closure mechanisms—covered in stage two—are related to the wider social and cultural settings (Bijker 1987: 27). The SCOT approach is directly inspired by EPOR and the three explanatory stages have furthermore been transferred to SCOT's analytical strategies or heuristics (relevant social groups, interpretative flexibility, technological frames and closure). For further insight in EPOR see e.g. Collins (1981).

22   The increased attention is necessary and relevant since SCOT in a large number of cases primarily focus on the process of design and production and not on what happens to the technological artefacts once they leave the assembly line. Critiques of such focuses have been addressed previously e.g. by Paul Rosen (Rosen 1993), Hughie MacKay and Gareth Gillespie (MacKay 1992) and even by Ronald Kline and Trevor Pinch (Kline 1996).

manifestations of the knowledge, ideas and meanings that constitute and define our behaviour (See also Berger 1966).

The institutionalised frameset is of course – just as the socio-cultural milieu – a complex entity to analyse, but since our social institutions are produced and reproduced by our various forms of interaction, it is my thesis that they appear or are referred to – directly or indirectly, intentionally or unintentionally – in our modes of expression, that is for instance in statements such as newspaper articles or in advertising campaigns. It is therefore necessary that our analytical interest once again is focused on the statements that form the new meanings. But this time around we must direct our attention towards the references made to the institutionalised frameset. We must observe whether institutional references are being made and which institutions these references involve. The argument is consequently that the references – whatever it is to institutions such as the state, matrimony, the education system or religion – reflect a set of ideas, which due to our social practises have been fixed as a set of rules and here provide the concerned social agents with stability, a sense of continuity as well as guidelines for social agency. This focus includes an analysis of the relevant statements and patterns of behaviour that characterize the social exchange related to the technological artifact in question. These statements and our behaviour can along these lines be seen as specific patterns of enunciation that form a discourse in which references to certain institutions to some degree are being made.

An analysis of the institutionalised frameset will elucidate some of the more insubstantial factors, which influence the social construction of the new meanings attributed to technological artifacts. As such, it is given that a close dialectical relationship exists between the institutionalised frameset and the technological frames, but also that either of these dynamic aspects at times may dominate the process of generating new meaning. The extensive body of knowledge, ideas, habits and practices, which define the ways that the authorities of delimitation perceive of, use and especially delimit and enable the social meaning of a given technological artifact is thus at the same time constituting the technological frames as well as it is influenced and determined by the institutionalised frameset. In relation to the aforementioned examples it is clear that the family and rural life were some of the institutions which could have influenced the reconfiguration of the automobile. For the Maori, the religious institution was of course the dominant institutional frameset, while mans ingenuity and strive towards progress can be recognised as an institution which governed the meanings generated in relation to electricity in the American public in the late nineteenth century.

Concerning text messaging, individual communication seems to be a dominant social institution, which in the late 1990s have become an even more clearly defined institution. With reference to these examples it furthermore seems reasonable to suggest that a connection exists between the institutionalised frameset and the specific rationality and codes utilized in relation to the surfaces of emergence.

The social institutions do as such not themselves define the constitution of the new social meaning, but are rather some of the crucial factors that enables it to appear in relation to other meanings and to the intention and telos, which originally was inscribed into the technological artifact. In this way the institutionalised frameset must be distinguished from the primary relations that invoked the new social meaning; that is the relevant social groups, the authorities of delimitation or in sum the parties directly involved in the construction of meaning.

3. Finally, we must specify and describe the grids of specification, which are the structures or systems by which the new social meaning is defined, arranged, categorized and justified; the new and existing taxonomies that governs the new meanings division, the degrees to which it is related to other meanings and the ways that it excludes other meanings. With the emergence of text messaging a distinct new mode of communication surfaced, but at the same time it was necessary that this new way of communicating with others were described in specific ways, which did not coincide with other modes of mobile phone-based communication. It was, in other words, required to establish relations of distance, difference, resemblance and so on between the new way of communicating and the multiple other ways. Such grids of specification could very well, e.g., be rationality, economy, ideology, law, fashion, professional knowledge, demography or religion and various specific connections between such factors. And at the same time there is naturally a god chance that the grids of specification will be closely related to the institutionalised frameset, such as it was the case in the Maori and Lego conflict: here the new meanings attributed to the Bionicle toy range were clearly rooted in a religious institution and were therefore also defined, categorized and justified in a religious grid of specification.

What this amounts to is that one might propose that if we are to analyse the social meanings attributed to technological artifacts, we must search for the social groups that warrant these meanings; we must show how these meanings find their place and which rules of emergence they follow. We must also illustrate the relations that exist between the different layers of formation. In short, we must seek to analyse the complex constellation of *rules* that have governed a series of particular practices and, in this way, have defined the specificity of a given new socially constructed meaning. Because such meanings have not waited to be set free, they are not innate values that exist a priori. They are the result of human agency and exist under a range of productive and positive conditions such as social institutions, norms, various techniques, social agency and processes. As such these conditions are not present in the technological artifact, but are some of the crucial factors that enable the new social meanings to emerge.

A Brief Remark on Foucault's Notion of the Épistémè

In relation to the above mentioned brief discussion of whether the social meanings attributed to artifacts are to be perceived as purely rational, it is appropriate to touch on Michel Foucault's notion of the *épistémè* (henceforth episteme).[23] As mentioned afore SCOT explains the concept of technological frames as social group's shared interpretations of possible problems, solutions, ways of employment, goals and so forth; as such these frames are "concepts and techniques employed by a community in its problem solving" (Bijker 1987). Along these lines I rendered the technological frames as being predominantly rationally inclined and introduced the institutionalised frameset as a cognate concept for better including and describing the various *socio-cultural factors*, which influence the not necessarily rational motifs or strategies implicated in the construction of new social meanings. But at the same time I acknowledge that rationality or more specific goal-oriented rationality in fact might be a cornerstone in the construction of the new social meanings. If I am to describe the reason to this acknowledgement I wish to include Foucault's account of the episteme, which he describes in the following manner:

> This episteme may be suspected of being something like a
> world-view, a slice of history common to all branches of knowl-
> edge, which imposes on each one the same norms and postu-
> lates, a general stage of reason, a certain structure of thought

---

23   The term episteme seems by large to refer to the same thing as the "historical a priori" and the "archive." The relationship between these terms is brought up regularly for instance by Michael S. Roth (Roth 1981).

that the men of a particular period cannot escape – a great body
of legislation written once and for all by some anonymous hand.
By *episteme*, we mean, in fact, the total set of relations that unite,
at a given period, the discursive practices that give rise to epistemological figures, sciences, and possible formalized systems;
[...] As a set of relations between sciences, epistemological figures, positivities, and discursive practices, the episteme makes it
possible to grasp the set of constraints and limitations which, at
a given moment, are imposed on discourse (Foucault 1972:
191f).

Foucault's concept of the episteme can, along these, be understood as the
systematic understanding of a given domain and in wider terms as varying
historical frames of reference or historically fixed frames of thought and
knowledge.[24] Like so the episteme[25] imposes constraints and rules on what is
possible to say in certain discursive formations. And, if we apply this strain
of thought to our account it does indeed seem plausible to suggest that goal-
oriented rationality conditions and determines the genesis of technological
systems. Technologies are first and foremost designed and produced to solve
problems or to aid us in our various endeavours. Whether it concerns our
entertainment, cooking, transportation, working life, sex life (e.g., regarding
contraceptives) and so on, technologies are designed to optimise, rationalize,
improve, etc... our social practices. Because of such observations, I am inclined to propose that we can understand the way we behave in relation to
technologies as governed by a sort of episteme or a shared horizon of knowl-

---

24   Foucault distinguishes between two layers of knowledge, derived from the French
     savoir and *connaissance* where the usual French distinction between the two terms
     is that *savoir* means to know, while *connaissance* means to be familiar with. By us-
     ing *connaissance* Foucault refers to the conscious rules we in a given period of
     time justify our knowledge by, while *savoir* is the underlying essential conditions
     that renders these recognitions possible. *Savoir* is as such not to be reduced to po-
     litical, social, religious and economic conditions; it cannot be discovered within
     the historical period, but have to be constructed by the historian, who is seeking
     to understand the rules and conditions, which existed for the production of
     knowledge and hence the knowledge statements made during a specific and de-
     marked period.
25   For further insight on the episteme see e.g., (Maclean 1998) and (Foucault 1972).

edge and ideas,[26] which makes it obvious to us to understand technologies as being predominantly rational, practical, logical, reasonable and sensible artifacts because they above all are designed to serve us. But the episteme does however not necessarily bring the knowledge of a certain period of time into complete uniformity such that everybody thinks the same thing. Instead, it makes it possible to – on the basis of the same rules – to take different stands and to hold competing views on the same issues. Surveillance technologies, weapons, contraceptives, microwave ovens and so forth are all goal-rational technologies even though opinions on their eventual implications may be entirely different.

Technologies are from the start designed and produced to be bought, used and appropriated and are in that sense goal-rational or at least intended as goal-rational as they are instrumental. The goal-oriented rationality is thus inscribed in the functional constitution of the technological artifacts. And, when the technologies eventually are used in the social arena, the immediate processes of social assimilation manifest the goal-oriented rationality that is instilled in the respective technologies. At the same time, these processes of assimilation are naturally influenced by various factors such as advertising, trends, habits, institutionalised framesets and so on. The central argument, however, is that technological artifacts *a priori* are rendered as rational due to their functional, intentional or instrumental constitution. This means that this historical *a pri-*

---

26 Along these lines I understand the episteme as a shared horizon of knowledge, which evolves at a given time and in a certain societal setting and here governs our discursive practices and bind together the discursive formations (see also footnote 13). The episteme is thus regularities or a specific mode of discourse in which knowledge, truth and power are joined together but not mastered by the human subject. This means that the episteme is not a structure or a set of organizing principles, but rather a set of relations or, as mentioned above, a shared horizon, which gives rise to our production of knowledge and meaning. In connection to the notion of the episteme it is also appropriate to mention that Foucault has been said to eventually having abandoned the idea of the episteme because of the question of how epistemic cultures change over time. And while Focuault in his later works (after *Le Mots et les choses* in which he introduced the term episteme [Foucault 1966]) did not spend much time elaborating on the episteme, his continuing interest in the knowledge and power that runs through society, which eventually evolved into his theory of *biopower* (Foucault 1998) is clearly in line with the notion of the episteme. I will however not discuss this any further, but I do take into account that the question of how epistemic cultures change over time is highly relevant.

ori or "episteme" permeates and determines the technological frames, the institutionalised frameset and in general the views held on technologies in the social world. Following this argument I find it reasonable to suggest that such an episteme also constrains, enables and influences the new social meanings, which surface and are attributed to technological artifacts in the social arena. And in this regard it is imperative that the analyses of new social meanings imbued on technological artifacts take this episteme into account.

SOCIAL MEANING AND SOCIAL CONSEQUENCES

When the Internet entered the public purview in Denmark, a range of governmental publications[27] proclaimed it as liberatory and emancipating; as an economical propellant; and as a technology, which when used correctly, it would ensure Danish citizens more quality in their everyday lives, it was plain to see that such qualities did not reside inherently in the concerned technology. In the concerned publications, the Internet was being attributed with meanings that transcended its intended functionality. These and a number of other descriptions of the Internet were made with a clear intent; the Danish government wanted to secure the Danish welfare state and during the 1990s it seemed clear that the Internet was a technology, which could facilitate economic, social and cultural security in the years to come. Of course, such descriptions did not go on unnoticed; they were adopted, manifested and challenged in the media by reporters, laymen and experts and became part of the general and very extensive Internet discourse (See Vetner 2001). But the guidelines and recommendations made in these publications were at the same time incorporated in business strategies, in the educational system and in the public administration, since many of the initiatives put forth in the publications were realised.[28] This favourable reception of the In-

---

27   Two of the prominent publications were *Info-samfundet år 2000* (*The Information Society Year 2000*) (Forskningsministeriet 1994) and *Det Digitale Danmark* (*The Digital Denmark*) (Forskningsministeriet 1999). These reports were the key accounts in a range of IT and Internet related publications initiated by the Danish government. The two key publications contained a number of recommendations, advices and distinct plans, which Danish businesses, institutions and so forth were strongly encouraged to follow.

28   At the same time one may argue that some of the initiatives to some degree also determined or structured specific patterns of social practice, as the possibility to access public information through the Internet and the possibility to exchange and submit information, i.e. tax reports, with the public authorities via the Internet were heavily encouraged as well as made easier.

ternet manifested the general positive attitude towards the new technology that rapidly spread throughout Denmark.

Along these lines, it is clear that the social meanings or descriptions invested in the Internet were deeply rooted in the political system, in political ideology and in economical calculations; as such, they had had substantial social, economical and political consequences. But, at the same time, I find it sound to argue that this vast horizon of meaning – which of course also was nourished by the flourishing international Internet discourse – also had more widespread consequences for the ordinary Danish citizen. The increasing and very rapid uptake of the Internet in the ordinary Danish household thus happened simultaneously with a continuous stream of predominantly positive descriptions, ideas, presentiments, hopes, etc… related to the Internet.[29] And without jumping to any conclusions I find it rather straightforward to suggest that the multitude of social meanings, which in different ways were imbued on the Internet, have played a substantial part in the Danish uptake of this technology, as they have been a frame of reference on how to understand the Internet.

Alongside the necessity of understanding and studying the processes of design and production the social relations that technologies embodies and influence and the social, cultural, economic ramifications that technologies have, it is equally important to consider how technologies are perceived, altered, enunciated and appropriated by the users in the social arena. An adequate understanding of why a particular technology is or is not used; why people in different social settings and positions have dissimilar experiences with the same technology, or why the technology is used in distinct ways or has a specific impact; is unlikely to be achieved without taking all these areas into consideration. Following this assumption, I have discussed the social

---

29   The Danish Prime Minister from 1993 to 2001, Poul Nyrup Rasmussen was among those, who recommended the Danes to use the Internet. In his 2001 New Years speech he said [our translation]: "I want a Denmark that, plain and simple, is the worlds greatest IT-Nation. This is not an unrealistic dream. It entails that every Dane must have access to the Internet and have the possibility to have an e-mail address. The public authorities have to be at the forefront regarding the employment of computers and information technology." (Jeg vil gerne have et Danmark, der ganske enkelt er verdens bedste IT-nation. Det er ikke en umulig drøm. Det betyder, at alle danskere skal have adgang til Internet og mulighed for en e-mailadresse. Den offentlige sektor skal være med helt fremme med anvendelsen af computere og informationsteknik). (Nyrup Rasmussen www).

meanings which are constructed via the social exchanges and via the processes of assimilation because users – just as users do – react to the technologies that they meet and during such encounters embed new social meanings into the technologies. And for that reason I argue that it is imperative that we study these social constructions of meaning, because despite being shaped by us or by society, technologies are used and perceived in unintended and unpredictable ways. This happens because users socially construct technologies in ways that cannot be steered, prevented or foreseen. And because of this we cannot defend overlooking the users, when writing the story of technology.

FINAL REMARKS

In this article I have been concerned with proposing a suggestion on how to understand and analyse the social meanings that users, advertising agencies, politicians and other relevant social groups attribute technological artifacts. In doing so I have suggested a discourse analytical approach that extends some of the heuristics proposed in the Social Construction of Technologies method. I have argued that technological artifacts are endowed with meanings since they have a purposive constitution; these meanings are thus attributed to the technological artifact during the various processes of design and production. But furthermore technological artifacts are encoded with meaning and symbolic value in the social arena when they are marketed, deployed and used or rejected by a variety of social agents. Of course, different technological artifacts offer different possibilities for such a construction of meaning, but the possibilities are not limitless, depending on the artifact in question. And furthermore, it is evident that our freedom to create such patterns of social meaning is not absolute since we operate in communities, in discursive formation, and in historical periods that shapes or determines what we can say and do in complex and comprehensible ways.[30] Studies of such meanings are imperative as these meanings illustrate the active role of the users in the shaping and defining of the technologies, which exist in their everyday lives. In this way, these social meanings are indications of how the technologies are appropriated and entrenched in the social world

---

30 See also Karen Burke LeFevre's account on invention processes in *Invention as a Social Act*. Lefevre describes her thesis in the following way: "Invention is *social* in that even while it occurs in an individual, it is heavily influenced by that individual's relationship to others through the social entity of language as well as through social structures, forms, purposes, and practices" (Lefevre 1986: 119-20).

as well as examples on how the social world at the same time shape the social exchange between social agents and technological artifacts.

The title I have chosen for this article is partly intended as a comment on Langdon Winners article "Do Artifacts Have Politics?" (Winner 1980) in which the author argues that it indeed is possible for artifacts to have politics. I entirely agree. Technological artifacts have meanings, politics and ethic. However, the configuration and range of these meanings, politics, ethics etc... depend not only upon how they are designed and produced – and whether these meanings, politics, ethics etc... were intended or unintended – but also on how relevant social groups have constructed and attributed meaning to them once they were introduced in the social arena. Thus, my primary purpose with this article has been to demonstrate the necessity of analysing these meanings. This is because the meanings of technological artifacts come about in all stages of their lifespan. This is the case during the stage of invention, design and production, during the various stages of externalisation such as marketing and during the appropriation by the users. Technological artifacts are social constructions and it is obligatory that we analyse them on all stages of their existence.

I believe that the approach I have suggested in this article confirm the necessity for the continuing analysis of technological artifacts. And along the way, I have tried to extend the scope of the SCOT method, and in a wider perspective I have tried to extend the range of social constructivist oriented technology analysis. The premise for this article is however undoubtedly that the conclusions I have reached and the suggestions I have put forth primarily are based on a few examples and on theoretical deliberations. As such it is clear that further confirmation and adjustments of these hypotheses and analytical guidelines are to be made via further empirical studies.

Works Cited

Akrich, Madeline and Bruno Latour (1992): *A Summary of a Convenient Vocabulary for the Semiotics of Human and Nonhuman Assemblies.* In Wiebe Bijker and John Law /ed.: *Shaping Technology/ Building Society : Studies in Sociotechnical Change.* – Cambridge : The MIT Press.

Benedict, Ruth (1959): *Patterns of Culture.* – Boston : Houghton Mifflin Company (Originally 1934).

Berger, Peter L. and Thomas Luckmann (1966): *The Social Construction of Reality: A Treatise in the Sociology of Knowledge.* New York : Anchor.

Bidou, Catherine, Marc Guillame and Véronique Prévost (1988): *L'Ordinaire de la Télématique: Offre et usages des services utilitaires grand-public.* – Paris : Editions de L'Iris.

Bijker, Wiebe E. et al (1987): *The Social Construction of Technological Systems : New Directions in the Sociology and History of Technology.* – Cambridge : The MIT Press.

Bijker, Wiebe E. and John Law /ed. (1992): *Shaping Technology/Building Society : Studies in Sociotechnical Change.* – Cambridge : The MIT Press.

Collins, Harry M. (1981): *Stages in the Empirical Programme of Relativism.* in *Social Studies of Science* Vol. 11: 3-11. – London : Sage.

Collins, Harry M. (1985): *Changing Order : Replication and Induction in Scientific Practice.* – London : Sage.

Feenberg, Andrew (1995): *Alternative Modernity: The Technical Turn in Philosophy and Social Theory.* – Berkeley : University of California Press.

Feenberg, Andrew (1999): *Questioning Technology.* – New York : Routledge.

Fischer, Claude (1992): *America Calling – A social history of the telephone to 1940.* – Berkeley : University of California Press.

Forskningsministeriet (1994): *Info-Samfundet år 2000.* – Copenhagen : Forskningsministeriet.

Forskningsministeriet (1999): *Det Digitale Danmark.* – Copenhagen : Forskningsministeriet.

Foucault, Michel (1966): *Les Mots et les choses.* – Paris : Editions Gallimard.

Foucault, Michel (1972): *The Archaeology of Knowledge : and the discourse on language.* – Tavistock, 1972.

Foucault, Michel (1998): *The Will to Knowledge : The History of Sexuality, Volume 1.* – London : Penguin, 1998.

Grint, Keith and Steve Woolgar (1997): *The Machine at Work : Technology, Work and Organization.* – London : Polity Press.

Herder, Johann Gottfried von (1965): *Ideen zur Philosophie der Geschichte der Menschheit.* – Berlin: Aufbau-Verlag (Originally 1784-1791).

Jantzen, Christian (1997): *Fra evolution til strukturation : rids af nogle kulturteoretiske positioner.* – Aalborg : Aalborg Universitet. Unpublished working paper.

Kline, Ronald and Trevor Pinch (1996): *Users as Agents of Technological Change : The Social Construction of the Automobile in the Rural United States.* – In *Technology and Culture*, October 1996; 37, 4. – Johns Hopkins University Press.

Knorr-Cetina, Karin D. (1981) *The Manufacture of Knowledge : An Essay on the Constructivist and Contextual Nature of Science.* – London : Pergamon.

Knorr-Cetina, Karin D. and Michael Mulkay (1983): *Science Observed : New Perspectives on the Social Study of Science.* – London : Sage.

Kuhn, Thomas S. (1962): *The Structure of Scientific Revolutions.* – Chicago : University of Chicago Press.

LeFevre, Karen Burke (1986): *Invention as a Social Act.* – Southern Illinois University Press.

Lipartito, Kenneth (2003): *Picturephone and the Information Age : The Social Meaning of Failure* in Technology and Culture Vol. 44, No. 1, 2003: 50-81.

MacKay, Hughie and Gareth Gillespie (1992): *Extending the Social Shaping of Technology Approach : Ideology and Appropriation.* In *Social Studies of Science* Vol. 22: 685-716. – London : Sage.

Maclean, Ian (1998): *Foucault's Renaissance Episteme Reassessed : An Aristotelian Counterblast* In *Journal of the History of Ideas*, Vol. 59, No. 1, January 1998: 149-166.

Mead, Margaret (1923): *Coming of Age in Samoa.* – New York.

Motorola (www1): http://motoinfo.motorola.com/motoinfo/20th_anniversary/docs/ 20thAnnouncementRelease.doc (last visited June 23. 2004).

Motorola (www2): http://motoinfo.motorola.com/motoinfo/20th_anniversary/docs/ how_its_changed.pdf (last visited June 23. 2004).

National IT and Telecom Agency, Denmark (www): http://www.itst.dk/ image.asp?page= image&objno=135226277 (last visited June 23. 2004).

Nye, David (1990): *Electrifying America : Social Meanings of a New Technology, 1880-1940*, Cambridge, MIT Press.

Nyrup Rasmussen, Poul (www): *New Years speech 2001*: http://www.nyrup.dk/ taler/2001 /01.html (Last visited June 23. 2004).

Osborn, Andrew (2001): *Maoris say Lego has no right to use their words.* – The Guardian, May 31, 2001. See also http://www.guardian.co.uk/print/0,3858,4 195290-103681,00.html (last visited June 23. 2004).

Rosen, Paul (1993): T*he Social Construction of Mountain Bikes : Technology and Postmodernity in the Cycle Industry.* In *Social Studies of Science*, Vol. 23: 479-513. – London : Sage.

Roth, Michael S. (1981): *Foucault's "History of the Present"* in *History and Theory*, Vol. 20, No. 1 February 1981: 32-46.

Tylor, Edward B. (1958): *Primitive Culture.* – New York (Originally 1871).

Vetner, Mikael (2001): *Internetdiskursen : Viden, ideologi og magt (The Internet Discourse : Knowledge, Ideology and Power)*, unpublished Masters thesis, Aalborg University 2001.

Wilska, Terhi-Anna (2003): *Mobile Phone Use as Part of Young People's Consumption Styles* In *Journal of Consumer Policy*, December 2003; 26: 441-463.

Winner, Langdon (1980): *Do Artifacts Have Politics?* in *Daedalus*, Vol. 109, No. 1, Winter 1980. Reprinted in *The Social Shaping of Technology*, Donald McKenzie and Judy Wajcman / ed. – London : Open University Press, 1985 and second edition 1999.

"What Does it Mean to Theorize Media?"

Of Questions and Positions, or What Does it Mean to Theorize Media?

Steen Christiansen
Department of Languages and Intercultural Studies
Aalborg University

One may wonder about the existence of this essay, if not the existence of this entire collection. Since this is a volume released by and for a university, is it not to be expected that any object, be it media or anything else, is meant to be analysed and theorised? Why question this practice and why discuss it, is the university not an institution that is designed specifically for these activities with the hopeful payoff that the student will later be able to get a job?

Since this volume deals explicitly with the activity of the university, it would be natural to investigate the institutional practices which surround the university and discuss not just what it means to theorise media, but also ask about the relevance of this theorization. In doing so, one must examine all parts of the question and reveal the assumptions which lie beneath, bringing to the fore any hidden codes which are taken for granted.

Here we must realise that the form of the question becomes relevant, simply because the question asked will determine to a large extent the answer given. Because of this, we should proceed slowly and continually reflect on the question as well as the answer. Before moving on, then, we need to take into account the word "theorize" and "media." Since my answer will depend on my understanding of both these terms, let us not assume that the question of media can be answered simply.

Let us begin with this question: what is media? How do we separate, if we must, media from, for instance, literature? Is literature not a medium, e.g., the book, the magazine, the Internet? This is, of course, of particular interest to me, due to my more or less schizophrenic division between literary and media studies. The question here must be whether this schizophrenia is relevant, or if it is artificial.

We might reform the question: what do we mean when we say media? It seems to me that it points to art, which is dependent on newer technology than the pen. Yet, this definition also strikes me as peculiarly false. Is the concept of media bound up with an existence in more than one medium, such as audio and visual? In that case the term should be multimedia, yet that is also misleading, as most would regard multimedia as belonging to the field of what the computer can do.

If text is part of media when it is placed on a website or in a comic book, why is it not when it is placed in a book? Or, are media dependent on a particular interplay between the visual and the verbal. Even this dividing line becomes problematic when we realize that there are plenty of novels, which include visual elements, such as the most typical novel of them all, *Tristram Shandy* (Laurence Sterne, 1767). And what of plenty of poetry where the visual form of the text is particularly relevant? The reason that this question of the definition of media is at all relevant is of course due to the institutional division between media and literary studies, which, rightly I believe, continues to assert the difference between the two fields.

Marshall McLuhan has defined media as any extension of man (McLuhan, 1964), but since we are most likely to not deal with bicycles, neither as objects for analysis nor theorisation, this definition must be discounted as too extensive. Furthermore, it would not differentiate at all between literature and media. Other definitions might suggest something along the lines of being one or more semiotic systems which serve for transmitting or expressing cultural "messages" or contents; a sign system which makes sense to someone else. But even here, we are not distinct from literature and we have the further problem of dealing with media as a form of communication, which is certainly problematic in some instances of media texts.

In the end, it seems that the definition of media is inherently problematic and that its definition must become central to the study of it, and certainly also its theorization. So far, we must perhaps be satisfied with the answer that media is whatever I point to when I say the word "media." Or more properly for our concerns here, what the director of the Culture and Media Studies at Aalborg University points to when s/he says the word "media." Or we could go a bit further and let you answer the question, if only for yourself.

DEFINITION OF MEDIA

There was another choice at the inception of this essay (remember, it is necessary to be aware of all the facts), and that was to write about what it means to analyse media (I here skip completely over the fact that media could have been replaced with culture in both instances), rather than theorize it. It is a peculiarity in our field (and surely no fault of the editor's) that these two things are seen as separate entities and practices.

Can we analyse without theory? If so, what do we need theory for? Can we theorize without analysis? If so, what do we need analysis for? Could we have reached the level of sophistication we have today without the existence of theory? All these questions are of vital importance and reflect back on the original question. I certainly have no expectations to end discussion on these matters, and in fact would rather regard it as critical that we continually engage in these questions, so that we are intimately aware of the status of theory and analysis at every point in history.

Can we separate our definition of media from our definition of theory? This is the basic problem which I am dealing with here and since textual media in a book is constituted as linear by institutional practices, one definition must follow the other.

First of all, however, we need to turn our gaze to the question of theory before we can answer the question of theorisation. This definition must mirror the one I just took regarding media and its definition, but with the added realisation that our understanding of theory is connected to our definition of media. And, most certainly, the opposite is also the case, perhaps even more so.

It is here that the difference between theory and analysis must be discussed as it is the position theory holds in relation to analysis which gives theory its particular status. This status is inherently problematical, always already under suspicion. Is theory prior to analysis and even more problematical, is it prior to the text? If theory is prior to text, what is theory based on? If we believe this, we must continually question the basis of the theory, asking if that basis is relevant to the text, how this relevance is judged and who determines the relevance.

Still, however, if theory is anterior to text, then theory is derived from text and so cannot hold any authority over text, since it then depends on text for its existence. Yet this peculiar bind makes theory basically meaningless, having no particular power over the text and so theory is left impotent, with no particular use and no real status other than what text may confer upon it.

We encounter the same problem with the question of analysis: if we analyse before theory, do we need theory at all? Or, if we need theory to analyse must we then discount the analyses which are not based explicitly on theory? Or does that apply only to analysis based on theories we do not agree with? To extend this question even further, when exactly are we dealing with a theory? Since we all have experience in dealing with media, we can all deduce certain things intuitively from these media texts. These intuitions are not simply based on loose assumptions, though certainly they also are that, but there are also specific structures in the way we approach media texts. This opens for another point: can a theory based on another medium be used in a different medium? How much of the theory must be altered and fine-tuned?

We can hardly argue that every reader has what amounts to a personal theory constructed from all these intuitions, experiences, and so on. We would not call this a theory but rather competence. So when can we say that there is actually an existing theory, what are the requirements for a theory? David Bordwell, for example, argues that theory is "…a system of propositions that claims to explain the nature and functions of cinema" (Bordwell, 1989: 4). He is writing specifically about cinema, yet his claim works well enough for a definition of theory in any media.

Let's look at this a bit further. Bordwell's basic claim is that theory is used to explain. This means that everybody must have some form of theoretical basis in order to even understand texts. Much of theoretical basis can be based on experience, so that we need not discount non-academic understandings of texts. If theory is used to explain a text, how does it do this? We must assume that the theory will point out certain areas which are of critical importance, places in any text which must be examined. We can also assume that the theory will be used in similar ways on pretty much all texts, with only very little variation.

If we look at a variety of theories, then this is exactly the way that they do work. There are specific, though always different, parts of a text which are placed under specific scrutiny, such as textual unity for New Critics (Wimsatt and Beardsley, Cleanth Brooks, etc.), textual repressions for psychoanalytics and so on. A variety of arguments are then used to show how these specific parts are the most important and relevant for the study of texts.

A theory needs to be convincing. This is achieved through a variety of strategies, the most important being what Bordwell argues that: "A theory has conceptual coherence, and it is designed to analyze or explain some particular phenomenon" (Bordwell, 1989:5). The conceptual coherence is the relevant part right now, for it is this coherence which means that the theory will take on a convincing look, as being a form of totality, complete in a sense.

What Bordwell argues is that we understand texts based on familiarity with the codes that control, govern and create the texts. This seems inherently true to me, even if we must as theorists and academics be aware of these codes and never assume that they are natural in any way. Nonetheless, equally interesting in the above quotation is that Bordwell equates analysis and explanation. This is perhaps not so large a leap as the fact that he also sees analysis as flowing from theory. In this way, analysis is the practical result of applying a theory to a given text. In this way, theory becomes a way of explaining rather than describing the text. In this way, theory is justified because it brings us greater knowledge of a text, more than we would have known had we not had theory.

This conception of theory not only makes theory of vital importance, it also means that theory becomes liberating. Through the use of theory we remove ourselves somewhat from the textual power that any text must have, perhaps even in order to be called a text. This textual power (the term, if not the concept, is Robert Scholes') is both alluring and dangerous. We consume texts in order to experience the textual power, to be moved, entertained, engaged and so forth by the text, yet when we analyse we are meant to step outside this power. This is where theory can and must help us.

Regardless of the conditions under which theory emerges, however, it seems to me that it represents a level of abstraction greater than analysis. This does not mean that theory is more difficult than analysis; simply that it is an activity which is at least somewhat separate from analysis, and must be identified as such. The result of this is that theory, by abstracting and generalising from a large field of texts, attempts to give us access to the more or less invisible forces which control textual production. This textual production must be understood from both sides of the text, so to speak, which is the act of making and consuming, in order to give proper space to those theories which only take for valid the reception part of a text.

This access to textual production should not be simply understood as enabling the creation of new texts, though it may well also do that, but rather to allow to expose what can be called "deep structures." Most ideological theory, such as Marxist or feminist theory, is centred specifically on this activity, asking who speaks and just as emphatically who does not speak and why? In this way, by posing certain general, critical questions, theory should provide a way of exposing the underlying cultural and social codes which are in place, often with the notion of trying to critique them and do away with them.

Theory thus becomes a way of discovering how and why we choose when we respond to texts. This is the notion of the textual power which is to some extent dispelled by the approaches of theory. It is because of this attempt at dispelling the textual power that a lot of theory has been brought in from other academic disciplines other than simply media studies themselves. Philosophy, cultural studies, psychoanalysis and so on, all represent areas where media studies have achieved great progress by borrowing the discourses and insights from these fields.

This means that theorization has brought about a very relevant point; that every act of mediation, in whatever form, is always cultural to some extent. We may say, paraphrasing Derrida's "there is not outside text" (1992: 58), that there is no outside culture. Any disbelief in this inherently false and we would not have reached this insight without theory. What theory can do, and has done, is create a way for to expose what is taken for natural and to reveal that it is not natural at all but rather cultural.

There are two other major insights brought to us by theory which are worth emphasising here, the first being the question of what to "apply" theory to. What theory has shown us is the fact that choice is just as excluding as including and that one should consistently discuss the "objective" worth of the media texts studied. Can we separate value from aesthetics and by what demands? While choice may always be a matter of preference and taste, what is vital is to disclose the process of selection. The discussion over a canon has been of great worth in literary studies and the same concerns need to be focussed in media studies, although here the canon has had less of a chance to establish itself.

What that means, however, is that there is a danger of not discussing the canon, of making it implicit and so hiding the choices made. It seems to me that no education interested in dealing with media and culture can afford to reinstate a form of high/low cultural divide between the texts studied. Commercials, reality TV, cartoons, web-animations, all these things say as much, if not more, about the culture they originate in, than the films of Peter Greenaway, Mike Leigh or Oolang. This should not be confused with aesthetic merit, for certainly the latter figures have a greater emphasis on formal innovation and may also be considered explicitly more critical of the surrounding culture. Still, a culture's popular entertainments certainly speak volumes about the state of said culture, and it is precisely theory which has brought us this insight. Theory, then, must always question why we choose to deal with specific texts over others, in order to ensure that none of these choices become too natural.

What this means is that it is often too easy to choose complex, detailed, canonical texts in order to emphasise and underscore many theoretical points, but this will often skew the reality of what is going on in the specific culture. Disney's animated features have a predilection for Expressionistic images, constructing many of their films around these visual conventions. Is this not as significant as Kieslowki's intertextual references?

In the same vein, Alan Moore's *Watchmen*, a superhero comic book, has pushed the boundaries not just of what is allowed within the genre itself, but also what we can expect of the medium of the comic book. That serious questions of identity, life, death, etc. are suddenly introduced into what is often regarded as entertainment for children, clearly displays not just changes in the cultural environment for this to happen at all, but also the falsity of claiming that any medium or artistic form is inherently of less quality than others. Again, theory has allowed us not to discard entire artistic fields simply because the majority of the output is of a low quality, and this is a good thing for what would be left to study if it had not?

The question of selection leads into the next insight, which is whether theory can, or even should, remove the personal in analysis. I have throughout this essay constantly drawn attention to the personal because I do not believe that there is any way to remove the personal in analysis. It may well be disguised better, but that act is itself suspicious, for what is there to hide? For instance, should I reveal how many revisions this essay has gone through? Should I also reveal which things the editor has asked me to change? The questions are as relevant as the answers, but what is more relevant is the realisation that this essay is not "authored" by a single voice and that it is written within a particular institutional practice where certain activities are required.

Here we come upon the great challenge to and for theory. It comes by way of Michel Foucault and the realisation that power is not something unitary which exists outside us (Foucault, 1984), and what is theory if it is not itself a form of textual power? We know from Barthes and on that the response to a text is itself a text, but this brings the added insight that the process which enables us to produce text on text, is also another text and that as such it needs to be analysed and questioned as much as the primary text itself. This also finally reveals that a theory does not hold mastery over a text, but merely grants access to the text in a different, more questioning manner.

Theory does not exist in any pure realm, and always requires the notion of being theorized itself. Theory must not be excepted from theorization. Barthes may despair over a metatheory (Barthes, 1989: 33), but we need not. While we may realise that interpreters can ascribe an indefinite number of meanings to a given textual element (see for instance Umberto Eco's *Interpretation and Overinterpretation* for illuminating examples), this should not make us doubt the possibility for theory to question itself, but rather require that theory continuously questions itself.

In this way, theory must always be, and *is* always a meta-commentary – a self-aware construction. As such, it must always question itself rather than regarding itself as the final result of a logical progression towards a final truth. Theory must always be self-reflexive and because of that I believe that meta-theory is redundant, since it makes no sense to speak of degrees of self-reflexivity. Of course, one might ask, if one is self-aware, how can one be more self-aware? Self-awareness does not happen by degrees but by a particular stance. As I regard theory, it is precisely a self-questioning stance, interested not in answers but rather in the question itself. Complacent theory loses its edge when it becomes self-indulgent and regards itself as affirmative and true.

Theory must ask the questions which analysis must then seek to answer. Therefore, when we analyse we should also realise that we only get answers to the questions we pose. That results in theory being both enabling and disabling, since there are questions we get answers to and others where we do not. It is because of this that theory needs to question itself and move forward.

I mentioned that theory may well serve as another instance of textual power, but this form of power is one which can to some extent be said to be deeply ingrained in the institutional practices of the humanities. Theory often serves as a way of asserting authority not just over a text but also over the analysis of said text. I have argued the inherent falsity of this claim, but this simply brings on the question of the students.

Perhaps the primary question, then, is how we teach students theory and how do we use theory when teaching. I can see no other option than to follow Scholes' argument which says that we must teach them the codes or access to the texts, but not in such a manner that theory becomes mastery over the students. We may well understand theory better than the students, but this is no excuse for not showing them the codes, rather it is the implicit requirement that we do show them the codes and reveal to them the questions (Scholes, 1985).

If theory is, as I have argued, a basic questioning position towards any cultural object, whether it is a media text or not, it is our responsibility to show how to adopt this questioning position, as well as to always turn this questioning position towards ourselves, our field and our practices. By remaining aware that none of what we do is natural in any sense of the word; we can continually revise ourselves and our positions.

Of course, none of this should tempt us to reinstate theory as a form of grand narrative, or regard theory as more important than the media texts we deal with in our daily work. We must avoid theories which create 'fearful symmetries', i.e. theories which seem too convincing. Instead, we must always remain critical and never believe that theory can create automatic responses or analysis. Theory becomes empty without analysis, turning us back to the question I posed in the beginning, if we could separate theory from analysis. To some extent, yes, they are distinct practices, but on the other hand none would survive without the other.

Analysis must always be more than a testing ground for theory, or a form of verification which shows that the theory was correct. This way of using theory can only be acceptable from students who are learning how to use the codes of theory and analysis, and of texts themselves. Such a way of using analysis would stultify it; drain it of any value it possesses. Analysis must be more than theory, must extend further in order to show how the object under analysis is created. Many of these codes can be illuminated and dug out through theory, but few texts are made to accord to a theory. Therein, analysis needs to push beyond theory, to show where theory is lacking.

As I have already pointed out, theory needs to question itself. It needs to continually reintegrate the findings of analysis, so that it will not retract into some ivory tower of pure reason. We need theory to expose and clarify the cultural codes which penetrate not just texts but all of us – a universality which is the reason for examining texts in the first place. To theorize media, or to simply theorize anything, then, is to pose questions about the process of making and understanding these texts, always with the realisation that none of these processes could exist outside the culture in which they are part. Theory must always locate the difficult questions so that we can analyse texts more clearly, use theory to explain the state of things. Theorizing, then, is neither something done prior to analysis nor abstracted from analysis, but is always already at work in the process of trying to understand and analyse texts.

In this way, to theorize means to contextualize in the manner that we do not complacently accept that things are a particular way but instead try to dig out the reason for why things are the way they are. Only a dialectical movement between theory and analysis can do this and this is why the two must never be separate, but rather seen as two sides of the same coin.

WORKS CITED

Barthes, Roland (1989). *The Rustle of Language*, Berkeley: University of California Press.

Bordwell, David (1989). *Making Meaning*, Cambridge & London: Harvard University Press.

Derrida, Jacques (1992). *Of Grammatology*, Baltimore: The Johns Hopkins Press.

Eco, Umberto (1992). *Interpretation and Overinterpretation*, Cambridge: Cambridge University Press.

Foucault, Michel (1984). *The Order of Things*, New York: Vintage Books.

McLuhan, Marshall (1964). *Understanding Media: The Extensions of Man*, London: Routledge,
    2001.

Scholes, Robert (1985). *Textual Power*, New Haven & London: Yale University Press.

Diplopia, or Ontological Intertextuality in Pastiche

Jørgen Riber Christensen
Department of Communication
Aalborg University

In the TV-commercial from September 2001[1] for the Mercedes "E-class" cars, tigers, elephants, giraffes, zebras, great Danes, penguins and camels are seen entering the Ark two and two. Potted plants of all sorts are carried into the Ark as well. However, great works of art, such as Michelangelo sculptures, paintings by Rembrandt and van Gogh, scores by Mozart and J.S. Bach and "The Best of Jazz," as well as canonical literature such as Goethe's *Faust* are also carried to safety into the Ark. After, a close-up of the heads of two Lipizzaner stallions and a long shot of the Ark still standing on dry ground with long rows of all creatures marching into it a surprising close-up of a running silver-metallic car wheel suddenly appears, and a medium shot then reveals that Mercedes cars can *also* enter the Ark two by two – apparently a male and a female Mercedes. The rain then starts to fall, and before the gates of the Ark close behind the Mercedes cars, their rain sensors have automatically switched on the windscreen wipers.

What is interesting about this opening scene is that the hectic biological and cultural rescue work is accompanied by dynamic and varied film language. There are nineteen cuts and three dissolves in the commercial, which only lasts thirty-four seconds. The film language, with its pans, cross-cutting and tilts ensures that a connection is created between the animals, the works of art and the two Mercedes cars so that they all attain the same status as worthy of preservation. The argument or premise of the commercial is established: the new Mercedes E-class is just as valuable and worthy of survival as animal and plant species, and the works of art are the connecting links between the world of nature and the world of the expensive and carefully designed cars. In this way the cars are imbued with aesthetic values, and the commercial defines its target group through its cultural taste. The aspects of culture that the commercial sets about to rescue from the Flood

---

1   The TV-commercial is available on the cd-rom in the book *Medietid, Dansklærer-foreningen*, Copenhagen 2002.

*Still from TV-commercial for Mercedes cars of the E-class with rain sensors, Springer &
Jacoby, Germany, September 2001*

belong to the culture of the upper classes. There is no room aboard the Ark
for Britney Spears CDs or flatpack furniture from Ikea. The people who prefer the cultural treasures aboard the Ark may also be the people who prefer
Mercedes cars.

What we can note is that this commercial is heavily intertextual as it is a
pastiche of the Genesis myth of the Flood, and it uses the Flood myth as an
argument to sell cars. Though the commercial is ironic and quite funny, it is
a reformulation of the myth of the Flood in so far as the grand narrative of
sin, retribution of Biblical proportions and also salvation for the select few is
turned into ontology as it depicts the values that may define the good life or
the kind of life that should be preserved from disaster. These values are not
only nature preservation, but also aesthetics. What is beautiful must be pro-
tected and preserved, as it is the foundation of life. The grand apocalyptical
narrative of the Bible has been reformulated in the Mercedes commercial as
a more limited, local narrative of life as consumption with taste and aesthetic discernment, a cultured hedonism. The Mercedes commercial has articulated an ontology different from the biblical one, yet, at the same time the
old grand biblical narrative has been retold or even told again, and this is the
crucial point. The Mercedes narrative is dependent on the Biblical narrative,
and the two come to co-exist within the narrative frame of the TV-commercial.

DEATH OF THE GRAND NARRATIVES

In the Mercedes commercial two ontological systems meet and co-exist. There is the grand narrative of the Deluge, which is backgrounded, and there is the local narrative of aesthetics and consumerism, which is foregrounded. Jean-François Lyotard has proclaimed the grand narratives dead, and that the little or local narratives have taken their place. Lyotard's importance for the conception of postmodernity is hard to deny, yet this chapter will question how dead the grand narratives actually are? In especially *La Condition postmoderne: rapport sur le savoir*, 1979, and also *Le Postmoderne expliqué aux enfants*, 1982, Lyotard concludes through an epistemologically founded analysis of the circulation and conditions of knowledge that the grand narratives have become delegitimized, and that their function in human ontology has in part been taken over by the little or local narratives. One consequence is for instance that history has lost value as a source of human experience. Lyotard's thinking has this movement starting from epistemology but ending in ontology, and the movement has resulted in the end of a worldview based on a secure knowledge of the world and existence. In other words, the delegitimization of the grand narratives has resulted in a postmodern condition, or existence where nothing can be taken for granted, and where we perceive the world and ourselves with ironic detachment, or put even more negatively with insecurity.

Lyotard defines the grand narratives (*grand récits* also called metanarratives) as the basic sources of understanding of existence, and they claim to provide universal explanations:

> "The dialectics of Spirit, the hermeneutics of meaning, the
> emancipation of the rational or working subject, or the creation
> of wealth"[2]

In continuation of these concepts, for instance, dialectical materialism posits all human behaviour and history as the history of the class struggle, and it denies all other explanations their validity. The ultimate goal of this process is communism, where individuals are no longer being exploited. Most religions have the same all-embracing worldview and explanations and projects. Yet Lyotard sees neither Christianity nor Marxism as the most important grand narratives in modern European history and culture. It is the Enlight-

---

2   Lyotard 1979, p. xxiii.

enment narrative "in which the hero of knowledge works toward a good ethico-political end – universal peace."[3] European thought since the Age of Reason or the Enlightenment with the climax in the French Revolution in 1789 has been basically optimistic. History moves forward, and with the help of reason, human endeavour, work and science the world can become a better place. The world is improvable. This thought or grand narrative with its optimism has since the end of the nineteenth century reached a crisis of legitimisation.

One aspect of this crisis is epistemological. Science in a wide sense, i.e., "objective" knowledge, has needed to legitimise its role in society. It has done this through narratives, and already here the scientific discourse meets with a paradox, as it defines itself in a positivist way as exactly not consisting of narratives, but of empirical facts and truths. Another attempt of epistemological legitimisation is the use science makes of a meta-discourse: philosophy. In Lyotard's view, philosophy became in German idealism the general meta-narrative that unites all part-sciences into a rational meta-discourse. Philosophy thus only served itself, and seen in the light of philosophy science is legitimised by itself. Therefore, true knowledge becomes indirect knowledge, and not just empirical knowledge. Here, the view of knowledge becomes almost anti-phenomenological in the sense that the philosophical study of objects perceived by the senses seems to have lost validity. Science is now capable of defining the state and society, not by knowing about them and referring to them, but by possessing knowledge about this knowledge about state and society at a higher level, by being speculative. Science then becomes legitimised by being incorporated in the grand totality of the meta-narrative of philosophy.

What this meant is that the grand narrative of knowledge was delegitimized by its position in society as well. The grand narrative of knowledge is a democratic and ideological narrative: man is the subject and has a right to knowledge and science. If man does not have this right it is because a tyrant has taken it away from him. The paradox is that it is the modern state which guarantees this right to knowledge (through education), and this state points to its function as a guarantee of freedom of knowledge each time it regulates the access to knowledge. Knowledge is not disinterested, but is has after all close ties to the system of power. To this extent, then, Lyotard claims that the grand narrative of science with its emancipatory and democratic

---

3   Lyotard 1979, p. xxiv.

ideals is no longer valid, as there is an inherent weakness in the great narrative of science from the nineteenth century: the speculative apparatus is based on positivist knowledge, which is knowledge that was only recognized by the speculative or philosophical apparatus when the speculative discourse repeated it or incorporated it in itself. The outcome is the death or decline of the grand narratives as ontological certainties.

Now, Lyotard has not used a positivist-empirical argumentation to disband the grand narratives. Rather, he employs a purely epistemological mode of argumentation. It must be noted however, that in 1982 *Le Postmoderne expliqué aux enfants* Lyotard is empirical and used modern European history as arguments. In his view, the death of the grand narrative of emancipation is called Auschwitz. At this point in European history with its mass-murder of six millions Jews it became impossible to see history as progress and as moving forward. Instead of the grand narratives as a way of understanding and accepting existence, then, Lyotard points to the little or local narratives as ontological foundations, and as such Lyotard's description of postmodern existence is not pessimistic or nostalgic, as the daily language games, daily communication take over the role of legitimisation. It is the little or local narratives, the – *petit récits* – which have risen from the ashes of the grand narratives that have taken over:

> "We no longer have recourse to the grand narratives – we can resort neither to the dialectic of Spirit nor even the emancipation of humanity as validation for post-modern scientific discourse. But as we have just seen, the little narrative [petit récit] remains the quintessential form of imaginative invention, most particularly in science"[4].

As examples of dominant little narratives today, one can mention personal love and family values, or as it was demonstrated in the Mercedes commercial above, consumerism may constitute another example. Here, consumerism must not be confused with the grand narrative of capitalism, as consumerism is not a societal system. Rather, it must be considered as a mode of behaviour found on the personal level. It is only a "little narrative." In the same sense tourism may be compared to the exploration expeditions in the historical period of imperialism, where the former is a little narrative whereas the latter is part of the old grand narrative of Enlightenment.

---

4   Lyotard 1979, p. 60.

INTERTEXTUALITY AND PASTICHE

Intertextuality seems to be the one defining trait of postmodern culture. Postmodern texts are open, not only towards their readers as reader-response criticism[5] has demonstrated, but even more so towards other texts.[6] When intertextual quotes are not written into the postmodern texts at the stage of production, then in the process of reception audiences and readers very often choose to perceive and understand scenes in an intertextual light, perpetually inferring references to other texts such that intertextuality may be understood as the dominant postmodern mode of reception. Quite often intertextuality is an inherent and structuring narrative device in postmodern texts. For instance in much fairly recent postmodern art, film and literature we have a two-tier structure where a present-day discourse is combined with an older one. We have seen it in the Mercedes commercial. Other fairly recent examples may be presented here in a schematic form:

The postmodern two-tier text:	The older source text:
Francis Glebas, *Fantasia 2000*, segment »Pomp and Circumstance«, Walt Disney Corp., USA 1999	*The Flood, Genesis, The Holy Bible*
John Madden, *Shakespeare in Love*, UK 1998	William Shakespeare, *Romeo and Juliet*, 1594-95
Sara George, *The Journal of Mrs Pepys*, 1998	*Samuel Pepys' Diary*, 1659-69
J.M. Coetzee, *Foe*, 1986	Daniel Defoe, *Robinson Crusoe*, 1719
Jean Rhys, *Wide Sargasso Sea*, 1966 / D.M. Thomas, *Charlotte The Final Journey of Jane Eyre*, 2000	Charlotte Brontë, *Jane Eyre*, 1847
Peter Ackroyd, *The Great Fire of London*, 1982	Charles Dickens, *Little Dorrit*, 1857
Jeff Noon, *Automated Alice*, 1996	Lewis Carroll, *Alice in Wonderland*, 1865
Stephen Frears, *Mary Reilly*, USA 1996 (novel Valerie Martin, 1990)	Robert Louis Stevenson, *The Strange Case of Dr Jekyll and Mr Hyde*, 1886
Will Self, *Dorian*, 2002	Oscar Wilde, *The Picture of Dorian Gray*, 1891
Steven Spielberg, *Hook*, 1991	James Barry, *Peter Pan*, 1904
Stephen Daldry, *The Hours*, 2002	Virginia Woolf, *Mrs Dalloway*, 1925
Zbigniev Rybczynski, *Steps*, USA 1987	Sergei Eisenstein, *Battleship Potemkin*, 1925

5   Iser 1976, 203-212.
6   Eco 1979, 21-22.

The archetypal postmodern two-tier text is probably the film based on John Fowles' *The French Lieutenant's Woman* from 1969. Harold Pinter adapted the novel, and the film was directed by Karel Reisz in 1981. Typically, the film is metafictional in the sense that the action is centered on the production of a film. The subject of the film being produced is the melodramatic love affair between the geologist and biologist Charles Smithson and the elusive Sarah Woodruff of poor reputation, and the setting of the film is the late Victorian Period with its Darwinism and strict, yet sensual morality. The other tier of *The French Lieutenant's Woman* is the present-day love affair between the actors, Anna and Mike, who play the two Victorian lovers. In Karel Reisz' film both the Victorian lovers and the present-day ones are played by Meryl Streep and Jeremy Irons. The film uses extensive cross-cutting between the scenes from the film under production with similar scenes from the lives of the present-day film crew, so that invariably the ontologies of the two periods are confronted with one another.

It is part and parcel of a well-constructed two-tier text that is has a focal point in which the two tiers intersect one another. In *The French Lieutenant's Woman* this focal point is found near the end, when the film crew celebrate the finished shooting with a garden party. When Anna leaves the party to go home to her family in the USA, Mike who is seriously in love with her, shouts after her, and the two tiers then meet, when he does not shout her name "Anna!"; but instead he shouts "Sarah!", the name of the Victorian woman, and at this moment the two tiers are tied together. The Victorian worldview is connected to the present-day one, and the audience is forced to compare the two ontologies. The audience has to realize that there is another worldview than its own, which must be considered in the light of the earlier historical period.

It is the pastiche genre that best embodies the double vision, or what is defined as *diplopia*, of two ontologies within one single text. The origins of the pastiche go back to the Renaissance in Rome where the term was first used to describe an artistic process of synthetic copying where element from diverse often Classical paintings and murals were combined into a new painting, and pastiche with time came to mean a literary, artistic, or musical work that imitates the style of previous works or a musical, literary, or artistic composition made up of elements borrowed from various sources. The pastiche is in other words highly mimetic in the sense that is does not imitate reality, but rather other works, and as such it is intertextual. The pastiche is related to parody, but where parody imitates other works or the style of other writers or artists in order to ridicule them, the pastiche is loyal to the source text, and in recreating the older text the pastiche implicitly states that the older text is of such value that it deserves a rebirth in a new form. The hybridity of pastiche is many-sided. Pastiche reaches back in time and history to its source text. It may also transgress genres, as it was seen above where the Biblical myth was recreated as a television commercial, and the pastiche may also hold various strata of taste. Pastiche is a truly postmodern genre. It values intertextuality much higher than originality, and it also exploits the huge archive of cultural history, which is the foundation on which the pastiche is built. However, the pastiche is not totally without originality and ambitions of being original. The way in which the old source text is recreated may be highly original, surprising and shocking. The focus of originality has moved away from thematics to form, physical material and technique. This aspect of the formal originality of the pastiche is postmodern, as it is an element of metafiction. The textuality and artificiality of the pastiche text is highlighted, not only by its intertextuality, but also by the processing of the original historical material that is the source of the new pastiche text. The audience is confronted explicitly with the creation process of the postmodern pastiche so that the pastiche text is never natural or given.

Fantasia 2000

Francis Glebas' »Pomp and Circumstance«- the seventh segment in *Fantasia 2000* from 1999 – is like the Mercedes commercial a pastiche of the Biblical story of the Flood. In this segment Donald Duck is Noah's assistant, and so *The Bible* has been merged with the world of the Walt Disney Corporation. The apocalyptic theme of the grand Biblical narrative is established in the prelude of the segment, which opens with a close-up of a ram's horn seen from a low angle while the blaring of a trumpet is heard. As a matter of fact it is not the trumpets from the Apocalypse that are sounded, but rather Noah, who from the prow of the recently finished Ark, calls the animals together. As the incidental music now becomes a compositions made up from Edward Elgar's *Pomp and Circumstance Marches – 1, 2, 3 and 5* reaction shots of pairs of animals are shown, and the animals quickly converge around the enormous Ark two and two. However, everything is chaotic, and Noah has to fetch his assistant to organize the embarkation of the animals. The assistant, Donald Duck, is lounging, naked and with a drink, in a hammock in front of his house, which is made out of a large egg. Donald is quite embarrassed, but his wife Daisy brings his him clothes, and Noah shows Donald a blueprint of the Deluge. Donald ridicules him and points to the clear sky and the burning sun; but right then the storm breaks loose. Daisy kisses Donald lovingly good-bye as he goes to work. Helped by the storm Donald manages to lead all the animals aboard the Ark in an orderly fashion. Only the now-extinct animals dragons, griffins and unicorns refuse to take part in the rescue. During the embarkation Donald and Daisy get out of contact with one another, and tragically, though mistakenly, they each think that the other has not managed to get aboard the Ark to safety before their world is engulfed by a huge wave. During their stay on the Ark they again and again miss discovering each other. The camera on the other hand quite elegantly reveals how close they are to each other, so that tilts, pans and cross-cuttings demonstrate that they are united by their strong love, but also how futile their search for each other each is, so that they sink into deeper and deeper sorrow and despair. All of this happens against the background of the awesome powers of the Flood, and the Ark, huge as it is, seems tiny in the big waves. When the storm finally subsides and the sky becomes clear, the animals enjoy the cruise, and the Ark becomes a love boat where the animals two and two do not hesitate to show their love, so that only Donald and Daisy are lonesome, and their loss becomes even more pronounced.

Still from Francis Glebas, Fantasia 2000, segment »Pomp and Circumstance«, Walt Disney Corp., USA 1999

When the Ark goes aground and the animals with a pair of lions leading the way march into the new Promised Land, Donald and Daisy again dejectedly just miss seeing one another, and it is not until Donald is cleaning out the Ark after anyone has left and Daisy comes back to look for her golden heart with a picture of her and Donald in it, which she has dropped, that the two lovers are reunited, and now they can go into the reborn world under the rainbow hand in hand.

The Flood segment with its camera movements, its editing and its action is structured by Elgar's music, arranged by Peter Schickele, so that very often a so-called "Mickey Mousing-effect" is achieved, when the movements of the images are totally synchronized with the music. The director Francis Glebas says about the relationship between images and music:

> "The real challenge with this piece has been to tell the story to the beat of the music... We've rearranged it slightly but you still have to basically go with the flow of it. The other thing is that it's like making a silent movie without subtitles, in a sense. You have to figure out how to say something on the screen without any words. And I think our animators have achieved that brilliantly. Donald's personality comes across very clearly even without his characteristic quacking. He doesn't say a word and yet you still know its Donald."[7]

Elgar's *Pomp and Circumstance Marches* work as underscoring in a double way. The sheer pomposity of the music defines the Biblical story as sublime, and the full emotional register is used from awe to pathos and sometimes sentimentality as when Kathleen Battle's soprano and the Chicago Symphony Chorus add an extra layer of emotions to Elgar's instrumental marches. This aspect of Elgar's music is part of the mythical proportions of this *Fantasia 2000* segment. At the same time *The Pomp and Circumstance Marches* are the background to Donald Duck's tantrums and many mishaps. The segment has a large amount of quite funny details, as for instance when Donald with justified concern sees two non-anthropomorphic ducks boarding the Ark, and this humour is strengthened or sometimes even produced by the relationship between the animated duck and the pompous music as this re-

---

7   http://www.animationartist.com/movies/fantasia2000/Production/production.
     html (as viewed 21.5.2004).

lationship is one of pathos with frequent descents from the sublime of the underscoring music to the absurd antics of a toon.

The "Pomp and Circumstance"-segment is a pastiche of the Biblical myth. It is a retelling of the original story, and as such the grand Biblical narrative is given new life. However, this new version of a grand narrative is reformulated. A new element has not only been added, but is has been foregrounded. The biblical myth is the background to the love story between two ducks, Donald and Daisy, but no more a background than an essential and causal element. The narrative of the Flood and the love story of Donald and Daisy are intertwined down to the most minute camera movement. The universal losses of the Flood are renegotiated in the sense that they are focused and distilled into the sense of loss which the two protagonists suffer aboard the Ark, and in the same vein the joy and hope of the post-Deluge world are not only expressed through the triumphant animals, but more so when Donald and Daisy enter it hand in hand. Within the Disney version of the Biblical myth there is room for both the old grand narrative of the Flood and for the new, little and local narrative of personal love between two protagonists. The grand narrative is combined narratologically and intertextually with a little, local narrative, and in this way the grand narrative is not dead and obsolete. It has not kept its all-embracing ontological status, but it has nevertheless enough vitality to enter into a dialogue with the little narrative, so that the little narrative necessarily is not absolute or universal. In this pastiche the little narrative has to be measured against the grand narrative, and it is this dialogue between the two that has achieved the ontological function, which neither of the two can lay claim to. The inherent intertextuality of the pastiche genre thus combines two historical periods, one of the grand narratives and one of the little and local narratives, and by including these two periods with each their own ontology into one text, a new ontological dialogue is created.

A HISTORY OF THE WORLD IN 10^1/$_2$ CHAPTERS

The first chapter in Julian Barnes' novel *A History of the World in 10_ Chapters* is called "The Stowaway." Again, we have a pastiche of The Flood. This pastiche is not totally loyal to its source story, as it sets about rewriting the Genesis text purporting to tell the story as it really happened, and in this way the pastiche is used within the genre of metafictional historiography – with tongue in cheek, as the crucial narrative device is that the point of view is changed from third person to first person, as the narrator at first is anonymous, and not until far into the chapter it is revealed that it is the lowly woodworm that is behind the first person voice, and who is the stowaway of the title. The premise of "The Stowaway" is to correct the historiography of the Ark. The character of Noah is entirely rewritten. According to the wood-worm he was "an old rogue with a drink problem,"[8] who with God as his role model was a despot; saw the Ark as a floating cafeteria. The fate of the uni-corn was that "the Noahs had him casseroled one Embarkation Sunday." [9] And the woodworm describes all the species that became extinct because Noah and his family slaughtered and ate them. The woodworm's point of view seems realistic and cynical: "It wasn't a nature reserve, that Ark of ours; at times it was more like a prison ship."[10] Other corrections to the biblical text are made. It was not just one ship, but a flotilla, which even included a brothel ship, and the time span of the Flood was 53 years, not a hundred and fifty days as the Bible would have it. The metafictional character of this pas-tiche becomes apparent when it refers to its source text, which is called "your own archives."[11] By rewriting history in this way the mythical truth-value of the grand narrative of the Bible is questioned, and so the ontological status is reduced to a textual one. The Bible becomes one (hi)story among others, and the ideological premise of the Biblical history is questioned, as the ideo-logical point of view of "The Stowaway" is egalitarian and democratic. Noah is deconstructed as a patriarch and along with him the patriarchal and an-thropocentric worldview. Julian Barnes' pastiche becomes a discourse about present-day extermination of animal species, and not about Noah's mythical rescue of the animal kingdom. The two discourses of "The Stowaway" are nevertheless combined. The discourse about the ecological problems of the present day are tied to the biblical extinction of practically all life, and in this way the old grand mythical narrative lends strength to a more local narra-tive. This narrative is local too, in the sense that its point of view literally speaking is biological, as it is a woodworm that is the narrator.

THE NARRATOLOGICAL REBIRTH OF THE GRAND NARRATIVES

It is the point of this article that Lyotard's grand narratives are not quite as dead or extinct as it may seem. They have been resurrected in textual form through the narrative device of intertextuality, in particular in the postmod-ern pastiche genre where they coexist with the little local narratives in a dia-

---

8   Barnes, p. 6.
9   Barnes p. 16.
10   Barnes p. 4.
11   Barnes p. 16.

logue. This dialogue has an ontological function. The very structure of the pastiche ensures the inclusion of an older text, and this older text belongs most often to a period in history when the grand narratives were thriving and well. The two tier-structure of the pastiche that contains two discourses produces new meaning. One discourse is from the old source text, and it contains traces of a grand narrative. The other discourse is from the time of production of the pastiche, which is Postmodernity characterized by an absence of ontological grand narratives. Yet the postmodern discourse in the pastiche contains a little and local narrative. The focal point in the postmodern two- tier pastiche is where its grand narrative is confronted with its local narrative in a dialogue. We might then ask whether the postmodern predilection for the pastiche genre is not based on a need of an ontological nature, so that the postmodern pastiche becomes the field where present-day local narratives are measured against the old grand narratives.

WORKS CITED

Barnes, Julian, *A History of the World in 10¹/₂ Chapters*, Picador, London 1990 (1989).

Eco, Umberto, *The Open Work*, Harvard Cambridge, Massachusetts 1989 (1962).

Eco, Umberto, *The Role of the Reader*, Indiana University Press, Bloomington 1979.

Hoesterey, Ingeborg, *Pastiche*, Indiana University Press, Bloomington 2001.

Iser, Wolfgang, *The Act of Reading*, The John Hopkins University Press, Baltimore 1978 (1976).

Kristensen, Jane and Jørgen Riber Christensen, *Medietid*, Dansklærerforeningen, Copenhagen 2002.

Lyotard, Jean-François, *The Postmodern Condition: A Report on Knowledge*, Manchester University Press, 1997 (1979).

Lyotard, Jean-François, *The Postmodern Explained to Children*, Turnaround, London 1992 (1986).

"What Does it Mean to Practice Media Analysis?"

METHODS AND MODELS
An Essay on Media Analysis

Ove Christensen

Department of Communication

Aalborg University

In our daily lives we are surrounded by images and messages of all kinds. We move swiftly from one situation to another, demanding very quick responses from us. We have to navigate in an urban iconography reading texts, images and signals at a pace not comparable with any other time in history. And, normally we are pretty good at it – well equipped, with sophisticated reading skills. We are living in a media saturated environment but tend to have few problems, it seems, decoding the messages when trying to find our way through the urban landscape.

What we are doing in these situations is practicing semiotics. We consider the signs as a means to obtain something from us or make us do something. Whenever we consider the signs relevant we take the sign in and try to understand it. Normally we do this without even considering that we are trying to decode a message which has been designed to communicate with us. The buzz from the alarm clock is immediately recognized as a signal telling us that the evening before we intended getting up at seven in the morning. The message is read without any conscious effort, understood simply by default. When the steam from the bath is clearly visible we take it as an indexical sign that we now can enter the shower compartment without getting a shock from cold water. The red light on the coffee machine convinces us that the coffee is processing.

In the street we continue to read messages as signs. The traffic signs, posters, shopping windows, the other driver's or biker's way of behaving and so on. All the signs are for us situated in a context where we are trying to understand what is going on by reading the signs relevant in our situation. The relevance can be our safety or convenience but, whatever the case might be, we are figuring that the signs are telling about what we are to do to make things happen and, hence, take control over the situation. We also tend to be convinced that the signs and signals are intentional in some way, which is to say that signs are directed at us with a purpose no matter if the address is for us personally or as a member of a larger group of citizens.

This somehow abstract description above is but one way of trying to understand how we manage to survive in a complex situation that is our everyday life. That is to say, that it is the description that is semiotic. Semiotics is just one way of trying to understand social practices and the individuals' ways of making meaning by their surroundings. Every analysis is thus somehow determined by the chosen system of description which is decisive for what features is drawn to attention and which are not. Also the interdependences of features and different layers of information are to some extend determined by the practical and theoretical framework put at work. Our mode of understanding puts reality in a certain perspective. And it is precisely the perspective that makes our surroundings mean something for us and thereby gives our disposition for acting accordingly.

In the following, I will try to suggest different points of focus that are important in media analysis. I will moreover suggest an overall understanding of methodology within media analysis. It will be a leading idea in this chapter that media analysis and understanding of cultural products and processes in general are not to be understood within just one theoretical framework. I will argue that analysis will benefit from pluralistic and eclectic approaches – just as it is important that our understandings be guided by a systematic approach is to obtain some coherence that makes analysis worthwhile.

METHODOLOGY, METHOD AND SYSTEMATIZATION

Dealing with methods within an analytical framework, a first step is to decide what is meant by method. In student assignments what is understood by method is often – and misleadingly – a presentation of the steps taken in the assignment: e.g., "first I introduce this theoretician and then the next which is followed by an analysis of the chosen media product." This is not a method, although it can be a starting point for methodological considerations if it is combined with theoretically discussions about different theories and their advantages and applicability within the problems sketched out in the assignment.

Method in its strict sense, as methodology, means the epistemological framework within which research can take place. One has to find out the way the world is functioning on a fundamental level as well as how human thinking is related to this level of being. What is knowledge according to which principles? How does human knowledge relate to reality? It is presupposed that the ontology of reality on the one hand and epistemology on the other is somehow connected and that this connection in some respect is stable. It is this strong sense of method that Roland Barthes rejects when he claims that method is more likely to ward off research than research is to gain from method:

Some speak greedily and urgently about method. It never seems rigorous or formal enough to them. Method becomes Law, but as this Law is deprived of any effect that would be outside of itself (no one can say, in the 'human sciences,' what a 'result' is) it always falls short… As a result, a work that unceasingly declares its will-to-methodology always becomes sterile in the end. Everything takes place inside the method, nothing is left to the 'writing'… the researcher repeats that his text will be methodological, but this text never arrives. There is nothing more sure to kill research and sweep it off into the leftovers of abandoned works, nothing more sure, than method. At some point one has to turn against method, or at least to treat it without any founding privilege.[1]

What Barthes has in mind, besides that rigorous thinking within a stable system is bound to repeat the system in stead of letting the system open to hitherto unknown insights, is that the idea of method in itself is a way of thinking that close off reality and method hereby becomes self-sufficient. Both its repetitive character and its closure principle is a problem because it exactly prevents what should be the idea with research, namely enabling new insights. For Barthes, research is an involvement with its material not a simple translation of reality into texts or vice versa. That is why he is stressing "writing" which is an interpretation that relate to the object without nullifying it.

Methodology is a way of maintaining the relation between an ontological and an epistemological understanding. In its whole idea is built in an understanding that it is possible scientifically to grasp (the meaning of) reality or at least building philosophical stable ideas and concepts concerning the reality and human understanding. But, thereby, it neglects the historical level of knowledge and the more pragmatic understanding that nothing simply *is* but always is in a certain respect for someone according to its practical or theoretically usefulness. Both the understanding of reality and of knowledge is situated in history and in concrete considerations directed at practical ends.

Methodology in the above understanding is a matter of religious beliefs and, it has its fundamentalists as have religious beliefs proper. Arguments about grounding principles might lead to improvements of methods within

---

1   Roland Barthes quoted by J. V. Harari in 'Preface' p.10, J. V. Harari (ed.): *Textual Strategies*, Ithaca 1979. The quotation is from *Tel Quel* 47, 1971, p. 10f.

the human sciences. However, if the method becomes and end in itself then methodological discussions will be barren. An example of this is the ongoing "battle" between semiotics and cognitivism. By recurs either to some fundamentals within psychoanalysis or cerebral research they claim different theories to be in concordance with reality and real processes whereas the opponent is deemed to be under the influence of false believes – heretics. The core of the disagreement is the basis of human understanding. Is our way of understanding our surroundings determined by culture – the paternalistic society and family structure – and codes or is it determined by nature and evolution? Put differently the debate revolves around how to understand human perception: is it signs or data?

Both positions stress the importance of perception but differ in their understanding of the way in which perceptions are processed to understanding. Are cultural codes involved in making perceptions cohere and establishing a relation to other people and reality, or are the processing guaranteed by the evolution of the human brain and its mental schemata? This debate, however, is not at all a real one in that human traits are much more complex than either of the theories recognize. They preestablish a context for their reasoning and support this with recurs to scientific discourses. But their contexts and perspectives differ in part because they address different parts of the whole question about meaning in relation to text and addressees. What is more, they seemingly do not acknowledge that their descriptions exactly are descriptions with certain perspectives and not directly related to the reality they describe. In that theories are *ways of description*, they form an interpretation of relations and establish a *mode* of understanding. Semiotics and cognitivism are modes of understanding which have serious consequences for what they regard important and how they relate to analysis and texts.

Without claiming a possible reconciliation between the two "master theories" or methods it is obvious that a lot of their disagreements is caused by the fact that they are not speaking of the same "object," let alone use the same vocabulary. More often than not, they address different layers of meaning when analyzing for instance texts. Semiotics is dealing with how to understand a message from the sign and its paradigmatic and syntagmatic relations i.e., the way meaning is generated from a bigger vocabulary and from the way an order between the different signs are established. Cognitive science is dealing with how an expression is processed by the receiver's cerebral capacity for recognition and collection of data. This is a highly generalized description of the disagreement, but it points to that different theoretically viewpoints "frames" analysis differently which will bring about different interpretations.

They will work with different questions and prioritize different features.

To avoid two obvious misunderstandings as the possibility of a neutral analytical position and of the rejection of theory altogether, two clarifications will be appropriate. First of all it is impossible to read or analyze a text without founding beliefs of sorts. Every interpretation or analysis is biased in many different ways, and I am not suggesting the possibility of a neutral approach. One has to be aware that one holds something to be true and certain relations to be the case and that these beliefs influence what one makes out of a text – as well as which theories may be chosen as guiding principles. Secondly, although no theory holds the whole truth, it is not possible to claim that no theory thereby is false and founded on false grounds. Theories have to prove their relevance, and some theories go out of style because they are no longer helpful in focussing our way of relating to reality and the texts in this reality.

Given these observations, however, I should also point out that I am also not suggesting a meta-theory by which it is possible to judge different theories and their viability. Within the humanities, theories are competing on the ground of what they manage to explain and make relevant within different professional sub-systems. Theories are generalizations of experiences and they have to meet pragmatic ends.

From the above, I have developed ten theses on my perspective on method and methodology:

1. There is no indisputable epistemological theory in our attempt to analyze audio-visual sign systems. Hence, there is not one method that can be applied for every analysis and there is no methodology securing a way to choose the best theories to implement.
2. Fundamentally, there are three decisive points in determining which theories and methods one wants to engage for analytical purposes:
   a. The questions that the analysis is trying to answer (external logic)
   b. The demands put forward by the analysis of the text (internal logic)
   c. The text's resistance to analysis as well as theory (violation of logic)
3. It is important to maintain a pluralistic approach to methods and theories. It is not important that there is a common epistemological or scientific basis for theories and methods implied. To claim otherwise is to assume that the objects in the world are made out of our theories. Theories may be mutually contradictory, but still helpful in the analysis if the analyst is able to bring something interesting – new

insights – forward by the use of different theoretically frameworks. It is likewise important that the analyst is aware of the different aspects and levels that different theories privilege.

4. It is important to recognize that the world and objects for analysis are not structured *by* theories but that theories are attempts to systematize earlier perceptions and understandings. To think that the world is mono-theoretically structured is an aspiration of God. Theories are simply helpful in guiding our attention enabling us to notice certain interesting features in the text. (Ontological claim: Objects *exist*).

5. The world and objects are exactly structured by our theories and methods. That is why we read it according to some principles and not other. The objects for analysis are to be constructed in a way that makes them approachable for us. We thereby translate objects of images and sounds to logically structured phenomena consisting of words. (Epistemological claim: Objects are *constructed* for analysis).

6. Theories and methods are only important because they give us a way of looking at objects and a way of discussing our observations. Theories points at different elements within an otherwise obscure text. Theories thereby give us a vocabulary making us able to name phenomena.

7. What is important with theories and methods is the language or system of language they give rise to. It is important to have a certain language to be able to describe and discuss objects in the world. Theories and methods bring us very elaborate and specific vocabularies which make us able to see objects as very rich, diversified and composite entities and it also make us see resemblances and differences between objects.

8. What is most important with method is the analyst's capacity to look beyond it and therefore also the capacity to see every method's limitation. Furthermore, every method is a kind of restriction of vision and understanding, in that it determines what we can see and say. It is important to acknowledge the repression by method. The critically aware scholar will always pay attention to the role of methods and theories.

9. If a text is analyzed and shows a remarkable accordance with the theory used for analysis it is almost for certain that analytical mistakes have been made. The analysis has been determined by the theory with the consequence of exterminating the object.

10. The interesting part of theories and methods is their failure and loss of power to explain phenomena. When that happens something new

and different may occur, something that will have a returning effect on the theories and methods. It is the resistance from the object for analysis that improves or falsifies theories and methods and, hence, it is failures that make us wiser. A method is successful if it fails to explain the text in its entirety. Unfortunately is the reverse not true. An unsuccessful explanation of text features does not prove an analysis.

These theses are to be regarded as some general ideas about the relation between methodology and media analysis. They are not aspiring to be laws but merely a list of important points to consider avoiding confusing methods, theories and analysis. What a specific text means to different people using it with different purposes and in different situations is not to be accounted for in most analyses. Therefore, an analysis will always only take issues with limited aspects of a text neglecting others. The thesis recommends a humble attitude towards the scope of explanatory values of analysis.

Secondly the thesis points to the independence of text in relation to the theories addressing specific textual features and general ideas about human understanding and perception. Again the situational aspects are important both when it comes to the texts in question and the theories implied. No text, no analysis and no theory exist in a void. The different contexts have to be taken into consideration if one wants to explain what, how and for whom a text means.

THE COMMUNICATION PARADIGM AS A GUIDELINE FOR MEDIA ANALYSIS

Instead of a methodological grounded model for analyzing media texts, I will suggest a systematization of the kind of questions to pose to an analysis. The purpose is not least to differentiate between different dimensions of an analysis. The proposed model is less a method than a guideline for systematization the different steps and perspectives on media analysis. This guideline is purely pragmatic and has no claims on "truth," "good" or "beauty." There may be other ways of approaching media and text analysis. The suggested model, however, is an easy way to obtain a focus on what to analyze.

Text analysis in general consists of three or four steps. First, it has to be figured out what kind of text the analysis is dealing with. This first step also constitutes a preliminary understanding of the text as an address in that it suggests that the text purvey a meaning – a content, as such. By this first step the analyst should obtain some general ideas of the text as a totality. An analysis never starts from scratch but is initiated by some provisional understandings and ideas about what the text means for someone and how the text generates this understanding. Normally, we have no problems in deciding the meaning of a text. An analysis should start from this point by questioning how and why the process of understanding seems effortless and be able to generalize the observations regarding this process. The first step leads to the questions one is inclined to work with. Not everything concerning a specific text calls for attention – therefore the analyst decides what kind of text features is interesting in the concrete analysis. It is also of importance that the analyst makes clear for him or herself what the analysis shall obtain and what the goal for the analysis is. It is possible to analyze a text in any number of ways. However, it will confuse and obscure an analysis if the specific reasons for an analysis are not clear from the beginning.

The second step is to dissect the text into pieces and separate its different elements to investigate what they consists of and how they are interrelated. Very much like taking apart an engine, one has to take a closer look at the single elements which make out the text. This endeavor is guided by the initial understanding of the text as a totality and the goal set out for the analysis, but the text may reveal something not immediately anticipated. It is almost impossible to analyze a text if it is not guided by specific questions put forward by the preliminary understanding. This also means that an analysis only answers to what initially is estimated to be relevant and interesting. An analysis sets out a specific perspective for the analysis which excludes other perspectives.

The third step reestablishes the connection between the elements and it presents the analyzed text as an explained totality. It is crucial that the new understanding in some respects is better than the initial understanding. The overall goal with analysis is to provide a better understanding of the text or a better explanation of how it works either internally, from the perspective of the addresser, or with different readers, receivers. This third step collides with the presentation of the analysis. The two steps previously mentioned are steps in the way one has to work with the text. When the results of this work are obtained it is possible to present the analyzed text as a totality, and the presentation will therefore be to bring to light the logic of the different text features understood from a theoretical standpoint where the structure of the text and its different elements are explainable. In most cases it is crucial that these three steps are not confused.

A possible fourth step is to establish a cultural understanding of the text in a broader perspective. The totality of the text as a discourse concerning ideas and values in the cultural formation it is taking part in. To take a look on the text's ideology in its broader sense is the goal for a final, overall interpretation of the text as a cultural utterance. It is here one normally finds the interest governing ideological critique and cultural studies programs which addresses mutual influences of culture, products and people.

The above description of analytical steps has as a leading principle the idea that (media) texts include a communication paradigm as it is suggested by Roman Jakobson. In its simplest form, a communication act is defined by three instances: a sender (addresser), a message (text) and a receiver (addressee), which gives three levels of analysis or three perspectives from which to analyze on the horizontal axis: what is the intention with the message, what does the message consists of, and how does the message affect the receiver (or: what does the receiver do with the message)? Furthermore, the model points at three different relations and sites of transformations, namely between the instances.

This simple formal structure of communication has to be understood within a larger scale of a cultural context, defining the roles within the communicative situation as a whole. That is to say that communication requires relatively stable agent functions and rules governing the communication process. The parts communicating have to share the implied codes if the communication is to be efficient. Normally the cultural context and the implied codes are taken for granted, but whenever a communication is experienced as unsuccessful the preconditions become visible. Meeting a foreigner with whom one shares no common language makes one aware that the process of communication is not at all a simple matter but is built into a system of prerequisites. In the example with two strangers not sharing a language it is easy to figure out what prevents a successful communication. They do not share common language codes normally provided by the upbringing, education and cultural conditions.

Nonetheless, we might note that misunderstandings between people with equal formal language skills happen all the time. Shared codes simply means that people share some of the elements within the code but not necessarily all its implications. Class, sex, age, education, social position or other demographic differences may be of great importance. Different people never share all codes and therefore understanding is reached by what might be coined as "creative misunderstanding." Communication agents infer meaning by focusing on some aspects which are regarded most relevant and pertinent, yet never get fully insight in the production of meaning.

With communication in the absence of face-to-face encounters, it is difficult to find out the reasons for unsuccessful communication. It is furthermore difficult to anticipate how addressees will respond to a text if the addressees are forming a more or less heterogeneous group as is mostly the case with communication in the public sphere. Analytical approaches can deal with the problems with communication explaining why it succeed or not, and it can deal with what meaning is produced by the text itself or by its receiver independently of the intention put forward in the message. Especially with analysis of products understood as artistic artifacts the communicative intention is often down played at least in the three first steps within the analytical practice. In respect to the ideological dimension different traditions foreground either the intention of the producer or the hidden societal effect on the producer. In the last case the ideological message is normally not known to the producer him or herself, but is a cultural meaning within the communicative practice which has ideological bearings as it is often stressed within ideological critique or cultural studies where the focus often is transference of hegemonic ideas and patriarchy.

Roman Jakoson's model is a good starting point for understanding the communicative processes by its implied dimensions because it points to the different instances that may be analyzed. The foregrounding of these instances works as a guideline for where to look to explain a text, its functioning and its possible impact. Moreover, the three grounding instances of a sender, message and receiver, the model points toward a context implying that the message conveys information about something outside the message. Messages are connected to the world in that a message almost always in some respects is assertive about states of affaires whether it concerns hard facts, interpersonal relations or inner feelings and emotions.

Communication never exists in a vacuum. Communication is derived from Latin *communicare* which means sharing within a community; connecting people, and it is further derivative of *communis*, meaning "shared." The root of the word "communication" points to the communality implicit in all communication processes. The connection in communication is not only between members of a group it also includes the connection to the surroundings, the environment and the reality which has an influence on the individual group members. Communication is, hence, always understood as communication of something to someone. And the communicative actions establish an understanding of the surroundings, making it mean something instead of just being. Human society is to some extent only so by its practices of making sense of the reality, the society and the individual and in that process communication plays a decisive role.

Even though a message always is assertive in its broadest sense, the assertive nature of a message can be put in parenthesis as in fiction where assertions mainly exists in a second degree nature, i.e., assertion about something made up; something not existing. However, even within fiction the text is communicating something about the world. First of all, an artistic work of art or a commercial product of entertainment is related to the outside world in a metaphorical manner. One has to presuppose that the work is communicating something to its receiver even if it is more abstract than a direct communication about reality. Secondly, a piece of fiction is establishing a diegetic world that is fictitious but no less has to be constructed by the text (the message) itself. In that sense, a work of fiction has to be assertive even if it is in a secondary degree. Even the most recognizable fiction is to be understood as an indirect communication about states of affairs within the culture it is part of. It is a common mistake to understand fiction as a direct mirror to the reality without taken into consideration the principle of second nature assertions.

Jakobson's model point to three different instances, and each of these may be of special analytical interest. What is important is firstly to be aware of which instance is under scrutiny. Talking about a text's meaning by referring to what the producer has said was the intention with the text is to mix two instances – the message and the sender. In this example the analysis will be blurred because of a lack of awareness of what instances is the subject of analysis.

It is not fundamentally problematic to talk about what was intended with the message and focus on the sender. In such contexts, it would be obvious to go deeper into the sender's motivation and perhaps professional, social or psychological issues relating to the message according to its genre, the chosen media, the sender's position etc. In the example it also will be necessary to question the motives behind the claim of the intention if the sender could have motives to give a special impression of him or herself. Neither is it a problem to try to figure out what the meaning of a text may be, but in that endeavor one has to refer to features of the text. It is thirdly not a problem to see how successful the sender is in transforming an intention of meaning into a text. Here the focus of analysis will be the process of transformation from an idea (intention) to a message. And if the addresser's intention reaches further than the production of textual meaning and want to affect the addressee in certain ways, it is also necessary to account for the second process of transformation from utterance (message) to receiver.

It is also a confusion of instances when a textual meaning simply is determined by associations in that it mixes the text with the receiver (here, the analyst). This does not mean that association is not part of an analysis, but it must be made clear what the relation is between the text and the association, and further it must be addressed how a specific association is pertinent within a larger group of receivers who for example share some group specific codes. An analysis can never be legitimized with references to private experiences, although one can use one's own experiences as a general model for a cultural determined receiver. We must make the distinction between what is pertinent for a historical situated receiver within a cultural framework and what is private and hinge on a person's life history. Ideally an analysis is directed toward what is understood within a community and not what is the personal outcome. A personal account is not qualified as analysis even if it may be of great interest and eye opening. For an analysis to be so it has to address relevance for more than the analyst him or herself.

Jakobson's model may also guide other aspects of analysis in that it points to the media (contact or channel) used in the communication. Certain logical features are implied by the chosen media for sending a message. In written language – as a letter, a novel, or an essay – the message has to take into consideration the way written language works and the conventions for messages of different types within written texts. The media is not just and not even primarily setting technical standards, but is itself determined by historical, institutional, social and cultural parameters. The channel is also indicative of how the message is understood in that it involves a specific relation between the media, its user and its uses. Awareness of media specificity is a leading principle within analysis of texts.

For aesthetic analysis, media is predominant in that messages are not regarded as their content but more so by their form. The form is never a mere vessel whatever is communicated. A message is besides being a message also presented in a certain way dependent on the media and that also has an impact on its "content." But in most informative communication the focus is on *what* is communicated and not *how* it is communicated. This separation of content and form is only working on a theoretical level. There is no message without a form, and no form is purely form without content. Furthermore, the form is part of the content as well as content is shaping (forming) the message.

FUNCTIONS AND GENRES

Content analysis has been dominant within the humanities for ages. For content analysis, the most important dimension is the text itself. Also, when it comes to content, Jakobson's model points at important dimensions by emphasizing the functions of the message. Jakobson talks about six fundamental functions of language. The functions are emotive, conative, phatic, referential, poetic, and metalingual. Texts will normally engage more or all the functions which are not mutually exclusive but one of the functions will typically be dominant.

The emotive function of a message is an attempt to convey to the receiver the emotional state of the sender. It is the function which most closely establishes a connection between the message and the sender although this connection might be questioned by the tendency in media research to downplay a direct connection between message and sender. One of the lessons from structuralism is that it is impossible to make inferences about the author from his or her text. The text becomes autonomous when it has left its producer. But that is only relevant when the text's meaning itself is in focus. If the sender is in focus motivations and intentions are legitimate subjects for analysis.

The *conative* function reversely points to what the text is intended to cause the receiver to do. It is obvious that a sign saying "No Trespassing" is directed to the reader, making him or her behave in a certain manner. The intention of a message is also important in campaigns against smoking or for recycling. The *phatic* function is the ways in which the message keeps the communication process running. Different markers either from the sender or the receiver only devised for confirming that the communication is going on as the nodding of a listener is telling the sender that he or she is listening and trying to grasp what is told.

When speaking of the message's *referential* function we are at the heart of the difficulties in analysis. It is impossible not to presuppose content directed outside a message. But it is very difficult to specify the exact rules governing the ways in which a text is pointing to its outside. The idea of representation and, hence, the referential function has been strongly debated throughout the twentieth century and many skeptics have claimed the impossibility of reference. This skepticism is by no way substantiated by ordinary experiences and praxes which succeed in making mutual understandings prevail over lack of understanding. Skepticism on behalf of different language systems' ability to create a relation between what is stated and what is the actual situation referred to, is often caused by a belief that two parts must understand the same in the exact same way to obtain real mutual understanding and that is never the case. From a pragmatic standpoint less than all is necessary for obtaining mutual understanding. When two people agree in their understanding it does not matter if their understandings are "the same" in all respects but only that they understand the same in the relevant aspects. Understanding is, from a communicative point of view, much more a pragmatic question than a philosophical question.

It is an often discussed problem with referentiality that words, images or other sign systems in no way directly relates to the reality they in some sense call forth. But before discussing all the problems involved with the talk of reference, one has to accept that the discussion must take as its point of departure, that something is questioned. Before the problems with reference may be addressed it has to be accepted that some sort of meaning is generated although it might be only loosely founded if at all. A process of meaning making is acknowledged by skeptics as well as its opponents. And for now it suffice to say that an analysis must work from the idea that by communication something is stated about something and that involves reference in some sense – may it be even so weak.

The *poetic* function is very important for media analysis when it comes to fiction. But also for other messages it is of importance how the message is construed. The rhetoric is part of a text's poetic functioning and, as I have stated above, it participates in the construction of meaning. This function is in most communication subordinated other aspects, but within fiction it becomes a dominant function.

The last function mentioned by Jakobson is the *metalingual.* It highlights the ways in which a message points its own codes. This function is pointing to a reflexive dimension within language, and it is also a function put at work when discrepancies arise in the process of communication. If misunderstandings are acknowledged, the first step out of the misunderstanding is addressing the codes involved in communication.

By focusing on the different functions of language Jakobson also calls attention to different functions of different texts which has great importance for what an analysis should try to come to grips with and reveal. The different functions are decisive for determining what kind of text is in question. The dominant functions are determining the overall genre of a specific text.

Jakobson's language functions points to a division of texts in different groups each with different functions as dominant. And when dealing with texts whether oral, written, visual or combinations thereof it is crucial to consider the specific kind of text in question and the purpose for engaging with it. One can investigate into the aesthetics of a telephone book, but normally one would not do so because the text is not understood as an artistic expression. But questions about its layout are important in dealing with its communicative usefulness. Here it becomes important what kind of letters are used, the layout and the organizing principles in the presentation of information.

Telephone books, for example, are not normally scrutinized for their ability to generate meaning. They are considered to be lists with practical purposes making the user able to look up a telephone number from name and address. In this example it is the specific use that makes the text signify and the text is legitimized by its usefulness. Although the telephone book may be an odd example, it is indicative of a very important dimension in the understanding of text generally and the academic analyses of text particularly because it shed light on the fact the relationship between text, meaning and use. A text maintains meaning only in respect with a use. For the sender's perspective the text is a means to achieve certain goals as informing, teaching, warning, complaining, selling products, entertain, convincing or whatever. From the receiver's point of view, the use may be equivalent of the sender's as to be informed, learn, avoid danger and so on, but it is not necessarily so.

The different purposes for making messages or texts and different uses of the texts available has in the run of history made a whole system of markers exactly addressing the different areas of concerns and the different situations for use. One of the most fundamental distinctions between texts that have evolved is *genre*. Genre is important because genre determines the purpose behind the text as a message. Within genre, it is first of all important to make distinctions between what kind of reference is implied by the text. If the text directs attention toward the world surrounding it or entities within reality, the dominant feature of the text is its referentiality in that the text makes claims about an outer reality. If the text conversely refrain from making statements immediately related to reality the text will be dominantly fictitious.

These two fundamental genres exist in numerous hybrids and mixes. However, for most texts it is possible to determine what feature is dominant. What is shown and recounted in a new program refers to reality, but the way in which this is done will depend on the presentation. The mode of representation does not stem directly from reality but is the way the presenter has chosen to present it and the connection thus induced are not necessarily in concordance with reality itself, but is instead a creation of the presentation. This kind of interference with reality, however, does not suggest a kind of fictionality of news. Instead the verbal translation of occurrences is a condition in the way in which humans interrelate with reality. But one cannot, contrarily, say that the assertions within the news programs are objective in the sense without human interference in the recounting of what has happened in reality.

What is essential to non-fiction is that it is making assertive claims about reality and, hence, these claims may in principles be examined by others. In non-fiction the relation between statements and the state of affairs is regulated by classical virtues as "truth," "good" and "beauty," but in its more modern dress as truth, fairness and trustworthiness to cite the guiding principles in Jürgen Habermas' understanding of communicative action. Media products dealing with reality are bound to establish a metonymic relation to reality.[2] It is the journalistic principles that guarantee the receiver that what

---

2   "Metonymic" is defined here as a relationship that works by proximity (closeness) and, hence, recognizability.

is shown and recounted is in accordance with what really has occurred, or that an interview is not misleading and manipulative in respect to what the interviewed person said during the interview. Assertive claims are more easily examined than are claims of, for instance, political motivations. That is why that claims on what actually happened in a certain case is up for dispute. That a presentation is disputable is not to say that it thereby is just a subjective view point, having no general objectivity. On the contrary – that a presentation is a matter of different opinions is indicative of the mutual and shared world that is referred to, and that it is possible to appeal to a common way of negotiating how we are to understand this mutual shared world.

Contrary to non-fiction, there are no immediate assertions involved in fiction because the text is not bound to something outside its own standards. It is not possible to examine the claims made within fiction in that there is not outer reality to check it against and therefore truth, right and trustworthiness does not exist as points of reference. It is not possible for fiction to lie. Instead, fiction mostly works by imitation of the assertive structures of language, and, hence, it makes claims within its own world: its diegesis. But since the diegetic world only exists as a consequence of the telling of it, it is not possible to check what is asserted against what actually has happened. There exist no witnesses or otherwise involved people to interpret occurrences differently from what is immediately available within the fiction itself.

Some fictions are playing with the dividing line between fiction and non-fiction by different devices as, for example, insertions of newsreel footages within a fiction setting as is the case in Oliver Stones' film *JFK*. This textual strategy has been used throughout the twentieth century and it has the effect of destabilizing the distinction. But the reader has to make a decision about the status of the insertions whether they are newsreel footages, agendas from workers meeting, excerpts from existing diaries or what else.

Although many fictions are very skilled and complex in structures and devices for meaning, giving rise to questions about the truth of the fiction, it cannot escape the fundamental distinction between fiction and non-fiction about assertions as bound or not bound to an external reality with competitive interpretations.

Similarly, a pervasive trend within television programs is to engage directly with a reality that is created by television itself. I think here of the phenomena of different reality shows. But although these programs are not showing reality proper it does not make these programs less referential – but perhaps their specific relation to reality is of a different kind than for instance classical documentary programs. In media programs, reality is always presented in a specific mode which shows reality in some of its aspects and with some respect.

My point in presenting Jakobson's model here is not that it should be a theoretical method for analysis of media products, but instead that it points to certain dimensions or levels of analysis. Every dimension (sender, message, receiver, channel, code, and context) in the model may be of interest and thereby indicating how one should analyze a text. Likewise it directs attention to the interrelatedness of the dimensions. It also directs our attention to the functions and thereby the dominant function of a message; text. It points to the importance of integrating a genre perspective firstly because genre is indicative of the dominant language function of the text, and secondly because genre establishes a specific relation between text and receiver. The system of genres are noticeably more complex than my presentation demonstrates and, of course, a specific analysis has to integrate a way more fine grained genre concept dealing with the different subgenres within media texts. Each of Jakobson's language functions point to different genres but the functions are not in themselves sufficient to decide genres.

An analysis is always addressing specific problems, and it may respectively make use of every theoretically ideas and frameworks that enable the analyst to gain insight in the text and help explain what and how the text communicate for whom. That's where quarrels begin in determining which analyses work best and explain the most relevant materials.

SUGGESTED READINGS

Altman, Rick: *Film/Genre*. BFI, London 1999.

Aumont, Jaques et.al: *Aesthetics of Film*, University of Texas Press, Austin 1992.

Barthes, Roland: *Selected Writings*. (Edited and selected by Susan Sontag), Fontana Paperbacks, Oxford 1983.

Calabrese, Omar: *Neo-Baroque. A Sign of the Times*. Princeton University Press, Princeton 1992.

Cook, Pam & Mieke Bernink (ed.): *The Cinema Book*. BFI, London 1999.

Creeber, Glen: *The Television Genre Book*. BFI, London 2001.

Eco, Umberto: *Semiotics and the Philosophy of Language*. Indiana University Press, Bloomington 1986.

Fiske, John: *Television Culture*. Routledge, London 1987.

Harari, J. V. (ed.): *Textual Strategies*, Ithaca 1979.

Jakobson, Roman: "Linguistics and Poetics" in T. A. Sebeok (ed.): *Style in Language*, Harvard University Press, Cambridge MA 1960.

Stam, Robert et.al.: *New Vocabularies in Film Semiotics*, Routledge, London 1990.

Stam, Robert: *Film Theory. An Introduction*. Blackwell, Malden MA 2000.

The Moment of Interpretation

Peter Allingham
Department of Communication
Aalborg University

Felinin

HOOC—CH–NH₂
|
CH₂
|
S
|
H₃C——C–CH₃
|
CH₂
|
CH₂
|
OH

Bio Site 10/4.03

– http://www.biosite.dk/staabi/felinin.htm[1]

"He has a square, flat, matte-black cassette tape recorder on the table in front of him. He puts in the tape. The sound comes from distant speakers on the perimeter of the room. Now that my eyes are becoming adjusted to the darkness, I can sense the way the walls curve along with the sides of the ship.
He listens for half a minute with his head in his hands. Then he stops the tape.
"Mid-forties. Grew up near Angmagssalik. Very little formal education. On top of the East Greenlandic there are traces of more northern dialects. But up

---

1   Other names: S-(3-Hydroxy-1,1-dimethylpropyl)-L-cystein
      Felinin is a special amino acid, which is found in the urine of cats, especially the urine of tomcats. The concentration in urine of cats is between 0,4-3,6 g/L (tomcats) and 0,2-0,25 g/L (tabby cats) (Hendriks 2001). Felinin is synthesized from cystein and enters into the tripeptide ?-glutamylfelinylglycin. Felinin breaks down into strong smelling solphurous compounds (Asferg og Ujvari, 2003).
      MV= 207,29; gross formula: C8H17NO3S [...] (my translation).

there they move around too much to say which exactly. He has probably never been away from Greenland for any appreciable length of time."

He looks at me with light-gray, almost milky eyes, with an expression as if he's waiting for something. Suddenly I know what it is. It's the applause after the first act.

"Impressive," I say. "Can you tell me more?"

"He's describing a journey. Across ice. With sleds. He's probably a hunter, because he uses a series of technical terms, such as anut for the dog harnesses. He's probably talking to a European. He uses English names for locations. And he seems to think he has to repeat many things."

He has listened to the tape for a very short time. I wonder whether he's pulling my leg.

"You don't believe me," he says coldly.

"I just wonder how you can conclude so much from so little."

"Language is a hologram."

He says this slowly and firmly.

"In every human utterance lies the sum total of that person's linguistic past."
– Peter Høeg: *Smilla's Sense of Snow.* Totonto: Seal Books 1994, p.157-58.

I. INTRODUCTION

The combination of humanistic theories of interpretation (e.g., Wolfgang Iser 1976, Umberto Eco 1990) and sociological and anthropological mapping of life styles, patterns of values and attitudes in commercial culture (Pierre Bourdieu 1979, Mary Douglas 1996, Grant McCracken 1990, Henrik Dahl 1997, et. al.) has provided a preferred strategic foundation for many editors of e.g., market communication during the last ten to fifteen years.

However, in recent years studies in media aesthetics (e.g., Agger & Jensen 2001; Allingham 2003) and studies in aesthetics of organizational communication (e.g., Stjernfelt & Thyssen 2000, Schultz, et. al. 2000, Thyssen 2003), especially the huge interest in branding and storytelling as strategic tools (e.g., Jensen 2002, Fog et. al. 2002, Kjærbeck 2004) and renewed interest in the relationship between aesthetics and effect[2], has drawn attention to the fact that moments of interpretation contain complex cognitive patterns of exchange of meaning which have a decisive impact on communication.

---

2   See e.g., the research group MAERKK at Aalborg University: http:// www.maerk-k.aau.dk/index.html.

Therefore, it seems worthwhile submitting processes of interpretation to further theoretical study.

By looking closely at the complicated processes of the moment of interpretation, which to a large extent determine the lived experiences of interpreters, it appears that it contains separate formations of meaning that go beyond cultural-anthropological mappings.

With point of departure in theory of interpretation with a historical perspective from theories of psychoanalysis to recent theory of cognitive semiotics, and through short analytic examples the aim of this article is to demonstrate what it means to practice media analysis so that differences between leading contemporary theoretical trends will appear. This will be done by focusing on a nodal point of mutual interest and difference among theoretical approaches, viz. the structures and dynamics of moments of interpretation on which, e.g., the success of storytelling depends. It is also the aim to suggest a possible synthesis of conflicting approaches by paying attention to a unifying matrix of the relationship between narrative structures and structures of reading.

But before entering the presentation a short survey of the relationship between the field of commercial cultural studies and cultural studies in a more general sense is necessary.

An important early modern approach to cultural studies in general was delivered in the 1930s by the Frankfurt School's sociological critique of the mass media, which pointed out how increasing commodification undermined democratic communication and led to oppression and stupidity (e.g., Horkheimer & Adorno 1949). Worth mentioning is also the development of modern theory of communication and information instigated by the interest through the 20th century in cybernetics, biology, system theory and communication (Norbert Wiener, Ludwig von Bertalanffy, Gregory Bateson, et. al.), a development which lead to the introduction of various linear models of communication by, e.g., Claude Shannon and Warren Weaver (about these models see Fiske 1982). From the 1950s until the late 1960s this linear 'school' of communication combined with behaviorist and cognitive psychological theories fulfilled growing needs within commercial life for a systematic communication theory which saw everything from the point of view of the addresser (see Buhl 1990).

The next steps towards the development of commercial cultural studies were connected to the introduction of structuralism, i.e., structuralist linguistics and semiotics (Roman Jakobson, Roland Barthes, Umberto Eco, et al.) into communication theory. Where the 'linear school' saw everything from the point of view of the addresser, the focus of the semiotic "school" was on the signs and the text in relation to its context, and furthermore the scope included steady and moving pictures and modern media, drawing the lines of correspondence between widespread conceptions and myths inside and outside texts, also texts and pictures within marketing (see Allingham 1997).

The next and third step towards commercial cultural studies brought the receiver into focus, so founding a multifacetted trend of reception theory. Various theories within post-structural literary studies (deconstruction, reader-response theory), mass communication studies (e.g., uses and gratification theory) and sociology and anthropology pointed to the fact that it is the reader of a text or a picture who to a very far extent decides what it means, and further that meanings and values can be related to various segments or groups of consumer "organized" in target groups (Pierre Bourdieu, Mary Douglas, Henrik Dahl, et. al.).

So, today a further and fourth step sees a return to cognitive-linear models of communication, due to a renewed interest in the cognitive functions of the mind (George Lakoff, Mark Johnson, et. al.) and the brain (Ernst Pöppel, et al.), a movement which to a large extent rejects linguistics and semiotics, which conceives meaning as based on discontinued distinctive units like phonemes (Roman Jakobson) or semes (A.J. Greimas), and turns to the pragmatic and realistic semiotics of the American philosopher Charles Sanders Pierce, whose pragmatic, anti-nominalistic philosophy conceives meaning as evolving through continued cognitive processes (see e.g., Thellefsen 2001).

So today, after the last fifty year's "swing" of focus within communication theory from the addresser to the text to the receiver it seems that we return to the problems and needs of the addresser and the question of: "what must we know about texts and receivers in order to become good strategic senders/addressers of communication?" But the dichotomy of the two semiotic trends, the linguistic and the cognitive, mentioned above is blatant, and has an impact both on practical media analyses, theoretical approaches to the nodal subject of interpretation, and on strategic thinking. Therefore, the following analysis of a printed advertisement below is set on confronting the two approaches, letting differences, similarities and possible crossovers stand out.

Finally, it must be mentioned that this article picks up from and continues my article "Marketing og semiotik" ("Marketing and Semiotics" Allingham 1997). In this article I presented some of the background to the present developments but I did not include the important approaches to the moment of interpretation, which is presented below.

Structure of Presentation

The presentation contains the following levels of discussion. First, a brief survey of trends and foci in modern theories of market communication is presented including a view of communication in an organizational perspective. Then the problem of the conditions and mechanisms of interpretation is presented. This will be followed by a survey of two contrasting approaches towards interpretation, which subsequently will be illustrated and discussed through analytical examples. This leads to the conclusion, which presents a model of interpretation, which combines psycho-semiotic and cognitive approaches. Finally, I set a perspective to various methodological problems.

II. TRENDS AND FOCI IN RECENT THEORIES OF MARKET COMMUNICATION – FROM SENDER TO RECEIVER

Interpretation and the relationship between aesthetics and effect have been pivotal points in discussions of communication in general and certainly within market communication since marketing became a necessity for commercial and later non-commercial organizations since World War II[3]. Most theories of communication have contributed to the understanding of these subjects but all in different ways.

A brief survey of the development of theories of communication from the Second World War till today reveals a change of focus with three stages ranging from the sender over the text to the receiver. Central to the change from the first stage (sender) to the second stage (text) was the break with the paradigm of information, the behaviorist S-R paradigm, and later also the cognitive S-O-R paradigm, like the Danish reader-response theorist Claus Buhl has described it (Buhl 1990 and Buhl 2000). For a while the break brought about a movement with the heading "Marketing and Semiotics," and later the heading "Humanistic Theories of Interpretation" summed up the rather heterogeneous endeavors of, e.g., combinations of quantitative and qualitative research of reception with or without a sociological perspective, cultural studies, and a variety of studies inspired by semiotics (see e.g., Buhl & Dahl 1993, Thwaites, et. al. 1994 or Allingham 1997).

Underlying this shift in focus has all the way through been a claim that the

---

3 Frandsen, et. al. (1997) distinguishes between three perspectives, the Production Perspective from before The Second World War until 1960; the Narrow Marketing Perspective 1960-1990; the Expanded Marketing Perspective 1990-? All years are approximations.

various theories of semiotics and reception were better than the behaviorist and cognitive theories at explaining and handling interpretation and the relation between aesthetics and effect because they in various ways were based on language and cultural context, cf. Frandsen et al. 1997. He takes a strong stand against among others Kotler 1967 and Ottesen 1992, introducing or launching the ideal model of the organizational employee of the future: the employee responsible for communication and language.

But the break was also accompanied by currents, which reflected and still reflect dynamics in the field of communications, which may be called postmodern (see Featherstone 1991 ad Firat & Venkatesh 1993). Traces of these dynamics can be seen in e.g., various demonstrations that even widespread strategic tools like RISC, Minerva, and others will fail confronted with the fact that consumers are unmanageable (Gabriel & Lang 1995), or "segmental nomads."[4] Furthermore a number of researchers noted early in the 1980s that new trends were appearing among consumers, which made it clear that the habitus of the individual receiver consisted of more than just "the lived network of objective social relations and situations." Researchers like Morris B. Holbrook and Elisabeth Hirschman wrote articles like "The Experiental Aspect of Consumer Fantasies, Feelings, and Fun" (1982), which drew attention to the experiential desire of receivers and pointed out that consumption is primarily a hedonistic state of mind of the subject. Michael Shudson in 1984 pointed to the fact that advertisements do not influence on consumption to the extent generally believed, and that changes in patterns of consumption are only rarely prompted by advertising. He verified this by showing that advertising only meant little to e.g., the prevalence of smoking cigarettes (Shudson 1984: 179). In the beginning of the 1990s the theorist of culture Dominique Bouchet discovered that symbolic, connotative meaning produced in texts apparently played a declining role in relation to e.g., the pleasing emotional experiences produced by images (Bouchet 1991). And last but not least Lars Thøger Christensen has carried out examinations in a perspective of organizational communication that among other details state that the belief in the external effects of advertising is grossly exaggerated

---

4   RISC means "Research Institute on Social Change." During the 1990s RISC referred to a market research value survey, which included the French sociologist Pierre Bourdieu's theories. It presented a model, which divided consumers into segments according to values and life styles. MINERVA is similar model developed by the Danish sociologist Henrik Dahl (see Dahl 1997).

(Christensen 1994 and 2001). Christensen exemplifies that advertising and other external communication issued by organizations apparently have a bigger effect internally in the organization than externally, i.e., the auto communicative effect of communication is what matters, which is why external market communication has an internally organizing effect. This point of view is supported in articles in the book *Modtageren som medproducent (The Receiver as a Co-producer)* by Helder & Pjetursson (1999).

Perhaps the most recent development in the conflicting transformations of the perspectives of strategic communication appears in the phenomena called "branding" and "storytelling" (see e.g., Aaker 1996, Mollerup 1998, Schultz et al. 2000, and Fog et al. 2002), which can be seen as profiling means through which e.g., internal values in an organization may be expressed externally (Schultz, et. al., 2000). Through storytelling, the core values in the 'depth' of the organization in question will rise to the 'surface' of the organization and present itself through, e.g., strategically molded brands, advertising, strategic behaviour or corporate architecture. Through the brands and the stories consumers with a hedonistic attitude and voracious hunger for identity can inscribe or insert themselves as loyal partakers of the aura of the organizations, as members of the corporations or – as the market communication researcher P. O. Berg describes it – enter the floating auditoria of the organizations (Berg 2000).

Phenomena and buzzwords like "Branding" and "Storytelling" represent two sides of the same coin (Jensen 2002). While the big narratives according to post-modern prophecy are disappearing, small narratives seem to be in demand, narratives that can index the branded product, e.g., inscribe the Nike sneakers and their contents into special mythological universes, e.g., the 'History of Sport' or 'The Spirit of Sport' (Schmitt & Simonsen 1997). The phenomenon of branding as an identity project can probably be understood as a symptom of a cultural state with a post-modern stamp. On the one hand branding is worshipped as a kind of strategic religion of communication (Kunde 1997, 2002) with strict demands to the organization operating on a multinational scale that in the organization there is only room for co-operators, not for 'counter'-operators, and that the almost divine top management has clarified, elaborated and implemented a strong visual and written identity in all links in the chain of the organization from parent to subsidiaries.

On the other hand, branding is the object of radical political criticism (Klein 1999), which tries to substantiate how branding functions as an accessory to a capitalist, globalized division of labour. One of the many reverses of the medal is the numerous EPZs – Export Processing Zones – and sweatshops in third world countries in Asia and Africa. Big corporations like e.g., Ford Motor Co. (Olins 2000), IBM, Nike and many more from the western countries lease or engage production units on a very favorable basis in these zones. Grossly underpaid often child workers produce the much-coveted branded consumer goods under conditions, which bring the horrors of the Industrial Revolution to mind. This scenario is claimed to remain invisible to the peoples and consumers of the rich western world, where the phasing out of industrial production units, i.e., factories, is substituted by parent enterprises connected to the grooming of the brands. According to Klein and others, branding and the commercial discourse of branding influence on, take over and control still larger parts of commercial and non-commercial public life, among others schools and universities. Klein presents grotesque examples and accounts for how e.g., the students movements of the 1970-80s for the rights of women and minorities and for equal representation retrospectively almost look like preliminary work for the branding projects of the big corporations, as pilot projects, guiding the marketers to the aesthetic characteristics of the later trend setting minority groups, often black communities in the American metropolises, who became the backbone of brand building throughout the 1990s.

III. Conditions and Mechanisms of Interpretation in Market Communication

Nonetheless, it seems that the breakaway from the cognitive paradigm to the advantage of the linguistic-semiotic textual theories and receiver and reader-response oriented theories of interpretation has carried along a blind spot. This spot has been referred to above as "dynamics" and has to do with identity and subjectivity, also a major point of interest to various theories of strategic communication involving branding and consumer research. Therefore, as I pointed out in Allingham (1997 p. 362): "As described marketing & semiotics rebelled against the positivist model of information, which was blamed for being fixated on needs and focusing on the individual separated from its context. However, it will be like throwing the baby out with the bath water to ignore that these theories after all deal with something, which is absolutely necessary and decisive, namely the subject." Although Claus Buhl had it out, for sympathetic reasons, with the outer – directed information – processing subject of the behaviourist and cognitive paradigms (Buhl 1990), a systematic theory of the dynamic subject was not presented as a follow up (see e.g., Buhl & Mick 1993).

The instance of the subject in the exchanges of meaning is present in most theories of communication. But as I pointed out in 1997, whether it was dynamically represented as "reading into the text" or "Horizontsammensmelt-zung" seen from a hermeneutic point of view, whether it was all about "symbolic equivalence" or "metaphorical identification" (McCracken 1990) seen from the point of view of the anthropologist, or it was a matter of "habitus" (Bourdieu 1979), which the sociologist Henrik Dahl defined as a translation of people's: "… basic living conditions into a semi-conscious semi-system of conceptions of values and objectives, which permeate the 'style of playing' within all possible fields of practice" (Dahl 1996: 11), it is quite obvious that most of these theories were and are lacking when it comes to theory of how the exchange of meaning takes place, the exact mechanisms and processes of meaning formation and interpretation.

Therefore it is necessary to bring into focus the psychological, mental and cognitive mechanisms of interpretation as well as the circulating meaning material in the form of discourses, which enter into the formation of meaning.

Focussing on the exchange of meaning, on the mechanisms and processes of interpretation seems absolutely necessary if we want to:

- go further into understanding of the processes of interpretation, including the relation between aesthetics and effect. This requires a further look into the question of the 'subjective habitus', the subject of cognition and discourse with its perceptual structures, batteries of schemata, mental logics and discourses.

- develop strategic tools of communication, which level with the conditions of communication in modern organizations in a culture of digitalized information where distinctions between internal an external communication are disappearing, borders between life-world and system-world are evaporating; where horizontal, hierarchical authoritarian relations seem to be abandoned to the advantage of horizontal relations of dispersed authority; where aesthetic and ethic principles confront economic criteria in relation to management; and where segments of consumers and the quantitative and qualitative thinking of segmentation are substituted by ideas of consumers and receivers as momentary interactive co-producers and elusive communicators of the floating auditoriums of companies (Berg 2000).

IV. TWO APPROACHES – THE RETURN OF COGNITIVE THEORY

What escaped my article in 1997 was first and foremost the elaboration of rather widespread psycho semiotic approaches to the role of the subject of discourse and interpretation in this connection. As a matter of fact this line of research played quite a role especially within the literary and textual sciences, and the science of film (Metz 1977) and media during the 1980s and 1990s both on an international and on a national Danish scale. In Denmark psycho semiotics flourished for fifteen years, from approximately 1975, peaking in Denmark around 1980 where the psychiatrist Bent Rosenbaum and the literary scholar Harly Sonne published *Det er et bånd der taler* (*The Language of psychosis*) (Rosenbaum & Sonne 1979), which was followed in 1980 by Danish semiotician Per Aage Brandt book *Den talende krop* (*The Speaking Body*) (Brandt 1980). Both books introduced appropriations of Freudian and Lacanian psychoanalysis, i.e., psycho-linguistic theory of the structures of the human consciousness in which the controversial, hermetic French psychoanalyst Jacques Lacan's re-writing of Sigmund Freud's psychoanalytic theory (Lacan 1966, 1973) with Ferdinand de Saussure's semiotics and Roman Jakobson's linguistics played a major role. The Danish psycho-semiotic effort resulted in among other things theory of text and textual aesthetics and its possible effects, i.e., in theory of interpretation although this was not developed very far.

This happened in two ways. First, a narrative theory was developed on account of Jacques Lacan's generative and structural models of the subject. The idea was, following Lacan's thought, that the infant subject enters social life, The Symbolic, through its inscription and admission into language, which carries the social order. This happens through a process of mental castration, which is supposed to tear the child out of it symbiosis, its phallic identification with the mother figure. Through this rupture the child is transformed from its narcissist secluded, imaginary existence where it identifies with what it sees to the threshold of social life. The psycho genetic development through the first years in the life of the child was thought to decide among other things the further development of the character of the child including its possible mental pathological dispositions. The point of Lacan's model is, however, that it is also a model of the structure of the subject, its mental structure being established with the first running through of the stages of the development.[5]

As mentioned, the genetic, structural model of the subject gave rise to the development of various narrative text models, among them models of diegesis developed by Brandt 1980 using the Greek term for narrative. His model

---

5   For further descriptions see Brandt (1980); Rosenbaum & Sonne (1979; Sonne & Grambye (1987); Grambye & Sonne (1997); Rosenbaum (2004).

was later expanded by Christian Grambye and Harly Sonne (1987) into the 3-D model and applied with interesting results to literary texts (Grambye & Sonne 1992) and to TV-spots (Grambye & Sonne 1997). Both versions of the model focus on the dynamic relationship between the level of the 1st and 2nd person, i.e., the subject of enunciation (or discourse) and its implied receiver which can be understood as the identity of he or she for whom the text has been written, the "Model Reader" (MR) in Umberto Eco's terms (1990). The 'narrative' level of diegesis is obviously not identical with the narrative on the level of the third person, i.e., the story, which is often summed up by Greimas' Actant Model (1966). The point of both diegetic models in this connection is the fact that they present us with a possible explanation of textual effects, i.e., aesthetic effects. In short the idea is that whenever a reader or viewer experiences something through an aesthetic object, a text or a picture, steady or moving, i.e., identifies with the implied model reader(s) of the aesthetic object, the reader lives through, re-enlivens, or repeats the emotional qualities of his or her own psychogenetic crises and dramas, crises and dramas which have been anticipated through the aesthetic structures of the aesthetic object. These structures were already an object of interest to Sigmund Freud who in a famous text "Der Dichter und das Phantasieren" (Freud 1908) asked about the secrets of the poet, from where he gets his material, and how he succeeds in making it affect, move and touch the readers. He thought that:

> "[...] in the technique which conquers the [...] repulsive effect [of the basic fantasies], which has got something to do with the barriers between the single I and the others, the true *ars poetica* lies. Among the devices of the poetic technique we can distinguish two kinds: The poet tempers the work's character of egoistic daydream through changes and disguises, and he bribes us with the pure formal, i.e., aesthetic pleasure which the presentation of the fantasies offer to us. Pleasures like that which we are offered in order that a bigger desire can be released from mental sources, which are deeper, are called a Verlockungsprämie or a fore-pleasure. In my opinion the aesthetic feeling of pleasure which the poet gives us, has the character of fore-pleasure and the real pleasure of a work of art is due to the fact that it releases mental tensions in us" (Freud 1908: 29-30, my translation).

Secondly, a theory of the decentered subject of enunciation/discourse inside and outside fiction had since the end of the 1960s been developed inspired equally by linguistic theory on shifters, deixis and origo, speech acts and other linguistic universals (Sonne 1978; Rosenbaum & Sonne 1979, Rosenbaum 2000; Allingham, Brandt & Rosenbaum 2002), theory of formations of discourses, the history of signs and signification (e.g., Foucault 1966), and theory of psychoanalysis of Freudian and Lacanian origin. This theory of enunciation presents a model of the subject, which claims that the subject of enunciation is split into a conscious register and a primarily unconscious part or register. In the conscious register of enunciation the subject is represented by the 1st person "I" of enunciation, whereas in the primarily unconscious register, in the register of the discourse, the subject, compared by Lacan to a stupid grinding motor of desire, is obliged to express its (stupid) desires according to the expressive material of its more or less complete battery of signifiers, of discourses, which the subject has inscribed into his or her register of discourse through his or her life up to the moment of enunciation (See Sonne 1978; Rosenbaum & Sonne 1986).

With these findings the psycho-semiotic theory of the 1980s and 1990s were able to account on a systematic basis for various aesthetic and interpretational effects, one of the points was that interpretation especially in fiction had to do with reconstructing the intention of the text through identification with or assumption of the identity of its implied model receiver. It all seemed to some extent to supplement and fill out the gaps in Freud's lacking explanation of the *ars poetica*, accounting for aesthetic structure as the structure of enunciation, which in much fiction and literature consists of several layers of enunciation embedded into each other, founded on the substratum of fantasy or phantasmatic formations in consciousness, characterized by

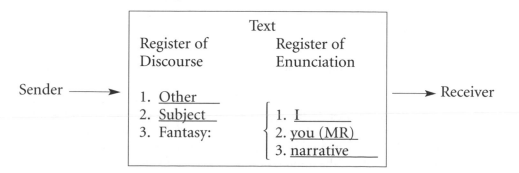

Figure 1: Model of Discourse-Enunciation with exterior pragmatic instances of communication:

lack of knowledge. It also seemed to explain that what happens when a reader experiences a meaning or interprets, is the fact that the reader "uploads" or records his or her psycho genetically grounded emotional experience into the gaps or empty spaces of a "downloaded," text, which for its part has organized and distributed these gaps in an aesthetic pattern, connected to narrative and enunciative structure (see e.g., Eco 1990 chapter 3).

As noted in the introduction accounting for the subjective component of interpretation must further include attempts to understand reception and interpretation and the relationship between aesthetics and effect on the basis of cognitive theory. This theory has since the 1980s taken a further step towards dealing with objects with an appeal to humanistic scholars, objects like literature, metaphor and a cognitive, realistic theory of the subject.

The core of the cognitive science since the 1980s can perhaps be summed up by suggesting that, in fact, human beings experience the world with the whole body and all senses and interact at the same time with the world.[6] But the worlds of perception and interaction are not identical. Meaning makes a difference. We perceive through our senses, sight, hearing and taste, with our olfactory and tactile senses, various aspects of our environment. But the environment only presents itself to us mentally as environment after having been processed through various complicated processes in the brain.[7] To be present in a situation requires that the brain presents the experiencing subject with a meaningful totality in a stable frame of space, time and identity. Ernst Pöppel, head of the Institute of Medical Psychology at The University of Munich, who has studied the phenomenology of time, has put forward a theory of the temporal dynamics of cognitive processes in order to understand the neuronal processes that decide phenomenal reality (Pöppel 1994). He claims that the neuro-cognitive machinery is controlled by three distinct temporal processing systems in different time domains. The integration in-

---

6   In the following paragraphs I draw heavily on texts from Bundgaard, Egholdm & Skov (2003).

7   According to neuro-physiological research the brain processes app. 11 million bit/sec from the five senses. To these the processing of the information of the interior functions of the body and the brain must be added, which is estimated to at least – but probably much more than – 10 billion bit/sec. Since the general channel capacity or bandwidth of the mind is estimated to only 10-30 bits/sec, it seems that a major task of the mind in order to produce conscious experiences is to throw away information. For an inspiring summary of this research see e.g., Nørretranders (1991).

tervals are of different duration and separated by a factor of 1:10, spanning from 30 msec to 300 msec to 3 sec.

In the "temporal window" of 30 msec the most basic operations take place. Here percepts are bound together in three stages, and the outcome is recognition of contours of surfaces, object binding within one sensory modality for different qualities and object binding from several modalities or inter sensory binding. This level of consciousness is characterized by an intrinsic absence of temporal order, which means that delays between, e.g., the different senses – the auditory system being faster than, e.g., the visual modality – are not perceived by the perceiver. At the next level of consciousness objects are perceived as something in the temporal windows of app. 300 msec, and at the final level, the temporal window of three sec we reach what Pöppel calls "the subjective present," the level of phenomenal awareness where pre-conceptual binding operations are supposed to take place.

Therein, to be present in a situation requires that a subject within three seconds have gestalted and integrated actual categorized objects in time, space and identity to its attention, including attitude and affection (passion and emotion). This is what defines a "moment," inherent in expressions like "one moment, please" or to motor activities like "throwing a glance" in order to level or acclimatize with a situation, fundamental to any kind of interpretational activity, or whatever.

This is what cognitive theory of late years have been trying to combine: processes taking place in the brain and experiences taking place in conscious mental life. Cognition, then, can be understood as the experienced connection between thought and the world in the phenomenology of the perceiving mind. Cognition is most certainly active while we perceive. Percepts are already concepts at the moment of experience and relation. The question is: how it can be?

A number of researchers within pragmatically oriented cognitive semantics have been working in this field. We find researcher like Eleanor Rosch and Barbara Lloyd who have presented a theory of categorization (e.g., Rosch & Lloyd 1978), George Lakoff and Mark Johnson have presented extensive cognitive research in metaphor (Lakoff & Johnson 1980; George Lakoff 1987; Mark Johnson 1987), George Lakoff and Mark Turner on poetic metaphor and literature (George Lakoff & Mark Turner 1989; Mark Turner 1996), Leonard Talmy on grammar and force dynamics, Charles Fillmore on frame semantics (Filmore 1982), Eve Sweetser on modality and semantic composition (Sweetser 1999), Gilles Fauconnnier has presented a theory of mental spaces and blending (Fauconnier 1994, 1997). At Aarhus University researchers like Per Aage Brandt, Svend Østergaard and Peer Bundgaard have presented research in cognitive semiotics in syntax, narratology, force dynamics, catastrophe theory, causation, literary theory et al. (Bundgaard, Egholm & Skov 2003).

One answer to the above question is theory of semantic domains and blending theory. Here linguist researchers like Lakoff & Johnson (1980), Lakoff & Turner (1989), Gilles Fauconnnier have found that linguistic metaphors – and not only in poetry, but in everyday language – represent and refer to cognitive operations which enable human beings to understand one subject or target "through" another subject or source. Target and source belonging to separate concepts in separate semantic domains, the formula of the metaphor will be in George Lakoff's terms:

A is B

The concepts in the operation do not merge or re-categorize. The operation is more like a momentary and automatic, floating inference.[8]

(1) Fredsforhandlingerne strandede.

(2) The peace negotiations ground to a halt.

In the Danish issue we are told:
A: [Negotiations] is B: [a(n unsuccessful) voyage]

In the English issue we get:
A: [Negotiations] is B: [a machine (seizing up)]

Metaphors like these are present in everyday language and present no problems in ordinary communication unless they attract too much attention in a discourse by being e.g., too numerous or extensive. E.g., certain politicians or TV-announcers are from time to time blamed for being too "poetic." It seems that discourses draw on batteries or lists of metaphors (schemas).

In view of Pöppel's theory of temporal windows, blending must play a decisive role in the pre-conceptual operations at the levels of consciousness ranging from categorization (300 msec) to the discursive level depending on the degree of compression. Conceptual blending and mapping are essential

---

8   Inference: the process of drawing a conclusion based on other conclusions.

operational components of mental spaces, which are conceptual integrated wholes at the conceptual level of consciousness.[9] Gilles Fauconnier writes, that they are:

> [...] constructs distinct from linguistic structures but built up in any discourse according to guidelines provided by linguistic expressions. In the model, mental spaces will be represented as structured, incrementable[[10]] sets – that is, sets with elements (a, b, c, ...) and relations holding between them (R_1ab, R_2a, R_3cef, ...) such that new elements can be added to them and relations established between their elements. (In a technical sense, an incrementable set is an ordered sequence of ordinary sets, but it will be convenient to speak of the mental space as being built up during ongoing discourse, rather than to refer to the corresponding sequence of sets.) (Fauconnier 1994 p. 16)

Various analytic models of Mental Spaces have been presented. Gilles Fauconnier and Mark Turner (1998) present a network model for conceptual integration. The network model deals with the dynamic on-line work, which we carry out cognitively in order to construct meaning in local thinking- and acting relations. Conceptual projection is essential in the activity and its central process is conceptual blending, a set of operations for combining cognitive models in a network of mental spaces. Mental spaces are small conceptual packages, which are constructed while we think and speak, in order to procure local understanding and action (Fauconnier in Bundgård 2003: 457). They are connected and can be modified, as thinking and discourse are unfolded. The prototypical integration network consists of four mental spaces, one for each input domain, one for the blended domain, and a generic space. The generic space contains what is common to the two input-spaces, e.g., abstract properties that apply to structure in all of the spaces. The input spaces make out partial structures, but they are connected through partial mapping lines between the input spaces indicated by lines

---

9   Conceptual blending is a set of operations for combining cognitive models in a network of mental spaces. Mapping or mental space connection is the understanding that an object or element in one space corresponds to an object or element in another space (Coulson & Fauconnier 1999).

10   Incrementable: gradually growing or increasing.

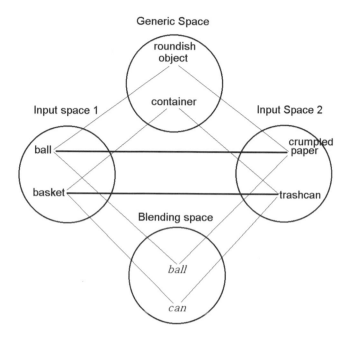

Figure 2: Mental Space Network Model 1

between the two input spaces. In the fourth room, the blending space, the mutually corresponding identical qualities are mapped.

At the NASS-conference in Copenhagen in 2000[11] Gilles Fauconnier gave the following "Trashcan basketball" example:

> Two college students are up late studying for an exam. Suddenly, one crumples up a piece of paper and heaves it at the wastepaper basket. As the two begin to shoot the 'ball' at the 'basket', the game of trashcan basketball is born.[12]

"Trashcan basketball" is a product of conceptual blending as it integrates knowledge structures from different domains into a hybrid frame, a blend, that contains partial structures form each input, e.g., the input domains are 'trash disposal' and 'basketball'.

---

11 NASS stands for Nordic Association of Semiotic Studies.
12 Quoted from Coulson & Fouconnier (1999).

The starting point is a generic space where the communicative action of throwing objects into a container emerges in a phenomenological reality. The two input spaces present us to two "worlds." In Input Space 1 we have the domain of the sport basketball. In Input Space 2 we have the domain of thrash disposal. In the blending space "ball" makes the two worlds blend so that the world of basketball becomes present in the world of the trash disposal through analogy. So it seems that it is through the abstract processes of conceptual projection from one domain to another that the features of the combined concept of 'trashcan basketball' emerge, i.e., through the system of correspondences that speakers can establish between various domains.

This way of analysing conceptual integration in networks is taken further and expanded by the researchers at the Center for Semiotics at Aarhus University (see Bundgaard, Egholm & Skov 2003; Brandt 2002 and 2003). The following example introduces the expanded model:

> I am in my living room in front of the TV. The announcer says:
> "Today the peace negotiations in X ground to a halt."

As in the above example the statement and its context makes out a generic space, here called Base Space, the space of communication, where the conceptual integration begins and ends. From Base Space the announcer refers to peace negotiations that have stopped. So, this subject must exist in a space of reference with a time frame, which is more extensive than the one in Base Space. The announcer uses the words "ground to a halt" which is an image, a metaphor, which presents in a space of its own, a space of presentation, timeless objects like old and badly maintained, run down, rusty, squeaky machines with creaky bearings finally seizing up with a grinding sound. These objects connect, i.e., map, with counterparts in referential space: the process of negotiations with the running of the machine, the agenda with e.g., production plan, the uncompromising attitudes of delegates with rust or lack of lubricants, the loud complaints with the grinding sound, and so on. However, the two sets of subjects, the negotiations and the mechanical movement, express the same thing. The two expressions blend so that the contents of the presentation (the inert moving machine) are used as a kind of staging or casting of the contents of the reference (negotiations). We then see in the first blending space the slack, sluggish movement of the exchange of demands and refusals, the bureaucratic structure of meetings, the dismissive attitudes of delegates, the delaying tactics, etc. Further, this drama works according to a dynamic schema, e.g., the democratic system or 'drama' of public opinion, which is introduced in a Relevance Space. Here the wanting and attempting of the agents of peace, e.g., "craftsmen" from the "political scene" or public agents from the media are opposed to, or alert to, the antagonistic uncompromising delaying, impeding forces of resistance. This gives rise to a second blend where we see the intervening agents, e.g., political craftsmen, trying to 'get the process back on the track', 'out of the deadlock' – by 'oiling the wheels', etc., trying to overcome or repair the opposing aspects. The dramatic blend contains, however, an aspect of communicative exchange. The appeal of the intervening agents for means of motive power is directed towards to the public. This is where the receiver of the message, where "I" come into the picture. Since I, who am watching the news, called to attention, invoked by the announcer's metaphor, am a part of public opinion, i.e., a potential helper, I will enter the new blend between the material from the first blend and the dynamic scheme in relevance space. In this way the last blend is projected back into Base Space.

The metaphoric process between mental spaces in communication forms

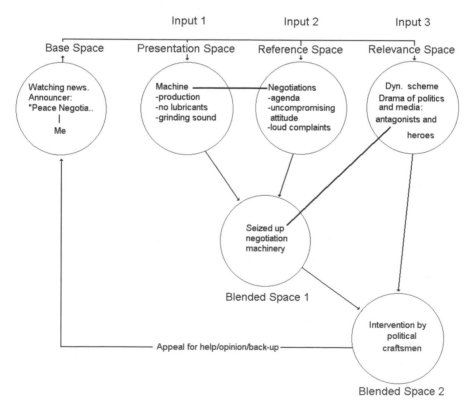

Figure 3: Mental Space Network Model 2:

a circuit in which meaning is built up, dramatized, and finally fed back into Base Space. I have invested the following Aarhus model of blending summing up the above analysis:

A conclusion to this is that metaphors always create conceptual networks, often much more complicated than this one. The point is, however, that the design of the network presumably represents a mental procedure for momentary formation of meaning on a semantic conceptual level. Therefore, the formation of conceptual networks must be a basic component in any narrative or interpretational activity.

So, what did not enter my article on Marketing and Semiotics in 1997 were these theories of the subjective components of discourse and interpretation which are at best only rudimentarily present in early cognitive, anthropological and sociological theory of communication, market communication and otherwise. Humanistic theories of interpretation, i.e., hermeneutics and much reception theory deal in these matters, but very often on a pragmatic level of usage, where qualitative and quantitative methods and combinations of these are prevalent in e.g., Mick and Buhl (1993), Kvale (1997), Schrøder (2000), and others. A researcher who has reached interesting results through combination of hermeneutic principles and semiotic theory in order to understand the processes of interpretation is Umberto Eco in e.g., *The Limits of Interpretation* (1990), but also Eco (1992) and Eco (2000) which throw interesting light on levels and processes of interpretational activity.

So after all, cognitive theory seems to be seriously breaking back into theory of communication.

IV. ELIZABETH ARDEN EXCEPTIONAL LIPSTICK – A PREFACE

Above was mentioned the fact that the worlds of perception and interaction are not identical, and that meaning makes the difference, cf. the TV-news watching example above. Viewing and listening to news about peace negotiations is not the same as partaking in them, although you may feel yourself emotionally involved.[13] Metaphors and the dynamics of media make a difference. This is why it is so important to stress that, e.g., watching a beautiful girl in reality is not the same as watching a beautiful girl in an advertisement, although it may produce almost the same effect. The frame of

---

13   See e.g., Stjernfelt (1994): "Metaphors Are Keeping Clinton out of Bosnia."

watching, i.e., the representation of an intermediary gaze through which the girl appears makes a difference. This gaze has its certain dynamics of relevance, its specific genre features or schemata, which set a scene and cast the players. Therefore cognitive theory, which put realistic phenomenal experience and experiences through texts and pictures on the same level, is missing the important point that in the human realm experiences mediated through signs are incremental. In the animal kingdom, experiences mediated through signs are apparently not incremental.

The following example taken from the kingdom of cats contrasting with the ensuing analysis illustrates the point:

The amino acid Felinin[14] has a decisive function in the life of cat. Because of its presence in the urine other cats can judge features of the identity and qualities of its fellow species in a certain territory. A strong concentration of it reveals that there is a big, strong, often red tomcat in the neighborhood. The concentration of Felinin warns other tomcats and rivals that a powerful opponent is present, and tabby cats are told that close by an attractive mate can be found, because the high concentration of Felinin refers to the fact that the tomcat is a good hunter, capable of catching prey which is difficult to catch, the eating of which causes the high concentration of Felinin. A tabby cat mating this tomcat will have a good chance of offspring with a high quality of genes, although the cats do not know that.

According to this explanation natural selection works through signs, in this case of cats pheromones are a part of it. In Nature among the species there seem to be an infinite number of sign systems, which communicate messages of genetic quality. The point seems to be that attractiveness certifies biological quality.

The same system seems to exist among the human species. Visual beauty and the judging of it seems to play a major role in conveying messages of genetic quality like health, fertility and resistance to diseases to fellow members of the human species. According to recent research (Jones 1995; Johnston 1999) bilateral symmetry of, e.g., facial bones and the placement of weight on the body seems to play an important role as signs of genetic quality, whereas asymmetrical features or lopsidedness revealing low resistance to e.g., parasites or germs are found to communicate signs of low genetic quality. But in culture the expressions of ideals of beauty, taste and fashion vary from era to era. Unlike cats, reading the steady messages of

14   See note 1.

Elizabeth Arden

Alt for Damerne no. 16. 17 April 1997

På alles læber.....
En exceptionel nyskabelse.
En exceptionel følelse.
Et exceptionelt look......

Nyhed!
Exceptional Lipstick

Den føles exceptionel
fra det øjeblik den
rører dine læber.

pheromones, human beings are subject to a constant awareness of themselves as objects of the judgment of others. Consequently they try to reflect what they look like in the eyes of others, trying to adapt to what they imagine others find attractive, the use of mirrors, images and texts being essential in this connection. This means that human beings, like companies, find themselves posited in a perpetual of lack of identity[15] to back up their "marketing activities." Further it means that an essential part of the dramatic dynamics of human life consists in covering up the chronic existential and bodily lacks by chasing suitable signs to cover up defects and insufficiency. But these signs seem to be constantly changing, to be metaphors on the move, slipping and incremental. However, the dynamics or syntax, which channel the evaluations of taste and values, forms an essential part of interpretation.

V. TWO ANALYSES OF ELIZABETH ARDEN EXCEPTIONAL LIPSTICK

In order to illustrate some of these observations and claims it would be suitable to present an analysis of an advertisement in an attempt to scrutinize further on the processes of the moment of interpretation.

Like many advertisements this one also combines elements of fiction and fact. One way of viewing its layout is to understand it as an argument, an argumentative structure, that the reader must buy the product in question.[16] The conclusion of the argument could be paraphrased: "Dear reader, this is why you should buy this product." The premises, the reasons why, are all the listed in the means of persuasion in the major codes of pictures and text. They consist of on the one hand an iconic picture code and on the other hand of a printed arbitrary symbolic code and a causal indexical code, which have been distributed throughout the primary functional fields of the advertisement[17], indicating a possible rhythm or dynamics of reading the realization of which is quite up to the empirical reader, of course.

Looking at the ad we find two pictures. First the main illustration to the left and to the right a picture of the product placed in a special marginal field to the right. Let us take a look at the main illustration.

---

15 See also Douglas (1996).
16 See Jantzen 1993).
17 According to Alsted (1988) there are five functional fields: caption, text, illustration, signature and price which may be used.

First a few iconic key signifiers must be localized. The illustration shows a woman in an evening or a party dress. Apparently she is standing in a lift or elevator of the kind, which runs on the outside of skyscrapers. Through the window of the elevator the blurred reproduction of tall buildings and a street below appear, at first sight an unidentified metropolis. The woman is turning her back to the observer of the scene her attention focused on a mirror on the wall of the elevator. She is putting on lipstick.

Until now we have listed four or five key signifiers that further can be qualified paradigmatically. The first signifier is the woman in her party dress. According to a "paradigm of women" her figure and appearance qualifies her as young, apparently not a teenager, but probably at the age of twenty-five to thirty-five years old. Her carriage or posture shifting to one leg, curving her back in a certain way emphasizes her elegance and beauty, this way of standing falling into classical codes of the way that beautiful women stand, cf., e.g., Botticelli's Birth of Venus:

The posture demonstrates an elegant, reserved, discreet attraction and not e.g., vulgar sensualism. The party dress she is wearing must be related to a "party dress paradigm." Judged according to its looks the dress must fit to the fashionable end of this paradigm scale, as it seems to be cut rather elegantly. It is obviously more creation than ready-made.

Sandro Botticelli: The Birth of Venus. C. 1485.

The elevator must also be placed at the fashionable end of an "elevator paradigm." An elevator on the fronts of fashionable buildings in metropolises make out a 'display of fashion' in public space from which – according to popular assumption – different types of VIPs or executives from the business world have an opportunity to express power and social superiority. Besides, the elevator has the character of connection, link or communicator. It splits the related universe into two or three poles. There is an "up" and a "down" and something "in between" which could be called the stage of "going."

The signifier of metropolis may at a first glance belong to the abstract end of a paradigm of metropolises, before the geographical locality reveals itself even to the not informed reader through various signs like the Empire State Building in the background. We are in New York the home city of skyscrapers and Elizabeth Arden. But to the less informed reader we are perhaps present in the type of nowhere or everywhere transit sphere characteristic of metropolises in the western world, a type of place which is close to airports, interstate highways, shopping centres, etc... At any rate, this icon has, due to its metonymic character, a certain index quality. This assures us that it is true that "we" are in some metropolis, in which case the fictive part of the ad is supplied with an effect of reality or truth.

How does a mirror-paradigm look? It is difficult to answer, but in this case the mirror gets its meaning through its context. Mirrors are normally attached to identity, identification and as we shall see a certain distribution of vision. Mirrors establish a certain connection to the social field, the eyes of the others, looking at you. In the ad the girl looking at herself in the mirror, discovering her defective or insufficient coat of lipstick, re-making it up, establishes the connection. In other words, she re-produces herself according to "a special gaze" directed at her from the outside, a gaze from eyes she wants to be caught by as someone special or as it says "exceptional." Apart from the fact that this gaze might belong to the members of the social circles or party, which she might be going to, the mirror in this ad is also a link to the gaze from the outside belonging to the beholder of the scene. In this way the reader of the ad is directly drawn into the socio-scopic dimension of the ad.

Certainly, it is by virtue of the reflection of the girl's face that the viewer appears as an identity belonging to a circle, a viewpoint, which can be compared to the possible social circle, implied by the scene, but whose identity is more doubtful. This means that the ad itself in a certain phase of the appropriation of it has the quality of a mirror in which the reader of the ad imagines being reflected. This mirror effect is broken through the reference to the exterior gaze, which the reader gradually becomes aware of, which leads to a crisis. So, the reader is assigned to a special point of view. We shall return to this crisis below.[18]

After having decoded certain key signifiers in the picture through paradigmatic appropriation we shall turn to the combination of the signs in possible syntagms. In doing that, the narrative contents of the picture will appear. The combination of signifiers, i.e., the syntagm: "young woman in elegant evening dress going by elevator on skyscraper in western metropolis" indicates a narrative with several ins and outs. Above has already been suggested during the analysis of the sign of the elevator a possible spatial polarization of qualities in the related universe of "up," "down" and "between" or "going." The picture clearly presents the middle one of the three stages in a narrative about life in the metropolis, where the positions "up" and "down" opens up a possibility of a thematic investment so that "up" connotes "socially superior." Tops of skyscrapers, penthouses, or fashionable sky-lounges and restaurants are mythologically speaking places where top managers, VIPs, business executives, and celebrities hang out. "Down" is mythologically speaking a place where everything from ordinary people, be it the man on the shop floor or the man or the woman in the street, are staying, to those who are "down and out", i.e., those who must live by selling their manpower or whatever they have for sale. In the middle we find those, who are either going up or down.

In order to proceed we must pose the question of which way the elevator is going, up or down? The up-story is obvious: "the young businesswoman wearing her elegant evening dress is going to a party in the fashionable surroundings on top of a skyscraper in a western looking metropolis." On her way up she checks her looks and makes sure that it is immaculate and complete by freshening up her lipstick. If the elevator is going down another story will be possible. It may sound: "On her way down in the glass elevator from the fashionable premises on top of a skyscraper in the metropolis the young woman in the evening dress gets an opportunity to freshen up her lipstick." This might be a story of a young woman of easy virtue who moves in high circles among the rich and famous, referring to myths and stories of e.g., the happy hooker known from film like *Pretty Woman*. More stories are possible, e.g., "the young elegantly dressed woman in the elevator on the fashionable skyscraper controls her vertigo by freshening up her lipstick." A vast number of stories will be possible; the question is which story is selected as the preferred one.

---

18 See also Messaris (1997, 34ff).

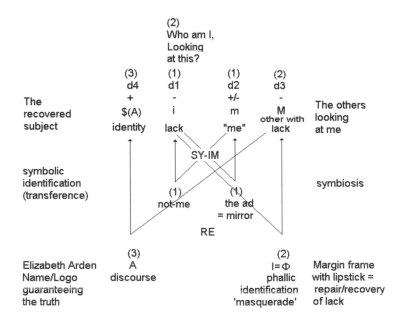

Figure 4: The diegesis of reading.

Of course, this is completely up to the reader although the text narrows down the polysemi of the picture to some extent. However, no wonder if those who have paid for the ad would prefer that the readers extract something in the direction of the first of the three stories mentioned above.

In order to verify this we have to return to the separation of the gaze of the receiver through the reference to the mirror effect and examine its function more closely. As written above this gaze contains and produces a crisis, because the question is: who is watching? Who is looking at this scenario? Hardly the one or ones at the company or party she may be going to. But the gaze of the picture catches the woman exactly in an inconvenient moment, where the cover, the appearances, the makeup is not quite in order, as a peep into an intimate, private situation where what lies beneath the smooth shiny surfaces appears in a sudden glimpse. Obviously, the ad in an extremely fleeting glimpse plays on fear of what must be hidden, be kept out of sight. In ads what must be kept out of sight has until recently been abject things like dirt, fat, references to bodily secretes like sweat, bad breath, menstruation blood, signs of ageing and decomposition, e.g., cracked, pale thin, bloodless lips, etc. What the beholder is watching is the covering up of the "misery," note the shy posture of the body, halfway turning the back towards the beholder, meanwhile the repairs showing the nicely proportioned back emphasized by the straps of the dress. But who is watching? The slight bird's eye view refers upwards perhaps in the direction of the mythological masculine power, money and managing director level. The elegant appearance of the woman supports this – she wants to look like this. The gaze, however, is interrupted on the page to the right by a pragmatic golden section, a closure, producing a further frame, which instructs the feminine beholder showing and telling what to do if there is a crack in the façade. The exceptional object of recovery is held out in the frame to the right, and the excellence of the lipstick is further framed and anchored by direct textual address to "you" arguing "It feels exceptional from the moment it touches your lips."

The final decisive effect is connected to the printing, the signature of the proper name Elizabeth Arden. The proper name is the last link in the chain of arguments producing the effect of truth due to the indexing quality of the proper names as signatures being metonyms of the person or organization which signs. In this case, the effect is strengthened as the signature also has a quality of a logo. [19]

VI. 2-D

Even though the ad is open to several readings and interpretations and it is up to each empirical reader to do with the ad whatever she or he would like to do, any reading into the ad will be met with an opposing "counter-reading" from the aesthetic and rhetorical structure inherent in the ad.

First we note that the ad contains two kinds of narrative structure. The **first** one is attached to the implied narrated fictive story applied mostly to the iconic representation, the story of the young woman in the elevator no matter if it is the story of the young career woman, the happy hooker, the vertiginous lady, or whatever. At this level we find the "storytelling" story of the ad.[20]

The **other** narrative structure is attached to the reading of the ad in which the attention of the reader is traveling among the function fields of the ad in

---

19 This is the reason why proper names, logos and brands are so important. They always refer to the truth which guarantees what has been stated. This is why contracts to be legal require a written signature. A signature is a metonym, i.e., part of the real person.

20 A "level" that at the moment is subject to dubious worship as the answer to the strategic problems of corporations and marketers of the future (e.g., Jensen 2002).

Alt for Damerne, March 1997

quest of meaning, a process where the diegetic structure of the ad and the interpretational quest of the reading are intertwined, a process which seen
from the strategic point of view of the addresser with the proper name is
successful if it stops there, at the proper name, in which case the argument of
the ad has been carried through.

This process of reading, the hermeneutical trace, according to the layout
of the ad, can be summed up by one of the psycho semiotically inspired
models. I suggest the following 2-D-model:[21]

The trace begins in the specific context (d1) where magazines are found. A
possible feeling of absence or lack can be momentarily relieved by e.g., a magazine in which among others our Elizabeth Arden ad is present. The glossy ad

---

21   For the sake of the especially interested I have retained some of its early Lacanian
     algebra. I repeat the reference to the presentation of these models in Brandt
     (1980); Grambye & Sonne (1987 and 1992).

resembles a mirror in which the viewer "sees herself" in a perfect aesthetic montage. This imaginary effect of méconnaissance[22]: "me" (d2) in a short glimpse relieves the lack of d1. It lasts until the alienating awareness: this is "not-me." Thus, a gaze from the exterior is watching the girl: I am watching her. This is returning to the initial lack, which now has been critically aggravated: "Who am I looking at this?" The answer in the first round measured against the aesthetic scale of the scene: somebody who is lacking all, which the scene and the ad cover. Consequently, I represent what she is covering up: evil-smelling transpiration, bad breath, wrong clothes, in short the perspective is a doomed, decaying body. In the second round the awareness arrives: "Like I am looking at others, others are looking at me" (d3). Their critical eyes, in which I would like to find favour, refer to a special perfection, materialised in a certain object (_), which is held out or indicated in a special frame, an object by means of which I can cover or sign up what is not perfect, the cracked lips, the faded colours, the incomplete body, which means recovery.[23] And that this is true is vouched by the proper name (d4), like in a religious discourse: "In the name of Elizabeth Arden, you are granted this exceptional favour."

This model founded in a psycho-semiotically conceived theory of the subject in perpetual existential lack and its consequent mental crises seems to account for exactly the dynamic relationship between the level of the first and second persons, i.e., the subject of enunciation (or discourse) and its implied receiver. The implied receiver must be understood as the identity of he or she for whom the text has been written, the Model Reader in Umberto Eco's terms. This process of building up reader identity has the character of "Identity-telling" more than storytelling.

VII. GLOSSING OVER

How does it look then if not only the "model reader" is drawn into the picture, but also the factual, phenomenal reader who perceives and conceives the meaning? In order to get an idea of this we have to turn to the cognitive theory and its conception of the moment of "subjective presence" according to e.g., Pöppel, in which a subject within three seconds have gestalted and integrated actual categorized objects in time, space and identity to its attention including attitude and affection (passion and emotion). In order to do (part

---

22   Systematic misunderstanding of one's own practice.
23   I.e., a specific mise-en-signe attached to gender, see e.g., Andersen & Engberg (1994).

of) that we shall apply the image-based analysis of the blending of mental spaces to the ad. But before doing that let us take a look at another edition of the same ad:

This edition reveals more information, especially of the context of the motive. Under the left arm of the girl we see in more detail than in the first edition of the ad a street apparently with one-way traffic stretching towards the horizon, one-way because we see as far as the street goes that it is lit by the taillights of cars moving downtown in the twilight, the break between day and night. This street is 5th Avenue in New York[276], because further to the left in the picture we see almost parallel to the avenue a fragment of a piece of architecture that seem to distinguish itself remarkably from the surrounding architecture of the New York skyline including the Empire State Building at distance and the Rockefeller Plaza to the right. This is one of the towers of the gothic cathedral St. Patrick's Cathedral on 5th Avenue. Besides, we note that the dimmed, blurred appearance of the background in the picture is due to at least three things. First the weather seems misty, second the twilight, and third especially at the top of the picture we see very indistinct reflections of the room behind the girl, i.e., what looks like squares of roof panelling and contours of room due to surfaces of changing light reflecting from the window, light which does not come from the outside.

Now, let us try to read the mental spaces of this edition of the ad in the Fauconnier-Aarhus manner. It starts in Base Space where we find the partners of phenomenal communication. Here I browse through a magazine, my eyes being caught by the picture on the back of the cover with the girl applying lipstick to her lips in front of a mirror standing somewhere above 5th Avenue. The situation contains (at least) two in inputs. In Reference Space we find: The body of the girl, her lips, evening dress (black) and the gloss of lipstick (red). In Presentation Space we have: the city of New York, 5th Avenue, twilight, red taillights, and the skyscraper Empire State Building. In the first blending space, city and body infers the girl and her body corresponds to or maps with New York city, her lips with 5th Avenue, the black evening dress appearing with the white of her back to the twilight, the lipstick to Empire State Building. In the first blending space what we see, what is conceived, is a "story" about how at the break between day and night, at twilight time in the metropolis the avenues *"put on"* their (red) taillights making ready for

---

24   To people familiar with or to connoisseurs of the discourse of lipsticks, it is common knowledge that Elizabeth Arden and New York 5th Avenue go together.

nightlife just like the girls dress their bodies in their black evening dresses and *gloss over* their lips with red lipstick. In this blending we see elements from the two input spaces come to the front when we imagine what it is like and what is needed to dress up for nightlife in New York. However, this selection happens according to a dynamics, a protocol of schemata, which substantiates the selection in this case by spelling out what advances and what hampers, what is needed in order to dress up: the glossing over of one's faults, the coat, the cover and the makeup for what looks defective in broad daylight. This Cinderella dramatic schema of problem solving, the filling out of gaps, complementing – a common genre in advertising and in fairytales – is introduced in a Relevance Space and is mapped on the first blend. But if the metaphor of putting on, of glossing over, of complementing is also relevant for me the reader of the magazine we must assume that the dynamics of the Relevance Space will blend and infer with the material from the first blend in which case there is a second blend, presenting itself as the lipstick in the frame. The shape and the style of the lipstick resemble the Art Deco of The Empire State Building, and also contain the gloss that evokes the feeling of exceptionality "the moment it touches your lips." This is the moment of completion where city, "body" and reader will infer. So, through this circuit the moment of the ad will anticipate the moment of consumption. The moment of the ad will – in the name of Elizabeth Arden – bring this momentary relief to the reader of the magazine, provided, of course, that the reader is subjectively present in this moment of interpretation. Below the analysis has been summed up in a model:

VIII. CONCLUSION: THE DYNAMICS OF INTERPRETATION – A MODEL

Above we have presented two approaches to what happens at or in the moment of interpretation. The psycho-semiotic diegetic approach shows us the build up of a text internal Model Reader Identity through the stages in the diegetic dynamics of a text (Identity building). The cognitive approach took its point of departure in the factual peceptive-cognitive, phenomenal reader, which perceives and conceives the meaning of e.g., in the moment of "subjective presence."

It seems possible to conclude that both approaches will be necessary to get a more thorough understanding of what is essential to the moment of interpretation. It seems that the perceptive-cognitive approach sheds light on the basic neurologically generated "automatic" effects of, e.g., aesthetic beauty as involving a question of e.g., visual symmetry, the question of conceptual blending of mental spaces in, e.g., metaphors, and also the question of how various conceptual dynamic schemes or genres integrate

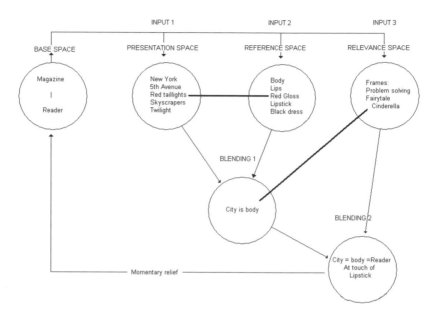

Figure 5: The Elizabeth Arden Network Model.

into blending processes. The psycho semiotic approach seems to account for stages in the dynamic build-up of model reader identity and has some explanatory strength in connection with effects of the symbolic and indexical stages.

It seems, then, quite obvious and easy on the basis of the diegetic code of narration and reading to extract a generalized matrix [of the integrated dynamics of producing and re-producing meaning]. It can be presented as an application of Lacanian theory of psychogenesis, but the model seems to suggest general cognitive dynamic qualities, which shall be discussed in further detail below. The matrix is quite simple and contains three stages:

Figure 6: Matrix of interpretation

1.↓ Opening: me – not-me: the mirror structure of méconnaissance connected to iconicity.
2.↓ Complementing: iconic or symbolic signs that can cover up or fill out gaps.
3.↓ Closure: indexing of the truth in the name of which the previously signified is valid.

Of these three stages especially the opening stage, the mirror stage, seems verifiable. A vast number of ads and other kind of marketing communication seem to concentrate on the effects of this stage and leave the others to the complementing activity of readers. In fact it seems that the possible mirror effect has inspired several magazine editors. The picture below is an excerpt from the magazine stand at the newsagent's at Odense Central Station from 14 May 2003:

Note how many magazines, e.g., *Sirene* at the bottom shelf, which feature face-to-face reflections with simulated eye contact like in a mirror, exploiting the possible effect of the attraction of the visual symmetry of the beautiful face or body. A circle of headings anticipates the filling of the aggravated lack after the – in our terms – "not-me"-crisis.

In the Elizabeth Arden ad the success of the mirror effect of the opening stage has to do with the means through which the receiver is situated or positioned in a lack. The means are especially the aesthetics employed from the photogravure of the glossy paper to the luxury, elegance and beauty of the presentation to the uses of the framing and cutting of the motive. Of course, the aesthetic exposure can be used with different value. In the Elizabeth Arden ad we are presented with a superior fashion or high society universe where the imaginary euphoric mirror identification (me) with the girl with the lipstick anticipates the rupture (not-me). The rupture accentuates the lack of the initial position of the reader by virtue of her youthfulness and beauty. Her – according to a certain taste – attractive geographic and social position can be measures against the reader's own everyday situation. Stated shortly, the aesthetics is an important means for establishing and accentuating any reader's perpetual initial state of lacking. It seems that the greater the aesthetic means the greater the effect of lack. Therefore, the universes of ads often present e.g., extreme superiority, beauty or cleanness. The extreme aesthetic qualities produce their opposites: inferiority, ugliness, and uncleanness. Exaggeration and over-indulgence seem to promote understanding.

After having been caught in the iconic traps of reflection the stage of complementing starts from the question of the identity of the reading subject. If the reading subject realizes its own faultiness in the eyes of others, the increasing knowledge that it is object of critical observation from others may make its gaze wander or shift to the object of rescue, the product, which is exposed and described.

In the Elizabeth Arden ad, the stage of completion is anticipated by the application of an interesting aesthetics. Unlike the magazine covers shown above, there is in this ad no simulated face-to-face eye contact between the reader and the girl. This contact has, so to speak, been displaced so that we see the girl having face-to-face eye contact with herself in the mirror, but the symmetry effect has been preserved through the body and the reflection of it in the mirror. Perhaps this is a means of accentuating the crisis of the rupture of méconnaissance and advancing the need of complementing. The theme of "rupture" or "breaking" is present in many ways in the ad: the twilight as the breaking point between day and night, the girl's white back against her black dress, the break between the girl as iconic motivated representation in the colours of black, skin white, and red and the iconic symbolic arbitrary representation of the lipstick to the right, which has almost the same colours. Further the misty twilight view of 5th Avenue is broken by the slight reflections of the room in the windows casting doubt on the iconic space.

The closing stage seems invariably tied to proper names or logos and their effects of truth. In fact it is difficult to find any ad without a signature.

Finally, it is absolutely important to emphasize that this is an idealized model of the integrated structure of narration and reception. In fact, no factual phenomenal reading of the ad will realize what has been spelled out here. It seems probable, that the process of reception or reading may unfold or realize only few or even fragments of the stages of the matrix.

Browsing through a magazine a glance at an ad for e.g., one second may only reach the opening stage and lead to an iconic perception of "beautiful girl." However, it perhaps gives us no New York, no lipstick, no proper name, no model reader identity. Or, perhaps, only the proper name will be noted and a full-fledged lipstick concept will be evoked on account of that if we, e.g., deal with a connoisseur of the magazine lipstick discourse. In fact it

The Olympic Tower and St. Patrick's Cathedral seen from 5th Avenue New York

seems that interpretation is the combined processing of multi modal sensory and conceptual input and projections of signs. Production and reception do not seem very far apart. And it certainly seems that it is possible for receivers to be present at many levels at a time in a moment. How this can be is still the question, which this paper has only accentuated.

Finally, the reason why this question has been put is among other things due to the point that there is no elevator on the Olympic Tower on the corner of East 51st Street and 5th Avenue in New York. Between the Olympic Tower on 5th Avenue, and the ad on the cover of the copy of the magazine there is only meaning. On several occasions, when asked by me, almost half of the students in classes where I have used this ad have claimed that their first impression was that the girl is in an elevator.

FINAL REMARK

This combination of elements of psycho semiotic and cognitive approaches to meaning understands reception as basically production of meaning, where meaning is produced or reproduced as a result of the projective semiosis of the individual. However, private semiosis is carried by sets of collective schemata of a perceptive and cognitive nature whose symbolic and social expressions in, e.g., metaphors has been described and mapped in the extensive sociological research of researchers like Pierre Bourdieu, Mary Douglas and Anthony Giddens, which the Humanistic Theories of Interpretation and the Consumer Culture theories through the 1990s with great success have drawn on. This research, however, has relied on mainly a semantic approach to meaning, except when rhetorical theory of persuasion has been applied (e.g., Dahl 1993) or discourse analysis (Fairclough 1995, et al.). However, it seems crucial that the theory of schemata apparently lacks ideas of the dynamics through which they are (re)produced. Furthermore, the cognitive theories also need to explain the connection between e.g., the information organizing operational protocols in media and the dynamics which sustain the social metaphors, although within theory of film comprehensive theories of e.g., narrativity has been presented (Bordwell 1985; Grodal 1994).

Where the linguistically based theories of aesthetics with or without psycho- have been blind to the fact that there prior to textual meaning exist mental processes of a pre-linguistic character (cf. Sonesson 1992), cognitive theory can be blamed that it is without a theory of the status of language in the human condition, which is the case with Lakoff and Johnson's theory of metaphors.

BIBLIOGRAPHY

Aaker, D. (1996): *Building Strong Brands.* New York: The Free Press.

Agger, G & J.F. Jensen (eds.) (2001): *The Aesthetics of Television: Medie & Cultural Studies 2.* Aalborg: Aalborg University Press.

Allingham, P. (1997): "Marketing & Semiotik," in: Jørgensen 1997.

Allingham, P., P.Aa. Brandt & B. Rosenbaum (2002): *Set fra sidste punktum.* København: Borgen.

Allingham, P. (2003): "Visual Deixis In Alfred Hitchcock's Psycho." Impact Online http://www.impact.hum.auc.dk.

Andersen, J.Ø. & C. Engberg (1994): *Masken som repræsentation.* Århus: Aarhus Universitetsforlag.

Andersen, H (red.) (1990): *Videnskabsteori og metodelære* bd. 2. Frederiksberg: Samfundslitteratur.

Asferg, T. og Ujvari, M. (2003): *Katten.* Natur og Museum. Marts.

Alsted, C. (1988): *Semiotik og retningslinjer for valg af annoncetype*, København: Working Paper, Institut for Afsætningsøkonomi, Handelshøjskolen i København.

Berg, P.O. (2000): "Fra image til aura. Nogle overvejelser over den strategiske kommunikations begrænsninger og muligheder" in: Stjernfelt & Thyssen 2000.

Bordwell, D. (1985): *Narration in the fiction film*. London: Routledge.

Bouchet, D. (1991): "Marketing as a Specific Form for Communication" in: Larsen, Mick & Alsted 1991.

Bourdieu, p. (1979) [1984]: Distinction: *A Social Critique of the Judgement of Taste*. London: Routledge & Kegan Paul.

Brandt, L. (2000): *Explosive Blends*. Roskilde: Speciale ved RUC.

Brandt, P. Aa. (1980): *Den talende krop*, København: Rhodos.

Brandt, P. Aa. (2002): "The Architecture of Semantic Domains – A grounding hypothesis in Cognitive Semiotics." http://www.hum.au.dk/semiotics/docs/epub/arc/paab/SemD/Semantic Domains.html

Brandt, P. Aa. (2003): "Kognitiv Semiotik – et forskningsparadigme for humaniora" in: Bundgaard, P., J. Egholm & M. Skov 2003.

Buhl, C. (1990): "Forbrugerteorier i videnskabsteoretisk belysning" in: Andersen 1990.

Buhl, C. (2000): "Æstetisk kommunikation i reklamer" in: Stjernfelt & Thyssen 2000.

Buhl, C. & D. Mick (1993): "A Meaning-based Model Of Advertising Experiences" in: *Journal of Consumer Research, Inc.* Vol 19, December 1992. Also: Research Paper. Copenhagen Business School Marketing Institute.

Bundgaard, P., J. Egholm & M. Skov (2003): *Kognitiv Semiotik*. Haslev: Haase.

Christensen, L.T. (1994): *Markedskommunikation som organiseringsmåde*. København: Akademisk Forlag.

Christensen, L. T. (2001): *Reklame i selvsving*. København: Samfundslitteratur.

Coulson, S. & G. Fouconnier (1999): "Fake Guns and Stone Lions: Conceptual Blending and Privative Adjectives" in: Fox, et al.

Dahl, H. (1993): *The Pragmatics of Persuasion*. Samfundslitteratur.

Dahl, H. & C. Buhl (1993): *Marketing & Semiotik*, Akademisk Forlag Semiotikserie.

Dahl, H. (1996): "Sociologi og målgrupper. Nogle erfaringer med at operationalisere Bourdieu." In: *MedieKultur* nr. 24. Aarhus: SMID.

Dahl. H.(1997): *Hvis din nabo var en bil*. København: Akademisk Forlag.

Douglas, M. (1996): *Thought Styles*. London, Thousand Oaks, New Delhi: Sage Publications.

Eco, U. (1990): *The Limits of Interpretation*. Bloomington And Indianapolis: Indiana University Press.

Eco, U. et. al. (1992): *Interpretation and overinterpretation*. Cambridge: Cambridge University Press.

Eco, U. (2000): *Kant og næbdyret sprog og erkendelse.* København: Forum.

Fairclough, N. (1995): *Media Discourse.* London: Arnold.

Fauconnier, G. (1994): *Mental Spaces: Aspects of Meaning Construction in Natural language.* Cambridge: Cambridge University Press.

Fauconnier, G. (1997): *Mappings In Thought And Language.* Cambridge: Cambridge University Press.

Fauconnier, G. & M. Turner (1998): "Conceptual Integration Networks" in: *Cognitive Science* 22 (2), Danish translation in: Bundgaard, P., J. Egholm & M. Skov 2003.

Featherstone, M. (1991): *Consumer culture and postmodernism.* London: Sage.

Fillmore, C. (1982): "Frames Semantics" in: Linguistic Society of Chorea (red.): *Linguistics In The Morning Calm.* Seoul: Hanshin.

Firat, A.F. & A.Venkatesh (1993): "Postmodernity: The Age of Marketing" in: *International Journal of Research in Marketing,* 10 (3).

Fiske, J. (1982): *Introduction to Communication Studies.* London And New York: Methuen.

Fog, K., C. Budtz & B. Yakaboylu (2002): *Storytelling: branding I praksis.* København: Samfundslitteratur.

Foucault, M. (1966): *Let Mots et les choses.* Paris: Éditions Gallimard.

Fox, B., D. Jurafsky & L. Michaelis (Eds.): (1999): *Cognition and Function in Language.* Palo Alto: CA: CSLI.

Frandsen, Finn, m.fl. (1997): *International markedskommunikation.* Systime.

Freud, S (1908): "Digteren og fantasierne" in: Johansen 1977.

Gabriel, Y. & T. Lang (1995): *The Unmanageable Consumer.* London, Thousand Oaks, New Delhi: Sage Publications.

Grambye, C. & H. Sonne (1992): "For det hjælper alligevel ikke at man bliver tømmerhandler" in: Østergaard 1992.

Grambye, C. & H. Sonne (1997): "Kompas" in: NyS 22. København: Dansklærerforeningen.

Greimas, A.J (1966): *Sémantique Strucrurale.* Paris: Librairie Larousse.

Grodal, T. K. (1994): *Cognition, Emotion and Visual Fiction.* Copenhagen: University of Copenhagen, Department of Film and Media Studies.

Helder, J. & L. Pjetursson (red.) (1999): *Modtageren som medproducent.* København: Samfundslitteratur.

Hendriks, W.H., S.M. Rutherfurd & K.J. Rutherfurd (2001): "Importance of sulfate, cysteine and methionine as precursors to felinine synthesis by domestic cats (Felis catus)." *Comparative Biochemistry and Physiology* Part C. 129:211-216.

Holbrook, M.B. & E.C. Hirschman (1982): "The Experiential Aspect of Consumer Fantasies, Feelings, and Fun" in: *Journal of Consumer Research* vol. 9.

Horkheimer, M. & T. W. Adorno (1944): *Oplysningens dialektik.* København: Gyldendals Logbøger 1972.

Iser, W. (1976): *Der Akt des Lesens. Theorie ästetischer Wirkung*. München: Wilhelm Fink.

Jantzen, C. (1993): "Strictly for Men" in: Jensen, Rasmussen & Stigel 1993.

Jensen, J.F, T. A. Rasmussen & J. Stigel (1993): *Reklame – Kultur*. Aalborg: Aalborg Universitetsforlag, FISK-serien.

Jensen, R. (2002): *Heartstorm*. Haslev: Jyllands-Postens Erhvervsbogklub I JPBøger.

Johansen, J. D. (red.) (1977): *Psykoanalyse, litteratur, tekstteori* bd 1 og 2. København: Borgen.

Johnson, Mark (1987): *The Body In The Mind*. Chicago And London: The University of Chicago Press.

Johnston, V. S. (1999): *Why we feel : the science of human emotions*. Cambridge Mass.: Perseus.

Jones, D. (1995): »Sexual selection, physical attractiveness and facial neoteny« in: *Current Anthropology*, 36.

Jørgensen, K. G. (red.) (1997): *Anvendt semiotik*. København: Gyldendal.

Kjærbeck, S. (red.) (2004): *Historiefortællling i praktisk kommunikation*. Roskilde: Roskilde Universitetsforlag.

Klein, Naomi: (1999): *No Logo*. New York: Picador.

Kotler, P. (1967): *Marketing Management*. London: Prentice-Hall International.

Kunde, J (1997): *Corporate religion: vejen til en stærk virksomhed*. København: Børsens Forlag. Kunde, J (2002): *Branding: skab bedre resultater – fokusér din virksomhed med branding*. København: Kunde & Co.

Kvale, S. (1997): *InterView : en introduktion til det kvalitative forskningsinterview*. København.: Hans Reitzel.

Lacan, J. (1966): *Écrits*. Paris: Éditions du Seuil.

Lacan, J. (1973): *Det ubevidste sprog*. København: Rhodos.

Lakoff, G. (1987): *Women, Fire And Dangerous Things: What Categories Reveal About The Mind*. Chicago: Chicago University Press.

Lakoff, G. & M. Johnson (1980): *Metaphors We Live By*. Chicago: Chicago University Press.

Lakoff, G. & M. Turner (1989): *More Than Cool Reason*. Chicago: Chicago University Press.

Larsen, H. H., D.G. Mick & C. Alsted (eds.) (1991): *Marketing and Semiotics*. København: Handelshøjskolens Forlag, Nyt Nordisk Forlag Arnold Busck.

McCracken, G. (1990): *Culture and Consumption*, USA: Indiana University Press.

Messaris, P. (1997): *Visual Persuasion : The Role of Images In Advertising*. Thousand Oaks, London New Delhi: Sage Publications.

Metz, C. (1977): *Le significant imaginaire.Psychanalyse et cinema*. Paris: Union générale d'Éditions.

Mollerup, Per (1998): *Marks of Excellence*. London: Phaidon.

Nørretranders, T. (1991): *Mærk verden.* København: Gyldendal.

Olins, Wally (2000): »How Brands are Taking over the Corporation." In: Schultz, m.fl. (red.) 2000.

Ottesen, O. (1992): *Markedskommunikasjon – strategisk helhetsplanlegging for økt lønnsomhet.* København: Handelshøjskolens Forlag.

Pöppel, E. (1994): "Temporal Mechanisms in Perception" in: *International Review of Neurobiology* (37).

Redeker, G. & Janssen, T. (1999): *Cognitive Linguistics: Foundations, Scope, and Metodology.* Berlin – New York: Mouton de Gruyter.

Rosch, E. (1978): "Principles of Categorization" in Rosch & Lloyd 1978.

Rosch, E. & B. B. Lloyd (eds.) (1978): *Cognition and Categorization.* Hillsdale (New Jersey): Lawrence Erlbaum.

Rosenbaum, B. & H. Sonne (1979): *Det er et bånd der taler.* København: Gyldendal.

Rosenbaum, B. & H. Sonne (1986): *The Language of Psychosis.* New York & London: New York University Press.

Rosenbaum, B. (2000): *Tankeformer og talemåder:en undersøgelse af skizofrenes udsigelse, tankeforstyrrelser og kommunikation.* København: Multivers.

Rosenbaum, B. (2004): "Psykosemiotik" in: Thellefsen & Dinesen 2004.

Schmitt, B. & A. Simonson (1997): *Marketing Aesthetics – The Strategic Management of Brands, Identity, And Image.* New York, London, Toronto, Sydney, Singapore: The Free Press.

Schrøder, K. (2000): "Pionerdagene er forbi! Hvor går receptionsforskningen hen?" in Borker, L. et.al. (red.): *Medie Kultur* nr. 31. Aarhus: SMID.

Schultz, M. et. al. (eds.) (2000): *The expressive Organization.* Oxford University Press.

Shudson M. (1984): *Advertising, The Uneasy Persuasion.* London: Routledge.

Sonesson, G. (1992): *Bildbetydelse.* Lund: Studentlitteratur.

Sonne, H. (1978): "Hvad er udsigelse?" in: Allingham, Brandt og Rosenbaum 2002.

Sonne, H. og C. Grambye (1987): "3-D-Fortælling og forløb" in: Sv. Bøggild Jensen: *Det fortalte forløb.* København: Basilisk.

Stjernfelt, F. (1994): "Metaforer holder Clinton ude af Bosnien" ("Metaphors are keeping Clinton Out of Bosnia") – interview with George Lakoff in: *Weekendavisen* 24-30 June 1994.

Stjernfelt, F. & O. Thyssen (eds.) (2000): *Æstetisk kommunikation.* København: Copenhagen Business School Press. Handelshøjskolens Forlag.

Sweetser, E. (1999): "Compositionality and Blending: Semantic Composition in a Cognitively Realistic Framework" in: Redeker & Janssen (1999).

Talmy, L. (2000): *Towards A Cognitive Semantics.* Cambridge (Massachusetts): MIT Press.

Thellefsen, T. (red.) (2001): *Tegn og betydning.* København: Akademisk Forlag.

Thellefsen, T. & A.M. Dinesen (eds.) (2004): *Semiotiske undersøgelser*. København: Hans Reitzels Forlag.

Thwaites, T., L. Davis & W. Mules (1994): *Tools For Cultural Studies – An Introduction*, MacMillan Education, Australia.

Thyssen, O. (2003): *Æstetisk ledelse – om organisationer og brugskunst*. København: Gyldendal.

Turner, M. (1996): *The Literary Mind*. New York Oxford: Oxford University Press.

Østergaard, A. (red.) (1992): *Skud*. Viborg: Amanda.

Pictures:

P. 15: Elizabeth Arden ad: *Alt for Damerne*, March 1997.

P. 21: Elizabeth Arden ad: *Alt for Damerne* no. 16. 17 April 1997.

P. 16: Sandro Botticelli: *The Birth of Venus*. C. 1485-86. http://www.ibiblio.org/wm/paint/auth/botticelli/venus/

P. 24: Photo by P. Allingham: Magazine stand at the newsagent's at Odense Central Station from 14 May 2003.

P. 26: Photo by P. Allingham: The Olympic Tower and St. Patrick's Cathedral seen from 5th Avenue New York, October 2001.

STUDYING NEWSPAPER DISCOURSE

Torben Vestergaard
Department of Languages and Intercultural Studies
Aalborg University

I. INTRODUCTION

It is a basic tenet of journalism that "report" and "comment" should be kept separate, which is to say that those items in a newspaper (or one of the electronic media) that convey information about events to its readers should do just that, and be clearly distinguishable from those items that offer opinions about and comments on those events. And, on the face of it, this does indeed seem to be the case. In the first place, newspapers keep the two types of material physically separate, with articles offering analysis, comment, background and opinion appearing on special pages. It is also the case that these items are often clearly labelled as such, carrying superscripts like "Comment," "Analysis" etc., or, in the case of the opinion article par excellence, the leader/editorial, occurring under the paper's logo or being superscripted by e.g., "Mirror Comment," or "The Sun Says." Thirdly, there is a clear difference between "report" and "comment" even at the discourse level. In 1. and 2. below I reproduce two paragraphs from the treatment of the same event, namely reactions to revelations of torture and other forms of abuse of Iraqi prisoners in American military prisons. One comes from the front page news report of the event, the other from the same paper's editorial comment. No reader could be in doubt which is which:

1. The US military yesterday announced that it had launched an overarching investigation into interrogation procedures and the role of private contractors in military prisons across Iraq after revelations of torture and sexual abuse at an army-run jail near Baghdad (*The Guardian*, 01.05.04: 1).

2. A single image retains the power to shock, even in this multi-media, broad-band, 24-hour rolling news age. The picture of an Iraqi prisoner held by US forces in Abu Graib prison, forced to stand on a block with electrical wires attached to his body, clothed in a Ku Klux

> Klan-style hood, is more than just another embarrassment for the
> Bush administration (*The Guardian*, 01.05.04: 19).

It would thus seem that every precaution has been taken lest readers should confuse the two types of material. Yet scholars working in the tradition of "Critical Discourse Analysis" or "Critical Linguistics" (e.g., van Dijk 1988a: 5) claim that the journalistic allegiance to the separation of fact and opinion is ideological (i.e., based on belief rather than reality), and in the same vein Fowler (1991: 208) characterizes the devices referred to above as "*seeming* [my emphasis, TV] to partition off the "opinion" component of the paper," implying that the presentation of values and beliefs is not restricted to editorials.

To address the plausibility of such claims, the central question with which we shall be concerned here is whether news reporting represents reality in a neutral, unbiased way, or whether it too offers values and beliefs. This general question can be broken down into two more specific ones: (1) are newspapers "neutral" in their selection of the events they report, and (2) are they "neutral" in the presentation of the events selected? In what follows, we shall see that the answer is "No" in both cases, but also that it could not possibly be otherwise. First, this is because to be reported in the press, an event has to be both sellable and tellable and, second, this is because there is no representation without interpretation.[1]

II. THE PRODUCTION OF NEWS

The number of events happening around us every day is of course infinite, whereas there are limitations of space on the number of events a single newspaper could report.[2] Newsworkers have to make choices, then, and these choices are naturally and inevitably conditioned by the fact that news is a commodity produced by an industry for consumption on the mass market, where it will compete with other mass cultural products for consumers' attention. Not everything that happens therefore stands the same chance of becoming transformed into a "news story" let alone of hitting the front page. The factors determining these chances of selection are referred to as "news values." Below, I pres-

---

1   This chapter will be concerned exclusively with the news article, in many ways the central product of the printed press. For discussion of the leading article/editorial see Bolívar (1994), Vestergaard (2000a, 2000b).

2   It would therefore seem slightly disingenuous to claim, as done by Hodge (1979: 160), that the decision not to publish an item that is available to the paper constitutes an act of suppression of the item for the readers.

ent the most important news values in random order, not wishing to imply any order of priority among them. (This analysis of news values was originally suggested by Galtung & Ruge 1973; for detailed discussion, see Allan 1999: 60 ff., Bell 1991: 155 ff., Fowler 1991: 12 ff., van Dijk 1988a: 119 ff., White 1997).

Recency. "News" has to be new, of course, but news production (at least in the print media) is further subject to a 24-hour constraint imposed by its production cycle. So events that can be located between the publication of yesterday's and today's copy of the paper are more newsworthy than more protracted processes and issues. Thus, "ethnic cleansing" of African tribes by Arabs in western Sudan has been going on for over a year almost unnoticed by the outside world (see *The Economist*, 15-21 May 2004: 10, 21-24). And events happening during weekends are less likely to get reported than events happening on weekdays.[3]

Negativity. Bad news is good news. That is, events "threatening to damage, disrupt or rearrange the social order in its material, political or normative guise" (White 1997: 104) range higher on the scale of newsworthiness than corresponding positive events.

Proximity and relevance. Events taking place in our immediate surroundings are more newsworthy to us than more distant ones, and events that could happen to ourselves are more newsworthy than less likely ones. Viewed from Northern Europe, where earthquakes do not happen, the recent terrorist attack in Madrid (11 March, 2004) scores higher than the earthquake in Iran (26 December, 2003) and predictably, received far greater press coverage in this part of the world, although in terms of human suffering and deaths, the latter event was of a far greater scale of magnitude than the former.

---

3   This means that Saturday night after the Sunday papers have gone to press is the worst possible time for an event to happen seen from the newspapers' point of view, as was the case with Princess Diana's death on the night between 30 and 31 August, 1998. The British national papers chose to stop press and clear the front pages in the early hours of the morning of 31 August, see Allan (1999: 76-77). In Denmark, where the event would score lower, at least on the proximity count, the papers did not carry the story until the ensuing Monday, by which time it wasn't "news" any more.

Magnitude. An event has to have a certain size or volume to be worth noticing, except in its immediate surroundings. Thus, a car accident involving only a single death may be front page material in the local paper, without being mentioned at all (except as a statistic) in the national press.

Unexpectedness. The mathematical theory of information as developed by Shannon and Weaver (for an introduction, see Fiske 1990: 6ff) defines the information value of an item as inversely proportional to its predictability, and "unexpectedness" as a news value can be seen as a direct manifestation of this. In fact it is likely that on closer analysis, "unexpectedness" could be shown to be the most general of the news values, from which some of the others, e.g., negativity and magnitude, derive.

Consonance. Perhaps paradoxically, in view of the preceding criterion, events that are in conformity with our socially shared norms and expectations (and accordingly easier to accept) make better news than less congruent ones. Thus, to a Danish audience, stories about Italian olive producers swindling with EC subsidies are more acceptable than stories of Danish meat producers committing similar offences, and may get more extensive coverage in Denmark, although they score lower on the Proximity and Relevance scales.

Eliteness. An otherwise trivial event, such as, e.g., a car crash with only a minimum amount of injury, may become a national news item if it involves a "public figure," a rock musician or a politician, for instance. Similarly, some nations and organizations are inherently more newsworthy than others. Since September 11, the Al-Qaida network is one of them – a fact that may also have contributed to the disparity in the press coverage received by the Madrid terrorist attacks and the Iranian earthquake.

Facticity. What the papers say should be true, of course, but it should also have the appearance of truth. It is probably for this reason that the news is so given to citing exact names, dates, places, sums of money and figures of all kinds, even participants' age, regardless of the relevance of this factual information.

Personalization. Events that can be related as involving identifiable persons are more newsworthy than events seen in terms of abstract processes and relations. Thus, the existence of AIDS, poverty and drug addiction is not news in itself, but the story of an individual hit by one or more of these tragedies may be.

Sources. Since journalists are only very rarely personal eye-witnesses to the events they write about, much depends on the quality of their sources. In the fields of finance and politics, these sources are naturally members of the financial and political elite, or persons authorized to speak on their behalf, but even a piece of "spot news" like a road accident, will have its newsworthiness enhanced by being witnessed by a celebrity, in particular if the person in question can be prevailed upon to offer a few comments (on the use of eye-witness accounts in reporting on September 11 see Silberstein [2002: 61 ff.]).

I want to make three comments on this list. First note that the same event may well be newsworthy on several counts, in which case it is the cumulative effect of the features that matters. The Madrid terrorist attack, for example, combines several features.

Second, observe that several of the features are not objective features of events, but subjective, culturally conditioned features of the stories *about* those events. This is obviously true about "eliteness," "sources," "personalization," and perhaps less obviously so about "facticity" (but recall that the issue is not about, say, the injury and damage figures in an accident but rather about the availability of information about those figures).[4]

Thirdly, a second group of features, viz., "unexpectedness," "consonance," "relevance," "proximity" and even "recency" are in a certain sense features of an event, but only in relation to a given audience.

III. THE NEWS STORY

The products of journalism, as well as the events on which these products are based, are customarily referred to as "stories," and in the preceding section I have occasionally used the term "news story." As Bell (1991: 146) puts it: "Journalists do not write articles. They write stories." This is to say, (*a*) there are structural as well as semantic similarities between the news story and other narratives, (*b*) to qualify as "story material" an event must possess certain characteristics and (*c*) as several writers have noted, see e.g., Hartley (1982),

---

4   Galtung and Ruge (1973), who first propounded the concept of news value on which the above account is based, also regarded the feature of "negativity" as culturally determined: why should success be less newsworthy than disaster? There are, however good reasons why this should be so. If we take into account that the information value of an item is inversely proportional to its predictability (see, e.g., Fiske, 1990: 9 ff), it is not difficult to see why we should be grateful that the plane crash is more newsworthy than the successfully completed air trip.

that the news story in our culture has the same functions as oral narrative in pre-literate societies. The idea that news stories follow a recognizable, recurrent pattern comparable to that of other types of narrative has been developed in detail by van Dijk (1988a: 49 ff) with his theory of "news schemata." The account below is based on van Dijk but with modifications suggested by Bell (1991: 163ff; 1998). For a general introduction to narrative, see Toolan (1988).

The Structure of a News Story

Text 1 below reproduces an "in brief" news story:

The story has three segments: headline, location and four sentences of text. The headline and the first sentence summarize the story, they make up the abstract. Note, however, that sentence 1 also contains the clause "it was reported yesterday." This clause does two things of interest: it indicates that there are sources, although it is pretty vague about who they are, and it emphasizes the recency of the story, "yesterday." Then in sentences 2 and 3 follow the main event. Sentence 4 finally contain two elements that very frequently round off news stories: result "She suffered puncture wounds" and expectation "[she] is expected to recover." We are not told who does the expecting, but the fully fledged news story, as we shall see, is typically rounded off with comments expressly attributed to outside sources.

There are quite close similarities between this story and the spontaneous oral narrative as studied by Labov (1972), which has the following six components:

1. **Abstract;** what is this story about?
2. **Orientation;** specifies the participants and main circumstances: who, when, where, what?
3. **Complicating action;** then, what happened?
4. **Evaluation;** why is this story important?
5. **Resolution;** what finally happened, how did it end?

Girl pulled from jaws of crocodile

► **AUSTRALIA:** A tour guide pulled an 11-year-old girl from the jaws of a 10ft crocodile, it was reported yesterday. Anne Thompson was swimming at a beach north of Cairns when grabbed. Roy Turner heard her screams, raced over in his boat, then jumped on top of the reptile, gouged its eyes, forcing it to flee. She suffered puncture wounds but is expected to recover.

The Independent 08.04.04: 28

6. Coda; marks the return from the narrative to the ongoing conversation

Abstract, orientation and complicating action recur in our brief news story and in that order, and the functions of resolution and coda can be said to have been taken over by the Result and Expectation components of the final sentence. Only Evaluation seems to be missing as a component in its own right, possibly because the girl's rescue is sensational enough as it is.

Let us now see to what extent the components of a narrative can be identified in a fully-fledged news story. Consider the story in text 2:

The story consists of the following elements: headline; by-line identifying the journalist; illustration; caption, giving the name of the missing woman; and main text. The main text in its turn consists of ten paragraphs, the first of which, the lead or "intro," together with the headline make up the abstract. Note again how the opening sentence of the story emphasizes its recency: *last week*. The circumstances of the discovery and identification of the body, the Main Event, are now given in the following paragraphs, but characteristically, interspersed with paragraphs serving different purposes. Thus after paragraph 2 has given us the basics of the discovery, paragraphs 3 and 4 take us back to the time of her disappearance, Previous Events, with a sudden leap in the last sentence of 4 to something that must have happened after the discovery, Subsequent Events, whereupon we return to Main Event in 5, to be given more details about the discovery. In 6 we get the Verbal Reactions of an eye-witness, viz., the man who found the body (note that his age and name are mentioned: the facticity value), and in 7 and 8 we now move on to an account of how the body was identified and foul play was ruled out, Subsequent Events. Comments on this latter aspect are again given as the Verbal Reactions of an attributed source, this time the police officer in charge of the investigation, presumably. Finally, much along the same lines as the previous story, the text closes with Resolution, her family have been informed, and expected Future Events, the inquest. As was the case with the previous minimum news story, there is no single segment that expressly has a function corresponding to the Evaluation of oral narrative. Considering, or perhaps exactly because of, its subject matter the story is in fact quite restrained in that respect. There are, however, two items of evaluative vocabulary (see Thompson and Hunston 2000): "the *badly* decomposed body" (1) and "The *gruesome* find" (5), neither of them attributed and thus the journalist's responsibility. Finally we might stop to consider the function of the Verbal Reactions. Since the whole account presumably is based on interviews with people who were there, the only reason to cite one of them directly is to

Woman lay dead by road for 3 years

MISSING: Kathleen

THE BODY of a pensioner lay hidden on a ring road's central reservation for more than three years, it emerged last week.

Workers discovered the badly decomposed body of Kathleen Childerley while clearing bushes on the ring road in Wolverhampton.

Widow Kathleen went missing from the town's Park Avenue Nursing Home in May 1996, aged 64. She was suffering from depression at the time.

Her disappearance led to a widespread media campaign. But police said last week they are not treating her death as suspicious.

The gruesome find was made on the central reservation near the

BY MARTIN STOTE

ring road in Stafford Street – about half a mile from the nursing home. A handbag and purse were also found close to the scene.

The man who found the body, 29-year-old highways worker Kevin McGloin, said: "Basically, it was just bones and clothing."

Detectives examined missing persons files in a bid to establish the woman's identity and the remains were examined by a pathologist. Forensic archaeologists were also drafted into the investigation.

Mrs Childerley's body was identified as a result of the forensic examinations and items of property

belonging to her, found at the scene. Detectives at first believed she was a victim of a road crash or had been killed and dumped there, but they have now ruled out any suspicious circumstances.

Detective Inspector Karl Bradburn, of West Midlands Police, said: "There is no evidence of injury on the body, in other words, there is nothing to indicate that Mrs Childerley came by her death violently or by way of a road incident. There is also nothing at the scene which would lead us to believe that her death is suspicious."

Her family have been informed and an inquest will be held.

International Express 11.01.00: 7

add dramatic detail to the narrative, i.e., direct speech in itself has an evaluative function. Note also that TV interviewers can often be observed to egg on eye-witnesses whom they feel to be too sober to provide more drama and more personal evaluation (cf. Silberstein 2002: 61 ff).

In conclusion, we may note first that oral narrative and newspaper stories exist in widely differing context. It should thus come as no surprise that one category is peculiar to each genre (the by-line and the coda, respectively, although there are coda-like elements in the news story), second, that the news story and the oral narrative do share so many features that treatment of the news story in terms of narrative categories may be fruitful. And, third, that they differ in one major respect: whereas the organization of the material in the oral narrative is linear, in the news story it is cyclic.

The Cyclic Principle

Labov (1972: 361) defines a minimal oral story as "a sequence of two clauses which are temporally ordered," and Polanyi, (1985: 189), states that "the order in which events are mentioned mirrors the order in which they are to be interpreted as having taken place." In the news story we saw that this was only the case in the case of the minimum story. In the fully-fledged news story, things are more complicated – and the narrative in text 2 is still a very simple one. The story opens with a brief account of a situation that has lasted for three years and only recently been discovered. Paragraph 1 deals with the discovery, the *now* of the story, time zero, then in 3 and 4 we move back into the past, Zero –, and in the last sentence of 4 we jump from the narrative past to something that took polace later than the narrative now, Zero+. In 5 we are back at time Zero; the eye-witness report in 6 was undoubtedly given only after the police had finished their investigation, i.e., later than the events reported in the two subsequent paragraphs, 7 and 8. The remarks by the leading police officer in 9 are of course given after the investigation they comment on, 7 and 8, but, out of consideration for the relatives undoubtedly only after they had been informed, 10. In comparison with oral narrative, the structure of the news story is highly complex. In fact, there is some evidence that this structure makes news stories more difficult to follow (Bell 1991: 230ff), and van Dijk (1988b) has similarly found that the popular press tends to use a more chronological structure than the elite press. The question now arises as to why news should be structured in this complex way. Why, we may ask, cannot newspapers relate events the way they happened and in the order in which they happened? There are several answers to this.

First, the criterion of news value dictates that the most newsworthy piece of information should be mentioned first, and this will very often be a recent event. Many previous events only gain newsworthiness thanks to their connection with a more recent one. This applies to the Previous Events reported both in our minimal news story and our full news story. Secondly, the cyclic principle ensures that the reader who for some reason stops reading the story will have got at least a gist of the information offered by the whole article. Interested readers, on the other hand, will know that if they read on, more details will follow. The final reason has to do with the production of news. After the journalist has handed in his story, it is subjected to further editing (most often cutting) by copy editors, who tend to "cut from bottom up ... which is a great incentive to get what you believe to be the main points in early" (Bell 1991: 154).[5]

IV. LANGUAGE AND REPRESENTATION

I said in the introduction that there is no representation without interpretation. This is most obviously true in the case of vocabulary: what to me is a "terrorist" may be a "freedom fighter" to you, and much research on media language has in fact been concerned with vocabulary (see Carter 1988).

Less obvious is the fact that also syntactic choices reflect, and in turn invite, different interpretations. As an introductory example, return to text 1.

---

5   However, the fact that "verbal reactions" and "expected events" figure so frequently as the final elements in a news story seems to indicate that although copy editors may cut from bottom up, they do not do so indiscriminately.

The headline and the first two sentences all relate what are essentially the same facts, though in increasing detail, namely that a man has saved a girl from the jaws of a crocodile. This process, which in the text is denoted by the verb *pull*, notionally involves three participants, viz., the rescuer (the Agent), the girl (the Goal) and the crocodile, which, however, is not linguistically treated as a participant but rather as a location: she was pulled *from the teeth of a 10ft crocodile*. The headline has the form of a non-finite passive clause, which allows the Goal of the action, the girl to figure in subject position with the effect that we feel that this is a story about her rather than her rescuer, let alone the croc.

Processes and Participants, Themes and Rhemes

Sentences can be analysed syntactically in terms of Subjects, Objects, Verbs, Adverbials, etc. But as the above analysis shows, texts are not just formal syntactic units: they are also semantic constructs by means of which we talk about things and events in the world around us. In Halliday's terms, the component of linguistics that handles this the referential capacity of language is called the Experiential component (Halliday 1994, for an easily accessible introduction see, e.g., Halliday 1973, Thompson 1996); its units are not formally defined units like Subjects, etc. but information units such as Processes and Participants.

Processes can be the deliberate Actions of Agents, such as *examine, grab, pull, swim*, or they can be events that just happen, e.g., *disappear fall, hear, die*, finally they can be "relational," indicating simply that two objects or phenomena are related to each other, as in "John *resembles* his mother," "the purse *contained* silver coins," "her remark *caused* a scandal."

We have already seen two types of Participant, namely Agent and Goal. In addition we need Phenomenon, the participant occurring with verbs of communication, cognition, etc: "Roy Turner heard *her screams*," "police said...*they are not treating her death as suspicious*."

Unlike the two central categories of the Experiential component of grammar, Process and Participant, the third, Circumstantial, is more marginal. These information units are expressions of time, place, reason, etc...: "it emerged *last week*," "Anne...was swimming *at a beach north of Cairn*...."

The categories of the Experiential component of grammar allow us to state whether a given unit is represented as Actor, Goal or Circumstance, etc. But we are still not able to account for how these information units are stringed together to form a text, and, as we have seen, our intuitions about what the text is about are influenced by the sequence in which the units are presented: it matters whether we say "Workers discovered the badly decomposed body" or "The badly decomposed body was discovered by workers," although the two are "cognitively synonymous," (i.e., if one is true, so is the other). The grammatical component dealing with the sequence of elements is called the textual component, and for present purposes it has the two categories "theme" and "rheme" (treatments of spoken language also have to account for the placement of accent), with Theme being the first unit in the sentence, and the Rheme all that follows. In notional terms, the Theme is what we feel the sentence is about, the Rheme is what is said about it. Finally, in unmarked cases, the Theme will contain only known, or "given," information, whereas the new information that is added will be contained in the Rheme.

The Burger Bug Story

In the final section of this chapter, I shall show how "the same event" was reported in different ways in two different papers. In accordance with the tradition of "critical linguistics/discourse analysis," I shall claim that the differences are ideologically significant. My treatment is going to differ from the standard practice of critical linguistics in two respects however: First, where it is customary to compare papers from different ends of the political spectrum and/or from different ends of the up market – downmarket range, the two stories we are going to analyze come from two papers that are both considered conservative and up market, viz., *The Times* and *The Daily Telegraph*. Second, whereas, traditionally, critical linguistics tends to deal with the journalistic treatment of politically significant events (see e.g., the articles by Tress and Hodge in Fowler et al. 1979 as well as Fairclough 1995), the events reported in the two news stories we shall be concerned with are quite trivial.

On February 15, 1991, several British national papers reported the outbreak of food poisoning in the North of England caused by eating infected hamburgers bought from the McDonald's restaurant chain. The story was a major front page item in the popular papers, one of which, *The Daily Mirror*, ran it as its main front page story under the headline "BURGER BUG ALERT." In the up market papers, its treatment was considerably more subdued. *The Times* (text 3) printed the first few paragraphs on the front page and continued it on page twenty-two, whereas *The Daily Telegraph* (text 4) relegated it to page four. As we learn from the two articles, the actual cases of poisoning had occurred on January 19. What made the story newsworthy about a month later was a press conference given by the Chief Medical Officer on the occasion of the release of a Health Department report on the poisoning. Identical quotations indicate that journalists from both papers must have had access to the same material, namely statements by the Chief Medical Officer (and possible other official representatives), the report, and statements by a McDonald's representative.

In spite of the fact that the two stories are based on identical material, the two headlines make us expect two quite different stories: *The Times'* story promises to be about an Actor (the Government) taking Action (warning) because of a Circumstance (food poisoning), whereas *The Telegraph* tells of a Relation (link) between a Phenomenon (food poisoning) and an Object (McDonalds). This expectation is borne out by the Main Event summarized by the two leads and related in somewhat greater detail in the first sections: "A Government representative has taken action;" *The Times*) and "An occurrence has been related to a place" *(The Telegraph)*.

Table 1 shows an analysis of the two first sentences of the two articles in terms of the distribution of participant roles. In accordance with what we would by now expect, *The Times* tells the story in terms of Agents and Actions, whereas *The Telegraph* is concerned with Relations and Events. Even more striking, however, is the fact that in terms of the arrangement of the information, the two first sentences are almost exact inverses (mirror images) of each other. The following items of information are given by both

a. the chief medical officer issued a warning
b. food poisoning has been related to McDonalds

(A third item – the meeting between meat industry and Health Department representatives – is only given by *the Times*.) The striking fact is now, that although both papers, in the first two sentences, convey these two items of information, their choices in terms of the experiential component of grammar are the exact opposite: In *The Times*, the information in (a) is given the status as Participants and Process, whereas *The Telegraph* downgrades it to Circumstantial. The information in (b), on the other hand, is accorded Participant-and-Process status in *The Telegraph* but pushed down to Circumstantial by *The Times*.

Distribution of Information

	participants and processes	circumstantials
Telegraph	food poisoning related to McDonalds	medical officer issues warning
Times	medical officer issues warning	food poisoning related to McDonalds

Table 2

The impression left by this analysis is corroborated by the following statistics: *The Times'* story consists of 18 sentences, 10 of which have a unit referring to a Government representative/institution in the role of Actor (but not always in thematic position). In comparison *The Telegraph's* story consists of 16 sentences, but only 5 of them with a Government representative as Actor.

V. CONCLUSION: CRITICAL OR DESCRIPTIVE?

Most readers will probably agree with me that the features about the two articles that we have discussed are ideologically significant:[7] we are apt to feel reassured when we are told that the Government is taking action in the face of a mysterious disease. We are also apt to feel informed, and possibly in a better position when it comes to making decisions, when we hear that the source of an infection has been found. I am not going to apportion praise or blame: after all, both papers give, roughly, the same information, and the decision between representing some units as either Participants or Circumstantials is a decision that language forces upon us. I do want to point out, however, that, in a sense, it is *The Times* that gives the most neutral representation of "the facts." Recall that the actual poisoning had happened about a month previously, and that it is the press conference that made the event newsworthy at this time. One could say that *The Times* sim-

---

7   I am referring to the concept of ideology in the sense of 'social representations in the mind' representing 'the basic principles that govern social judgment – what group members think is right or wrong, true or false.' (van Dijk 1998: 24-25) rather than in the orthodox Marxist sense of false consciousness legitimizing existing powerf relations.

participant 1	process	participant 2	circumstantials
Times			
1 agt the...medical officer	act issued a warning	phen that beefburgers should be cooked	yesterday in response to an outbreak...
2 agt Sir Donald Acheson	act gave	phen the warning	after a meeting with... meet retailers
Telegraph			
1 phen an outbreak of food poisoning	rel was linked to	obj the McDonalds restaurant chain	last night
2 phen the connection	event emerged		as Sir Donald ... issued a warning about cooking beefburgers

Table 1

Government warning on burger food poisoning

By THOMSON PRENTICE, MEDICAL CORRESPONDENT

THE government's chief medical officer issued a warning yesterday that beefburgers should be thoroughly cooked, in response to an outbreak of food poisoning among customers of a McDonald's restaurant.

Sir Donald Acheson gave the warning after a meeting on Wednesday with representatives of meat retailers, manufacturers and catering chains selling beefburgers. An investigation by the department's laboratories found that 14 people who ate beefburgers in or near Preston, Lancashire, last month suffered a rare and potentially serious form of food poisoning.

Nine of them had bought burgers at a branch of McDonald's in Preston around lunchtime on January 19. There was a "highly significant association" between the illness and eating beefburgers from the restaurant, the department said.

Another six people with the same distinctive strain of the illness, caused by *Eschericia*

Continued on page 22, col 4

Warning issued after beefburger poisoning

Continued from page 1

coli 0157 bacteria, have been identified nationally. Although some of them had eaten beefburgers, the restaurant chain is not implicated.

The health department is asking environmental health officers to check the cooking procedures for beefburgers when visiting restaurants and cooked food outlets. Sir Donald said there had been a steady increase in cases of illness caused by the bacteria in the past few years, with about 380 cases reported in Britain last year.

"Fortunately, the number of cases is relatively small, but the organism can lead to bloody diarrhoea and, occasionally, go on to kidney failure," he said. Until the Preston outbreak, public health specialists had been unable to identify possible sources of the infection.

"This organism is heat-sensitive and can be readily destroyed by proper cooking. I have been delighted by the positive response of those who have met and discussed this matter with the department and I see no reason why consumers should not continue to enjoy their products," Sir Donald said. "As far as the domestic consumer is concerned, there is no need for further precautions other than ensuring that the beefburgers are thoroughly cooked right through." A statement issued by McDonald's Hamburgers Ltd in north London yesterday said tests carried out at its Preston branch and meat suppliers had not detected the bacteria.

"The health department is satisfied with McDonald's quick response to this problem," it said. "McDonald's strives at all times to serve only the highest quality products quickly and efficiently in clean and hygienic surroundings."

Health officials believe the source of the Preston outbreak was an infected animal carcass and that the infection was spread through the meat during the mincing process.

ply and fairly reports what went on at that press conference, whereas *The Telegraph* goes out of its way to talk about something else. On the other hand, the press has been criticized for its tendency to talk about events in terms of what elite representatives have to say about them (Fowler, 1991: 120ff). This, in its turn, is caused (*a*) by the fact that journalists get a large part of their material from elite sources, and (*b*) by the general personality

Food poison link with McDonalds

By Nigel Bunyan

AN OUTBREAK of a rare and potentially serious form of food poisoning was linked to the McDonalds restaurant chain last night.

The connection emerged as Sir Donald Acheson, Chief Medical Officer, issued a warning about cooking beefburgers.

The Department of Health said that nine out of 13 people who became ill in Lancashire during six days last month had eaten at McDonalds in Preston.

Six other people with the same strain of illness were later identified. A number of them had eaten beefburgers.

Sir Donald said that illness from this form of food poisoning had shown a steady increase in Britain.

"A similar rising trend, preceding that in this country, has been noticed in North America where an association with beef burgers has been made."

The number of UK cases was still relatively small, with about 380 cases last year. The disease is most common in infants and young children.

Sir Donald said he now wanted to issue advice to caterers so they could review their cooking procedures.

Domestic consumers needed to take no further precautions, other than to ensure that beefburgers were cooked right through until the juices ran clear and there were "no pink bits inside".

He emphasised that the organism was heat sensitive and could therefore be "readily destroyed" by such cooking.

A spokeswoman for McDonalds Restaurants said: "Tests have been conducted at our Preston restaurant and in the premises of our meat supplier and the bacterium that causes this particular type of food poisoning has not been detected.

"The Department of Health have advised us that there have been no other reports of this illness following this outbreak."

The Department was satisfied with the company's "quick" response to the problem.

factor (cf. section 2, above). [8] From this point of view, then, we should be glad whenever a paper reports not a press conference as such, but rather what the press conference was about.

In his celebrated 1985 paper Fairclough argues that discourse analysis that is "merely" descriptive is bound to be non-explanatory or at best "locally" explanatory, i.e., capable of explaining discourse with reference to features in the immediate situation. Only a critical discourse analysis that sees any given piece of discourse in the context of its ideological-discursive formation, it is argued, will be able to attain "global" explanatory goals. Others, e.g., Stubbs (1997), Widdowson (2000), have argued that much "critical" discourse analysis is at worst prejudiced and at best misguided and possibly circular, fixing on a particular linguistic feature and assigning to it "ideological significance without regard to how it might be understood in the normal indexical process of reading" (Widdowson 2000: 166). If the stance taken in the present chapter is accepted, the question of critical versus non-critical will be seen as a non-issue. For if any event can be experienced, interpreted and represented in any number of ways, and none of them by definition is more "neutral" or more "correct" than the others, then the first step in a comparative analysis of journalism as a mode of media representation will be simply to note if and in what ways two journalistic reproductions of "the same event" are different, but the second question that will inevitably pose itself, then, is why one rather than the other representation of the event was chosen, and that question is in essence a critical one. The point that I am making is that simply by asking for explanations, one is entering critical territory. By this, I mean "critical" not in the Faircloughian sense of exposing supposedly hidden relations of power and dominance. Rather, I mean "critical" in the sense of seeking explanations lying outside the object under investigation and not taking immediately obvious explanations at face value.

---

8   Hodge (1979), finds that the tendency towards personalization is most pronounced in the popular press, whereas the quality press is more willing to talk about events and abstract relations.

WORKS CITED

Allan, S., 1999. *News Culture.* Buckingham: Open University Press.

Bell, A., 1991. *The Language of News Media.* Oxford: Blackwell.

___ 1998. The discourse structure of news stories. In Bell, A. and P. Garrett (Eds.) 1998, 64-104.

___ and Garrett, P. (Eds.) 1998. *Approaches to Media Discourse.* Oxford: Blackwell.

Bolivar, A., 1994. The structure of newspaper editorials. In, Coulthard, M. (ed.), *Advances in Written Text Analysis.* London: Routledge.

Carter, R., 1988. Front Pages: Lexis, style and newspaper reports. In M.Ghadessy (Ed.), 1988. *Registers of Written English.* London: Pinter Publishers.

van Dijk, T.A., 1988a. *News as Discourse.* Hillsdale, N.J.: Lawrence Earlbaum.

___ 1988b. *News Analysis: Case studies of International and National News in the Press.* Hillsdale, N.J.: Lawrence Earlbaum.

___ (Ed.), 1985. *Handbook of Discourse Analysis.* vol. 1-4.London, etc.: Academic Press.

___ 1998. Opinions and ideologies in the press. In Bell and Garrett (Eds.) 1998, 21-63.

Fairclough, N., 1985. Critical and discriptive goals in discourse analysis. *Journal of Pragmatics* 9, 739-763.

___ 1995. *Media Discourse.* London: Arnold.

Fiske, J., 1991, *Introduction to Communication Studies.* London and New York: Methuen.

Fowler, R., 1991. *Language in the News.* London and New York: Routledge.

___ et al. 1979. *Language and Control.* London: Boston and Henley.

Galtung, J. and M. Ruge, 1973. Structuring and selecting news. In S. Cohen & J. Young (Eds.). *The Manufacture of News.* London: Constable

Halliday, M.A.K., 1994. *An Introduction to functional Grammar.* London: Edward Arnold.

___ 1973. *Explorations in the Functions of Language.* London: Edward Arnold.

Hartley, J., 1982. *Understanding News.* London: Routledge.

Hodge, B., 1979. Newspapers and Communities. in Fowler et al (eds), 1979, 157-174.

Labov, W., 1972. *Language in the Inner City.* Philadelphia: University of Pensylvania Press.

Polanyi, L., 1985. Conversational Storytelling. in van Dijk, T.A. (ed), 1985, 183-201.

Silberstein, S., 2002. *War of Words.* London: Routledge.

Stubbs, M., 1997. Whorf's children: critical comments on critical discourse analysis. In Ryan, Ann and Alison Wray (eds). *Evolving Models of Language. British Studies in Applied Linguistics, 12.* Clevendon: BAAL/Multililngual Matters. 100-116.

Thompson, G., 1996. *Introducing Functional Grammar.* London: Arnold.

Thompson, G. and S. Hunston, 2000. Evaluation: an introduction. In Hunston, S.

and G. Thompson (Eds.) 2000. *Evaluation in Text.* Oxford: Oxford University Press, 1-27.

Toolan, M.J., 1988. *Narrative: a Critical Linguistic Introduction.* London and New York:

Trew, T., 1979. Theory and Ideology at Work. In Fowler et al. (eds) 1979, 94-116.

Vestergaard, T., 2000a. That's not news: persuasive and expository genres in the press. In Trosborg, A. (Ed.) *Analysing Professional Genres.* Amsterdam: John Benjamins, 97-120.

___ 2000b. From genre to sentence: the leading article and its linguistic realization. In Ungerer, F. (Ed.) *English Media Texts Past and Present.* Amsterdam: John Benjamins, 151-176.

White, P., 1997. Death, disruption and the moral order: the narrative impulse in Mass media 'hard news' reporting. In Christie, F. and J.R. Martin (Eds.) *Genre and Institutions. Social Processes in the Workplace and School.* London: Cassel. 101 – 133.

Widdowson. H., 2000. Critical practices: on representation and the interpretation of text. In Sarangi, S. And M. Coulthard (Eds.) *Discourse and Social Life.* London: Longman. 155-169.